# Korean Neo-Confucian Perspectives on Laozi and Zhuangzi

by

Tae Hyun Kim

Three Pines Press
St Petersburg, FL 33713
www.threepinespress.com
threepinespress@gmail.com

EU Representation
R. Vencu
Negoi 58b, Sibiu, RO-550275
richard.vencu@gmail.com



9 8 7 6 5 4 3 2 1

Printed in the United States of America
This edition is printed on acid-free paper that meets
the American National Standard Institute Z39. 48 Standard.
Distributed in the United States by Three Pines Press.

Cover Design:
Kyŏmjae Chŏng Sŏn (1676–1759). *Yangch'ŏn Sŏnyubong*. Public domain. Image courtesy of Wikimedia Commons, https://commons.wikimedia.org/wiki/File:Gyeomjae-Yangcheon-Seonyubong.jpg

---

Library of Congress Cataloging-in-Publication Data

Names: 880-70 Kim, Tae Hyun, 1981- translator editor | Yi, I, 1536-1584. Sunŏn. English | Han, Wŏn-jin, 1682-1751. Changja pyŏnhae. English
Title: Korean neo-Confucian perspectives on Laozi and Zhuangzi / Tae Hyun Kim.
Description: St Petersburg, FL: Three Pines Press, [2026] | Includes bibliographical references and index.
Identifiers: LCCN 2025052772 | ISBN 9781931483889 paperback
Subjects: LCSH: Yi, I, 1536-1584. Sunŏn | Han, Wŏn-jin, 1682-1751. Changja pyŏnhae
Classification: LCC BL1900.L35 K6713 2026
LC record available at https://lccn.loc.gov/2025052772

# Korean

# Neo-Confucian

# Perspectives

# on

# Laozi and Zhuangzi

# Contents

# List of Abbreviations

| | |
|---|---|
| DDJ | *Laozi Daodejing* |
| DZJ | *Daode zhenjing jijie*, by Dong Sijing |
| DZL | *Daode zhenjing lun*, by Sima Guang |
| DZSH | *Daode zhenjing jieyi*, by Song Huizong |
| ECYS | *Er Cheng yishu*, by Cheng Hao and Cheng Yi |
| LJ | *Laozi jie*, by Su Che |
| ZZ | *Zhuangzi* |
| ZZQS | *Zhuzi quanshu*, by Zhu Xi |

Dedicated

to

Shim Soon Ok

# Acknowledgments

Looking back, it is truly a strange thing. Ever since—over twenty years ago—I entered graduate school, made a vow to live as a professional scholar, and received my doctorate, the books I have read and studied most passionately, embracing with all my heart as guiding principles for my life, have been the Daoist classics *Laozi* and *Zhuangzi*. And yet, why did I never wonder what my ancestors—those who lived on the very land where I was born and raised—thought about these texts? I have read many commentaries, scholarly monographs, and academic papers on the *Laozi* and *Zhuangzi* but never once tried to find out what my grandfathers' grandfathers had written about my most beloved books. Nor had I ever thought that I needed to read them, study them, and reflect on them, just as I have done with the writings of many scholars from China, Japan, the United States, and Europe.

While teaching at several universities in the United States, I was often asked, as a Korean scholar trained in the study of premodern China, to cover a wide range of topics in premodern East Asia, with particular emphasis on Korean thought and culture. It was in this pedagogical context that my sustained scholarly interest in premodern Korean perspectives first took shape. Because my formal training lay in the intellectual history of premodern China, my courses on Korean thought and religion were necessarily framed through their profound historical, textual, and institutional entanglements with China.

Through this work, I came to appreciate a crucial insight: when studying thought, religion, and literature before the formation of modern nation states, we must move across regions now labeled China, Korea, Japan, Manchu, Mongol, and Tibet. This perspective reveals a world in which centers and peripheries were dynamically interconnected through political authority, textual transmission, ritual practice, and scholarly exchange, while also developing localized forms shaped by specific geographic, historical, racial, and political conditions.

One day, while teaching a course on the history of Daoism in Korea, I was introducing to my students the religious ideas, ritual practices, and state institutions in Korean history that may be identified as Daoist, situating them in comparative relation to their counterparts in premodern China. In the midst of that discussion, a question suddenly struck me with the force of a jolt of electricity: just as Chosŏn-era Neo-Confucianism unfolded along distinctive trajectories within its own historical and intellectual context, in what ways did premodern Korean scholars read, interpret, and rearticulate the *Laozi* and the *Zhuangzi* on their own terms?

The thought thrilled me, and at the same time, it deeply embarrassed me. How had I never once wondered what those who lived long ago in the land of my birth thought about these texts? Though I had accumulated scattered knowledge about Daoism in Korea, I knew almost nothing about how premodern Korean intellectuals actually engaged with Lao-Zhuang thought. The realization left me ashamed.

After this realization, I began collecting and studying premodern Korean texts related to foundational Daoist thought. It was during this process that I first encountered, from the perspective of a twenty first century, American trained academic, the commentaries on Lao Zhuang texts written by Chosŏn scholars of the Zhu Xi Neo-Confucian school. The sense of surprise I experienced while reading these works—the tension and excitement that brought a smile to my face, the intellectual fascination they inspired, and the deep respect they evoked—remains beyond the reach of words.

When I first read Yi I's 李珥 (1536–1584) *Sunŏn* 醇言 (Purified Words) and Han Wŏnjin's 韓元震 (1682–1751) *Changja pyŏnhae* 莊子辨解 (Analytic Interpretation of the *Zhuangzi*), both of which are closely examined and translated in this study, the intellectual shock and emotional exhilaration I experienced were unforgettable. Whether they set out to criticize or to defend Lao Zhuang thought, what impressed me most was the scholarly seriousness, sincerity, and intellectual honesty with which Yi I and Han Wŏnjin confronted the ideas articulated in these foundational texts. Their awe-inspiring intellectual posture compelled me to return to their writings repeatedly, reading them to the end again and again with the utmost care.

From that point on, I resolved to translate and introduce the works of Yi I and Han Wŏnjin to the English-speaking world. This book is the proud outcome of that resolution—proud not only because I was able to complete the project in book form, but also because it allows these important works to reach readers Yi I and Han Wŏnjin likely never imagined addressing when they first wrote them.

Yi I's *Sunŏn* is the earliest surviving Korean commentary on the *Laozi* and served as a conceptual model for later Chosŏn commentaries. More importantly, it reveals the remarkable integrity of Yi I, a leading Neo-Confucian thinker who, in an age when Zhu Xi's orthodoxy was unquestioned and Lao-Zhuang thought was condemned as heresy, boldly treated the *Laozi* as a sage's text. By reorganizing the traditional eighty-one chapters into forty sections, Yi presented a mature vision of philosophical integration between Confucianism and Daoism within the ideal of cultivating oneself and governing others (*sugi ch'iin* 修己治人). *Sunŏn* thus stands as a landmark work that invites us to move beyond viewing Chosŏn thought exclusively through the narrowly defined monolith of Zhu Xi Neo-Confucianism and to approach it instead through more dynamic and plural perspectives that emerge from within Neo-Confucianism itself.

The other work presented in this book, Han Wŏnjin's *Changja pyŏnhae*, has never been fully translated into any modern language, including contemporary Korean, despite its historical and intellectual significance. Little known in Western scholarship, Han was nonetheless a leading late Chosŏn Neo-Confucian thinker and a key figure in the eighteenth-century development of a distinctly Chosŏn articulation of Zhu Xi learning.

The *Changja pyŏnhae* is Han's commentary on the Inner Chapters of the *Zhuangzi*, written amid profound social and political upheaval. It reflects the pressures confronting conservative scholars of the time, namely the need to defend Zhu Xi orthodoxy while responding to Zhuangzian views that were gaining currency despite their long-standing status as heterodox. By engaging critically with the *Zhuangzi*, Han also sought to clarify his position in the Horak debate, one of the most consequential controversies in Chosŏn, particularly concerning the sameness and difference between human and non-human nature.

Unlike Yi I's commentary on the *Laozi*, which seeks synthesis, Han's *Pyŏnhae* treats the *Zhuangzi* as a heterodox work. It defends the Neo-Confucian view of human nature and the moral cosmos against both the *Zhuangzi*'s *qi*-based vision of undifferentiated oneness and those Neo-Confucians who, influenced by Daoism, argued for the essential unity of all beings. Han sought instead to affirm and justify the moral and ontological boundaries between humans and things, and between the Sage and the ordinary person.

Through this multifaceted work where complex intellectual tensions and personal convictions intersect readers encounter the critical gaze that Chosŏn Neo-Confucians cast upon the *Zhuangzi*, along with the challenges they faced in confronting and seeking to overcome its thought. Within this commentary on the Inner Chapters, a text on which even Zhu Xi left no systematic commentary, readers witness a rare and rigorous intellectual encounter between Zhuangzi and Zhu Xi thought in the history of East Asian philosophy.

In writing this book, I have incurred many debts of gratitude. Above all, I thank my parents, Kim Chŭnghoe and Yun Yŏngnam, who have been unwavering pillars of strength throughout the years. I am deeply grateful to my sister, Kim Soo Hyun, for her insight and wisdom, and to her three beloved companions, Super, Mimi, and Pori, who never fail to bring warmth and joy. I also thank my brother, Kim Taemun, and his wife, Pak Yŏngsun, whose companionship and wonderful meals have been a constant source of happiness. My deepest gratitude goes to my dearest friend, Shim Soon Ok, whose compassion and humanity sustained me through some of life's darkest passages. Finally, I extend my sincere thanks to Prof. Livia Kohn for her kindness, generosity, and support in bringing this book to publication.

—Tae Hyun Kim,
At Haegwangjae, 2025

# Notes on Translation

Except for the two main texts, *Sunŏn* and *Changja pyŏnhae*, which I manually transcribed, most premodern Chinese and Korean sources cited in this book are based on digital versions. Chinese texts are drawn from the Chinese Text Project (ctext.org) and verified against scanned images from original collections such as the *Siku quanshu* and *Zhengtong daozang*, or reputable printed editions when scans are unavailable. Korean texts come from the Comprehensive Database of Korean Classics (db.itkc.or.kr, ITKC), checked against scanned or printed originals; citations follow the traditional pagination of the "original images." URLs for other digital sources are listed in the bibliography.

The citation format for digital versions of texts works with the chapter or volume, followed by the section or page. When it is difficult to render consistently the relationships among composite volumes and individual works, as in the case of early Chinese classics, I cite sources by first giving the title of the text and the chapter, hexagram, or poem, followed by the relevant section or stanza.

Korean names and terms are rendered in McCune–Reischauer (MR), while Chinese terms use Pinyin. However, classical Chinese terms and phrases cited by Korean authors are romanized according to Korean conventions, reflecting how the commentaries read them in context. For certain key concepts in the main text, both Korean and Chinese romanizations are provided, with Korean first. When an author provides their name or a title in English, I preserve their usage without modifying it to the MR system.

Last, in translating the commentaries of Yi I and Han Wŏnjin on the *Laozi* and the *Zhuangzi*, a central issue concerns how to handle the base texts themselves. Given the long history of diverse and often controversial interpretations of these works, translation is not a straightforward task. However, since this book is concerned primarily with Yi I's and Han Wŏnjin's readings rather than with the original texts as such, I have adopted the following approach: I first present the text as understood by Yi I or Han Wŏnjin, and then, where necessary, situate their readings in relation to widely accepted exegetical traditions, such as those of Wang Bi and Heshang Gong for the *Laozi*, and Guo Xiang and Cheng Xuanying for the *Zhuangzi*. In some cases, I also make independent interpretive decisions as translator; these are indicated in the footnotes.

# Part One

# Yi I's *Sunŏn*

# Translator's Introduction

## Anti-Daoism in Chosŏn

The new class of Neo-Confucian scholar-officials (*sinjin sadaebu* 新進士大夫; lit. "newly promoted scholar-officials"), who founded the Chosŏn dynasty (1392–1897), regarded the fall of Koryŏ (918–1392) as the consequence of the mistaken understanding of humanity and the world instilled in the soteriological doctrines of Buddhism, which had been the state religion of Koryŏ. Naturally, with the founding of Chosŏn, the intellectual landscape of the country gradually reorganized itself around a new environment in which Zhu Xi's 朱熹 (1130-1200) Neo-Confucianism became the state-sponsored orthodox academic tradition. As it increasingly grew into the sole legitimate form of learning, both politically and intellectually, along with the systemic stabilization of Chosŏn, other traditional teachings, such as Buddhism and Daoism, that Zhu Xi had explicitly rejected were intensely criticized by Chosŏn scholar-officials as heretical doctrines that needed to be defeated, overcome, and replaced with Zhu Xi's views on humanity and the world based on his radical reinterpretation of early Confucian texts.

This new trend was already clearly evident among the scholar official class that led the political revolution in the early founding period of Chosŏn. Most notably, the revolutionary figure Chŏng Tojŏn 鄭道傳 (1342–1398) understood the ideological confrontation, namely the effort to overcome Buddhism and Daoism through Neo-Confucianism, as a central intellectual task. Grounded in the Zhu Xi Neo-Confucian worldview, Chŏng articulated a vision of Chosŏn as a new Confucian ideal state. In doing so, he established the basic framework of Chosŏn's intellectual order, in which Neo-Confucianism functioned as the sole orthodoxy and all other teachings were relegated to the status of heresy.

One of the works that most clearly expresses this line of thought is Chŏng's *Sim Ki Ri P'yŏn* 心氣理篇 (Book on Mind, *Qi*, and Principle), written only two years after the founding of Chosŏn (see *Sambong-jip* 10.1a-11b). In this work, Chŏng characterizes Buddhism as a teaching focused on the mind, Daoism as oriented toward the vital energy of *qi*, and Confucianism as grounded in principle (Korean *ri*; Chinese *li* 理). From the standpoint of Zhu Xi learning, he seeks to demonstrate how Buddhism and Daoism, through their mutual theoretical contradictions, reveal their own internal inconsistencies and limitations, and ultimately why they are inferior to Confucian teachings.

In his critique of Daoism, Chŏng identifies *qi* as the core of its doctrine, treating the *Laozi Daodejing* 老子道德經 (hereafter DDJ) as the central text of Daoist theory and the *Zhuangzi* 莊子 (ZZ) as a secondary reference. According to Chŏng Tojŏn, the world of primordial *qi* described by Laozi and Zhuangzi, a realm of absolute indifference where there is neither good nor evil, neither right nor wrong, fails to recognize the existence of the fundamental ontological principle that determines why the world exists as a world and why humans exist as humans, the principle that lies beyond the perceptible, sub-phenomenal realm of *qi.* Chŏng also contends that Daoist teachings, which prioritize the pursuit of personal purity and longevity, are ultimately selfish. Because of this, he argues, the theories of Laozi and Zhuangzi offer a view of humanity no different from that of beasts, making their doctrine fundamentally unfit for human society.

> The teachings of Śākyamuni and Laozi revere purity and quiescence, and therefore, even the most significant moral principles of human relationships and the greatness of ritual and music, they seek to discard and utterly extinguish. Though those who harbor no desires in their hearts may seem different from those who chase after profit, they still do not understand how to uphold the impartiality of the heavenly principle and restrain the selfishness of human desire.
>
> Therefore, their daily words and actions constantly fall into the realm of self-interest without their realizing it. Furthermore, there is nothing people desire more than life, and nothing they fear more than death. Yet, when we examine the doctrines of these two schools, we see that the Buddhists seek to transcend life and death; this is nothing but a fear of death; and that the Daoists pursue longevity; this is nothing but a craving for life. If this is not self-interest, then what is? (*Sambong-jip* 10.6b-7a)[1]

According to Chŏng Tojŏn, Buddhism and Daoism, though they appear to promote purity and detachment, ultimately reject essential moral principles and the civilizing functions of ritual and music. While they may differ outwardly from those who pursue profit, they fail to uphold the impartiality of the heavenly principle or restrain selfish human desire, causing their actions to remain self-centered. Their doctrines, such as the Buddhist quest to transcend life and death and the Daoist pursuit of longevity, are driven by fear of death and desire for life, revealing, at their core, nothing but self-interest.

Although Chŏng Tojŏn's argument does not significantly differ from the typical anti-Daoist stance of orthodox Zhu Xi school scholars, his position as the intellectual architect of Chosŏn and his historical significance ensured that his critique became the core rationale by which orthodox Confucian scholars throughout the Chosŏn period came to regard the Daoist thought of Laozi and Zhuangzi as heretical.

---

[1] 若夫釋老之學，以清淨寂滅為尚。雖彝倫之大，禮樂之懿，亦必欲屏除而滅絶之。是其胸中無欲，與趨於利害者，疑若不同矣。然不知主天理之公，以裁制人欲之私，故其日用云為，每陷於利害而不自知也。且人之所欲，無甚於生；所惡，無甚於死。今以兩家之說觀之：釋氏必欲免死生，是畏死也；老氏必欲求長生，是貪生也。非利害而何哉？An alternative translation of this is found in Muller 2015, 50-52.

Kwŏn Kŭn 權近 (1352–1409), a founding contributor to the establishment of Chosŏn alongside Chŏng Tojŏn and a leading figure in promoting Zhu Xi's thought within the Chosŏn intellectual world, likewise explicitly denounced Daoist thought, particularly that of Laozi, as something that ought to be rejected. In the preface he wrote for Chŏng Tojŏn's *Sim Ki Ri P'yŏn* (*Sambong-jip* 10.9a-11a), Kwŏn Kŭn characterized the fundamental aim of Laozi's teaching as "nurturing life" (*yangsaeng*; *yangsheng* 養生), condemning it as a selfish doctrine that, without any discernment between right and wrong, focuses solely on protecting and preserving one's own life. He declared it a heretical teaching that abolishes human ethics and plunges society into disorder.

> Confucians take principle as the foundation, by which the mind and *qi* are governed; thus, with principle as the root, the other two are cultivated. Laozi, [on the other hand,] takes *qi* as central, regarding the cultivation of life as the Way (*dao* 道). Śākyamuni takes the mind as central, making non-moving (*pudong*; *budong* 不動) its essential doctrine. Each holds firmly to one element while discarding the other two. Laozi, desiring non-action (*muwi*; *wuwei* 無爲), avoids discerning right from wrong in affairs and seeks to eliminate all of them. He fears that the toil of action may harm his *qi*. But if *qi* is properly cultivated, the spirit becomes concentrated and stabilized, and even when one engages in activities, they will not harm one's life. …
>
> The teachings of these two schools, if they do not fall into withered emptiness and quiescent extinction, inevitably drift toward indulgence and unchecked permissiveness. In either case, they are the same in undermining benevolence and righteousness, destroying moral order and human relations, and becoming guilty of opposing the teaching of the sagely tradition, the great balance (*taejung*; *dazhong* 大中).[2] (*Sambong-jip* 10.10a-10b)[3]

Whereas Chŏng Tojŏn emphasized the theoretical inferiority of the *qi*-centered worldview of Laozi and Zhuangzi in comparison to the *li*-centered worldview of Zhu Xi's learning, Kwŏn Kŭn focused his critique on the ethical dimension of Daoist practice, specifically, on how Daoist obsession with preserving life and pursuing longevity reflected a narrow and self-centered understanding of humanity and the world, one that would lead to harmful consequences in the real world.

This strict Zhu Xi Neo-Confucian stance by both Chŏng Tojŏn and Kwŏn Kŭn, the architects of Chŏson politics and intellectual culture, rejected all non-

---

2 Commonly translated as "middle" or "center," the character *chung* (*zhong* 中) is rendered in this book mostly as "balance," understood in a more philosophically interpretive way.

3 儒主乎理而治心氣，本其一而養其二。老主乎氣，以養生為道。釋主乎心，以不動為宗，各守其一而遺其二者也。老欲無為，不計事之是非而皆去之，恐勞其身以弊其氣也。氣苟得養，則精神凝定；雖有所事，而不害吾之生… 是二家之學，不陷於枯槁寂滅，則必流於放肆縱恣，其賊仁害義，滅倫敗理，得罪於聖門大中之教，則一也。See also Muller 2015, 52-53.

Confucian teachings as heretical and laid the groundwork for a political and social climate in which Buddhism and Daoism could no longer be studied or debated as respected intellectual and cultural traditions, as they had been prior to Chŏson. As the Chŏson's scholar-official class in Zhu Xi school consolidated political power, this stance gets increasingly institutionalized. Throughout the Chŏson period, scholars aspiring to pass the civil service examinations and participate in public office found themselves in an structural environment where the public and open study, writing, or publication of Buddhist or Daoist thought and texts was repressed and condemned.

## Daoist Commentaries in Chosŏn

Despite the implicit, and at times explicit, ideological suppression and persecution of non-Confucian thought, the circulation, reading, and study of Daoist texts were not entirely prohibited in Chosŏn. In terms of textual transmission, Daoist works continued to be widely read and studied among both Confucian official literati and Daoist practitioners throughout the Chosŏn period. According to the research of Lee Sangyong, who examined bibliographic catalogues from both private individuals and public institutions circulated among Chosŏn intellectuals, they read not only the DDJ and ZZ, but also other foundational texts such as the *Liezi* 列子, *Baopuzi* 抱樸子, *Zhouyi cantongqi* 周易參同契, *Huangting neijing jing* 黃庭內景經, and *Yinfu jing* 陰符經 (Lee 2013).

Nevertheless, the Daoist texts circulated in Chosŏn appeared to be limited in both number and variety, and largely confined to the basic writings of Daoist thought. This can be attributed to two main factors. First, in a social climate where the reading and study of Daoist texts was not welcomed, there were likely few scholars who seriously engaged with Daoist literature. This would have hindered the importation of a wider range of texts from China. Such a social context likely contributed to the narrow scope of Daoist works available in Chosŏn intellectual circles. Second, it is also possible that a greater variety of texts were actually in circulation, but the prevailing social atmosphere made it difficult to publicly disclose ownership or study of such works, resulting in their exclusion from official bibliographic records of individuals and institutions. As will be discussed later, the case of Yi I 李珥 (1536-1584) demonstrates this point. Yi based his study on the *Daode zhenjing jijie* 道德真經集解 (hereafter DZJ), a Northern Song (960-1127) commentary by the Daoist monk Dong Sijing 董思靖 (fl. 1246–1260), and consulted various other commentaries on the *Laozi* by figures such as Sima Guang 司馬光 (1019–1086), Su Che 蘇轍 (1039–1112), and Emperor Huizong (r. 1100–1125). This suggests, indirectly but compellingly, that Chosŏn intellectuals may have engaged with a far broader range of Daoist literature than the extant records alone would indicate.

Beyond merely reading Daoist texts, there were also—albeit rarely—cases in which specialized works such as commentaries were published. Based on extant texts, a total of five commentaries on the DDJ were produced by five different scholars throughout the Chosŏn period, and four scholars authored commentaries on the ZZ.

With regard to the *Laozi*, the earliest surviving commentary is by Yi I's *Sunŏn* 醇言 (Purified Words), discussed and translated in here. Following this, four additional commentaries are known to have been written: *Sinju Todŏkkyŏng* 新註道德經 (A New Commentary on the DDJ), also known as *Noja chuhae* 老子註解 (Commentary and Explanation of the DDJ) by Pak Sedang 朴世堂 (1629–1703); *Todŏk chigwi* 道德指歸 (A Corollary of the DDJ) by Sŏ Myŏng'ŭng 徐命膺 (1716–1787); *Ch'owŏn tamno* 椒園談老 (Chowŏn's Discourses on the DDJ) by Yi Ch'ung'ik 李忠翊 (1744–1816); and *Chŏngno* 訂老 (Rectifying with the DDJ) by Hong Sŏkju 洪奭周 (1774–1842).

As for the ZZ, a total of four commentaries are known to survive to this day: *Namhwagyŏng chuhae sanbo* 南華經註解刪補 (A Commentary and Editing of the *Nanhua Scripture*) by Pak Sedang; *Ch'irwŏn ch'aegi* 漆園采奇 (Selections of Wonders from the Lacquer Garden) by Kwŏn Hae 權瑎 (1639–1704); *Changja pyŏnhae* 莊子辨解 (Analytic Interpretation of the ZZ) by Han Wŏnjin 韓元震 (1682–1751), which is introduced in this book; and *Munjang chunch'ik Changja sŏn* 文章準則莊子選 (Selected Writings from the ZZ as a Model of Composition) by Sin Kyŏngjun 申景濬 (1712–1781), a work newly discovered and made public by Kim Namhyŏng in 2014.

## Commentaries on the *Laozi*

Yi I's *Sunŏn* is a re-edited compilation of phrases and chapters from the DDJ, reorganized into forty new chapters. A prominent Neo-Confucian scholar and reform-minded statesman of mid-Chosŏn, the author chose passages that he believed either aligned with original Confucian ideals or faithfully reflected the true intent of the DDJ. This is the earliest extant Korean-authored commentary on the DDJ. In this work, Yi boldly breaks with nearly two hundred years of Neo-Confucian position, first institutionalized by Chŏng Tojŏn and Kwŏn Kŭn, that had branded Laozi as heretical.

Instead, he seeks the core meaning of the DDJ in the Confucian ideal of "cultivating the self and ordering others" (*sugi ch'iin*; *xiuji zhiren* 修己治人), presenting a striking and, at the time, radical interpretation that compares the spirit of the DDJ to the vision of a Confucian sage. In many cases, Yi's interpretation closely aligns with the perspective of DZJ, a commentary by the Northern Song Daoist Mr. Dong Sijing, which Yi used as his base text and was likely much influenced by. Yet, considering the originality and clarity with which Yi articulates his vision in his own language, it is reasonable to conclude that Yi's interpretation was not merely derivative from Dong but a product of his independent thought. Yi's bold declaration that the DDJ is not a heretical work preaching nihilism, but a sage's text sharing in the Confucian Way, became a powerful source of intellectual inspiration for later scholars.[4]

However, Yi I's commentary was limited by the fact that it did not cover the entirety of the DDJ, but only less than 40% of the original text—those passages he selected and edited based on his conviction that they aligned with Confucian teachings. The first complete commentary on the DDJ by a Chosŏn scholar was Pak Sedang's *Sinju*. Like Yi I, Pak was a reform-minded scholar-official, but he was more explicitly critical of the Zhu Xi-centered orthodoxy that dominated Chosŏn intellectual life. He advocated a return to the original spirit of Confucianism as found in Confucius and Mengzi, rather than in Zhu Xi's metaphysics. Pak Sedang's commentary on the DDJ reflects a distinctive interpretive approach shaped by his Confucian background while simultaneously embracing the practical value of Daoist thought. As a Confucian scholar, he fundamentally upheld Confucian values and ethics, and thus his reading of the DDJ does not depart from a Confucian framework.

Instead, he explores how Daoist ideas can be meaningfully integrated into it. He sought to go beyond a merely critical stance toward the DDJ, actively engaging with those aspects of Daoist philosophy, such as non-action and natural spontaneity (*chayŏn*; *ziran* 自然), that could serve the Confucian aim of self-cultivation and ordering others. For Pak, the ultimate goal of his commentary was to investigate how Daoist thought might be harnessed to support moral self-cultivation and the governance of society. He believed that the teachings of the DDJ could contribute to the enhancement of individual morality and the maintenance of social order. Importantly, Pak did not blindly follow Zhu Xi's interpretations; instead, he adopted a critical stance, arguing that Zhu Xi's readings were overly rigid and that the classics should be open to diverse interpretations. In sum, Pak Sedang's interpretation remains grounded in a Confucian worldview, but it also recognizes the value of Daoist ideas as a means of achieving the Confucian ideal of self-cultivation and social order (Kim 1999).

Unlike Yi I and Pak Sedang, who emphasized the practical aspects of Laozi's thought and discovered in them the spirit of self-cultivation and ordering others in continuity with Confucius, Sŏ Myŏng'ŭng took a more systematic approach by examining Laozi's metaphysical worldview through the lens of a Zhu Xi style cosmology.[5] In doing so, he explored their points of convergence and sought to overcome the longstanding Neo Confucian prejudice dating back to Chŏng Tojŏn that "the Way of Lao Zhuang is merely *qi*," by advancing the proposition that "the Way of Laozi is the Supreme Ultimate (*t'aegŭk*; *taiji* 太極)," a claim first acknowledged by Zhu Xi (ZZQS 31.140) and also confirmed by Yi I

---

[4] Yi I's *Sunŏn* was first translated into Korean by Yi Chuhyang in 1993, and has since been rendered into Korean by several scholars such as Kim 2001; Yu 2002; Cho 2022; and Sŏ 2023, listed the "Translations" section of the Bibliography below.

[5] Sŏ Myŏng'ŭng's *Todŏk chigwi* has been translated into Korean twice by two different scholars: Cho 2008; Kim 2023.

in the *Sunŏn*, as we will see below. Through this reinterpretation, he not only defended the philosophical legitimacy of Laozi and Daoist thought but also enabled a more grounded and immediate understanding of self-cultivation, not as an abstract or hollow ideal buried in the complexities of Neo-Confucian metaphysics, but as a concrete practice of becoming a sage (Kim 2003; 2006).

More boldly, Yi Ch'ung'ik's *Tamno* steps outside the interpretive framework imposed by the Neo-Confucian orthodoxy of his time. Instead, it offers a commentary on the DDJ grounded in the interpretive perspectives of Yangming thought and Hwaŏm (*Huayan* 華嚴) Buddhism. Rejecting the dualistic worldview of *li* and *qi*, and of the metaphysical and the phenomenal, as found in Neo-Confucianism, Yi approached the DDJ from a perspective that emphasized the unity of all things under a single root of unity (*il*; *yi* 一). He appreciated the profundity of the DDJ's worldview for its holistic orientation and argued for an alternative vision of the cosmos and self-cultivation, one that was more unified and integrated than that offered by Zhu Xi's teachings (Kim 2013; Kim 2014).

Like Pak Sedang, Hong Sŏkju also composed his commentary on the DDJ with the aim of returning to the original spirit of Confucianism. Following in the footsteps of Yi I and Pak Sedang, Hong firmly maintained that Laozi was by no means a heretic. He believed that the core message of the DDJ, much like that of Confucius, lay in the ideal of self-cultivation and ordering others (Kim 2001).[6]

## Commentaries on the *Zhuangzi*

Although relatively fewer in number, commentaries on the ZZ were written and read by Chosŏn Neo-Confucian scholars, too. The earliest extant commentary on the ZZ by a Chosŏn scholar is *Namhwagyŏng chuhae sanbo* 南華經註解刪補 (A Commentary and Editing of the *Nanhua Scripture*) by Pak Sedang.[7] This work is not only the earliest known commentary on the ZZ in Chosŏn but also the only one that covers the entire text of the ZZ in full. He frequently cited and referenced the interpretations of Guo Xiang 郭象 (252-312) and Lin Xiyi 林希逸 (1193-1271). Like his commentary on the DDJ, this work was written from a Confucian perspective, aiming to supplement Confucianism with the strengths of Lao-Zhuang thought. He believed that although the teachings of Lao-Zhuang differed from the great method of the sage, they still contained aspects worth adopting, and that it was a mistake to reject them without discerning their value.

The second ZZ commentary written by a Chosŏn Confucian scholar is *Ch'irwŏn ch'aegi*, authored by Kwŏn Hae (Im 2014). As the title suggests, this work is a unique form of commentary that selectively annotates only key allegories and discourses from the ZZ. It uses *Nanhua zhenjing fumo* 南華眞經副墨

6 Kŭm Changt'ae provides a valuable overview of Chosŏn Neo-Confucian scholars' interpretations of the DDJ. See Kŭm 2006.

7 Pak Sedang's *Namhwagyŏng chuhae sanbo* has not yet been fully translated. To date, only the Inner Chapters have been translated into Korean twice by two scholars: Chŏn 2012; Pak 2012.

(Supplementary Notes on the *Nanhua zhenjing* (i.e., *Zhuangzi*) by Lu Xixing 陸西星 (1520–1606) as its base text. Although Kwŏn Hae was a Neo-Confucian scholar, he held a much more favorable view, both philosophically and practically, toward internal alchemy (*naedan; neidan* 內丹) and life-nurturing practices (*yangsaeng sul; yangsheng shu* 養生術) as methods of sage-like self-cultivation than most other ZZ commentators in Chosŏn. Philosophically, he also maintained a remarkably open view, holding that Zhuangzi's ultimate vision could, in essence, be compatible with the Confucian understanding of humanity and the cosmos. Thus, alongside Pak Sedang's commentary, Kwŏn Hae's *Ch'irwŏn ch'aegi* stands as one of the rare Chosŏn works that appreciate the value of Zhuangzi's thought as a source of self-nurturing and cultivation from a Confucian-informed perspective.

The third commentary, and the one translated and examined in this book, is Han Wŏnjin's *Changja pyŏnhae*.[8] This work is a commentary on only the Inner Chapters from the original ZZ, and it stands apart from the other Chosŏn commentaries in both content and purpose. This work was composed specifically to critique Zhuangzi's thought from a Neo-Confucian perspective. With the clear aim of overcoming Zhuangzi's *qi*-centered cosmology through a Zhu Xi-style *li-qi* dualistic worldview, the commentary exhibits a far more explicit philosophical confrontation between Zhuangzi's ideas and Neo-Confucian thought than is found in other Chosŏn commentaries.

The final commentary is *Munjang chunch'ik Changja sŏn*, a work newly discovered and made public in 2014 by Kim Namhyŏng and attributed to Sin Kyŏngjun (Kim 2014). As the title suggests, this is not a general commentary that broadly engages with Zhuangzi's philosophy, but rather a more specialized work that focuses on a particular topic—namely, Zhuangzi's elegant yet difficult prose style and diction, from the perspective of literary theory. Like several other commentaries, it does not annotate the entire ZZ text; instead, it offers commentary only on selected chapters: Chapter 1, "Free and Easy Wandering" (*Xiaoyao you* 逍遙遊); Chapter 2, "On Treating All Things Equally" (*Qiwulun* 齊物論)' and Chapter 3, "The Foundation of Nurturing Life" (*Yangshengzhu* 養生主) from the Inner Chapters; and Chapter 17, "Autumn Floods" (*Qiushui* 秋水) from the Outer Chapters. The composition of such a specialized commentary appears to reflect Sin's intellectual desire and ambition to challenge the speculative dogmatism of Neo-Confucian orthodoxy in Chosŏn and to advocate for the coexistence of diverse worldviews and values, an impulse shaped by and in tension with the dominant Zhu Xi–centered scholarly environment of the time. Sin Kyŏngjun stands out clearly from the orthodox Zhu Xi scholars of his era by, for instance, using Buddhist theory to explain Zhuangzi, affirming the excellence of

[8] Han Wŏnjin's *Changja pyŏnhae* has not yet been translated into any modern language. To explore the relationship between the works of Pak Sedang and Han Wŏnjin, see Kim Hangmok 2024. Here, Kim argues that Han's *Pyŏnhae* was written as a Neo-Confucian rebuttal to Pak Sedang's *Sanbo*, which was widely read among Chosŏn Neo-Confucians at the time.

Zhuangzi's philosophy, and repeatedly noting parallels between Zhuangzi and Confucian thought.

All these DDJ and ZZ commentaries produced in Chosŏn were written by Confucian scholars trained within the intellectual framework of Zhu Xi learning. Except for Han Wŏnjin's case, all the Chosŏn commentators on DDJ and ZZ used their commentaries to criticize, either directly or indirectly, the oppressive intellectual climate of the time that regarded only Zhu Xi learning as the sole truth and expressed the necessity for its reform. As exemplified by scholars such as Yi I, Pak Sedang, Kwŏn Hae, and Sin Kyŏngjun, most Confucian commentators on DDJ and ZZ sought through a more receptive understanding of these texts to restore the original spirit of Confucianism, centered on self-cultivation and practical governance, which had been lost under the repressive dogmatism of Zhu Xi learning in Chosŏn. Among them was even a more radical thinker like Yi Ch'ung'ik, who, through the marginal thought of DDJ, envisioned a new intellectual order beyond Zhu Xi learning. Ultimately, the commentary works on DDJ and ZZ in Chosŏn can be understood as an intellectual effort aimed at the renewal and reform of Chosŏn, much like the Buddhist critiques carried out by the newly rising Neo-Confucians at the end of the Koryŏ period.

From here on, the following sections will briefly examine, in order, the works of Yi I and Han Wŏnjin introduced in this book.

## Yulgok Yi I: Life and Thought

Yi I is regarded as one of the most representative philosophers and educators of Zhu Xi learning in Chosŏn. He also served as a statesman during the reigns of King Myŏngjong (r. 1545–1567) and King Sŏnjo (r. 1567–1608).[9] Born in 1536 in Kangnŭng to the famed mother Sin Saimdang 申師任堂 (1504-1551), he was said to have amazed people as a prodigy who learned to speak and write by age three and was composing poetry by age eight.[10] At age sixteen, Yi I lost his mother and, after three years of mourning at her grave, entered Pong'ŭn Temple, where he devoted himself to studying Buddhist scriptures. He later retreated to Mt. Kŭmgang for further Sŏn 禪 Buddhist practice, where he is said to have gained thorough insight into Buddhist doctrine. These formative experiences, occurring before his formal establishment as a Confucian scholar and political figure grounded in Zhu Xi learning, appear to have laid the foundation for his intellectually open mindset, one that allowed him to compose a commentary on DDJ and to engage in broader inquiry across rigid school boundaries.

Beginning at the age of thirteen, Yi I passed first place in the local preliminary civil examination for *chinsa* 進士 (State Examination Graduate) status, and over the course of his life, he would go on to place in various levels of the state

---

9 For an excellent introduction to Yi's life and thought in English, see Ro 2019, 179–196.

10 One of the poems he composed at age eight, titled "Hwasŏkjŏng" 花石亭 (Hwasŏk Pavilion) appears in *Yulgok sŏnsaeng chŏnsŏ* 栗谷先生全書 (Complete Works of Master Yulgok Yi I) 1.1b.

examinations a total of nine times. At the age of twenty-nine, he began his government career as Assistant Director at the Ministry of Revenue and subsequently held numerous high-ranking posts, including Royal Secretary, Vice Director of the Royal Academy, and Minister of Personnel, Revenue, Military Affairs, and Justice.

During his illustrious political career, he became known for his efforts to mediate factional strife and for advocating national defense against potential Japanese invasions, including his proposal to raise a standing army of 100,000 troops. He also championed key policy reforms such as the *Taedong* Law 大同法 that was a tax reform that simplified the collection of state tribute by converting various miscellaneous goods into a single grain tax, and the *Sach'ang* 社倉 System that was a community-based grain loan system in which stored grain was lent to people in need, all in pursuit of improving the livelihood of the populace.

Yi I was also a major scholar of Chosŏn Neo-Confucianism who offered a new interpretation of the relationship between principle and *qi* as well as between nature (*sŏng; xing* 性) and emotion/feeling (*chŏng; qing* 情) which Zhu Xi had left somewhat ambiguous. Departing from his predecessor Yi Hwang's 李滉 (1501-1570) formulation, where principle and *qi* were strictly distinguished as mutually exclusive (*pulsangjap*; *buxiangza* 不相雜) in a dualistic and austere manner,[11] Yi I preferred the notion that principle and *qi* are in a subtle and inseparable relationship (*pulsangni*; *buxiangli* 不相離). According to Yi I, principle and *qi* may be logically distinguished, but cannot be actually separated.

For Yi I, *qi* was not merely, as it had been for Yi Hwang, the "vital force of blood and energy" (*hyŏlgi-ji-gi* 血氣之氣) that conceals original nature and causes human corruption. Rather, he regarded *qi* in a more active and positive sense as something that can not only express but also help restore original nature. In this

---

[11] Known as "theory of the mutual arousal of principle and *qi*" (*rigi hobal-sŏl* 理氣互發說), Yi Hwang's theoretical position is most clearly articulated in the historic "Four-Seven Debate" (*sach'il nonjaeng* 四七論爭), conducted with Ki Taesŭng 奇大升 (1527–1572) over the relationship between *li* and *qi*, and between human nature and emotion. Yi Hwang advances a rigorously dualistic account in which principle and *qi* are distinguished as mutually exclusive. For him, principle possesses ontological priority, normative purity, and intrinsic intelligibility, whereas *qi* serves as the material substrate through which principle is actualized but is itself prone to turbidity and moral irregularity. This distinction is most evident in his analysis of the Four Beginnings and the Seven Emotions, where the former issue from principle and are inherently good, while the latter arise from *qi* and are morally indeterminate, requiring regulation. In contrast, Ki Taesŭng articulates a more integrated account that emphasizes the inseparability and co-presence of principle and *qi* in all concrete phenomena. While he does not deny the normative status of principle, he resists any strict bifurcation that would isolate it from the dynamic operations of *qi*. Against Ki Taesŭng's position, Yi Hwang insists on preserving the transcendence and purity of principle. The doctrine of non-mixture serves both metaphysical and ethical ends: it secures the absolute normativity of principle while explaining the variability of human emotions as conditioned by *qi*.

For a comprehensive and detailed introduction to Yi Hwang's thought in English, see Kalton 2019, 159–178; see also Kalton 1988.

view, *qi* is not limited to the material or emotional realm but extends to the more spiritual domain, encompassing even the faculties of the soul and reason.

Thus, whereas for Yi Hwang, concepts such as the heavenly principle (*ch'ŏlli* 天理) and human desires (*inyok* 人慾),[12] the human mind (*insim* 人心) and the mind of the Way (*tosim* 道心), the Four Beginnings (*sadan* 四端) and the seven emotions (*ch'iljŏng* 七情), and original nature (*ponyŏn-ji-sŏng* 本然之性) and material endowment nature (*kijil-ji-sŏng* 氣質之性) were fundamentally opposed and reflected the actual conditions of human life and the world, Yi I saw them as intricately interwoven and inseparable. For Yi I, self-cultivation did not lie in eliminating human desires to pursue heavenly principle, as Yi Hwang maintained, but rather in seeking and securing the heavenly principle within those desires.

Even sages, Yi I held, cannot avoid human emotions and desires. They are themselves an expression of the heavenly principle. According to Yi I, even what is called the "human mind," if properly regulated, "becomes the mind of the Way." In this light, he did not regard the seven emotions as merely belonging to the realm of the form-generating *qi* (*hyŏnggi* 形氣), nor did he believe that original nature exists completely apart from material endowment nature.[13]

> The Four Beginnings and the seven emotions are just like original nature and the nature of material endowment. The original nature is spoken of without reference to material endowment, whereas the nature of material endowment includes the original nature within it. Thus, the Four Beginnings cannot encompass the seven emotions, but the seven emotions do include the Four Beginnings. What Master Zhu called "arising from principle" and "arising from material force" was merely a general way of speaking—who would have thought later scholars would divide them too severely? Students should approach this issue with flexibility.
>
> Moreover, since Master T'oegye (Yi Hwang) attributed goodness to the Four Beginnings, and also said that none of the seven emotions are devoid of goodness, then it follows that outside of the Four Beginnings, there must also be good emotions. From where do these emotions arise? Mengzi presented only the broad outline and so mentioned only compassion, shame and dislike,

[12] The heavenly principle is the supreme and all-encompassing form of *li*, the underlying moral and ontological pattern that orders the cosmos and human life. While *li* denotes the inherent structure or normative principle present in all things, *ch'ŏlli* emphasizes its source in heaven and its role as the ultimate moral standard that governs rightness and harmony. In relation to human desires, the heavenly principle stands as their moral and rational counterpoint: it represents the objective order that should guide human conduct, whereas human desires arise from the sensory and self-seeking tendencies of embodied existence. The cultivation of virtue lies in preserving the heavenly principle within oneself by regulating the desires, ensuring that the cosmic order of *li* manifests in moral life.

[13] Interestingly, Yi I's philosophical position, despite differences in conceptual and categorical frameworks, structurally resembles both the Buddhist *Prajñāparamita* logic of "form is emptiness" 色卽是空 and the Laozi worldview of mutual generation and interdependence between being and non-being such as *yumu taedae* 有無對待 or *yumu sangsaeng* 有無相生.

> modesty and yielding, and a sense of right and wrong. As for other good emotions that may constitute the Four Beginnings, students must infer them by analogy. How could any human emotion that is truly good not be rooted in benevolence, righteousness, ritual propriety, and wisdom? This passage ought to be thoroughly investigated and deeply contemplated.
>
> If there are Four Beginnings that are good emotions, and there are also good emotions outside the Four Beginnings, then it would imply that the human mind has two roots. Can such a view be acceptable? (*Yulgok sŏnsaeng chŏnsŏ* 9.35a–35b)[14]

Yi's more optimistic understanding of the concept of *qi* came to be referred to by later scholars as *qi*-centered theory (*chugi ron* 主氣論), in contrast to Yi Hwang's *li*-centered theory (*churi ron* 主理論), which emphasized the absolute primacy of principle over *qi*. This *qi*-centric view of reality promotes a moderate and pragmatic approach that aims to address problems by confronting and correcting present conditions, rather than seeking an ideal world completely divorced from reality or attempting to radically overturn the existing order through essentialist or fundamentalist means. Many of the reformist policies Yi I proposed reflect this philosophical worldview.

Furthermore, rejecting Sŏ Kyŏngdŏk's 徐敬德 (1489–1546) *qi*-monistic theory (*ki irwŏn* 氣一元) that all things originate from *qi*,[15] Yi I also developed another important theoretical position called "principle is all-pervasive, while *qi* is delimiting" (*rit'ong kiguk* 理通氣局), as part of his effort to systematize Zhu Xi's idea that "principle is one, and its manifestations are diverse" (*riil punsu*; *liyi fenshu* 理一分殊). Whereas Sŏ interpreted both the metaphysical and the physical realms in terms of *qi*, associating "Non-Ultimate and yet Supreme Ultimate" (*mugŭk i t'aegŭk*; *muji er taiji* 無極而太極) with the innate and fundamental, and "The Supreme Ultimate in motion gives rise to yang" (*t'aekŭk tong i saengyang* 太極動而生

---

[14] 四端七情，正如本然之性、氣質之性。本然之性，則不兼氣質而為言也；氣質之性，則卻兼本然之性。故四端不能兼七情，七情則兼四端。朱子所謂「發於理、發於氣」者，只是大綱說，豈料後人之分開太甚乎？學者活看可也。且退溪先生既以善歸之四端，而又曰：「七者之情，亦無有不善。」若然，則四端之外，亦有善情也。此情從何而發哉？孟子舉其大概，故只言惻隱、羞惡、恭敬、是非，而其他善情之為四端，則學者當反三而知之。人情安有不本於仁義禮智而為善情者乎？此一段，當深究精思：善情既有四端，而又於四端之外有善情，則是人心有二本也，其可乎？See also Kalton 1994, 114-15.

[15] Sŏ Kyŏngdŏk articulates a *qi*-monistic theory in which all reality is grounded in the single, continuous, and self generating activity of *qi*. Rejecting any dualistic separation between principle and material force, he maintains that what later thinkers describe as *li* is not an ontologically distinct entity but simply the patterning or regularity inherent in *qi* itself. On this view, the cosmos is an unbroken process of transformation in which all phenomena, from the formation of heaven and earth to human cognition and moral awareness, arise through the dynamic condensation and dispersion of *qi*. Because there is no metaphysical gap between mind and world, moral cultivation consists not in aligning oneself with an external principle but in clarifying and harmonizing the *qi* that one already embodies.

For a helpful English introduction to Sŏ Kyŏngdŏk's thought, see Kim 2019, 135–158.

陽) with the acquired and functional, Yi I made a clear distinction: principle pertains to the metaphysical, and *qi* to the physical. For him, the Supreme Ultimate is principle itself, while yin and yang are manifestations of *qi*.

Yi I described principle as formless (*muhyŏng* 無形) and non-active (*muwi* 無爲), in contrast to *qi*, which is with form (*yuhyŏng* 有形) and active (*yuwi* 有爲). From this, he argued that when principle does not act and *qi* does, then *qi* activates itself, and principle rides upon it (*kibal risŭng* 氣發理乘); and because principle is without form and *qi* is with form, principle is all-pervasive while *qi* is delimiting (*rit'ong kiguk* 理通氣局). In this view, principle has no temporal priority, no shape, no function, and no movement; it is simply the inherent subtlety (*ponyŏn-ji myo* 本然之妙) present in all things. This universality is what is meant by "principle is all-pervasive." *Qi*, on the other hand, is a finite entity (*yuhan-ja* 有限者): it has precedence or posteriority, root and branch, and varies by clarity and turbidity (*ch'ŏngt'ak* 淸濁), thickness and thinness (*hubak* 厚薄), or refinement and dross (*chobak* 糟粕). It performs diverse functions such as imbalance and balance (*p'yŏnjŏng* 偏正), ascent and descent (*sŭnggang* 升降), or flight and elevation (*piyang* 飛揚). As *qi* is confined to particular individuals and cannot pervade all things, it is said to be "*qi* is delimiting." According to Yi I, just as a square vessel and a round vessel differ while the water they contain remains the same, the water may appear different because of the vessel's shape, but its subtlety does not change, but only its appearance does.

According to Yi I, the universe is unified through principle, and at the same time, the principle governing heaven and earth (*ch'ŏnji chi ri* 天地之理), all things (*manmul chi ri* 萬物之理), and human beings (*oin chi ri* 吾人之理) are all shared in common. The reason *qi* has a single root is due to the universality (*t'ong* 通) of principle, and the reason principle manifests in myriad distinctions is because of the particularity or limitedness (*kuk* 局) of *qi*. Yi I's theory of the universality of principle and the particularity of *qi* later developed into a major debate on the sameness and difference between human nature and nonhuman nature, and between the sage and the ordinary person, a nationwide controversy initiated and led by Han Wŏnjin known as the "Horak Debate."

## Sunŏn

The extant *Sunŏn* commentary was first edited by Hong Kyehŭi 洪啓禧 (1703–1771), who acquired a manuscript copy, wrote a postscript, and later published it in print. He notes that the manuscript already bore this title when he first obtained it, and it was believed that the title was given by Yi I himself.[16]

The character *sun* (*chun*) 醇, literally meaning "pure" or "unadulterated," is rarely used as part of a book title. It does not appear at all in the commonly

---

16 See postscript. "Master Yulgok's intention in editing and titling this book may perhaps have been inspired by this [i.e., Xunzi's case]" 先生編書命名之意，或即取於此耶。

circulated Wang Bi edition of the DDJ, and in the ZZ, it only appears once in chapter 33 ("Under Heaven"; *Tianxia* 天下).[17]

First, the concept of *sun* is a phono-semantic compound character combining the radical *yu* (*you*) 酉, which denotes alcohol or wine, and the phonetic component *sun* (*chun*) 享, which means "well ripened" or "well fermented." Its primary meaning is "well-aged, unadulterated wine" or "pure, undiluted liquor." Accordingly, the *Shuowen jiezi* 說文解字 explains this meaning as "wine not diluted with water" 不澆酒也 (15.9768). From this original sense, the character came to carry derived meanings such as "unadulterated," "pure," "simple," and "unsophisticated." Thus, *sun* in *Sunŏn* is used in this derived sense, and the title means "pure words." As discussed below, Yi I considered the work "pure" because he condensed and rearranged the original eighty-one-chapter DDJ into a forty-chapter version, removing what he saw as impure or toxic words. To emphasize this editorial intervention, I use *purified* rather than *pure* in the English title, as it better conveys Yi I's active role in reshaping the text while remaining faithful to its original sense.

One interesting point regarding the term of *sun* is that while the character does not appear in the commonly circulated version of the DDJ, it does appear in the Heshang gong 河上公 edition. This raises the possibility that Yi I may have consulted this text while composing *Sunŏn*. In the third paragraph of his commentary on Chapter 1, Yi I cites Dong Sijing's DZJ, referring to early versions of the DDJ, one of which is the Heshang gong version. While it is Dong who directly mentions this early text, and Yi I is merely quoting him, the fact that Yi I chose to include the reference, when he could have easily omitted it, suggests that he found Dong Sijing's interpretation reliable and helpful. Yi I, like Dong, may also have had access to and consulted the Heshang gong version. However, apart from this single passage, there is no explicit mention of the Heshang gong version elsewhere in the *Sunŏn*, so we cannot conclusively determine whether Yi I actually consulted it himself.

In Chapter 58 of the Heshang gong text, the phrase that reads "The government is muddled; the people are simple" 其政悶悶，其民淳淳 in the received text appears instead as "The government is muddled; the people become pure" 其政悶悶，其民醇醇. Heshang gong glosses the latter as: "The government's correction is generous, so the people become more sincere and prosperous, living in harmony with their parents and others" 政教寬大，故民醇醇富厚，相親睦也. Here, *sun* not only carries the meaning of "pure," but also, by derivation from its original sense of "rich-tasting wine," can imply "warm-hearted" or "deep in human feeling."

---

[17] "How complete the person of ancient times! They paired with the illumination of spirit, were as ***pure*** as heaven and earth, reared myriad things, harmonized with all-under-heaven, and extended grace to all people" 古之人其備乎！配神明，醇天地，育萬物，和天下，澤及百姓。(ZZ 33.1; emphasis added)

## Reception History

As a Neo-Confucian statesman and thinker who was widely respected across Chosŏn for both his political and scholarly leadership, it remains unclear why Yi I chose to write a commentary on the DDJ, a text that, at the time, was unanimously regarded as heretical from the Zhu Xi Confucian standpoint, and even went so far as to make the scandalous claim that studying this work as a sage's book could benefit students in their moral cultivation. The precise reasons or circumstances behind this decision are not known. Yi I's commentary on the *Laozi* is entirely absent from his collected writings, the extant *Yulgok sŏnsaeng chŏnsŏ*, and there is no single hint to indicate or suggest Yi I's authorship of the *Sunŏn* in the *Yulgok sŏnsaeng chŏnsŏ*, and the *Sunŏn* text itself contains no direct reference or indication that identifies him as the author.[18] Moreover, there is no mention in Yi I's biography or in nearly all contemporaneous historical records that he authored or published a commentary on the DDJ.

Unlike many other renowned Neo-Confucian scholars who devoted their entire lives solely to the study and practice of Zhu Xi's teachings, Yi I had a well-known history of engaging in heterodox thought, particularly during his formative years when he entered the mountains and immersed himself in Buddhist practice, which Neo-Confucians despised. This early deviation from orthodoxy was already widely known among his contemporaries and later generations. For his political rivals and opponents, this unorthodox past became a persistent excuse to attack and discredit him throughout his public career.

For those who supported Yi I, it became a burden to defend him against such accusations. The defense usually framed his youthful engagement with Buddhism as a moment of misguided wandering following the tragic loss of his mother, which later became the very reason he came to recognize the emptiness of such paths and fully dedicate himself to the study of Neo-Confucianism.[19]

This line of defense was, above all, a rhetorical repertoire that Yi I himself devised and repeatedly employed when he found it necessary to justify his past. For example, in 1568, at the age of thirty-three, when he was appointed associate counselor at the Royal Advisory Office, he wrote the following in his memorial requesting resignation, known as "Resignation Memorial as Associate Royal Counselor" (*sa pugyori so* 辭副校理疏):

---

[18] While the opening page of the manuscript includes the phrase "Compiled and explained and given oral reading marks by Master Yulgok" 栗谷先生鈔解口訣, the use of the title *sŏnsaeng*, which means Master, suggests that it was not written by Yulgok himself but was likely inserted later by a copyist or editor during the process of manuscript transmission.

[19] For instance, Song Siyŏl 宋時烈 (1607-1689), a major intellectual and political figure of seventeenth-century Chosŏn who was heavily influenced by Yi I's scholarship, justified Yi I's youthful mountain retreat as a confused choice made by a grieving young man. See *Songja taejŏn* "Purok" 宋子大全 附錄 10.18b-19a. For a rare yet helpful introduction to Song Siyŏl's thought in English, see Kwak 2019, 197–209.

> Struck by unfortunate times, I lost my mother early and tried to soothe my grief with reckless thoughts. Eventually, I became engrossed in Buddhist texts and immersed myself in their doctrines, falling into a path of delusion. As a result, my original mind became obscured, and I fled into the deep mountains, where I engaged in Sŏn practice for nearly a year. (*Yulgok sŏnsaeng chŏnsŏ* 3.21a)[20]

Given that Yi I had to publicly defend his earlier life in such terms throughout his official career, it is not difficult to understand why writing a commentary on a text like the DDJ that was considered heretical in Confucian orthodoxy would have posed a significant burden not only for Yi I himself, but also for the many scholars who admired and sought to defend him. This might help explain why the fact that Yi I wrote *Sunŏn* is virtually absent from most official and personal records made in the Chosŏn dynasty.

Although we find no direct testimony from Yi I himself, compelling evidence appears in a letter written by his close friend Song Ikp'il 宋翼弼 (1534–1599), who expresses deep concern about Yi I's work on the DDJ commentary. Although barred from government office because of his illegitimate birth (*sŏŏl* 庶孽), Song Ikp'il was a distinguished scholar of ritual theory (*yehak; lixue* 禮學) and was especially renowned for his commentary on Zhu Xi's *Jiali* 家禮 (Family Rituals). As one of Yi I's closest and trusted friends, Song Ikp'il did not hesitate to offer both encouragement and criticism regarding Yi I's scholarly pursuits.

In a letter supposedly dated to around 1580, Song criticizes Yi I's work on the DDJ commentary in strongly disapproving terms:

> The other day, I met with Howŏn (Sŏng Hon 成渾; 1535-1598) in Hyangyang-*ri* village, and there I saw a newly edited copy of *Sunŏn* 諄言.[21] It seemed to have been driven by your talent and flair, but I must confess it gave me pause. Could it be that you have inherited the lingering intention of Zhu Hui'an (i.e., Zhu Xi) in writing the *Zhouyi Cantongqi kaoyi* (Critical Examination of the *Cantongqi*)? Again, I lament on behalf of the Way of the world. You aim to subdue those who think differently and make them conform, yet there is a risk that you have lost the original intent of DDJ and forced it into agreement with our Confucian Way. Your commentary, too, seems strained and contrived. You have committed yourself to reviving the broken lineage of learning, and you should have no time to spare for such a thing, yet you have still made time to toy with words and ink. This is not what I had hoped from you. (*Kubong sŏnsaeng-jip* 4.35b)[22]

---

20 生丁不辰，早喪慈母，以妄塞悲，遂耽釋教，膏浸水潤，反覆沈迷；因昧本心，走入深山，從事禪門，迨周一年。

21 Here, Song Ikp'il writes the title as *Sunŏn* 諄言 instead of *Sunŏn* 醇言. It is unclear whether this deviation from the official title was simply his orthographic mistake. If not, the original title might also be interpreted as *Sincere Words* rather than *Purified Words*.

22 日者，與浩原相會於向陽，見兄新編《諄言》一帙，似為才氣所使，為兄致疑焉。抑無乃朱晦庵《參同契》遺意耶？重為世道興歎，屈異而欲同之，失老子本旨，而於吾道

This remarkable testimony, coming from one of Yi I's closest intellectual allies, strongly supports the possibility that Yi I indeed composed a DDJ commentary. At the same time, it also reflects how controversial and potentially damaging such a work could have been in the eyes of contemporaries committed to the purity and orthodoxy of the Neo-Confucian tradition in Chosŏn.

To Song Ikp'il, Yi I's writing of a *Laozi* commentary resembled Zhu Xi's effort to appropriate Daoist teachings by writing a commentary on the *Cantongqi*, a text on Daoist alchemical practices. Song saw Yi I's attempt to interpret the DDJ through a Confucian lens as a distortion of its original meaning, an act of forcing coherence, and criticized it as a frivolous indulgence in literary play rather than the kind of scholarly work expected from someone of Yi I's stature. For Song, the historic task of reviving the broken lineage of Neo-Confucianism after Zhu Xi should have taken priority, and Yi I's commentary on the DDJ was an unworthy distraction from that mission. The core portion of this criticism is in fact quoted by Hong Kyehŭi in the postscript he wrote for *Sunŏn*.

Based on the information in Song's letter, it appears that Yi I completed *Sunŏn* around 1580, when he was approximately 43 years old, and that figures such as Sŏng Hon already had access to the work. Considering that Yi I passed away in 1584 at the age of 47, *Sunŏn* may be regarded as a product of his later years. Nevertheless, despite the crucial fact that *Sunŏn* had been completed and was in circulation by 1580, Yi I's precise motivation, intention, or context for composing the work remains unknown.

Even if it is true that Yi I wrote a work titled *Sunŏn*, whether the version of *Sunŏn* currently in circulation is indeed the same work that Song Ikp'il once saw remains uncertain. Ultimately, this question hinges on whether we can trust the postscript attached to the end of the extant *Sunŏn*. That postscript was likely written nearly 170 years after the work's composition by Hong Kyehŭi, a prominent statesman during the reign of King Yŏngjo (r. 1724–1776). In the postscript, Hong clearly states that the work was authored by Yi I.

According to the postscript, Hong Kyehŭi, while serving as governor of Ch'ungch'ŏng Province, happened upon a manuscript of *Sunŏn* in 1749 during an inspection tour of the southern regions of the province. He acquired it from a descendant of Sindokjae 慎獨齋 Kim Chip 金集 (1574–1656), who claimed that Kim had copied the manuscript by hand. At the time, Hong was engaged in collecting scattered writings by Yi I that had not been included in the *Yulgok sŏnsaeng chŏnsŏ*, and 1749 marked the year in which this effort bore its first fruit: the initial publication of the *Yulgok sŏnsaeng chŏnsŏ sŭbyu* 栗谷先生全書拾遺 (Supplementary Collection of Master Yulgok's Writings).[23]

---

亦有苟同之嫌。註又牽合，兄以繼絶為期，宜日不暇及，而弄文墨於餘地，非吾所望於兄也。

[23] For the publication of the *Yulgok sŏnsaeng chŏnsŏ sŭbyu* by Hong Kyehŭi, see Kang 2024.

Given this context, it seems unlikely that Hong's acquisition of *Sunŏn* from a descendant of a prestigious family in his own jurisdiction was purely coincidental. Fearing that the manuscript might be lost, Hong had the book printed the following year, in 1750, after his promotion to Minister of War and his return to Seoul. According to this account, it may be partly thanks to Hong Kyehŭi that we are able to read and know of this book today.

As for the authenticity of the work, it appears that even Kim Chip's descendants, who had preserved the manuscript for nearly 170 years, believed it to be genuinely authored by Yi I. Although Kim Chip belonged to the next generation of scholars, he himself was a nationally respected Neo-Confucian scholar, who deeply admired Yi I. It is therefore not implausible that Kim came to possess a manuscript of Yi I's work.

One important fact to note here is that despite having directly uncovered *Sunŏn*, Hong Kyehŭi did not, in fact, include it in the *Yulgok sŏnsaeng chŏnsŏ sŭbyu*, which he was compiling and publishing in collaboration with close colleagues. The precise reason for this exclusion remains unknown. Since the exact dates of his acquisition of the *Sunŏn* manuscript and the compilation of the *Sŭbyu* are not clearly established, it is possible that he had not yet obtained or just become aware of *Sunŏn* at the time he was about to publish the *Sŭbyu*. Another plausible explanation, as mentioned earlier, is the burden of justification that Yi I's overt engagement with heterodox teachings placed on both himself and the many Chosŏn Confucian scholars who respected and followed him. For those aware of Yi I's impious project, there may have been compelling reasons either to defend it or to remain silent. From this perspective, excluding *Sunŏn* from the *Sŭbyu* might have been a deliberate decision made to protect Yi I and his supporters. Seen in this light, Hong Kyehŭi's act of publishing *Sunŏn* was likely motivated more by a concern for preservation than by a desire to widely disseminate it.

*Sunŏn* came to be reexamined within the intellectual history of Korea through a chance occurrence. In 1974, Dr. Ryu Ch'illo, a scholar of East Asian philosophy, happened upon the book in the Kyujanggak archives at Seoul National University and introduced it to Dr. Kim Kilhwan. It was through Kim's 1976 article, "Yulgok ŭi *Noja*-gwan," that the existence of the work was first made known to the academic community in Korea.

Taking this reception history into account, we cannot say that the authorship issue regarding Yi I and *Sunŏn* has been completely resolved. However, given the currently available evidence, including Song Ikp'il's letter that explicitly mentions Yi I's authorship of a *Laozi* commentary titled *Sunŏn*, the manuscript commentary on the DDJ bearing the same title that was acquired some 170 years later from a descendant of Kim Chip, the postscript by Hong Kyehŭi that records that event, and the broader anti-Daoist intellectual context of Yi I's time in which the work circulated, it is difficult to find compelling grounds to doubt or reject the attribution of this text to Yi I. Accordingly, this study follows the scholarly consensus in treating Yi I as the author of *Sunŏn*.

## Editions and Structure

To date, *Sunŏn* survives only in manuscript form from the Chosŏn dynasty, and four extant copies have been identified. These are held respectively at the Kyujanggak Institute for Korean Studies at Seoul National University, the Tōyō Bunko Museum in Japan, Chŏnnam National University Library, and the C.V. Starr East Asian Library at UC Berkeley. There are no significant textual differences among the editions, and the Kyujanggak version is generally regarded as the base text. The Kyujanggak, Tōyō Bunko, and UC Berkeley editions are all accessible online. Here, I have used the Kyujanggak edition as the primary source.

One intriguing fact concerning the editions is that although Hong Kyehŭi stated he had the text printed with movable type, all extant copies are handwritten manuscripts rather than printed editions. In other words, none of the currently surviving copies are from the edition printed by Hong. This raises the possibility that there may have been some differences between the original manuscript Hong obtained from Kim Chip's descendant and the versions that exist today. However, since Hong's original copy is now not confirmable, this possibility cannot be confirmed, either. That said, given the general textual consistency among the four extant manuscripts, it is unlikely that any major alterations occurred during the transmission of the text.

Among the various commentaries on the DDJ written by either Chinese or Chosŏn Confucian scholars, *Sunŏn* stands out for the distinctive way in which its content is organized. According to the postscript written by Hong Kyehŭi, Yi I selected only those lines and passages from DDJ that do not conflict with Confucian principles and recompiled them into a new structure consisting of 40 chapters. This indicates that Yi I did not adopt the traditional structure of standard DDJ, which is divided into two parts, the Way (Dao) part and the Virtue (De) part, and consists of a total of 81 chapters. Instead, he eliminated approximately three-fifths of the original text and restructured the remaining two-fifths according to thematic relevance and philosophical necessity. The content he excluded from the original text will be discussed below. First let us examine the content Yi I did retain and the principles on which he restructured it.

In fact, the attempt to interpret Laozi's message as being compatible with Confucian teachings was not unique to Yi I. Already during the Ming dynasty, when Yi I lived, Chinese intellectual circles were marked by a distinct trend of philosophical synthesis that sought to reconcile Daoism and Confucianism. Dong Sijing's DZJ, which Yi I used as the textual basis for his own commentary, had been written during the Northern Song dynasty, approximately four hundred years before Yi I's time. Given that Yi I frequently cited Dong's commentary in *Sunŏn* without sometimes adding much of his own interpretive input, it might be difficult to claim that his originality mainly lies in the pro-Daoist approach or perspective of the commentary itself.

Perhaps, instead, what makes Yi I's *Sunŏn* a truly unique contribution to the tradition of the long DDJ exegesis is not merely that he read the DDJ through the lens of Neo-Confucianism or sought to harmonize Laozi's message with Confucian thinking. Rather, he dismantled the traditional two-part, eighty-one-chapter structure of the standard DDJ and drastically abridged it, preserving only about 40 percent of the original content and reorganizing it into a new form. In doing so, the *Sunŏn* becomes a text that is at once the DDJ and yet no longer the DDJ, an independent work with a distinct textual identity of its own.

The structure and content of Yi I's *Sunŏn*, in which he dismantled and recompiled the original chapter divisions of the DDJ, are as follows.[24]

| ***Sunŏn*** | ***Daodejing*** | ***Sunŏn*** | ***Daodejing*** |
|---|---|---|---|
| 1 | 42 (part), 5 (part), 42 (part) | 21 | 45 |
| 2 | 51 (part) | 22 | 56 |
| 3 | 37 (part) | 23 | 55 (part) |
| 4 | 11 | 24 | 50 (part) |
| 5 | 12, 10 (part) | 25 | 34 (part), 63 (part) |
| 6 | 48 (part) | 26 | 54 (part) |
| 7 | 59 (part) | 27 | 81 (part) |
| 8 | 22 (part), 24, 22 (part), 24 | 28 | 27 (part) |
| 9 | 33 | 29 | 49 (part) |
| 10 | 44 | 30 | 29 |
| 11 | 47 | 31 | 57, 58 (part) |
| 12 | 46 | 32 | 43 (part) |
| 13 | 67 (part) | 33 | 30 |
| 14 | 76, 78 | 34 | 31 (part) |
| 15 | 9 | 35 | 60 (part) |
| 16 | 39 (part) | 36 | 64 (part), 63 (part) |
| 17 | 8 (part), 66 (part) | 37 | 73, 72 (part) |
| 18 | 68 | 38 | 77 (part), 79 (part) |
| 19 | 41 (part), 45, 81 (part) | 39 | 70 |
| 20 | 26, 23 (part) | 40 | 53 (part) |

Noteworthy in Yi I's reordering and editing of the original DDJ is that several of the most important chapters typically regarded as representative of Laozi's philosophy are excluded. Notably, the early chapters of the Way part, which encapsulate the core and defining traits of Laozi's thought, are entirely omitted, as is Chapter 38, which marks the beginning of the so-called Virtue part. On what basis did Yi I decide which passages to include and which to exclude? Do the chapters he chose not to adopt share any common themes or patterns?

According to the postscript by Hong Kyehŭi, the guiding principle of Yi I's editorial discretion was to discard any content that did not align with the Confucian Way. This explains why passages such as the early part of Chapter 5, as well as Chapters 18, 19, and 38, texts that explicitly deny or subvert core Confucian

[24] When only part of a chapter is excerpted, this is marked with "(part)."

values like benevolence (*in; ren* 仁), righteousness (*ŭi; yi* 義), ritual propriety (*ye; li* 禮), wisdom (*chi; zhi* 智), and filial piety (*hyo; xiao* 孝), were not included in *Sunŏn.*

Moreover, the exclusion may also relate to common Neo-Confucian critiques of Daoism and Buddhism at the time, particularly their association with moral relativism, cynicism, or nihilism stemming from the idea of non-being (*mu; wu* 無) as the ultimate origin of being. In this context, chapters such as Chapter 1 and Chapter 40, which focus on non-being in metaphysical terms, would naturally have been excluded from *Sunŏn.*

However, when the notion of non-being is not presented as a cosmological origin but rather as a practice of self-cultivation, such as emptying the self (*mugong; wugong* 無功; "non-achievement") or acting in accordance with, rather than against, natural principle (*muwi; wuwei* 無爲; "non-action"), then those sections could be included. For example, DDJ 11 (incorporated into Chapter 4 of *Sunŏn*) and DDJ 24 (appearing in Chapter 8) are accepted, as they reflect this more ethically compatible interpretation of *mu* (*wu*).

While examining the content of *Sunŏn*, Kim Hangmok observes that certain passages which could initially seem contrary to Confucian principles were nevertheless included, and further, that Yi I reinterpreted them in ways that aligned with Confucian teachings. As concrete examples, Kim points to DDJ 48 (*Sunŏn* Chapter 6), 50 (24), and 55 (23) (Kim 2001, 136-140). According to Kim, such examples suggest that Hong Kyehŭi's postscript subtly implies Yi I did in fact engage with material not conventionally aligned with the Confucian Way, when Hong quotes Song Ik'pil's accusation that Yi I seems to force to harmonize those teachings with Confucian ones. This, Kim argues, offers a concrete rebuttal to concerns, voiced by both Song and Hong, that Yi I might have distorted the original meaning of the DDJ in order to force it into a Confucian mold.

Ironically, this raises ambiguity regarding the phrase "content incompatible with the Confucian Way," which Hong Kyehŭi had originally presented as a guiding principle of Yi I's editorial intervention. If such anti-Confucian content could be interpreted into harmony with Confucian values, then the criteria for exclusion become far less clear. This suggests that Yi I's editorial discretion may not have followed a consistently objective or transparent standard, and that, aside from passages that explicitly reject fundamental Confucian values or positions, the notion of incompatibility with the Way is more of a broad rhetorical assertion than a precise analytical framework for understanding how *Sunŏn* was composed. Therefore, rather than assuming a definite standard of selection, it seems more reasonable to understand that Yi I selectively chose passages in a loosened manner from the original text of the DDJ that aligned with the themes and structure he envisioned for *Sunŏn*, as he outlines at the end of Chapter 40.

In the final section of *Sunŏn*, Yi I not only explains the overall structure of the text but also summarizes the key points at the end of each chapter. According to this last passage, chapters 1 to 3 address the Way's essence (*toch'e* 道體), chapter 4 the mind's essence (*simch'e* 心體), chapters 5 to 35 deal with self-cultivation (*sugi*

修己) and governing others (*ch'iin* 治人), chapter 36 concerns the beginning and end (*sijong* 始終), chapters 37 to 38 the heavenly Way (*ch'ŏndo* 天道), and chapters 39 to 40 the practice of the Way (*haengdo* 行道).

Yi I first begins with the essence of the Way as taught by Laozi, then discusses the essence of the human mind that contains that Way; these two together form a general overview and constitute the fundamental premise for his central message on how to cultivate oneself and govern others. From this general overview, Yi I moves to more concrete discussion about how to live and practice the Way in individual and communal life, covering chapters 5 through 35, which can be seen as the main part of the work. This main part resembles the concentric expansion structure of "self-cultivation and governing others" or "self-cultivation and bringing peace to others" (*sugi anin* 修己安人) emphasized by Zhu Xi's *Daxue* 大學 (Great Learning), understood as the original spirit of Confucianism. Passing through the structure of "self-cultivation and bringing peace to others," Yi I finally concludes by recalling once again the essence of the Way that undergirds this concrete practice of life, thereby ending his discussion. Therefore, while most of *Sunŏn*'s structure proceeds deductively from the principle of the Way to concrete practice, the last five chapters adopt an inductive approach that returns to the fundamental principle.

Through this radical reorganization, modeled in part on the *sugi anin* idea of the *Daxue*, Yi I's work, while preserving the content of the original DDJ, was transformed into an essentially new book fittingly named *Sunŏn*, distinct from the DDJ. More specifically, how did Yi I reconcile the DDJ with Confucian ideals?

## Yi I on Laozi in *Sunŏn*

Although we do not know the specific motivations, or context that led Yi I to compose a commentary on the DDJ, we may note that around the same period he was writing *Sunŏn*, he was also producing and publishing introductory Confucian texts intended for the basic education of young students and youth, such as the *Sŏnghak chibyo* 聖學輯要 (Collected Essentials for Sage Learning; 1575), *Kyŏngmong yogyŏl* 擊蒙要訣 (Essential Secrets for Awakening the Benighted; 1577), and the *Sohak chipju* 小學集註 (Collected Annotations on the *Xiaoxue*; 1579). Taking this into account, it is possible that Yi I may have regarded the DDJ as a work that preserved the teachings of an ancient sage and thus as a valuable text for transmitting the core principles of becoming a sage.

The fact that the DDJ has not been properly appreciated by Chosŏn Neo-Confucian scholars is largely due to the approximately 60% of its content that Yi I deliberately excluded in the making of *Sunŏn*. Yet, Yi I was firmly convinced that the ultimate message conveyed by the DDJ is not in conflict with the Confucian teachings of practicing the Way. For Yi I, the most important message of the DDJ is that only a morally cultivated individual, someone who has undergone self-cultivation and follows the path of the sage who has realized the Way, can bring peace to the state and the world.

The governance of the sage described in DDJ, as Yi I saw it, namely governance through non-action (*muwi-ji-ch'i*; *wuwei zhi zhi* 無爲之治), was not about nourishing one's life for the sake of self-preservation, nor was it a form of nihilism or misanthropy that refrains from doing anything for others and community. Rather, it was the rule of the ideal Confucian noble person (*kunja; junzi* 君子), who renounces selfish desires and self-interest and devotes himself to the benefit and well-being of others. In this respect, Yi I believed there was essentially no difference between the sage's governance in DDJ and the moral rule (*tŏkch'i*; *dezhi* 德治) of the Confucian noble person or Mengzi's ideal of kingly governance (*wangdo chŏngch'i*; *wangdao zhengzhi* 王道政治). He was convinced of this, and throughout the entire text, he repeatedly emphasizes this message.

As Yi I explains in the structure of *Sunŏn*, before addressing the central theme of self-cultivation and the governance of others in the DDJ, he begins with a general discussion of the Way and the human mind as the first topic of the work. Based on the thematic structure he lays out in *Sunŏn*, we will now examine how Yi I interprets the DDJ from the perspective of Neo-Confucianism and thereby aligns it with the foundational spirit of Confucian learning.

## Yi I's Understanding of Laozi's Way

Yi I begins his *Sunŏn* by first addressing the nature of Laozi's concept of Way. As noted earlier in the structural overview of the book, this is because Yi I intended to compose the work according to a deductive structure, starting from the essence of the Way and moving toward its realization and concrete application in daily life. The DDJ itself begins with highly abstract language, describing the essence, characteristics, and functions of the Way. And although somewhat nominal, the classic is divided into the Way part and the Virtue part, forming a structure that begins with understanding the Way and proceeds to its practical application. This textual feature of the DDJ may have further encouraged Yi I to adopt such a deductive framework.

However, this structure may simply reflect a more logical and persuasive method of exposition. Whether in Confucianism, Daoism, or Buddhism, the Way, as implied in its original meanings of "path one walks" or "to guide," refers to the fundamental orientation and guiding principle that human beings ought to follow and practice in life. Questions about how a person should exist, live, or act; how one should relate to others; and how one should connect to larger communities beyond the self and family all begin with correctly grasping the true nature of the Way and then embodying it in daily life. Thus, understanding what the Way is must precede any discussion of how we are to apply and practice it in real life; it is an essential first step.

Interestingly, however, when discussing the essence of the Way, Yi I makes no mention of Chapter 1 of the DDJ, which is typically regarded as one of the most representative chapters related to the concept of the Way in DDJ. As mentioned earlier, this may be because Yi I sought to avoid the misunderstanding of a kind of "primordial nothingness" that could arise from interpreting the notion of non-being as the origin of all things in a nihilistic light.[25]

Instead, at the beginning of *Sunŏn*, Yi I cites Chapters 42 and 5 of the DDJ, making clear that for Laozi, the Way is the ultimate source that gives rise to all things. In Laozi, the function of the Way is generative; it brings forth life and causes things to emerge within the world. All beings in the world originate from the Way, and therefore all beings share the same source.

> The Way gives rise to the One; the One gives rise to the Two;
> the Two gives rise to the Three; the Three gives rise to all things. (1; 42)[26]

> Between heaven and earth, it is like a bellows. (1; 5)[27]

As Han Wŏnjin later argues in his reading of the ZZ, Neo-Confucian scholars often understood the Daoist Way as a state of non-being: an empty, quiescent nothingness in which nothing yet exists. From this state of beingless non-being, the first thing (being) arises, and the generation of existence begins. If one equates the non-being in DDJ 1, described as the origin of all things, with the Way in DDJ 42, which gives rise to one, then it becomes possible to claim that Laozi's Way is likewise characterized as empty, quiescent non-being.

For Neo-Confucian thinkers, however, such non-being, though lacking concrete substance, is still understood as a kind of *qi*, the vital material force or energy capable of generating something. More specifically, since it is silent, still, and devoid of any determinate form, it is seen as a form of *qi* in the yin state (*ŭmgi*; *yinqi* 陰氣). Naturally, from the standpoint of Neo-Confucianism, which asserts the priority and superiority of yang over yin and principle over *qi*, Laozi and Zhuangzi's Way is flawed: it recognizes only *qi* and fails to grasp *li*.

Interestingly, however, Yi I, citing Zhu Xi, firmly asserts that the Way described in DDJ 42 as the primordial source that gives birth to all things is not *qi* but the Supreme Ultimate.

> Comment: Master Zhu commented, "The Way refers to the Supreme Ultimate as mentioned in the *Zhouyi* (*Xici* A11). 'One' represents the odd number of yang, 'Two' the even number of yin, and 'Three' the combination of both the odd and even numbers of yang and yin (*Xici* B4). The phrase 'The Two gives life to

---

[25] For example, the following line is often interpreted as a case of nihilistic non-being fundamentalism that Chosŏn Neo-Confucians were highly critical of and took the DDJ as a heresy for: "Non-being is called the beginning of heaven and earth; being is called the mother of all things" 無名天地之始，有名萬物之母。Traditionally, this line has also been interpreted as: "The nameless is the beginning of heaven and earth; the named is the mother of all things."

[26] The numbers in parentheses following the quotations indicate the chapter numbers in *Sunŏn* and the DDJ, respectively. The original sentence of the quoted lines is: 道生一，一生二，二生三，三生萬物。

[27] 天地之間，其猶橐籥乎。

Three' resembles the old saying, 'Two and one make three.'[28] 'The Three gives life to myriad things' indicates that the combination of the odd and even numbers of yang and yin brings forth all creation" (ZZQS 31.140).[29]

According to the full record in the volume 31 of the *Zhuzi quanshu* 朱子全書 (The Complete Works of Master Zhu; ZZQS), one day the disciple Cheng Renzhi 程泰之 (fl. mid-12th century) quoted DDJ 42 and asked Zhu Xi about that passage.[30] Zhu Xi is said to have interpreted that chapter in the way described above. In the part Yi I does not quote, Zhu Xi further affirms that Laozi's concept of Way is virtually the same as the Supreme Ultimate discussed in the *Zhouyi* stating, "If Laozi had regarded one as the Supreme Ultimate, then there would have been no need for him to say again that the Way gives rise to one." 若直以一為太極，則不容復言道生一矣. Zhu Xi clearly distinguishes between the Way and one, asserting that one is generated from the Way. For Zhu Xi, then, Laozi's Way is a state of pure potential for the emergence of life, prior even to the existence of one. By citing this record, Yi I makes it clear that Laozi's Way is not *qi*, but is in fact the same as the Confucian Way, the Supreme Ultimate.

For Zhu Xi and Neo-Confucian thinkers, the Supreme Ultimate is principle as one.[31] The concept of Supreme Ultimate first appeared in the Confucian worldview in the *Xici* of the *Zhouyi*, where it was used to explain the origin of the eight trigrams used in divination for fortune and misfortune.[32] Later, Zhou Dunyi 周敦頤 (1017–1073) of the Northern Song (960–1127) reinterpreted the Supreme Ultimate as the cosmic origin in his work *Taiji tushuo* 太極圖說 (Explanation on the Diagram of the Supreme Ultimate), and Zhu Xi later canonized Zhou's interpretation. As a result, within Neo-Confucianism, the concept of Supreme Ultimate came to be understood as the original source from which all things begin and are generated. Zhu Xi identified the Supreme Ultimate that Zhou Dunyi had posited as the ultimate origin of all things with the concept of principle, the inherent principle of being in all things, that he had learned from the brothers Cheng Hao and Cheng Yi.

According to this Neo-Confucian cosmology, every being already possesses an internal principle that makes it what it is, even before it assumes its external

---

28 The "old saying" refers to the following line: "One and Speech are two; two and one are three" 一與言為二，二與一為三。See *Zhuangzi* 2.9.

29 朱子曰：「道即易之太極，一乃陽之奇，二乃陰之耦，三乃奇耦之積。其曰二生三，猶所謂二與一為三也。其曰三生萬物，即奇耦合而萬物生也。」

30 "[Cheng] asked about the line: 'The Way gives life to one, one gives life to two, and two gives life to three" 問：「道生一，一生二，二生三。」

31 "The Supreme Ultimate is principle" 太極，理也。(ZZQS 49.41).

32 "In the change, there is the Supreme Ultimate. This gives rise to the two modes. The two modes give rise to the four forms. The four forms give rise to the eight trigrams. The eight trigrams determine fortune and misfortune, and from fortune and misfortune are born great undertakings"易有太極，是生兩儀；兩儀生四象；四象生八卦；八卦定吉凶；吉凶生大業。(*Xici* A.11).

form. Although Yi I does not explicitly state this in *Sunŏn*, the concept of *chayŏn* (*ziran* 自然), commonly translated as "spontaneity" or "to be so of itself," which frequently appears in DDJ, refers to an internal law by which all beings emerge, grow, change, develop, decline, and perish without the imposition of any external force or condition. From the Neo-Confucian perspective, this can be seen as all beings following *li*. In this light, even in DDJ, the Way should not be mistaken, as it often is, for *qi*, but rather understood as *li*.

After declaring that Laozi's Way is the Supreme Ultimate, Yi I follows Zhu Xi's explanation, interpreting the terms "one," "two," and "three" in DDJ 42 not as numerical quantities, one thing, two things, three things, but as ordinal positions: first, second, and third. He asserts that the "first" refers to yang *qi*, the "second" to yin *qi*, and the "third" to the union of yin and yang. This is a reading of DDJ from the cosmological perspective of the *Zhouyi*.

As previously noted, the *Xici* is the first to use the concept of Supreme Ultimate, stating: "In the change, there is the Supreme Ultimate. This gives rise to the two modes" 易有太極，是生兩儀. Traditionally, the "two modes" have been understood as referring to yin and yang, which constitute the smallest unit of a hexagram line (*hyo; yao* 爻) in the *Zhouyi*. Zhou Dunyi, in his *Taiji tushuo*, offers a more specific interpretation of this line:

> The Supreme Ultimate moves and gives rise to yang. When its movement reaches its limit, it becomes still. In stillness, it gives rise to yin. When stillness reaches its limit, it moves again. One movement and one stillness, each is the root of the other. In their differentiation into yin and yang, the two modes are therein established." (*Taiji tushuo* 6)[33]

Zhu Xi, along with Yi I who followed him, sought to explain how all things emerge from the Way in Laozi by applying the cosmological theory of the generation of the eight trigrams found in the *Xici*, as reinterpreted by Zhou Dunyi. According to this Neo-Confucian cosmology, Laozi's worldview includes not a formless void, but rather *li* or Way, which is both Non-Ultimate (*mugŭk* 無極) and yet Supreme Ultimate, non-being yet being, and being yet non-being. That principle or Way moves, giving rise to the *qi* of yin and yang, and through the combination and accumulation of yin and yang, all things come into being.[34]

---

[33] 太極動而生陽，動極而靜；靜而生陰，靜極復動。一動一靜，互為其根；分陰分陽，兩儀立焉。

[34] This cosmological theory has long provoked conceptual difficulties and debates since Zhu Xi. The first concerns the priority between *li* and *qi*. While the Supreme Ultimate's generative process seems to assume that *li* precedes *qi*, Zhu Xi also held that, just as there is no precedence between Non-Ultimate (non-being) and Supreme Ultimate (being), *li* cannot be said to precede or produce *qi*.

Second, if *li* precedes *qi*, how does the Supreme Ultimate move of itself? Since *li* is by nature still while *qi* moves and transforms, Zhu Xi's identification of the moving Supreme Ultimate with *li* raises the question: can *li* move and generate *qi*? This problem of the mobility

Simply put, the essential nature of this Way is that it is the source of all life. All beings come into existence from this Way. According to Yi I, the first characteristic of such a Way is that it is empty in itself. In the first chapter of *Sunŏn,* Yi I cites a passage from DDJ 5 to present the Way as something empty yet inexhaustible—a source that generates beings all the more as it moves. "While empty, it never exhausts itself. As it moves, it gives forth more (1; 5).[35]

That is to say, while the Way serves as the origin that gives birth to all things, it itself possesses nothing within; it is empty. Why, then, is Laozi's Way, which Yi I also identifies as the Supreme Ultimate, empty? Although Yi I does not explain this explicitly in his commentary, we can find a possible answer from the *Taiji tushuo.* According to this foundational text, the Taegŭk (taiji) is also Mugŭk (wuji). For Zhu Xi, who annotated the *Taiji tushuo*, this Non-Ultimate corresponds to Laozi's notion of non-being. Although Zhu Xi points out that Laozi treats being and non-being as two distinct entities, while Zhou Dunyi regards them as one, he nonetheless acknowledges that Zhou's Supreme Ultimate corresponds to Laozi's being, and Zhou's Non-Ultimate to Laozi's non-being.[36] Thus, even though Supreme Ultimate and Non-Ultimate are conceptually distinct, in Neo-Confucian framework, the Supreme Ultimate is the being that generates all things, while in itself it is empty, and its depth reaches the infinite non-being.

This Way operates by what is called "doing nothing" (*muwi*, *wuwei*). This is the second characteristic of Laozi's Way as seen by Yi I. In Chapter 3 of *Sunŏn*, Yi I quotes DDJ 37 to highlight that the Way functions through *wuwei.* "The Way constantly operates with non-doing, yet there is nothing it cannot accomplish" (3; 37).[37]

---

of *li* and *qi* became tied to issues of human nature, emotion, and moral cultivation, sparking intense mid-Chosŏn Neo-Confucian debates. Yi Hwang proposed the "mutual activation of *li* and *qi*," while Yi I rejected this as inconsistent with Zhu Xi, insisting that only *qi* moves while *li* governs its motion—"*qi* is activated, and *li* rides upon it in one pathway" (*kibal isŭng ildo sŏl* 氣發理乘一途說).

A third issue is whether *li* is one or many. If yin and yang *qi* arise from the Supreme Ultimate to generate all things, is *li* universal or individual to each being? Zhu Xi replied, "*Li* is one, but its manifestations are many" (*riil punsu* 理一分殊), like one moon reflected in many rivers. Yet he did not explain how *li* diversifies, leaving the problem unresolved. Many Chosŏn scholars sought answers; Yi I held that *li* is one but diversifies due to the uneven manifestations of *qi*. A century and a half later, the *li*'s diversification issue developed into the question of whether human nature and the nature of things are the same or different, which became the central issue of debate in the eighteenth-century debate. Han Wŏnjin, discussed later in this book, was a major figure who argued that they are fundamentally distinct.

35 虛而不屈，動而愈出。

36 "Zhu Xi also says, 'Laozi speaks of being and non-being as two, but Master Zhou speaks of being and non-being as one'" 朱子又曰：「老子之言有無，以有無為二；周子之言有無，以有無為一。」 (*Taiji tushuo* 6).

37 道常無為，而無不為。

What then exactly does "doing nothing" mean in the phrase "doing nothing, yet nothing cannot be undone"? Yi I understands the concept of non-action in two interconnected dimensions in *Sunŏn*.

First, as shown in Yi I's commentary on Chapter 3 (DDJ 37), non-doing does not mean literally doing nothing. Rather, the operation of the Way is so profound and mysterious that from the human perspective, it appears as if nothing is thought or done. Why, how, and what it accomplishes is beyond human perception and understanding. Yi I cites the famous phrase from the *Shijing*, *Daya*, "The operation of the high heaven is soundless and odorless" 上天之載，無聲無臭.[38] It stresses that the operation of the Way surpasses human senses and comprehension. From a human standpoint, the Way appears as if it did nothing.[39]

The second meaning of non-doing as Yi I understands it is acting without any conscious intention or thought of doing something for someone or something. By eliminating such consciousness and thought itself, one does not claim to have achieved it oneself, and thus it becomes no different from having done nothing. In Chapter 15 of *Sunŏn*, Yi I quotes DDJ 9 to clarify that this is how heaven accomplishes its tasks:

> To withdraw when the task is done, and fame has been followed — This is the Way of heaven. (15; 9)[40]

One accomplishes a merit yet does not think of it as one's own, withdrawing quietly so that no one can claim to have done it. Though no one claims to have done it, the work is already completed; thus, no one did anything, yet everything is done.

Embracing non-doing as how the Way of heaven works, Yi I, citing Dong Sijing's commentary, takes a further step to formalize *wuwei* as no-self.

> Not revealing oneself, one becomes illumined.
> Not asserting oneself, one shines forth.
> Not boasting, one gains merit.
> Not being proud, one endures.
> Because they do not contend,
> None under heaven can contend with them. (8; 22)[41]

> Comment: Mr. Dong said, "The character for 'to see' means 'to reveal,' and this points to a method of cultivating virtue. When one embraces the oneness, he no longer has [the sense of] self (*mua; wuwo* 無我). But if one reveals themselves,

---

[38] *Shijing* 詩經, *Daya* 大雅, "Decade of King Wen" 文王之什, 7.

[39] Yi I's commentary in Chapter 3 states: "For humans, nothing appears to be thought of and nothing to be done" 人則無思無為。

[40] 功成名遂，身退，天之道。

[41] 不自見故明，不自是故彰，不自伐故有功，不自矜故長。夫惟不爭，故天下莫能與之爭。

> insists on being right, boasts, and takes pride in themselves, it shows that the self is not forgotten yet. How, then, can he speak of the oneness?"[42]

The no-self in this context is different from the Buddhist notion of *anātman*, which holds that the self does not exist as a substantial entity but is merely a temporary composite of the five aggregates (*skandhas*). What Yi I means by no-self, borrowing Dong Sijing's interpretation, is the absence of self-consciousness in one's actions. One eliminates the awareness of "I" in what one does, such that even the agent himself forgets that he has done it, so no one can know who accomplished it. And yet, everything is properly done. Thus, Yi I asserts that the sage is one who has no consciousness of self.

> For this reason, the sage does not regard himself as great, and therefore, he is able to accomplish greatness. (25; 34)[43]

> Comment: The sage has no self and is able to merge with the Way. Therefore, even when accomplishing feats akin to the works of heaven, he ultimately does not entertain the thought that he himself is great. It is precisely for this reason that he is able to achieve such greatness.[44]

This concept of non-action as no-self is not unfamiliar to Confucians. Insofar as it involves eliminating selfish desires and the pursuit of empty fame from within oneself, it fundamentally aligns with the Confucian notions of self-cultivation and governing others, such as self-overcoming (*kŭkki; keji* 克己; *Lunyu* 12.1) or selflessness (*musa; wusi* 無私; *Liji* "Kongzi xian ju" 孔子閒居, 5).[45]

This second meaning of non-doing as no-self is not only the mode by which the Way operates, but also serves as an ideal and imperative for individual and collective human life, to be practiced in emulation of the Way. This leads into the next topic, which concerns Yi I's reading of self-cultivation and governing others in the DDJ, as discussed in the next section.

When we realize the true nature of the Way, what remains is the task of embodying its character and essence in both our personal and communal lives. But before discussing this next issue, one final question must be considered: Why must I embody and live in accordance with the characteristics and essence of the Way? How can I carry out that task? These questions require examining the nature of the connection between the Way and myself.

---

42 董氏曰：「見，顯也。此養德之方也。蓋抱一則無我，若更自見、自是、自伐、自矜，則是我見未忘，烏可以言一哉？」

43 是以聖人終不為大，故能成其大。

44 聖人無我，與道為一，故雖成如天之事功，而終無自大之心，此聖人之所以為大也。

45 "One of the Master's words says: '... When [emperor Yu] ruled over all-under-heaven, he had no self-interest. When he died, he did not enrich his son.'" 子言之曰：「…君天下，生無私，死不厚其子。」(*Liji* 禮記, "Biaoji" 表記, 31).

Yi I, in Chapter 2 of *Sunŏn*, cites Laozi 51 to introduce a new concept: *tŏk* (*de* 德; virtue). This refers both to the potential within oneself to practice the Way, and to the internal power that arises through the actualization of that practice. For, Yi I, virtue is "the manifested form of the Way," that is embedded within our innate nature. In Neo-Confucian thought, nature refers to the principle endowed by heaven that resides within us. This idea appears in the line "What heaven has mandated is called nature" 天命之謂性 in the text *Zhongyong* 中庸 (Balanced Harmony in Daily Life). Zhu Xi commented on this line as follows:

> "Mandate" (*myŏng*; *ming* 命) is a command. "Nature" is principle. Heaven gives birth to and transforms the myriad things through yin, yang, and the five phases, and shapes them through *qi*. With this shaping, principle is also endowed; this is like issuing a command. As people and things are born, each receives the principle allotted to them. That principle becomes the basis for strengthening and following the five constant virtues: benevolence, righteousness, ritual propriety, wisdom, and trustworthiness. This is what is called nature.[46]

According to Zhu Xi, as heaven brings forth all things, each being is endowed with its own fitting principle. That principle, as the potential and power to realize moral value, becomes what he calls virtue, which he identifies with innate nature. From this structure, principle, nature, and virtue are essentially different names for the same underlying reality.

Yi I, in commenting on the phrase "virtue nourishes" 德畜之 from DDJ 51, writes, "If it is not virtue, there is no way to follow principle and nourish oneself" 非德則無以循理而自養. Here, he points out that virtue is what allows a person to follow *li* and cultivate oneself. That is, the Way is embedded in each human being from birth as the reason for existence, taking shape in the form of principle, specific to each being. When this principle comes to be realized in life as a concrete value to be practiced, it is called virtue. In this sense, virtue is the foundation that enables us to live in accordance with the Way.

Because we are born with this virtue, we ought to live by it, follow the Way, and thereby nourish both our virtue and our lives. By interpreting the notion of *tŏk* in the DDJ through the concept of *sŏng* (innate nature) as understood in early Confucianism and in Zhu Xi's thought, Yi I discovers an inseparable connection between the Way and the human being. From this, he derives the answer to the question of why we embody and live out the Way's character in our lives.

---

46 Zhu Xi, *Zhongyong zhangju* 中庸章句, 1.
The original lines are as follows: 命猶令也。性即理也。天以陰陽五行化生萬物，氣以成形，而理亦賦焉，猶命令也。於是人物之生，因各得其所賦之理，以為健順五常之德，所謂性也。

## Mind and Self-Cultivation

By making clear that the Way is immanent within us in the form of virtue and innate nature, Yi I, building on the *Mengzi* and Neo-Confucian tradition, affirmed the fundamental premise of self-cultivation: that everything we ultimately need to realize is already fully present within ourselves. He believed that this inwardly centered spirit of cultivation was clearly expressed in the DDJ as well, and he refers to it repeatedly throughout *Sunŏn*. Its Chapter 11 is a good example of this. There, in interpreting DDJ 47, Yi I offers the following insight:

> Without stepping outside the door, one can know all-under-heaven;
> Without looking out the window, one can see the heavenly Way. (11; 47)[47]
>
> Comment: "All myriad things are already within me" (*Mengzi* 7A4), so why seek them elsewhere? By seeking to find the stray mind (*Mengzi* 6A11), one can come to perceive the Way. What Master Cheng (i.e., Cheng Yi) refers to when he speaks of one's ability to seek upward on one's own, beginning with learning from below and ascending to higher understanding (*Lunyu* 14.35). This is it.[48]

Looking at the latter part of DDJ 47, which Yi I does not quote here,[49] it becomes clear that this chapter is not primarily about the Way being fully present within oneself, as Yi I interprets it. Rather, it addresses the typical Daoist theme of the sage's non-action: acting without forced purpose, without self-consciousness of one's deeds, without revealing one's actions to others, and trusting the natural course of things so that the action is accomplished; an action that, when thus performed, is considered greater and more authentic. Therefore, the original meaning of the DDJ 47, which Yi I cites for Chapter 11 of *Sunŏn*, is that the sage's knowledge does not come from forcibly going outside to grasp the world with a purposeful or self-aware intention but is a natural knowledge that arises from entrusting oneself to the world as it is.

Yi I, however, interprets this passage in a Neo-Confucian framework. What originally symbolized forced action, excessive effort, or externalized behavior aimed at drawing attention or achieving a goal, such as going outside or peering through a window, becomes for Yi I an act of distraction, a turning of attention away from the inner self toward the outside world. In his commentary on Laozi 47, Yi I cites Mengzi and Cheng Yi, arguing that Laozi, like them, affirms the existence of truth already fully present within us. As Mengzi taught, the real task of self-cultivation lies in rediscovering the complete truth within that we have

---

47 不出戶，知天下；不窺牖，見天道。

48 萬物皆備於我，豈待他求哉？求其放心，則可以見道矣。程子所謂「自能尋向上去，下學而上達」者，是也。

49 This refers to the phrase: "Therefore the sage, without going out, knows; without being seen, becomes famous; without doing, accomplishes." 是以聖人不行而知，不見而名，不為而成。

forgotten due to external influences. Thus, by resisting the pull of external things and instead realizing what is already within, one comes to understand the mandate of heaven and thereby comes to understand heaven itself. Yi I draws from the DDJ this thoroughly Confucian message of "beginning with what is below and reaching up to what is above" (*Lunyu* 14.35).

For Yi I, then, the work of self-cultivation in the DDJ ultimately consists in knowing oneself, in more precise terms, in accepting the principle that is already embedded within, and awakening to its meaning. He finds this message in DDJ 33 and places it in Chapter 9 of *Sunŏn*. To know oneself, in Mencian terms, is to recover the mind that has been lost in the pursuit of external things (cf. *Mengzi* 6A11). This is precisely what Yi I points out in his commentary on DDJ 47 (Chapter 11 of *Sunŏn*).

What, then, does it mean to know oneself? And how can one come to know oneself? In Yi I's reading of the DDJ, to know oneself is simply another way of expressing self-cultivation. According to him, the DDJ presents self-cultivation as having two main aspects: first, the emptying or clearing out of the mind; second, treasuring what is already contained within the mind. This "cherishing" (*saek; se* 嗇) is also described using the phrase knowing contentment (*chijok*; *zhizu* 知足). Yi I believes that this "cherishing" begins with the self and with the mind, but it ultimately extends outward to include others and the state. In this way, he finds in the DDJ the same logic found in the *Daxue*: the legitimacy of moving from cultivating the self to governing others.

## Emptying the Mind

This begins with first recognizing whether or not one's mind is situated rightly in the present moment. Yi I begins his treatment of the issue of self-cultivation in Chapter 5 of *Sunŏn*, where he cites DDJ 12 to make the following point: when we become governed by external things and pursue them, we inevitably forget the noble qualities we originally possessed, and in doing so, we lose our Way.

In order to recover this lost mind, Yi I, in *Sunŏn* Chapter 9, draws on DDJ 33 to convey the message that we must overcome our present selves that are now dominated by external things. He interprets this as the same meaning as Confucius's phrase "overcoming oneself and returning to ritual propriety" (*kŭkki pongrye*; *keji fuli* 克己復禮; *Lunyu* 12.1). When Yi I says that in order to know oneself one must overcome oneself, this first means not yielding to human desires—namely, desires that are governed and pulled by external things. But he does not stop at merely resisting; through DDJ, Yi I proposes a more active mode of self-overcoming: it is to empty the mind that is filled with greed for external things. By emptying, one returns to the original state of the human mind.

Underlying this is Yi I's Neo-Confucian presupposition that the mind is originally empty. Just as the Way is empty, the mind is closest to the Way when it, too, is empty. Yi I insightfully points this out in *Sunŏn* chapter 4, where he cites DDJ 11 in his reflection on the true nature of the mind.

Thirty spokes converge upon a void hub.
It is the nothingness at the hub
That makes the wheel useful. (4; 11)[50]

According to Yi I's interpretation, the wheel's hub serves as metaphors for the mind. Just as the hub of a wheel must be empty so that the spokes can converge and the wheel can fulfill its function, the mind too, when understood as a vessel that receives the world, only truly functions as a mind when it is empty. If the mind is filled with something, whether produced from within or introduced from without, it can no longer serve as a vessel that contains the world. Therefore, for the mind to fulfill its role as a mind, just as the Way, being empty, gives birth to life without limit, it, too, must be empty.

In Yi I's view, then, this emptying or removing is the first essential of Laozian self-cultivation. In the DDJ, various terms are used to describe this process of emptying for self-cultivation, and the first concept Yi I introduces is to unload (*son; sun* 損) in *Sunŏn* chapter 6 where he cites DDJ 48.

In Yi I's interpretation, learning refers to acquiring knowledge—that is, accumulating information. In contrast, practicing the Way means realizing that learned knowledge through concrete actions in life. Interestingly, then, unlike Laozi's original critique of learning as something to be undone or rejected, Yi I does not see learning itself as something to be negated. Rather, much like in Zhu Xi's Neo-Confucianism, learning is a necessary prerequisite for practicing the Way. The distinction lies in their function: while learning increases one's intellectual grasp, practicing the Way involves reducing or simplifying human behavior in accordance with ritual propriety. What is to be reduced, in Yi I's view, is not knowledge or words, as Laozi might have originally intended, but rather the superfluous and unnecessary aspects of human action, especially when they deviate from proper ritual norms.

Yi I then goes further to broaden the meaning of Laozi's concept of unloading, extending it beyond merely trimming inappropriate actions. It also includes purging material desires that arise from *qi*. Thus, what must be removed in the practice of the Way is not only excessive behavior but also the defilements of the mind caused by desire.

For Yi I, goodness exists fully and self-sufficiently within human nature. What one must do is simply eliminate the accretions, namely, the physical endowment and material desires, that obscure that goodness. Through steady effort to cast these off, one eventually reaches a point where nothing remains to be discarded, thereby returning to one's original nature, which is inherently good.

---

50 三十輻，共一轂；當其無，有車之用。

## Cherishing

The second task of self-cultivation in DDJ, as understood by Yi I, is to cherish what is already fully present within us and not to waste or squander it in vain. The concept Laozi uses to express this cherishing is *saek* (*se* 嗇), which appears in chapter 59 of the DDJ. According to the *Shuowen Jiezi*, the character is explained as "to cherish and store away" 嗇 愛濇也 (7.3327). As this definition already suggests, the character contains two meanings that are distinct yet interconnected. One is "to cherish," "to value highly," or "to care much for," and the other is "to spare" or "to economize," that is, to keep and preserve something rather than use up or deplete it.

In Chapter 7 of *Sunŏn*, Yi I reads the line from DDJ 59, "governing people and serving heaven" 治人事天, as hinging on this very notion of cherishing.

> In ruling people and serving heaven,
> Nothing is like cherishing. (7; 59)[51]
>
> Comment: In my humble opinion, to 'serve heaven' means to 'govern oneself.' Mengzi said, "Preserving the mind and nurturing one's nature—this is how one serves heaven" (*Mengzi* 7A1). Thus, it is said that both self-cultivation and the governance of others must be rooted in the virtue of cherishing as the Way.
>
> "Cherishing" refers to sparing what has been gathered. In terms of self-governance, it means curbing greed and desire, nurturing one's essence and spirit, being cautious in speech, controlling food intake, maintaining reverence, and practicing simplicity—this is cherishing. In terms of governing others, it involves carefully implementing laws, simplifying directives, reducing burdensome taxes, eliminating extravagance and waste, attending to important matters with seriousness, and caring for the people—this is cherishing.[52]

Yi I interprets the DDJ's original expression "to serve heaven" by citing *Mengzi*, understanding it as referring to the cultivation of the self. This interpretation differs from that of Wang Bi, who understood the phrase as governing the state in accordance with the principle of nature, and of Heshang gong, who saw it as applying the Way of heaven and following the cycles of the seasons in governing the people. Yi I takes this passage to mean that, for Laozi, nothing is more important in the tasks of self-cultivation and governing others than cherishing. From the perspective of self-cultivation, to cherish means to restrain desires and to nurture the original mind.

---

51 治人事天，莫若嗇。

52 愚按：事天是自治也。孟子曰：「存其心，養其性，所以事天也。」言自治治人，皆當以嗇為道。嗇是愛惜收斂之意。以自治言，則防嗜慾，養精神，慎言語，節飲食，居敬行簡之類，是嗇也。以治人言，則謹法度，簡號令，省繁科，去浮費，敬事愛人之類，是嗇也。

When extended to the political sphere, this cherishing entails valuing others and caring for the community. In this context, the character *saek* does not mean "to grudge" or "to economize," but rather "to care for" or "to value highly." Specifically, it means to reduce things that burden the people, such as punishments and taxes, and to love and serve them. Here, the idea of cherishing is not limited to the preservation of one's own mind in the name of self-cultivation; it expands to include care, love, and respect for one's neighbors, society, and the broader national community.

As we will examine in more detail below, Yi I uses frequent discussions in the DDJ about what benefits the people and enables them to live in peace to reject the common Confucian accusation that Laozi's vision is a form of selfish individualism concerned only with one's own preservation (e.g., *Sunŏn* 5; DDJ 10). In Yi I's view, even in the DDJ, the final goal of cultivating the self is ultimately the governing of others. Self-cultivation in DDJ is not merely for one's own sake but for the sake of one's fellow members of the community. And the meaning of governing others lies in morally transforming others. Yi I regarded this as Laozi's compassion for the people and the spirit of good governance. Therefore, a person who preserves their mind through cherishing is led to commit themselves to ensuring the well-being and safety of others.

In *Sunŏn*, Chapter 12, citing DDJ 46, Yi I further expands the meaning of cherishing to the extent of guarding the Way present within oneself, overcoming selfish desires, avoiding arrogance through self-pride, and always knowing how to be content with what has been given. While this concept of cherishing is defined primarily within the scope of self-cultivation and does not explicitly extend to social or political dimensions, Yi I sees an equivalence in meaning between this idea of cherishing and the recurring Laozi notion of "knowing contentment."

In chapter 10 (DDJ 44), where the concept of knowing contentment first appears, Yi I cites Dong Sijing's commentary and defines knowing contentment. Knowing contentment means being able to distinguish between what is already possessed internally and what comes from the outside, and recognizing through such discernment that one's self-cultivation is already complete with what is innately within, and there is nothing further to be sought externally. In this respect, knowing contentment is fundamentally the same as emptying the mind of unnecessary things and cherishing what is already inherently present within. It is also essentially the same as ceasing the foolish and vain desires that have long sought things outside the self. This is akin to why Confucius's most beloved disciple, Yan Hui, despite living in poverty, never lost the peace and joy of his heart (*Lunyu* 6.11). Here, Confucian finding joy in simplicity and Laozi's knowing contentment reveal a shared spirit. For Yi I, once a person reaches such a state, one no longer worries about gains or losses, and can dwell in peace with what is always already given by one's nature and the mandate of heaven. In terms of self-preservation, this is what enables one to avoid disgrace and live a long life.

## The Ideal of Self-Cultivation

To thoroughly empty the mind, to preserve and observe the Way or principle already embedded within, and to reflect upon it inwardly. This, for Yi I, is Laozi's ideal of self-cultivation, and it is also the foundation of self-cultivation as understood in Confucianism. To realize that there is nothing more to be sought outside, because everything is already complete within, and this is the core.[53]

In *Sunŏn* 5, Yi I cites chapter 10 to describe what he considers to be the ideal state of self-cultivation in Laozi's thought.

> Cleansing your mind and profoundly gazing into it,
> Can you leave no blemish on it? (5; 10)[54]

> Comment: The phrase "to cleanse the mind" means to wash away material desires, while "to gaze profoundly" refers to contemplating and discerning the mysterious principle [within]. When one eliminates desires for sound, color, scent, and taste, the mind becomes empty, perception is purified, and learning progresses. When knowledge and action reach their highest refinement, not a single blemish remains.[55]

Here Yi I speaks inclusively of both stages of self-cultivation in Laozi's teaching. It is the cleansing of all desires for the external world from within, and the quiet contemplation of the subtle principle originally present inside oneself. Yi I says that when desires disappear, the mind becomes pure and learning can advance further. He expresses this as "knowledge and practice advance together to their fullest perfection." Of course, learning is not mentioned in the original DDJ text here; this reflects Yi I's Neo-Confucian conception of self-cultivation influencing his interpretation of DDJ. Regardless of whether Yi I's interpretation of DDJ and scholarship is, as Song Ikp'il pointed out, somewhat forced, it is clear that thoroughly eliminating material desires and nurturing one's self-respect is a fundamental task of practicing the Way. This is true beyond the labels of Daoism or Confucianism and applies universally.

---

[53] In the Zhu Xi school, "investigating things and extending knowledge" (*kyŏngmul ch'iji*; *gewu zhizhi* 格物致知) in the *Daxue* is taken as a directive to study the principles of external things, so self-cultivation must include both examining the external world and engaging in the internal moral work of "making the will sincere and rectifying the mind." This reading suggests that, contrary to Mengzi's claim that all things are complete within the mind, the principles of mind and world are distinct. Later, Wang Shouren 王守仁 (1472-1528), or Wang Yangming, resolved this dualism by interpreting "investigating things" not as studying external objects but as correcting the mind that perceives them. Had Yi I been a Yangming scholar, he likely would have seen Laozi's self-cultivation as much closer to that of Confucianism.

[54] 滌除玄覽，能無疵乎？

[55] 滌除者，淨洗物欲也。玄覽者，照察玅理也。蓋既去聲色臭味之慾，則心虛境清，而學識益進，至於知行並至，則無一點之疵矣。

## Governing Others

Yi I saw that the ultimate goal of self-cultivation is governing others, not only in Confucianism but also in the DDJ. The "governing by non-action" frequently mentioned in the DDJ represents the ultimate task and goal of the sage in the Laozi's thought (*Sunŏn* 5; DDJ 10). Once one has refined oneself and drawn close to the Way, the highest form of goodness one attains is the one that resembles water—benefiting all things while dwelling in the humblest of places (DDJ 8).

Furthermore, in the *Sunŏn* Chapter 26 where Yi I cites DDJ 54 that shows a vision of moral cultivation expanding outward in concentric circles—from the self, to the family, to society, and ultimately to the state—much like what is seen in the *Daxue* (2), Yi I points out that the Laozi's vision of self-cultivation ultimately leading to peace among all-under-heaven is, in essence, no different from the ideal presented in the *Daxue*.

> Cultivate it in the self, and its virtue will be authentic;
> cultivate it in the family, and its virtue will be abundant;
> cultivate it in the village, and its virtue will be enduring;
> cultivate it in the state, and its virtue will be flourishing;
> cultivate it in all-under-heaven, and its virtue will be universal. (54)[56]

> Comment: To be authentic means to be earnest and free from carelessness. With authentic and sincere principle, one cultivates oneself and extends what remains to govern others, regulating a household, the state, and all-under-heaven. The scope of self-cultivation extends no further than this.
>
> Honorable Wen (Sima Guang 司馬光; 1019-1086) noted, "All of this is a matter of governing the peripheral by following the foundational, and reaching the distant by starting from the near."[57]

Then how, concretely, is self-cultivation connected to governing others? What exactly does it mean to govern others? Yi I focuses on the actions of the sage as described in the DDJ. The sage in DDJ does nothing for himself, but acts solely for the sake of others. The sage, whose mind is fully emptied of desire for the external world and concentrated instead on the principle already present within, discovers fellow human beings within his emptied mind. He then shares what he has with them and acts on their behalf. In the end, he rescues the many who are suffering and trapped in hardship. This is the ideal of a person who is "utterly impartial and without selfishness" (*chigong musa* 至公無私) and who "acts without self and devotes himself to the public good" (*mua ponggong* 無我奉公)

---

56 修之身，其德乃真；修之家，其德乃餘；修之鄉，其德乃長；修之國，其德乃豐；修之天下，其德乃普。

57 真者，誠實無妄之謂也。以真實之理修身，推其餘以治人家國天下，不外乎是而已。溫公曰：「皆循本以治末，由近以及遠也。」

Here, Yi I points out that the Laozi's sage attains a level akin to what Confucians calls benevolence and even sageliness (*sŏng; sheng* 聖). In *Sunŏn* Chapter 27, he interprets a passage from DDJ 81 and cites *Lunyu* 6.30 to argue that the sage of DDJ shares the same moral vision as the sage of Confucianism.

> The sage does not accumulate.
> As he uses what he already has for others, he gets more.
> As he shares what he already has with others, he gets richer. (27; 81).[58]
>
> Comment: The sage uses his to connect with others. One who wishes to be established helps others to find his footing; one who wishes to be well-versed assists others in deepening his understanding. They give extensively and benefit many, yet nothing has been wasted on himself. Thus, his virtue grows all the more, and his virtue gets less solitary.[59]

In Yi I's reading, the DDJ's sage, in practicing "being utterly impartial and without selfishness," is exemplifying the method by which one achieves benevolence and reaches the sagely status of saving the people (*chejung; jizhong* 濟衆).

Mengzi believed that when one sees a child on the verge of falling into a well, a natural feeling of compassion arises in everyone's heart. This, he argued, is the beginning of benevolence (*in-ji-dan; ren zhi duan* 仁之端; 2A6). The "human mind that cannot bear to see the sufferings of others" (*purin injisim; bu ren ren zhi xin* 不忍人之心; 2A6) and the spontaneously arising compassionate heart are expressions of a capacity to deeply empathize with and understand another's situation by extending one's own experience and knowledge to that of others. Yi I saw this Mengzian explanation of benevolence realized in the DDJ's sage, who gives all of himself for the sake of others. For Yi I, the sage is someone who, grounded in his own experience, expands his heart to include the hearts of others. Such a person, who empathizes and commiserates, aims to rescue others by broadly spreading his virtue. This is the highest state of sagehood as envisioned by Confucius. A sage, because he always exists for others, is never lonely (*Lunyu* 4.25). Here, the common Confucian accusation that the Laozian sage is a selfish narcissist is overturned.

DDJ chapter 27 describes how the ultimate vision of the sage is the salvation of not only all people but all beings. Yi I cites a passage from the *Lunyu* 15.39 noting that Confucius accepted all who came to learn from him, regardless of the level of their learning, social status, or wealth. Drawing from this, Yi I emphasizes the indiscriminate and egalitarian nature of the sage's salvific work in the DDJ. He then interprets the concept of *sŭp* (*xi* 習; to practice or embody) found in the DDJ as suggesting that the sage's work of saving the people is not

---

58 聖人不積；既以為人，己愈有；既以與人，己愈多。

59 聖人以己及人，己立而立人，己達而達人，博施濟眾，而於己未嘗有費，其仁愈盛，而其德愈不孤矣。

only a spatial expansion across all sectors of society but also a temporal one, a transmission that endures across time. That is, this social salvation brought about by the sage is not a one-time event confined to a particular generation, but becomes an ongoing tradition stretching from antiquity into the future.

Through a continuous chain of awakened individuals enlightening those yet to awaken, the salvation of the world becomes a sustainable, living process. Just as the Way of Confucianism has been passed down for thousands of years; from the sage-kings Yao and Shun, to King Wen, King Wu, and the Duke of Zhou, and then to Confucius and Mengzi, and on to Zhou Dunyi, Zhang Zai, the Cheng brothers, and Zhu Xi, so too, the vision of governing others in the DDJ mirrors the sacred historical tradition of Confucian Way transmission.

## The Historical Significance of the *Sunŏn*

At the conclusion of *Sunŏn*, in the very last section of the last Chapter, Yi I briefly shares his reflections on DDJ and his own commentary on it. This final passage, which functions as a kind of personal postface by the author, can be read in two main parts. The first part reads as follows:

> In general, this book (i.e., DDJ) takes non-doing as its foundation. In its application, there is nothing that [the non-doing] cannot accomplish, and so [this book] is not something that drowns readers in emptiness or non-being. Its words are, for the most part, an invitation to advancement [of self]. However, since this book actively claims to speak on behalf of a sage and often discusses lofty matters, yet seldom addresses practical learning at the lower levels, it is naturally suited for scholars of high capacity, while those of intermediate or lower level find it difficult even to approach.[60]

Here, Yi I first strongly argues that the DDJ is not a text that leads people into nihilism. This is because the *wuwei* it advocates does not mean "doing nothing," but rather refers to a mode of effectiveness in which nothing is left undone. The DDJ, in fact, speaks in many places from the perspective of the sage about growth and development, and thus cannot be considered harmful. The problem, rather, lies in the fact that while the text discusses many lofty and elevated themes, it includes few topics directly related to practical implementation in daily life. For scholars below the middle or advanced levels, this makes it difficult even to know how to begin engaging with the book. To Yi I, this is why the DDJ remained so poorly understood among Confucians for such a long time.

So then, what is the DDJ really trying to say? In the next paragraph, Yi I succinctly summarizes what he believes to be the core message of the DDJ.

---

60 大抵此書以無為為宗，而其用無不為，則亦非溺於虛無也。只是言多招詣，動稱聖人，論上達處多，論下學處少，宜接上根之士，而中人以下，則難於下手矣。

> Nonetheless, it speaks of the meanings of overcoming the private self and curbing selfish desires, maintaining calm and guarding oneself, cultivating humility and self-governing, and attending to people with kindness and simplicity, all of whose topics are presented in a gentle and in-depth way, and there are many benefits for those who learn with this book. It cannot be considered not a book by a sage, yet no one reflects upon it.[61]

Yi I understood the DDJ as a profound work concerning the cultivation of the self and the ordering of society. Naturally, then, he believed it to be a text full of benefit for any serious student. At this point, Yi I ventures a remarkably bold claim—one well beyond what his era was prepared to accept: that the DDJ must not be dismissed as a non-sage's book, and yet no one has reflected on this issue. This statement is both a criticism of his contemporaries trapped within the orthodoxy of Neo-Confucianism and a sober admonition to those who blindly believed that only Zhu Xi's teachings is the sage's learning.

Here, we discover the historical meaning and value of *Sunŏn*. It may be one among many commentaries on the DDJ, but in a deeper sense, it is a commentary on human conscience itself, written in an age when only one teaching was considered absolute truth, and all other teachings were persecuted as heresy. It stands as a testament to the spirit of respecting and learning from different paths that, though distinct, ultimately aim toward the same destination.

[61] 但其言克己窒慾，靜重自守，謙虛自牧，慈簡臨民之義，皆親切有味，有益於學者，不可以為非聖人之書，而莫之省也。

# Chapters 1 to 10[1]

栗谷先生鈔解口訣[2]
Master Yulgok [Yi I]'s transcription and commentary [on the *Laozi Daodejing*], with annotations and oral reading marks.[3]

## Chapter 1 (DDJ 42; 5)[4]

> 道生一，一生二，二生三，三生萬物。
> The Way gives rise to the One;
> the One gives rise to the Two;
> the Two gives rise to the Three;
> the Three gives rise to all things.

朱子曰：「道卽易之太極。一乃陽之奇，二乃陰之耦，三乃奇耦之積。其曰二生三，猶所謂二與一爲三也；其曰三生萬物，卽奇耦合而萬物生也。」
Master Zhu (i.e., Zhu Xi) said: "The Way is the Supreme Ultimate of the *Zhouyi* (*Xici* A.11). The One is the singularity of Yang; the Two is the pairing of Yin; the Three is the product of the singularity and the pairing (*Xici* B.4). When it is said that 'Two gives birth to Three,' this is like saying that Two together with One forms Three.[5] When it is said that 'Three gives birth to all things,' this means that

---

[1] Dividing the forty chapters of the *Sunŏn* into four units of ten is the translator's own editorial decision, intended to distribute the text more evenly; such grouping does not appear in the original. As noted in the translator's Introduction, Yi I reorganized the eighty-one-chapter DDJ into forty chapters and explained its principles and thematic structure in a concluding note after chapter forty. Readers seeking a more integrated reading should consult Yi I's commentary, presented here under "Conclusion."

[2] Aside from the 1750 postscript by Hong Kyehŭi, which was written probably around 170 years later, there is no indication or explicit statement within the main text that attributes this work to Yulgok Yi I. In light of this, the opening line that names Yulgok as the author was likely added at a later time.

[3] In the Kyujanggak edition used as the base text for this book, reading marks known as *kugyŏl* are annotated in Korean to aid in segmenting phrases of the original DDJ, facilitating vocal reading and offering simple guidance for grasping basic logical connections. These reading aids appear only in the original text of the DDJ, not in Yi I's own commentary. However, since the reading marks are extremely simple and do not appear to reflect any distinctive contribution by Yi I to the reading of the original DDJ text, they have not been included in the main body of this book. For reference, the *kugyŏl* reading mark annotations for the DDJ text in *Sunŏn* are completely missing from the UC Berkeley edition.

[4] In the original *Sunŏn*, chapters are not numbered at the beginning; however, Yi I marks their divisions with numbers at the end of each commentary. For clarity, I have added Arabic numerals at the beginning of each chapter.

[5] It refers to the following line: "One and Speech are two; two and one are three" 一與言為二，二與一為三。See ZZ 2.9.

the singularity and the pairing combine, and from this all things are generated." (ZZQS 31.140).

> 天地之間，其猶橐籥乎。
> Between heaven and earth, is it not like a bellows?

董氏曰：「橐，鞴也；籥，管也，能受氣鼓風之物。天地之間，二氣往來屈伸，猶此物之無心，虛而能受，應而不藏也。」
Mr. Dong commented,[6] "The term bellows refers to a type of air blower, whereas a pipe denotes a woodwind instrument—things capable of receiving air and being blown upon. Between heaven and earth, the two *qi*-energies move back and forth, expanding and contracting, just like these objects: without intention, empty yet able to receive, responsive yet storing nothing" (DZJ 1.47).

> 虛而不屈，動而愈出。
> While empty, it never exhausts itself.
> As it moves, it gives forth more.

古本皆釋屈作竭。無形可見，而無一物不受形焉。動而生生，愈出而愈無窮焉。朱子曰：「有一物之不受，則虛而屈矣；有一物之不應，是動而不能出矣。」
Early commentaries [such as Heshang gong's or Wang Bi's one] consistently interpret the character "to bend" as meaning "to exhaust."[7] Although [the Way] has no visible form, there is nothing that does not derive its shape from it. As it

---

[6] Mr. Dong refers to Dong Sijing 董思靖 (fl. 1246-1260). Aside from his two major works, the DZJ and the *Dongxuan lingbao ziran jiutian shengshen zhangjing jieyi*, 洞玄靈寶自然九天生神章經解義 (Explanation of the Meaning of the Scripture of the Divine Generation of the Nine Heavens of Spontaneity from the Cavernous Mystery and Numinous Treasure Tradition), little is known about him. He was a Lingbao Daoist priest at Tianqing Temple 天慶觀 on Mount Gui 圭山 in Quanzhou 泉州 in the late Southern Song. A notable feature of his thought, evident in the DZJ, is his adoption of the emerging Neo-Confucian hermeneutic framework of Zhu Xi and his integration of it into his reading of the DDJ. Dong understood the DDJ as a manual for the self-cultivation of rulers and governing elites, and believed its core message could be harmonized with Confucian ideals. For a study of Dong's thought in the DZJ, see Liu Gusheng 2024, 329-350.

Dong's ecumenical reading of the DDJ seems to have shaped Yi I's thought and led him to compose this work, in which he presents his own position through both the DDJ and Dong's commentary. Because Dong's approach was relatively congenial to Confucian views, his work was sometimes read in Chosŏn despite the broader sense that engaging the DDJ was impious. Yet, as Yi I's complete reorganization of the text shows, even Dong's accommodating stance could be accepted only in part, given the DDJ's openly anti-Confucian statements and their tension with Chosŏn values. The selective adoption of even such a moderated reading reflects Chosŏn's complex attitude toward the DDJ. Thus, in drawing on Dong, Yi I largely avoids passages on metaphysics, cosmology, or criticisms of Confucianism, focusing instead on sections describing the sage or his methods of governance.

[7] Quoted from DZJ 1.49.

moves, it continuously gives rise to things; the more it brings forth, the more inexhaustible it becomes. [Thus,] Master Zhu remarked, "If there is anything it does not receive, it would be empty yet exhausted. If there is anything to which it does not respond, it would be moving yet unable to bring forth" (ZZQS 58.11).

> 萬物負陰而抱陽，冲氣以爲和。
> All things carry yin on their backs and embrace yang, achieving harmony through the empty *qi*.

董氏曰：「凡動物之類，則背止於後，陰靜之屬也；口鼻耳目居前，陽動之屬也。植物則背寒向煖，故曰負陰而抱陽，而冲氣則運乎其間也。」溫公曰：「萬物莫不以陰陽爲體，以冲和爲用。」
Mr. Dong explained, "All moving things have their backs behind them, where the still yin *qi* resides. The mouth, nose, ears, and eyes are positioned at the front, where active yang *qi* operates. Plants grow with cool *qi* at their backs and stretch toward warm *qi*. Thus, [Laozi] states, 'they carry yin on their backs and embrace yang in their chests,' meaning that 'empty *qi*' moves within this space between them" (DZJ 3.73).

Honorable Wen (On'gong; Wengong 溫公; Sima Guang 司馬光; 1019-1086) remarked, "All things take yin and yang as their essence and use empty harmony as their function" (DZL 3.42,10).

右第一章，言天道造化發生人物之義。
The passage above, Chapter 1, illustrates the workings of heaven's Way, which gives rise to humans and all things.

## Chapter 2 (DDJ 51)

> 道生之，德畜之，物形之，勢成之。
> 是以萬物莫不尊道而貴德。[8]
> 道之尊，德之貴，夫莫之爵，而常自然。
> The Way gives life, virtue nourishes, things take shape, and circumstances bring them to completion.
> Thus, among all things, none fails to honor the Way and esteem virtue.
> The Way is revered, virtue esteemed—yet no one grants them rank, and they remain ever naturally so.

道卽天道，所以生物者也。德則道之形體，乃所謂性也。人物非道，則無以資生；非德，則無以循理而自養，故曰道生德畜也。物之成形，勢之相因，皆本於道德，故道德最爲尊貴也。

---

[8] In the standard Wang Bi edition of DDJ, this phrase appears as *fu mo zhi ming er chang ziran* 夫莫之命而常自然 [not because it is mandated, but because it is ever so in itself].

The Way is the heavenly Way that gives rise to all things. Virtue is the manifested form of the Way, referred to as "[innate] nature." Without the Way, neither people nor things can have a foundation from which they emerge; without virtue, there is no way to follow principle and nourish oneself. Thus, it is said that "the Way generates, virtue nourishes." The formation of things and the interdependence of the current are all rooted in the Way and virtue, which is why the Way and virtue are regarded as the most noble.

右第二章，承上章，言道德有無對之尊也。
This passage serves as Chapter 2, continuing from Chapter 1 to convey that the nobility of the Way and virtue is unparalleled.

## Chapter 3 (DDJ 37)

> 道常無爲，而無不爲。
> The Way is always non-acting, yet there is nothing it does not accomplish.

上天之載，無聲無臭，而萬物之生實本於斯。在人則無思無爲，寂然不動，感而遂通，天下之故也。
The operation of the high heaven is soundless and odorless,[9] yet the birth of all things truly has its origin in this. In the human [realm], nothing appears to be thought of and nothing to be done, being in stillness and unmoving. But when it responds, it ultimately penetrates the causes of all-under-heaven (*Xici* A1).

右第三章，亦承上章，而言道之本體無爲，而玅用無不爲，是一篇之大旨也。
This passage serves as Chapter 3. Continuing from the previous chapter, it explains that the fundamental essence of the Way is non-action. Yet it is capable of such wondrous effects that nothing is undone. This is the main message of this chapter.

## Chapter 4 (DDJ 11)

> 三十輻，共一轂；當其無，有車之用。
> Thirty spokes converge upon a void hub;
> It is the nothingness at the hub
> That makes the wheel useful.

朱子曰：「無是轂中空處，惟其空中，故能受軸，而運轉不窮。」董氏曰：「謂輻轂相湊以爲車，即其中之虛，有車之用。」
Master Zhu remarked, "The term nothingness refers to the empty space in the hub, which, being empty in the center, allows the axle to fit and the wheel to rotate endlessly" (ZZQS 58.9).

---

[9] Quoted from *Shijing*, *Daya*, "Wenwang zhi shi" 文王之什, "Wen Wang" 文王, 7.

Mr. Dong explained, "The spokes and the hub come together to form the wheel, and it is due to the emptiness in the hub that makes the wheel useful" (DZJ 1.108).

> 埏埴以爲器，當其無，有器之用。
> When shaping clay into a vessel,
> It is the emptiness within
> That makes the vessel useful.

董氏曰：「埏，和土也；埴，粘土也，皆陶者之事。此亦器中空無，然後可以容物，爲有用之器。下意同。」
Mr. Dong said, "The term 'to shape' refers to kneading the clay, while the term for 'clay' means making it firm; both are tasks of the potter. Only after the center of the vessel is empty, and nothing is inside, it can hold anything and become a useful vessel. The next passage carries the same meaning" (DZJ 1.110).

> 鑿戶牖，以爲室；當其無，有室之用。
> Cut doors and windows to make a room.
> It is the emptiness within
> That makes the room useful.

鑿，穿也。
The term "to cut" means "to pierce."

> 故有之以爲利，無之以爲用。
> Therefore, being is that by which benefit is made;
> non-being is that by which usefulness is made.

外有而成形，中無而受物。外有譬則身也，中無譬則心也。利者，順適之意；利，爲用之器，用，爲利之機也。非身則心無所寓，而心不虛則理無所容。君子之心，必虛明無物，然後可以應物。如轂中不虛，則爲不運之車；器中不虛，則爲無用之器；室中不虛，則爲不居之室矣。
"Being" is externalized to form a shape, while "non-being" is internalized to contain a thing. "Being" externalized can be likened to the physical body, while "non-being" internalized resembles the mind.

The benefit signifies a smooth progression; the benefit serves as the vessel of usefulness, and usefulness forms the foundation of the value.

Without a body, the mind has no place to reside, and if the mind is not empty, principle cannot find acceptance. Only when the noble person's mind is empty and clear can he respond to things appropriately. It is like this: if the hub of a wheel is not empty, the wheel cannot turn; if a vessel is not hollow, it cannot hold anything; and if a room is not vacant, it cannot be lived in.

右第四章。三章以上言道體，此章以後始言行道之功，而以虛心爲先務。蓋必虛心然後，可以捨己之私，受人之善，而學進行成矣。
This concludes Chapter 4. The preceding three chapters discuss the essence of the Way, while from this chapter onward, the tasks of practicing the Way begin to be addressed, and the emptying of the mind is regarded as a priority. Only after one has first cleared the mind can one discard selfish desires, embrace the goodness of others, advance in learning, and complete one's practice.

**Chapter 5 (DDJ 12; 10)**

> 五色，令人目盲；五音，令人耳聾；五味，令人口爽。
> The five colors blind one's eyes,
> The five sounds deafen one's ears,
> The five tastes dull one's palate.

爽，失也。五色、五音、五味，本以養人，非所以害人；而人多循欲，而不知節。故悅色者，失其正見；悅音者，失其正聽；悅味者，失其正味也。
The character meaning "to reduce" is interpreted as "to lose." The five colors, sounds, and flavors arc originally meant to nourish people, not to harm them. However, most tend to follow their desires and do not know how to reduce them. Thus, those absorbed in colors lose true sight; those captivated by sounds lose true hearing; and those indulging in flavors lose true taste.

> 馳騁田獵，令人心發狂。
> Galloping and hunting drive one's mind into frenzy.

董氏曰：「是氣也，而反動其心。」愚按：好獵者，本是志也；而及乎馳騁發狂，則反使氣動心。
Mr. Dong said, "This is because of *qi*, which turns back and agitates the mind" (DZJ 1.119).

In my humble view, a passion for hunting begins as an act of will. But when galloping reaches the point of driving the mind into frenzy, one allows *qi* to cause *qi* in turn to stir the mind.

> 難得之貨，令人行妨。
> Hard-to-obtain wealth hinders one's practice [of the Way].

董氏曰：「妨，謂傷害也，於善行有所妨也。」
Mr. Dong explained, "The term 'to hinder' means 'to injure' or 'to harm.' Regarding good deeds, [hard-to-obtain wealth] causes hindrance" (DZJ 1.121).

> 是以聖人爲腹，不爲目；故去彼取此。
> Because of this, the sage works for the belly, not for the eyes.
> Therefore, he discards the latter and embraces the former.

董氏曰：「去，除去也。腹者，有容於內而無欲；目者，逐見於外而誘內。蓋前章言虛中之妙用，故此則戒其不可爲外邪所實也。」
Mr. Dong said, "The term 'to discard' means 'to remove' or 'to eliminate.' The 'belly' takes things inward without desire, while the 'eyes' follow external appearances and tempt what is within" (DZJ 1.123).

The previous chapter explained the marvelous function of empty space. Therefore, this chapter warns against filling the inside with external, evil things.

> 滌除玄覽，能無疵乎。
> Cleansing your mind and profoundly gazing into it,
> Can you leave no blemish on it?

滌除者，淨洗物欲也。玄覽者，照察玅理也。蓋既去聲色臭味之慾，則心虛境淸，而學識益進；至於知行竝至，則無一點之疵矣。
The term "to cleanse" means "to wash away material desires," while "to gaze profoundly" refers to contemplating and discerning the mysterious principle within. When one eliminates desires for sound, color, scent, and taste, the mind becomes empty, the realm of perception is purified, and learning advances further. When knowledge and action reach the highest refinement, not a single blemish remains.

> 愛民治國，能無爲乎。
> In loving the people and ruling the state, can you non-do?

修己既至，則推以治人，而無爲而化矣。
When self-cultivation reaches its highest point, you can extend it to ordering others. Then, you practice non-doing, and [people] are transformed.

> 天門開闔，能爲雌乎。
> The heavenly gate opens and closes—can you be the female?

開闔，是動靜之意；雌，是陰靜之意。此所謂定之以中正仁義，而主靜者也。
The term 'to open and close' signifies movement and stillness, while 'the female' represents the yin of tranquility. This refers to stabilizing oneself by aligning benevolence and righteousness with balanced correctness and maintaining a steadfast focus on tranquility.

> 明白四達，能無知乎。
> Bright and clear, penetrating the four directions—can you remain without knowing?

董氏曰：「此寂感無邊方也。」愚按：此言於天下之事，無所不知，無所不能，而未嘗有能知之心，詩所謂不識不知，順帝之則者也。夫如是，則上下與天地同流參贊育，而不自居也。下文乃申言之。

Mr. Dong commented, "This is a state in which, in both silence and responsiveness, one is without boundary" (DZJ 1.102).

In my humble view, it expresses that even though one may know everything and be capable of anything in the realm of worldly affairs, he [should] never harbor an intent to know or to act. As the *Shi* says, "Unknowingly and unwittingly, you follow the law of the *di*, Lord on High"[10] If one can be like this, he flows with heaven and earth above and below, taking part in the nurturing of the myriad things—yet without ever claiming credit. The lines that follow elaborate further on this idea.

> 生之畜之，生而不有，爲而不恃，長而不宰，(是謂玄德)。[11]
> [The Way] gives them life and nurtures them,
> Gives them life without possessing them,
> Acts for them without claiming credit for it,
> Raises them without ruling over them—
> This is called a mysterious virtue.

天地生物，而不有其功；運用造化，而不恃其力；長畜羣生，而無有主宰之心。聖人之玄德，亦同於天地而已。玄德，至誠淵微之德也。
Heaven and earth give birth to all things, yet they do not claim credit for their contributions. They operate in creation and transformation without taking pride in their power, raising and nurturing all living beings without any intent of presiding over them. The sage's mysterious virtue is also the same as that of heaven and earth. Mysterious virtue is the supremely sincere and deeply subtle one.

右第五章，此承上章，而始以初學遏人欲之功，終以參贊天地之盛。自此以後諸章所論，皆不出此章之義。
This concludes Chapter 5. This chapter continues the messages of previous chapters and begins with the discussion about the method for novices to restrain human desires, and ends with a description of gaining prosperity through participating in and assisting the works of heaven and earth. From this point onward, the discussions in all the following chapters will remain within the scope of this chapter's message.

## Chapter 6 (DDJ 48)

> 爲學日益，爲道日損；損之又損之，以至於無爲。
> Learning, one adds day by day;
> Practicing the Way, one unloads day by day.

---

[10] *Shijing*, *Daya*, "Wenwang zhi shi," "Huangyi" 皇矣, 7.

[11] The original text of *Sunŏn* does not include the final phrase from the DDJ, *shi wei xuande* 是謂玄德 (This is called mysterious virtue). However, since this phrase is clearly present in Yi I's commentary, it seems likely that it was accidentally omitted during the editing process of *Sunŏn*. Here, I have restored this last phrase in accordance with the DDJ original.

Unloading and unloading still more,
One arrives at the state of non-action.

學以知言，道以行言。知是博之以文，故欲其日益；行是約之以禮，故欲其日損。蓋人性之中，萬善自足，善無加益之理，只當損去其氣稟物欲之累耳。損之又損之，以至於無可損，則復其本然之性矣。
Learning is to understand words; [working for] the Way is to put the words in action. Knowing is to expand through written expression, and so one seeks to increase them day by day. Practicing is to reduce one's [words] through ritual, and thus one seeks to unload day by day.

Within the human innate nature, all goodness exists as self-sufficient, for goodness is the principle to which nothing needs to be added. One should simply remove the *qi*-based material desires that have accumulated. By continually unloading these, one eventually reaches a state where nothing remains to be shed, and thereby restores their original nature.

右第六章，承上章以起下章之義。
This is Chapter 6, continuing the previous chapter while also laying the groundwork for the message of the following chapter.

## Chapter 7 (DDJ 59)

治人事天，莫若嗇。
In ruling people and serving heaven, nothing is like cherishing.

董氏曰：「嗇，乃嗇省精神，而有歛藏貞固之意。學者久於其道，則心廣氣充，而有以達乎天德之全矣。」愚按：事天是自治也。孟子曰：「存其心，養其性，所以事天也。」言自治治人，皆當以嗇爲道。嗇是愛惜收歛之意。以自治言，則防嗜慾、養精神，慎言語、節飲食，居敬行簡之類，是嗇也。以治人言，則謹法度、簡號令、省繁科、去浮費、敬事愛人之類，是嗇也。
Mr. Dong stated, "Cherishing means to restrain and reduce the use of essence and spirit, drawing them inward to store and solidify. When one who studies devotes themselves to the Way over a long period, their mind expands and their *qi* becomes abundant, enabling them to completely embody the fullness of heavenly virtue" (DZJ 4.4).

In my humble opinion, to "serve heaven" means to govern oneself. Mengzi said, "Preserving one's [original] mind and nurturing one's innate nature—this is how one serves heaven" (*Mengzi* 7A1). It is said that both self-cultivation and the governance of others must be rooted in the virtue of cherishing as the Way.

"Cherishing" refers to sparing what has been gathered. In terms of self-governance, it means curbing greed and desire, nurturing one's vital essence and spirit, being cautious in speech, controlling food intake, maintaining reverence, and practicing simplicity—this is cherishing. In terms of governing others, it involves carefully implementing laws, simplifying directives, reducing burdensome taxes, eliminating extravagance and waste, attending to human affairs with deep respect, and caring for the people—this is cherishing.

> 夫惟嗇，是謂早復；早復，謂之重積德。
> Only cherishing, this is called "returning early."
> Returning early, it is called "accumulating virtue upon virtue."

董氏曰：「重，再也。」朱子曰：「早復者，言能嗇，則不遠而復。重積德者，言先已有所積，復養以嗇，是又加積之也。」愚按：人性本善，是先已有所積也。
Mr. Dong said that the term "to add" means "to do it again" (DZJ 4.6).

Master Zhu remarked that "returning early" signifies that if one can practice cherishing, he does not stray far and return [to the original nature]. The phrase "accumulating virtue upon virtue" means that what is already accumulated within oneself can again be nurtured further through cherishing, thus adding to what has already been built up" (ZZQS 58.21).

In my view, human nature is inherently good; therefore, this goodness is what is already accumulated within oneself.

> 重積德，則無不克；無不克，則莫知其極；莫知其極，可以長久。[12]
> When one accumulates virtue upon virtue, nothing cannot be overcome.
> When nothing cannot be overcome, no one will know his limits.
> If no one knows his limits, he can endure for a long time.

不遠而復，則己私無不克矣。克己復禮，則天下歸仁，其德豈有限量哉？德無限量，至於博厚高明，則是悠久無疆之道也。
By not straying far and returning to it, one completely overcomes one's private desires. When one overcomes oneself and returns to ritual propriety, all-under-heaven turns toward benevolence. How could such virtue have any limits? When virtue is without limit, it becomes broad and deep, lofty and luminous—this is the eternal and boundless Way.

右第七章，言入道成德，以嗇爲功，是損之之謂也。此下五章，皆申言此章之意。
This concludes Chapter 7. Entering the Way, fulfilling virtue, and valuing cherishing as a merit—this is what is meant by unloading. The next five chapters continue to elaborate on the message of this chapter.

---

[12] In the original DDJ chapter 59, there is an additional phrase, 可以有國，有國之母, appearing between the last two clauses, as follows: 重積德，則無不克；無不克，則莫知其極；莫知其極，可以有國；有國之母，可以長久。This phrase is preserved in Dong Sijing's commentary. It is unclear why Yi I omitted it in his commentary.

**Chapter 8 (DDJ 22; 24)**

少則得；多則惑。
With less, one gains; with much, one falls into confusion.

董氏曰：「道一而已，得一則無不得矣。凡事多端，則惑。」
Mr. Dong said, "The Way is simply oneness. If one attains the oneness, nothing cannot be attained. When affairs have many branches, confusion follows." (DZJ 2.21; 23).

跂者不立，跨者不行。
One who tiptoes cannot stand firm; One who overstrides cannot walk well.

跂則不能立，跨則不能行，疑惑於兩端，而不能主一者也。
If one tiptoes, he cannot stand firm; if one overstrides, he cannot walk well. Caught between two extremes, one cannot focus on the oneness.

是以聖人抱一，爲天下式。
For this reason, the sage embraces the oneness
And sets himself as a model for all-under-heaven.

董氏曰：「隨時趨變以道，而在乎以謙約爲主。抱一，則全體是道也。」
Mr. Dong said, "Following the times and adapting to change in accordance with the Way, one should take modesty and restraint as the guiding principle. By embracing oneness, one fully embodies the Way itself" (DZJ 2.25).

不自見，故明；不自是，故彰；不自伐，故有功；不自矜，故長。
夫惟不爭，故天下莫能與之爭。
Not revealing oneself, one becomes illumined.
Not asserting oneself, one shines forth.
Not boasting, one gains merit.
Not being proud, one endures.
Because he does not contend,
None-under-heaven can contend with him.

董氏曰：「見，顯也。此養德之方也。蓋抱一則無我。若更自見自是，自伐自矜，則是我見未忘，烏可以言一哉？惟無我則光明盛大，愈久愈新，何爭之有？」愚按：書曰：「汝惟不矜，天下莫與汝爭能；與汝不伐，天下莫與汝爭功」，卽此意也。
Mr. Dong said, "The character 'to see' means to reveal, and this is a method of cultivating virtue. When one embraces oneness, there is no [sense of] self. But if one reveals oneself, insists on being right, boasts, or takes pride in oneself, it shows that the self has not yet been forgotten. How then can one speak of oneness? When there is no self, one's [inner] light grows ever brighter and greater; it endures and renews itself continually. In this, what contention would there be?"

In my view, this echoes what the *Shu* says: "If you are not arrogant, none-under-heaven will contest your abilities; if you do not boast, none-under-heaven will dispute your achievements" ("Da Yu Mo" 大禹謨, 13) This is precisely the meaning intended here.

自見者不明，自是者不彰，自伐者無功，自矜者不長。
其於道也，曰餘食贅行，物或惡之，故有道者不處。
One who reveals himself is not illumined;
One who asserts himself does not shine forth;
One who boasts gains no merit;
One who is proud does not endure.
From the perspective of the Way, such conduct is like eating leftovers or behaving like a tumor.
All beings find it repulsive.
Therefore, one who is on the Way does not dwell on it.

溫公曰：「是皆外競，而內亡者也，如棄餘之食，附餘之形，適使人惡。」董氏曰：「有道者，足於內，而不矜於外也。」右第八章。
Honorable Wen said, "All these are instances of striving for the external while losing the internal. They are like discarding leftover food or attaching something superfluous to the body, which causes others to feel repelled" (DZL 2.24, 4–6). Mr. Dong said, "One who has attained the Way is content within and does not display himself outwardly" (DZJ 2.64).

This serves as Chapter 8.

## Chapter 9 (DDJ 33)

知人者智，自知者明。
One who knows others is knowledgeable;
One who knows himself is illumined.

知人之善惡，固智矣。自知之智，為尤明；明者，智之實也。
To know the good and evil in others is indeed [a form of] wisdom, but to know oneself is the higher illumination; for illumination is the substance of wisdom.

勝人者有力，自勝者强。
One who prevails over others has strength;
One who prevails over himself is truly strong.

勝人者，血氣之力也；自勝者，義理之勇也。克己復禮，則不屈於人欲，而强莫加焉。
One who prevails over others possesses strength of blood and *qi*, but one who prevails over himself has the courage of moral principle. By overcoming oneself

and returning to ritual propriety, one no longer yields to human desires and attains a strength to which nothing has to be added.

知足者富。
One who knows contentment is truly wealthy.

自知既明，無求於外而常足，則富莫加焉。顏淵簞瓢陋巷，孔子曲肱飲水，而其樂自如；舉天下之物，無以易其所樂，則豈非至富乎？彼牽於物欲，而有求於外者，則心常不足；雖富有天下，猶非富也。
If one knows oneself, one is already illumined; there is no need to seek anything from outside. Such a person is ever content, with no further wealth to be added. Yan Yuan lived on coarse food and dwelled in humble quarters (*Lunyu* 6.11), while Confucius rested his head on his arm and drank water (*Lunyu* 7.16); yet their joy remained constant. Even if one were to offer all the things under heaven, there would be nothing to exchange for his contentment. How, then, could they not be considered supremely rich? [In contrast,] those driven by material desires and who seek from the external remain perpetually dissatisfied. Even if they possess all the wealth in the world, they are not truly wealthy.

强行者有志。
One who strives to practice [the Way] possesses will.

董氏曰：「惟自勝，故志於道，而自强不息，則物莫奪其志，而與天同健矣。」
Mr. Dong said, "One who conquers only himself sets his will on the Way. By continually strengthening oneself without rest, nothing in the world can seize that will and becomes vigorous together with heaven." (DZJ 2.157).

不失其所者久。
One who does not lose their proper course endures.

董氏曰：「知道而能行，則自得其所而居安矣。」愚按：知之明而守之固，則素位而行，無願乎外，無入而不自得焉。此乃不失其所也，是悠久之道也。
Mr. Dong said, "If one knows the Way and can practice it, he will find his place and dwell in comfort" (DZJ 2.159).

In my humble view, if one's knowledge is clear and one's practice is steadfast, then one acts according to one's proper station, harbors no desires beyond it, and in every situation remains self-contented. This, precisely, is what it means to not lose one's place; it is the enduring Way.

死而不亡者壽。
One who has died yet does not fade away is truly long-living.

孔顏既歿，數千載，而耿光如日月，豈非壽乎？右第九章。

Confucius and Yan Yuan have been gone for thousands of years, yet they still shine and radiate like the sun and moon. How could they not be long-living?

This is Chapter 9.

### Chapter 10 (DDJ 44)

> 名與身，孰親？身與貨，孰多？
> Which is closer, name or the self?
> Which is greater, the self or wealth?

名者，實之賓，於身為外物也。身，一而已；貨財則眾多。若棄身而循名與物，則捨親而從賓，役一而求多，惑莫甚焉。
A name is merely a guest of one's substance, an external thing in relation to the self. The self is singular, while wealth and possessions are many. To forsake the self in pursuit of reputation or material things is like abandoning one's parents to follow mere guests. To burden the singular in order to chase the many—nothing could be more misguided.

> 得與亡，孰病？
> Which brings greater harm, gain or loss?

得名與貨，則身必亡，是乃亡也。得身，則雖亡名與貨，而不害乎為得也。然則得身與亡身，孰為病乎？
To gain name and possessions inevitably means losing the self, and that is true loss. But if one preserves the self, then even the loss of name and wealth does not diminish what has been gained. If this is so, then which is more harmful: gaining the self or losing it?

> 是故，甚愛必大費；多藏必厚亡。
> Therefore, excessive attachment inevitably leads to great expenditure;
> excessive accumulation inevitably leads to heavy loss.

愛名者，必損實，是大費也。藏財者，必失身，是厚亡也。
One who attaches to fame will inevitably diminish what is real—this is great expenditure. One who hoards wealth will inevitably lose his life—this is heavy loss.

> 知足不辱，知止不殆，可以長久。
> One who knows contentment is not disgraced.
> One who knows when to stop is not imperiled.
> Thus, he can endure long.

董氏曰：「惟審於內外之分，則知止知足，而無得失之患。故能安於性命之常，亦何殆辱之有？所以可長久也。」右第十章。

Mr. Dong said, "By discerning the distinction between inner and outer, one knows when to stop and how to be content, and thus has no anxieties over gain or loss. In this way, one remains at peace with the constancy of one's nature and mandate—how then could there be danger or disgrace? This is why one endures." (DZJ 3.93)

This concludes chapter 10.

# Chapters 11 to 20

## Chapter 11 (DDJ 47)

不出戶，知天下；不窺牖，見天道。
Without stepping outside the door, one knows all-under-heaven;
Without peering through the window, one perceives the Way of heaven.

萬物皆備於我，豈待他求哉？求其放心，則可以見道矣。程子所謂自能尋向上去下學而上達者，是也。
All myriad things are already within me (*Mengzi* 7A4); why then seek them elsewhere? By seeking to recover the stray mind, one can come to perceive the Way (*Mengzi* 6A11). This is what Master Cheng refers to when he speaks of one's ability to seek upward on one's own, beginning with learning from below and ascending to higher understanding (*Lunyu* 14.35; ECYS 1.22).

其出彌遠，其知彌少。
The farther one ventures outward, the less one truly knows.

溫公曰：「迷本逐末也。」愚按：心放而愈遠，則知道愈難矣。
Honorable Wen said, "This is because he is confused about the root and chases after the branches" (DZL 3.47,4).

In my humble view, the farther one's mind strays from the Way, the more difficult it becomes to truly know it.

是以聖人不行而知，不見而名，不為而成。
For this reason, the sage knows without venturing forth, is named without being seen, and accomplishes without doing anything.

此言聖人清明在躬，而義理昭徹，乃自誠而明之事也。學者不可遽跂於此，但當收斂放心，以養其知，而勉其所行也。右第十一章。
This passage describes how the sage's clarity and illumination reside within himself, while the moral principle shines forth and penetrates all things. In this way, he is sincere with himself and brings illumination to every matter. Learners, however, cannot reach this state suddenly; they must first recover their stray minds, cultivate their understanding, and diligently apply themselves in practice.

The above is Chapter 11.

## Chapter 12 (DDJ 46)

天下有道，卻走馬以糞；天下無道，戎馬生於郊。

When all under heaven has the Way, war horses are led back to haul manure.
When all under heaven lacks the Way, war horses are bred on the frontier.

董氏曰：「糞，治田疇也。戎馬，戰馬也。郊者，二國之境也。以內言之，心君泰然，則卻返氣馬，以培其本根；反是則，氣馬馳於外境矣。」
Mr. Dong stated: "[To haul] manure refers to plowing the fields, and warhorses denotes horses used in battle. The frontier signifies the border between two states. Viewed inwardly, when the mind assumes the role of sovereign and remains calm, it channels the restless *qi* like a running horse guided to nurture its foundational roots. If this is not the case, the restless *qi* rushes outward like an untamed horse" (DZJ 3.109).

禍莫大於不知足，咎莫大於欲得。
No misfortune is greater than not knowing contentment;
No disgrace is greater than the desire to acquire more.

董氏曰：「究其根本，原於縱欲。」
Mr. Dong said, "If one traces [misfortune and disgrace] to their root, one finds that they originate in the indulgence of desire" (DZJ 3.111).

故知足之足，常足矣。
Thus, the contentment born of knowing contentment
is the contentment that endures forever.

無求於外，則內德無欠，故應用無窮，而常足矣。
When one seeks nothing from the outside, inner virtue has no deficiency. Thus, one responds with inexhaustible efficacy and remains in constant contentment.

右第十二章。以上五章，言守道克己，不自矜伐，常知止足之義，皆推演嗇字之義也。
This is Chapter Twelve. The preceding five chapters discuss guarding the Way, overcoming the self, refraining from pride and boasting, and always knowing when to stop and how to be content. All of these unfold from the meaning of the character for cherishing.

## Chapter 13 (DDJ 67)

我有三寶，保而持之：一曰慈，二曰儉，三曰不敢先。[1]
I have three treasures, which I guard and preserve:
first, compassion; second, frugality; and third, not daring to take the lead.

---

[1] In the standard DDJ, the final phrase appears as *sam wal pul kam wi ch'ŏnha sŏn* (*san yue bugan wei tianxia xian* 三曰不敢為天下先). In contrast, Yi I omitted the three characters *wi ch'ŏnha* (*wei tianxia* 為天下) from the original phrase.

不敢先者，謙也。慈、儉、謙三者，持身接物之寶訣也。
Not daring to take the lead means humility. Compassion, frugality, and humility, these three are the treasured secrets for conducting oneself and engaging with others.

> 夫慈，故能勇。
> Being compassionate, one can thus become courageous.

董氏曰：「仁者，必有勇也。」
Mr. Dong stated, "The benevolent are necessarily courageous" (DZJ 4.72).

> 儉，故能廣。
> Being frugal, one can thus be broad-minded.

董氏曰：「守約而施博也。」
Mr. Dong said, "By holding to restraint, one extends generosity widely." (DZJ 4.74).

> 不敢先，故能成器長。
> By not daring to take the lead, one can thus become a vessel fit to be a leader.

器，物也。自後者，人必先之，故卒為有物之長也。董氏曰：「乾之出庶物，亦曰：見羣龍無首，吉。」
The term "vessel" refers to a being. One who puts themselves behind will ultimately be placed at the forefront by others. Therefore, one will be the true leader of other beings.

Mr. Dong said, "Heaven produces all things, and if one sees multiple dragons but does not take their lead, it is auspicious" (DZJ 4.76).[2]

> 今捨其慈且勇，捨其儉且廣，捨其後且先，死矣。
> If one abandons compassion and yet pursues courage, abandons frugality and yet seeks expansiveness, or abandons staying behind and yet tries to take the lead, he will die.

務勇，則必忮；務廣，則必奢；務先，則必爭，皆死之徒也。
Striving for courage inevitably breeds malice; striving for generosity inevitably leads to extravagance; striving to take the lead inevitably invites conflict—all are paths to death.

> 夫慈以戰則勝，以守則固；天將救之，以慈衛之。

---

[2] The last phrase appears in *Yijing*, Hexagram Qian 乾, The Use of the Number Nine 用九, 8.

> Compassion, when used in battle, brings victory; when used in defense, brings security. When heaven is about to save someone, it protects him with compassion.

董氏曰：「慈者，生道之流行，乃仁之用也，故為三寶之首。以慈御物，物亦愛之，如慕父母，效死不辭，是以戰則勝，守則固。故曰：仁者，無敵於天下也。苟或人有所不及，天亦將以慈救衛之，蓋天道好還，常與善人故也。」程氏曰：「去邠而歧，周以興，是其救也。」
Mr. Dong said: "Compassion is the flowing operation of the Way of life; it is the function of benevolence. Therefore, it stands first among the three treasures. When one governs things with compassion, the people also love him, as they long for their father and mother, and they do not refuse even to die in his service. For this reason, when he fights, he is victorious, and when he defends, he is secure. Hence it is said: 'The benevolent man has no enemy under heaven' (*Mengzi* 1A5). If someone should fall short in some respect, Heaven will likewise save and protect him through compassion. For the Way of Heaven favors returning good, and it is always with the good person" (DZJ 4.80).

Master Cheng said: "When (King Wen) left Bin and went to Qi, the Zhou thereby arose; this was its rescue."[3]

右第十三章，言三寶為修己長物之要道。其下六章，皆推廣此章之義，蓋因嗇字之義，而伸長之也。
This is Chapter 13, which explains how the three treasures serve as essential principles for self-cultivation and the development of others. The following six chapters all elaborate on this chapter's meaning, extending from the significance of the character for cherishing.

## Chapter 14 (DDJ 76; 78)

> 人之生也柔弱，其死也堅强；草木之生也柔脆，其死也枯槁。
> 故堅强者，死之徒；柔弱者，生之徒。
> When a person is alive, he is soft and pliant;
> when he dies, he becomes hard and rigid.
> When plants are alive, they are tender and supple;
> when they die, they become dry and withered.
> Therefore hardness and rigidity belong to the company of death,
> while softness and pliancy belong to the company of life.

沖氣在身，則體無堅强之病；以理勝氣，則事無堅强之失矣。
When empty *qi* dwells within the body, the body is free from the ailments of hardness and rigidity. By overcoming *qi* with principle, no task suffers from harshness or force.

---

[3] The source of this quotation is unclear. The story of King Wen relocating the Zhou capital to Qi appears in *Mengzi* 1B18.

> 是以兵强則不勝，木强則共；故堅强居下，柔弱處上。
> For this reason, an army that is too strong does not prevail;
> a tree that is too hard is cut apart.
> Thus the hard and rigid take the lower place,
> while the soft and pliant occupy the higher place.

董氏曰：「共，謂人共伐之也。」列子云：「兵强則滅，木强則折，是矣。物之精者，常在上，而粗者，常在下。其精必柔，其粗必强，理勢然也。」
Mr. Dong said, "The term 'cut apart' means that people jointly cut it down. Liezi stated, 'When an army is strong, it will perish; when a tree is hard, it will be broken' (2.17)—this is indeed so. Among all things, the refined is always placed above, and the coarse below. The refined is necessarily soft, and the coarse is necessarily hard—such is the natural course of principle" (DZJ 4.149).

> 天下柔弱，莫過於水；而攻堅强，莫之能勝，其無以易之。[4]
> Of all things soft and weak under heaven, nothing surpasses water.
> In overcoming the hard and strong, nothing excels it;
> Thus, nothing can take its place.

善下而柔弱，故必勝堅强，其理不可易也。
[Water] flows downward and is soft and yielding; therefore, it overcomes what is hard and strong—a principle that cannot be changed.

> 故柔勝剛，弱勝强；天下莫不知，莫能行。
> Thus, the soft overcomes the hard;
> The weak overcomes the strong—
> All-under-heaven know this, yet none practice it.

觀水之攻堅，則其理昭然，豈難知哉？非知之難，行之惟難，故人鮮克行之。
When one observes how water conquers the hard, the principle is perfectly clear—how could it be difficult to understand? The difficulty lies not in knowing it, but in putting it into practice; therefore, few people succeed in doing so.

> 是以聖人言：受國之垢，是為社稷主；受國不祥，是為天下王。
> For this reason, the sage says: "To bear the nation's filth is to become the lord of the altars of earth and grain; to endure the nation's misfortunes is to become the sovereign of all-under-heaven."

[4] The DDJ passage Yi I cites differs slightly from the standard Wang Bi edition. In Wang Bi Chapter 78, the line reads: 天下莫柔弱於水，而攻堅強者莫之能勝，其無以易之. The DZJ version is nearly identical to Wang Bi: 天下莫柔弱於水，而攻堅彊莫之能勝，以其無以易之也 (DZJ 4.156).

溫公曰：「含垢納污，乃能成其大。」愚按：仁覆如天，無物不容，是謂受垢與不祥也。
The Honorable Wen said, "By embracing filth and accepting contamination, one can accomplish greatness" (DZL 4.78,1).

In my view, when benevolence covers all as heaven does, nothing is excluded—this is what is meant by "embracing filth" and "bearing misfortune."

右第十四章，因上章戰勝之說，而推明慈柔勝剛暴之義。夫所謂柔者，只言仁慈之形耳，非一於柔弱而已。若一於柔弱，則豈能勝剛暴哉？且其勝之者，亦出於理勢之當然耳，非有心於欲勝，而故為柔弱也。
This is Chapter 14. Building on the previous chapter's discussion of triumph in battle, it expands the meaning: the compassionate and soft prevail over the hard and violent. "Softness" refers to the manifestation of benevolence and compassion—it is not mere weakness. If one were only soft and weak, how could one overcome the strong and aggressive? Moreover, its victory arises simply from what naturally follows from the principles and tendencies of things.; it does not stem from a deliberate desire to conquer, but from being soft and yielding.

## Chapter 15 (DDJ 9)

> 持而盈之，不如其已；揣而銳之，不可長保。
> Holding it full to the brim—better to stop in time.
> Sharpening it to a keen edge—it cannot be preserved for long. (9)

恐盈之或溢，而持固之，不若不盈之為安也；恐銳之或折，而揣量之，不若不銳之可保也。蘇氏曰：「無盈則無所用持，無銳則無所用揣矣。」
Fearing that what is full may overflow and therefore holding it tightly is not as safe as leaving it unfilled. Likewise, fearing that what is sharpened may break and therefore striking it with measured force is not as secure as leaving it unsharpened so that it may be preserved. As Mr. Su (Su Che 蘇轍; 1039–1112) said, "If there is no fullness, there is nothing that requires holding; if there is no sharpness, there is nothing that requires striking" (LJ A.51).[5]

> 金玉滿堂，莫之能守；富貴而驕，自遺其咎；功成名遂，身退，[6] 天之道。
> When gold and jade fill the hall, none can keep them safe.
> When wealth and rank give rise to arrogance, one brings ruin upon oneself.
> When merit is accomplished and reputation fulfilled, to withdraw oneself, this is the Way of heaven. (9)

---

5 Here "A" denotes the upper volume 上卷 and "B" the lower volume 下卷.

6 The standard DDJ has this as 功遂身退. Yi I added the phrase 名遂 to this line because his source, Dong Sijing's DZJ (1.88), contains it.

劉師立曰：「盈則必虛，戒之在滿；銳則必鈍，戒之在進；金玉必累，戒之在貪；富貴易淫，戒之在傲。功成名遂必危，在乎知止，而不失其正。」右第十五章，言儉之義。

Liu Shili (d. 640) said: "What is full will inevitably become empty; therefore, the warning lies in fullness. What is sharp will inevitably become dull; therefore, the warning lies in pushing forward. Gold and jade inevitably become a burden; therefore, the warning lies in greed. Wealth and rank easily lead to excess; therefore, the warning lies in arrogance. When merit is accomplished and reputation fulfilled, danger inevitably follows; the essential point lies in knowing when to stop and not losing what is proper."[7]

The above is chapter fifteen, explaining the meaning of frugality.

## Chapter 16 (DDJ 39)

> 貴以賤為本，高以下為基。是以侯王自謂孤寡不穀，此其以賤為本邪，非乎？
> Nobility takes lowliness as its root;
> the high takes the low as its foundation.
> Thus, lords and kings call themselves orphaned, widowed, and unworthy.
> Is this not because they take lowliness as their root?

夫惟自賤，則人必貴之；自下，則人必高之。是以賤為本，以下為基也。侯王之自貶，是自賤自下之道也。右第十六章，言不敢先之義。下章同此。

Only when one regards oneself as lowly will others surely honor him; when one places oneself below, others will surely raise him up. Therefore, lowliness serves as the root and the low as the foundation. The self-deprecating language used by lords and kings reflects the Way of lowering and humbling oneself.

The above is chapter sixteen, explaining the meaning of not daring to take the lead. The following chapter conveys the same idea.

## Chapter 17 (DDJ 8; 66)

> 上善若水，水善利萬物，又不爭；處眾人之所惡，故幾於道。
> The highest goodness is like water.
> Water benefits the myriad things and does not contend;
> it dwells in places that people despise.
> Therefore it is close to the Way.

董氏曰：「守柔處下，乃俗之所惡，而實近於道。」

---

[7] Quoted in DZJ 1.89. The original source of Liu Shili's statement quoted above has not yet been precisely identified. Although this saying is attributed to Liu Shili and appears in various Daoist texts and commentaries on the *Laozi*, its exact origin remains unclear. His biographies in the *Jiu Tangshu* 舊唐書 and *Xin Tangshu* 新唐書 make no mention of any writings. It is evident that Yi I cited Liu Shili's words from Dong Sijing's DZJ, where the passage appears almost verbatim.

Mr. Dong said: "To preserve softness and dwell in the lowly place is what the world despises, yet in reality it is close to the Way." (DZJ 1.68).

> 一一主[8] 江海所以能為百谷王者，以其善下之，故能為百谷王。是以聖人，以言下之，以身後之，是以處上而人不重，處前而人不害，天下樂推而不厭。
> Rivers and seas are able to become the kings of the hundred valleys because they are good at placing themselves below them; therefore, they can be the kings of the hundred valleys. For this reason, the sage lowers himself through his words and places himself behind others in his person. Thus, when he occupies a high position, people do not feel oppressed; when he stands before them, people do not feel harmed. Accordingly, all-under-heaven gladly support him and never grow weary of doing so.

水固近道，而江海又水之大者也。宋徽宗曰：「屯初九曰：以貴下賤，大得民也。得其心也。處上而人不重，則戴之也歡；處前而人不害，則利之者眾。若是，則無思不服，故不厭也。」
Water is indeed close to the Way, and rivers and seas are simply the greatest forms of water. Emperor Huizong of Song said: "[In the *Xiangzhuan* 象傳 of the *Zhouyi*] on the First Nine of the hexagram Zhun, it is said, 'By lowering the honored toward the humble, one greatly wins the people.' This means winning their hearts. When one occupies a high position yet does not weigh heavily upon others, those who support him do so with joy. When one stands before others yet does not harm them, many benefit from him. If it is thus, there is none who will not submit, and therefore they do not grow weary (DZSH 9.66,6).

董氏曰：「楊雄曰：自下者，人高之；自後者，人先之。故天下樂推戴，而無厭斁之心也。」右第十七章。
Mr. Dong said, "Yang Xiong (53 BCE-18 CE) states, 'One who lowers himself will be elevated by people, and one who puts himself behind of others will be brought forward by them' (*Fayan* 7.20). Thus, all under the world gladly elevate him and do not have feelings of dislike against him" (DZJ 4.67).

This concludes Chapter 17.

## Chapter 18 (DDJ 68)

> 善為士者，不武。
> One who is skilled as a warrior does not rely on force.

董氏曰：「不尚力也。」
Mr. Dong said, "It means such a person does not esteem force" (DZJ 4.83).

---

[8] In front of the original text of this chapter, there is a hyphen-like mark (一) combined with a character *chu* (*zhu* 主) written as 一一主, but the precise origin and intended meaning of this phrase are currently unknown.

善戰者，不怒。
One who is skilled in warfare does not act out of anger.

不得已而用兵，非出於血氣之怒也。
[Such a person] mobilizes his force only when necessary, never driven by rage born of blood and *qi*.

善勝敵者，不爭。
One who is skilled in winning over enemies does not compete.

只以征伐正其不正而已，非有爭奪之心也。
He employs military action only to rectify what is unjust; he does not harbor a mind of contention or seizure.

善用人者，為之下。
One who is skilled in managing others humbles himself.

致敬盡禮，屈己以下賢，然後能用賢。孟子曰：「湯之於伊尹，學焉而後臣之。」
By showing reverence and exhausting the rites, and by humbling oneself before the worthy, one is then able to employ the worthy. As Mengzi said, "King Tang of Shang learned from Yi Yin and only afterward made him his minister" (2B11).

是謂不爭之德，是謂用人之力，是謂配天，古之極也。
This is called the virtue of non-contention;
this is called the power to make use of others;
this is called being aligned with heaven—the ultimate state of the ancients.

謙卑自牧，與人為善，故人樂為用。其德配天，無以尚矣。右第十八章。極言慈柔謙下之德，可以配天也。
By cultivating oneself with humility and treating others with kindness, people gladly place themselves in one's service. Such virtue accords with heaven, and nothing surpasses it. This is chapter 18. It fully expounds the virtues of compassion, softness, and humility, with which one can accord with heaven.

## Chapter 19 (DDJ 41)

上士聞道，勤而行之；中士聞道，若存若亡；下士聞道，大笑之。不笑，不足以為道。
When the superior scholar hears of the Way, he diligently practices it.
When the middling scholar hears of the Way, it seems to him at times present and at times absent.
When the inferior scholar hears of the Way, he laughs at it loudly.
If it did not provoke laughter, it would not be worthy to be the Way.

上士聞道，篤信不疑；中士，疑信相半；下士，茫然不曉，反加非笑。若合於下士所見，則豈聖人之道哉？
The superior scholar hears of the Way and devoutly trusts it without doubt. The middling scholar is divided, partly believing and partly doubting. The inferior scholar is confused and uncomprehending, responding instead with criticism and ridicule. If it aligns with the understanding of the lowest scholar, how could it be the Way of the sage?

> 建言有之，明道若昧；進道若退，上德若谷，大白若辱。
> An established saying has it:
> The bright Way seems obscure;
> the advancing Way seems to retreat;
> the highest virtue is like a valley;
> the greatest purity appears sullied.

建言，古之所立言也。明道者，若無所見；進道者，退然若不能行。德之高者，自謙如谷之虛；潔白之至者，自處如有玷汚也。
Established sayings are words set down by the ancients. One who clearly understands the Way appears as though nothing is seen; one who advances in the Way seems to withdraw, as if unable to proceed. One whose virtue is highest humbles himself like the emptiness of a valley; one who is supremely pure places himself as though he bore some stain.

> 大器晚成。
> A great vessel is completed late.

積之久，然後發之洪，故大器不速成。
Only after long accumulation does it swell and emerge; thus, a great vessel is not quickly completed.

> 大成若缺，其用不敝。
> Great completion appears incomplete, yet its usefulness never diminishes.

董氏曰：「敝，敗壞也。體至道之大全，而盛德若不足，故其用愈久，而愈新也。」
Mr. Dong explains, "The term 'to diminish' means 'to be worn out or decayed.' When one fully embodies the great wholeness of the ultimate Way, their supreme virtue appears as if something is lacking. Yet as it is applied over time, it only becomes ever more renewed" (DZJ 3.96).

> 大盈若沖，其用不窮。
> Great fullness appears hollow, yet its usefulness is inexhaustible.

道備於己，而謙若沖虛，故積愈厚，而用愈不窮。董氏曰：「此兼用而言。」愚按：中間二句，言其用，上下則皆略文也。

When the Way is fully present within oneself, yet one remains humble as though empty and open, one's accumulation grows ever deeper and its application becomes inexhaustible. Mr. Dong said: "Here it is speaking of both in terms of their function" (DZJ 3.98).

In my humble view, the two middle lines refer to its function, while the lines above and below are both abbreviated expressions.

> 大直若屈，大巧若拙。
> Great straightness seems bent; great skill seems clumsy.

與物無競，故其直若屈；曲當而無跡，故其巧若拙。
He does not contend with others; therefore, his straightness appears bent. His adaptability is fitting and leaves no trace; therefore, his skill appears clumsy.

> 大辯若訥；善者不辯，辯者不善。信言不美，美言不信。
> Great eloquence appears awkward;
> Those who are good do not argue; those who argue are not good.
> Trustworthy words are not ornate; ornate words arc not trustworthy.

不事乎辯，而發必當理者，謂之大辯。吉人辭寡，故其辯若訥。以善為主，則不求辯；以辯為主，則未必善也。美者，華飾也。忠信之言，不必華美；華美之言，未必忠信。
One who does not pursue argument, yet whose speech always accords with principle, is called a great debater. An auspicious person speaks sparingly, so their argument may appear awkward. One who prioritizes goodness does not seek to argue; one who prioritizes argument is not necessarily good. "Ornate" refers to embellishment. Words that are faithful and trustworthy need not be adorned, and adorned words are not necessarily faithful or trustworthy.

> 大音希聲，大象無形，道隱無名。
> The greatest sound is rarely heard; the greatest image has no form.
> The Way is hidden and nameless.

希者，聽之不聞也。道本無聲無臭，而體物不遺；強名之曰道，其實無名也。體用一源，顯微無間之妙，豈中下士之所能聽瑩哉？
The term "rarely [heard]" means that one listens for it but does not hear it. The Way inherently has no sound or scent, yet as the substance of all things, it leaves nothing behind. We force a name upon it and call it the Way, though in truth it is nameless. Its essence and function arise from a single source, and the mystery of the seamless link between the manifest and the subtle—how could middling or inferior scholars perceive such radiant mystery?

右第十九章，推明謙虛之德，合乎道體之本然。文王望道，而如未之見；顏子以能問於不能，以多問於寡。有若無，實若虛，犯而不校，即此章之意也。申言十三章三寶之義者，止此。

The above is Chapter 19, which further clarifies that the virtue of humility and emptiness accords with the fundamental nature of the essence of the Way. King Wen perceived the Way yet behaved as if he had not (*Mengzi* 4B20). Yan Yuan, though capable, consults those who seem incapable; though fully knowledgeable, he questions those who appear unknowing. He acts as if he has nothing, though he possesses, as if empty, though he is full, and when wronged, he does not retaliate (*Lunyu* 8.5). This is the meaning of the chapter. It also extends the principle of the three treasures discussed in Chapter 13.

**Chapter 20 (DDJ 26; 23)**

> 重為輕根，靜為躁君；是以君子終日行，不離輜重。
> The heavy is the root of the light, and stillness is the master of restlessness.
> Because of this, though the noble person moves about all day,
> He never parts from the cart's weight.

重是本，輕是末，不可捨本而趨末。靜是君，躁是卒徒，不可捨君而逐卒徒也。董氏曰：「輜，大車也。君子之道，以靜重為主，不可須臾離也，如輜車之重，不敢容易其行。」

Heaviness is the foundation, lightness the tip; one must not forsake the root to pursue the tip. Stillness is the ruler, restlessness the subordinate; one must not abandon the ruler to follow the subordinate.

Mr. Dong explained, "Cart refers to a great wagon's [weight]. The noble person's Way is grounded in stillness and weight, which he must not leave even for a moment—like a heavily laden cart that cannot be moved lightly" (DZJ 2.83).

> 雖有榮觀，燕處超然。
> Even amidst splendid sights, [the noble] remains serene and detached.

雖在繁華富貴之中，而無所係戀，常超然自得於物欲之外也。董氏曰：「榮觀在物，燕處在己，惟不以物易己。故遊觀榮樂，而無所係著也。」

Even when the noble person find himself amid wealth and splendor, he is not bound by such things and remain detached from material desires.

Mr. Dong stated, "Dazzling attractions belong to the external thing, while detachment arises from within. He does not allow external things to alter [his mind]. Thus, even when faced with splendid and pleasurable sights, he is not swayed by them" (DZJ 2.85).

> 奈何萬乘之主，而以身輕天下？輕則失臣，[9] 躁則失君。

[9] In the standard DDJ, this phrase is written as 輕則失本.

How could the lord of myriad chariots treat all-under-heaven lightly for himself?
If a ruler is frivolous, he loses his ministers;
If a minister is hasty, he loses the ruler.

董氏曰：「萬乘之尊，不可縱所欲之私，而不顧天下之重也。君輕則失於臣，臣躁則失於君矣。近取諸身，則以心為君，以氣為臣；輕則心妄動，而暴其氣；躁則氣擾亂，而動其心。」

Mr. Dong remarked, "The lord of myriad chariots must not indulge in selfish desires while disregarding the gravity of the matters of all-under-heaven. If the ruler acts lightly, he loses the ministers; if the ministers act hastily, they lose the ruler. Looking inward, one takes the heart as ruler and the *qi* as ministers. Acting lightly comes from a heart that moves recklessly and disturbs the *qi*; acting hastily comes from disturbed *qi* that unsettles the heart" (DZJ 2.87).

飄風不終朝，驟雨不終日；天地尚不能久，而況於人乎？
A gusty wind lasts no morning; a sudden downpour lasts no day.
If even heaven and earth cannot endure for long, how much less can a human being?

董氏曰：「狂疾之風，急暴之雨，此陰陽擊搏，忽然之變，故不能久。自朝至中，為終朝。」愚按：人有輕躁之病，則必有急暴之行；暴怒者，必有後悔；以至暴富暴貴者，必有後禍，皆非長久之道也。

Mr. Dong said: "Gale-force winds and sudden torrential rains—these are the clashes of yin and yang, abrupt and unpredictable changes, and therefore cannot last. From morning until noon, they reach their end" (DZJ 2.34).

In my humble view, when a person is prone to haste and impulsiveness, his actions will inevitably be abrupt and violent; one who rages violently will surely regret it later; and one who gains sudden wealth or rank will inevitably suffer later misfortune. None of these follow the Way of enduring stability.

右第二十章，言君子主乎靜重，而不動於外物，亦嗇之義也。

The above is Chapter 20, which teaches that the noble person governs himself with stillness and weight, remaining unmoved by external things. This, too, reflects the meaning of cherishing.

# Chapters 21 to 30

## Chapter 21 (DDJ 45)

躁勝寒，靜勝熱；清靜為天下正。
Restlessness overcomes cold, stillness overcomes heat;
Clarity and stillness set all-under-heaven in order.

董氏曰：「動屬陽，靜屬陰。故躁勝寒，靜勝熱，皆未免於一偏也。清靜者，動靜一致，故為天下正。」愚按：清靜者，泊然無外誘之累，而動靜皆定者也。
Mr. Dong said, "Movement belongs to yang, and stillness to yin. Therefore, restlessness overcomes cold, and stillness overcomes heat; both inevitably lean toward one side. 'Clarity and stillness' means the union of movement and calm. Therefore, they set all-under-heaven in order" (DZJ 3.106).

In my view, "clarity and stillness" refer to a serene state untroubled by external enticements, in which both movement and stillness are in proper balance.

右第二十一章，因上章躁靜之義，而言清靜之正，恐人之偏於靜也。
The above is Chapter 21. This chapter builds upon the previous discussion of restlessness and stillness, emphasizing the uprightness of clarity and stillness. [I] fear that people may become partial to stillness.

## Chapter 22 (DDJ 56)

知者不言，言者不知。
One who knows does not speak; one who speaks does not know.

知道者，默而識之；有知輒言，非知道者也。
One who knows the Way grasps it in silence. Those who speak whenever they gain some knowledge are not ones who understand the Way.

塞其兌，閉其門。
Block the openings and close the gates.

兌，說也。塞其兌者，防窒意慾也。門，口也。閉其門者，淵默自守也。
The term "opening" means "to speak"; thus, to block the opening is to guard against [the stirring of] desires and intentions. The "gates" refers to the mouth; to close it is to maintain deep silence and preserve oneself.

挫其銳，解其紛，和其光，同其塵，是謂玄同。
Blunt the sharpness, untangle the entanglements,
Soften the radiance, merge with the dust.

This is called the mysterious union.

銳，英氣也。挫其銳者，磨礱英氣，使無圭角也。紛，眾理之肯綮也。解其紛者，明察肯綮，迎刃而解也。和光同塵者，含蓄德美於中，而不自耀立異於眾也。玄，妙也。既不隨俗習非，而又非離世絕俗，故曰玄同。
The word "sharpness" refers to exceptional *qi*. "To blunt his sharpness" means to refine his extraordinary *qi* so that no sharp edges remain. "Entanglements" denotes the intricate interconnection of principle, like the joints and tissues of the body. To "untangle the entanglements" is to examine these subtle connections with clarity and precision, resolving them as a blade meets and separates the joints with ease.[1] "Softening the radiance and merging with dust" means that he contains virtue and excellence within, without displaying them outwardly or setting himself apart from others. "Mysterious" means subtle and wondrous. Because he neither follows worldly custom in its errors nor withdraws from the world altogether, this is called "the mysterious union."

故不可得而親，不可得而疏，不可得而利，不可得而害，不可得而貴，不可得而賤，故為天下貴。
Therefore, it cannot be approached closely, nor kept at a distance; it cannot be advantaged, nor harmed; it cannot be exalted, nor demeaned.
thus, it is honored by all-under-heaven.

君子周而不比，和而不同，出處合義，動靜隨時，豈世人之私情所能親疏利害貴賤者哉？其所以然者，以通乎道，而無欲故也。為天下貴者，是天爵之良貴也。
A noble person is inclusive without being partisan (*Lunyu* 2.14) and seeks harmony without [blindly] conforming (*Lunyu* 13.23). He accepts or declines office according to righteousness, and moves or remains still in accordance with the times. How could such a person be drawn near or pushed away, advantaged or harmed, exalted or demeaned by the private sentiments of the world? It is because he aligns with the Way and is free from selfish desire. To be honored by all-under-heaven is to be granted a truly noble rank by heaven.

右第二十二章，承上章而言清靜自修之功，而因言其效。下二章，皆推說其效也。
The above is Chapter 22, which continues from the previous chapter by explaining the merits that come from clarity, stillness, and self-cultivation. It then discusses their effects. The following two chapters further elaborate on these outcomes.

## Chapter 23 (DDJ 55)

含德之厚，比於赤子。
One who embodies profound virtue is likened to a newborn child.

[1] Here Yi I alludes the story of Cook Ding in the *Zhuangzi* (3.2).

含懷至德之人，誠一無僞，如赤子之心也。
One who harbors supreme virtue is sincerely single-hearted and free from deceit, like the heart of a newborn child.

> 毒蟲不螫，猛獸不據，攫鳥不搏。
> Venomous insects do not sting him; wild beasts do not seize him; birds of prey do not strike him.

董氏曰：「全天之人，物無害者。」右第二十三章。
Mr. Dong said, "One who is fully aligned with heaven cannot be harmed by anything" (DZJ 3.176).
The above is Chapter 23.

## Chapter 24 (DDJ 50)

> 蓋聞，善攝生者，陸行不遇兕虎，入軍不被甲兵。兕無所投其角，虎無所措其爪，兵無所容其刃。夫何故？以其無死地。
> It is said that one who excels in nurturing life encounters neither rhinoceros nor tiger on land, and is not struck by weapons on the battlefield.
> The rhinoceros finds nowhere to gore, the tiger nowhere to claw, and weapons nowhere to pierce.
> Why is this so? Because he stands beyond the reach of death.

善攝生者，全盡生理，故所遇皆正命，必無一朝之患也。或疑聖賢亦有未免禍患者，曰：「此只言其理而已，若或然之變，則有未暇論也。」
One who excels in nurturing life fully realizes the principles of life; therefore, all he encounters aligns with the proper mandate, leaving no cause for sudden misfortune. If one objects, pointing out that even sages and worthies have sometimes been unable to escape calamity, the answer is this: these words concern only the principle itself; in cases of exceptional contingencies, there is no occasion for detailed discussion.

右第二十四章，與前章皆申言全德之效。七章所謂嗇以事天者，其義止此。
The above is Chapter 24. Together with the preceding chapter, it further elaborates on the effects of completed virtue. The notion of serving heaven through cherishing, introduced in Chapter seven, is developed more fully here.

## Chapter 25 (DDJ 34)

> 大道汎兮，其可左右。
> How vast is the great Way! One can turn left or right.

(董) 氏曰：「汎，無滯貌。惟不麗於一物，不離乎當處，無處不有，無時不然，是以左右逢其原也。」

Mr. Dong said, "'Vast' means being diffuse and free flowing, with no appearance of stagnation. It means being unrestricted by any single thing, never departing from its proper place—yet it is nowhere absent and never fails to be so. Thus, whether it turns left or right, it always meets its source" (DZJ 2.164).

> 萬物恃之以生，而不辭；功成，不名有。
> The myriad things rely on it to live, yet it does not refuse them;
> when its work is accomplished, it does not claim them as its own.

萬物之資，始生成；莫非此道之流行，體物不遺，而不自有其能也。
The source on which the myriad things depend—by which they first come into being and are generated—is nothing other than the flowing operation of this Way. It embodies things without omitting any, yet does not regard its capacity as its own.

> 是以聖人終不為大，故能成其大。
> For this reason, the sage never makes himself out to be great;
> therefore, he is able to accomplish his greatness.

聖人無我，與道為一。故雖成如天之事功，而終無自大之心，此聖人之所以為大也。
The sage has no [awareness of] self and is one with the Way. Therefore, although he accomplishes achievements as vast as those of heaven, he never harbors a mind of self-aggrandizement. This is precisely why the sage is great.

右第二十五章，以聖人體道之大，為修己之極，而起下章治人之說也。
The foregoing, Chapter 25, takes the greatness of the sage's embodiment of the Way as the ultimate in self cultivation, and thereby gives rise to the discussion in the following chapter on governing others.

## Chapter 26 (DDJ 54)

> 善建者不拔，善抱者不脫，子孫祭祀不輟。
> One who establishes well cannot be uprooted;
> one who holds fast well cannot be loosened;
> the sacrifices of his descendants will not cease.

建中建極，是謂善建。如保赤子，是謂善抱。溫公曰：「不拔者，深根固蒂，不可動搖；不脫者，民心懷服，不可傾奪；不輟者，享祚長久，是也。」
Establishing the balance and setting up the ultimate is what is meant by "establishing well." Just as one protects a newborn baby, this is what is meant by "holding fast well."

Honorable Wen explained: "Not being uprooted means having deep roots and a firm base that cannot be shaken. 'Not being loosened' means that the hearts of the people are attached in submission and cannot be taken away. 'Not ceasing' means that the enjoyment of blessing and tenure endures long" (DZL 3.54,1-6).

> 修之身，其德乃真；修之家，其德乃餘；修之鄉，其德乃長；修之國，其德乃豐；修之天下，其德乃普。
> Cultivate it in the self, and its virtue will be authentic;
> cultivate it in the family, and its virtue will be abundant;
> cultivate it in the village, and its virtue will be enduring;
> cultivate it in the state, and its virtue will be flourishing;
> cultivate it in all under Heaven, and its virtue will be universal.

真者，誠實無妄之謂也。以真實之理修身，推其餘，以治人、家、國、天下，不外乎是而已。 溫公曰：「皆循本以治末，由近以及遠也。」右第二十六章，始言治人之道，而推本於修身。此下六章，皆申此章之義。

To be authentic means to be sincere and without falsity. By cultivating the self according to the principle of authenticity, one extends his surplus to order others, the family, the state, and all-under-heaven. The scope does not go beyond this.

Honorable Wen noted, "All of this is a matter of governing the peripheral by following the foundational, and reaching the distant by starting from the near" (DZL 3.54,10).

The above is Chapter 26, which begins to explain the Way of governing others, tracing it back to the foundation of self-cultivation. The following six chapters all elaborate on the meaning of this chapter.

## Chapter 27 (DDJ 81)

> (爲一作與)[2] 聖人不積，既以為人，己愈有；既以與人，己愈多。
> The sage does not accumulate.
> As he uses what he has for others, he gains even more.
> As he gives what he has to others, he becomes richer.

聖人以己及人，己立而立人，己達而達人，博施濟眾，而於己未嘗有費，其仁愈盛，而其德愈不孤矣。

The sage extends himself to others. He who seeks to be established helps others find their footing; he who seeks understanding helps others deepen theirs (*Lunyu* 6.30). He gives widely and benefits the many, yet nothing is ever lost to himself. Thus, his benevolence grows, and his virtue is no longer solitary (*Lunyu* 4.25).

> 天之道，利而不害；聖人之道，為而不爭。
> The Way of heaven benefits without causing harm.
> The Way of the sage acts for others but does not contend.

---

[2] Yi I's original comment: The character *wi* (*wei* 爲), meaning "to be for" here, is rendered as *yŏ* (*yu* 與), meaning "to be with," in some versions.

天道只生物為心，故利而不害；聖人順理而無私，故有所為而不爭，此聖人所以與天為徒者也。右第二十七章。
The Way of heaven takes giving life to all things as its sole concern. Thus, it benefits and does not harm. The sage follows principle and harbors no selfishness. Thus, he acts yet does not contend. This is why the sage is a companion of heaven. The foregoing is Chapter 27.

## Chapter 28 (DDJ 27)

> 善行無轍跡，善言無瑕謫，善計不用籌策。
> One who acts well leaves no trace.
> One who speaks well leaves no flaw.
> One who plans well requires neither cunning nor strategy.

從容中道，而無跡可見；發言為法，而無瑕可指；不思而得，泛應曲當，此聖人之事也。
Moving with ease in the balanced Way, yet leaving no trace that can be seen; when he speaks, it becomes a model, yet no flaw can be pointed out; without deliberation he attains, and in responding he is everywhere fitting—this is the work of the sage.

> 是以聖人常善救人，故無棄人；常善救物，故無棄物，是謂襲明。
> For this reason, the sage is always adept at saving others, and thus no one is abandoned; he is always adept at saving things, and thus nothing is abandoned. This is called inheriting illumination.

有教無類，而人無不容，物無不化；以先知覺後知，以先覺覺後覺，故其明傳襲無窮也。
In teaching there are no distinctions of kind (*Lunyu* 15.39), and so no person is not included, no thing is not transformed. By means of those who know first awakening those who know later, and those who are awakened first awakening those who are awakened later, his illumination is thus transmitted and carried forward without end.

> 故善人，不善人之師；不善人，善人之資。
> Therefore, the good person is a teacher to those who are not good;
> The one who is not good serves as a resource for those who are good.

因其不善，而教之使善，則我之仁愈大，而施愈博矣，此之謂善人之資也。夫善者，吾與之；不善者，吾教之，則天下歸吾仁矣。民吾同胞，物吾與也之義，於此可見矣。
Because of their lack of goodness, I teach them so as to make them good; thus my benevolence becomes all the greater, and its extension all the broader. This is what is meant by a resource for good person. As for the good, I associate with

them; as for the not good, I teach them. Then all-under-heaven will return to my benevolence. The meaning of "the people are my fellow beings, and things are my companions" can be seen here. [3]

右第二十八章，言聖人有善行、善言、善計，故能化不善之人。下章同此。
The above is Chapter 28. It explains that the sage acts well, speaks well, and plans well, and thus can transform those who are not good. The following chapter continues in the same vein.

## Chapter 29 (DDJ 49)

> 聖人無常心，以百姓心為心。
> The sage has no constant mind;
> he takes the minds of the people as his own mind.

聖人於天下，無一毫私心，只因民心而已。
Toward all under Heaven, the sage harbors not the slightest selfish mind; he simply follows the minds of the people..

> 善者吾善之，不善者吾亦善之，德善；信者吾信之，不信者吾亦信之，德信。
> Those who are good, I treat as good;
> those who are not good, I also treat as good—thus my virtue is goodness.
> Those who are trustworthy, I trust;
> those who are not trustworthy, I also trust—thus my virtue is trustworthiness.

人之有生，同具此理；聖人之於民，莫不欲其善信。故善信者，吾既許之；不善不信者，亦必教之，以善信為期。若棄而不教，則非所謂德善德信也。宋徽宗曰：「舜之於象，所以善信者至矣。」右第二十九章。
When people come into being, they all equally possess this principle; the sage, in relation to the people, never fails to desire that they be good and trustworthy. Thus, those who are good and trustworthy, I already affirm; those who are not good and not trustworthy, I must also teach, taking goodness and trustworthiness as the aim. If one were to abandon them and not teach, this would not be what is meant by "virtue as goodness" and "virtue as trustworthiness."

Emperor Huizong of Song said: "In Shun's treatment of Xiang, his goodness and trustworthiness reached the utmost" (DZSH 7.47,28).

The foregoing is Chapter 29.

## Chapter 30 (DDJ 29)

> 將欲取天下而為之，吾見其不得已。天下神器，不可為也；為者敗之，執者失之。

[3] Quoted from Zhang Zai 張載 (1020-1077), *Ximing* 西銘 (Western Inscription) 1.

> If one would seek to take all under Heaven and act upon it,
> I see that he will not succeed.
> All under heaven is a sacred vessel and cannot be acted upon.
> Those who act upon it ruin it;
> those who grasp it lose it.

天下乃神明之器也。帝王之興，自有歷數，不可有心於取天下也。欲為天下者必敗，欲執天下者必失矣。三代以上，聖帝明王，皆修身盡道，而天下歸之，非有心於天下者也。後之帝王，或有有心於天下而得之者，此亦有天命存焉，非專以智力求也。
All-under-heaven is a mysterious and luminous vessel. The rise of an emperor or king follows its own ordained course; one must not harbor the intent to seize all-under-heaven. Those who desire to act for all-under-heaven will surely fail; those who desire to grasp it will surely lose it.

Before the Three Dynasties [i.e., Xia, Shang, and Western Zhou], sage emperors and illumined kings cultivated themselves and fully practiced the Way; thus, all-under-heaven came to them, though it was never their intent to possess it. In later times, some emperors and kings did have intent for all-under-heaven and succeeded in acquiring it, yet even then, the mandate of heaven was at work, not purely the result of their own intelligence and force.

> 故物或行，或隨；或煦，或吹；或強，或羸；或載，或隳。
> Therefore, things sometimes lead and sometimes follow,
> Sometimes are warm and sometimes are blown upon,
> Sometimes grow strong and sometimes weaken,
> Sometimes are whole and sometimes fall apart.

董氏曰：「煦，暖也；吹，寒也；強，盛也；羸，弱也；載，成也；隳，壞也。有為之物，必屬對待，消長盈虛，相推不已。」
Mr. Dong said: "'Warm' means to be heated; 'blown on' means to be cooled; 'to flourish' means to grow strong; 'to weaken' means to decline; 'whole' means to reach fulfillment; 'to fall apart' means to be ruined. Everything's actions and states belong to the interplay of opposites—growth and decline, fullness and emptiness—each influencing the other in an endless cycle" (DZJ 2.118).

> 是以聖人去甚，去奢，去泰。
> For this reason, the sage removes the extreme, the extravagant, and the excessive.

去，除也。聖人之治天下，因其勢而利導之，因其材而篤焉，只去其已甚者耳。所謂裁成天地之道，輔相天地之宜，以左右民者也。右第三十章，言以無事為天下也。
"To remove" means to eliminate. In governing all-under-heaven, the sage follows its tendencies and guides them to advantage, follows its capacities and firmly develops them, merely removing what has become excessive. This is what is meant by "Trimming and completing the Way of heaven and earth, [the sage]

assists and supports the appropriateness of heaven and earth, and thereby guides the people" (*Xiangzhuan*, Hexagram Tai 泰, 1).

The foregoing is Chapter 30, which speaks of ordering all-under-heaven through non-action.

# Chapters 31 to 40

## Chapter 31 (DDJ 57; 58)

> 以正治國，以奇用兵，以無事取天下。
> Govern the state with uprightness;
> employ the military with stratagem;
> take all-under-heaven through non action.

蘇氏曰：「古之聖人，柔遠能邇，無意於用兵。惟不得已，然後有征伐之事。故以治國為正，以用兵為奇。夫天下神器，不可為也。是以體道者，無心於取天下，而天下歸之矣。」愚按：成湯非富天下，為匹夫匹婦復讎，而東征西怨，是也。
Mr. Su said, "The sages of ancient times reached the distant with gentleness and those nearby with skill, without harboring thoughts of employing the troops. Only when circumstances made it unavoidable did they engage in expeditions. Thus, they governed the state with uprightness and employed the military with stratagem. All-under-heaven is a mysterious vessel, and one cannot act upon it at will. For this reason, one who embodies the Way has no intent to seize all-under-heaven, yet all-under-heaven returns to him" (LJ B:133).

In my humble view, King Cheng Tang did not seek to enrich all under Heaven, but to avenge the grievances of common men and women. Thus, when he campaigned eastward, those in the west voiced their resentment [at being left behind].[1] This is what is meant here.

> 天下多忌諱，而民彌貧；人多利器，國家滋昏；人多伎巧，奇物滋起；法令滋彰，盜賊多有。
> Under heaven, the more prohibitions there are, the poorer the people become.
> The more profitable tools the people get, the more benighted the state becomes.
> The more skills and crafts the people have, the more strange things arise.
> The more laws and regulations are enforced, the more thieves appear.

蘇氏曰：「人主多忌諱，下情不上達，則民貧困而無告矣。利器，權謀也。上下相欺以智，則民多權謀，而上益眩而昏矣。奇物，奇怪異物也。人不敦本業，而趨末伎，則非常無益之物作矣。患人之詐僞，而多出法令以勝之，民無所措手足，則日入於盜賊矣。」
Mr. Su said, "When the ruler imposes many prohibitions, the true conditions of the people below fail to reach him above. As a result, the people grow poorer and have no outlet to voice their grievances. 'Profitable tools' refer to schemes and stratagems: when the upper and lower classes deceive one another with cunning, the people become skilled in intrigue, and those above grow increasingly

[1] *Shujing*, "Zhonghui zhi gao" 仲虺之誥, 2; Also, *Mengzi* 3B10.

benighted. 'Strange things' are bizarre and extraordinary things. When people neglect their proper work and pursue trivial skills, unnecessary and unhelpful things are produced. Concerned with such deceit, the authorities impose numerous laws to suppress it. The people are left without a place to stand, and day by day, fall into banditry" (LJ B:133–37).

> 故聖人云：「我無為而民自化，我無事而民自富，我好靜而民自正，我無欲而民自樸。」
> Thus, the sage says:
> "I practice non action, and the people transform of themselves;
> I engage in no affairs, and the people become prosperous of themselves;
> I cherish tranquility, and the people become upright of themselves;
> I am without desire, and the people become simple of themselves"

董氏曰：「此自然之應，而無為之成功也。」
Mr. Dong remarked, "This is the response of things as they are, and the accomplishment of non-doing" (DZJ 3.204).

> 其政悶悶，其民淳淳。
> When governance is unobtrusive,
> The people remain simple and sincere.

悶悶，寬仁不察之象也。董氏曰：「為政以德，則不察察於齊民。以俗觀之，若不事於事；然民實感自然之化，乃所以為淳和之至治也。」
The term "unobtrusive" signifies a broad-minded and benevolent disposition that avoids meticulous scrutiny.

Mr. Dong said, "When governing with virtue (*Lunyu* 2.1), [the ruler] does not inspect every detail in managing the people. From the perspective of mundane custom, it may appear as though he is neglecting his duties. Yet in truth, the people experience spontaneous transformation; this is the ultimate form of governance, marked by simplicity and harmony" (DZJ 3.207).

> 其政察察，其民缺缺。
> When governance is meticulous and intrusive,
> The people become deficient and anxious.

董氏曰：「不知修德為本，而專尚才智，欲以刑政齊民，則必有所傷，故缺缺也。」
Mr. Dong said, "If [the ruler] does not understand that cultivating virtue is the foundation [of governing], and he values only skill and cleverness, and seeks to govern the people through punishments, the people will inevitably be harmed, and as a result, they will become deficient and anxious" (DZJ 3.209).

> 禍兮福所倚，福兮禍所伏，孰知其極。

Misfortune is that on which fortune depends;
fortune is that within which misfortune lies concealed.
Who could know their ultimate limit?

一治一亂，氣化盛衰，人事得失，反復相因；莫知所止極，而惟無為者，能治也。右第三十一章，承上章，而言無為之化也。
Once in order, once in chaos: the waxing and waning of *qi*, the gains and losses in human affairs—all repeat and depend on one another. No one knows their ultimate limit, yet only those who practice non-action can bring about order.

The above is Chapter 31, which continues from the previous chapter and explains transformation through non-doing.

## Chapter 32 (DDJ 43)

不言之教，無為之益，天下希及之。
The teaching without words, and the benefits of non-action—
Few in all-under-heaven reach them.

聖人不言，而體道無隱，與天象昭然，常以示人，此謂不言之教也。無所作為，物各付物，而萬物各得其所，此謂無為之益也。
The sage does not speak, yet embodies the Way without concealment. Like the image of heaven, he shines clearly, constantly revealing lessons to the people—this is called the "teaching without words." He deliberately does nothing; each thing is left to itself, yet all the myriad things attain their proper place—this is called the benefits of non-action.

右第三十二章，申上章無為之義，而結之。夫以無為治人，亦嗇之義也。推說二十六章之義者，止此。
The above is Chapter 32, which develops the meaning of non-action from the previous chapter and ties it together. In showing how non-action governs the people, it also illustrates the significance of cherishing. In explaining the meaning of Chapter 26 up to this point, it stops here.

## Chapter 33 (DDJ 30)

以道佐人主者，不以兵强天下，其事好還（○旋）。[2] 師之所處，荊棘生焉；大軍之後，必有凶年 。
One who assists the ruler with the Way does not use arms to coerce all-under-heaven; such actions are apt to rebound.
Where armies are stationed, thorns and brambles grow;
in the wake of great forces, there are surely lean years.

宋徽宗曰：「孟子所謂反乎爾者，下奪民力，故荊棘生焉；上干和氣，故有凶年。」

---

[2] Yi I's original comment reads: "The character *hwan* (*huan* 還) means to return or rebound."

Song Huizong says, "[This is] what Mengzi meant by 'what [comes from you] returns to you (1B19).' [Such a ruler] underestimates and exploits the people's strength of the people. Therefore, thorns and brambles will grow, and since the harmonious *qi* is disturbed above, famine will occur" (DZSH 5.30,5; 8).

> 故善者，果而已，不敢以取強。
> Therefore, one who excels is resolute and no more;
> he does not dare to use it to seize strength.

董氏曰：「兵固有道者之所不取，然天生五材，亦不可去，譬水火焉，在乎善用。惟以止暴濟難，則果決於理而已，何敢取強於天下哉？」
Mr. Dong said, "Arms are truly not something one who follows the Way would take up. Yet heaven produces the five elements (i.e., earth, wood, metal, fire, and water), none of which can be discarded. Like water and fire, their use depends on proper application. Only when employed to halt cruelty and relieve suffering can arms be used resolutely in accordance with principle. How, then, could one dare to seek strength over all-under-heaven?" (DZJ 2.126)

> 果而勿矜，果而勿伐，果而勿驕，果而不得已，是果而勿強。
> Be resolute, yet do not be self regarding; be resolute, yet do not boast; be resolute, yet do not be arrogant; be resolute, yet only when it cannot be avoided.
> This is being resolute without being forceful.

董氏曰：「果以理勝，強以力勝。惟果則有必克之勢，初非恃力好戰。故臨事而懼，好謀而成，不得已後應之，勿強而已。」
Mr. Dong said, "When resolute, one wins by principle; when forceful, one wins by strength. To be resolute is to have the momentum of inevitable victory, not to rely on strength or take pleasure in waging war from the outset. Therefore, when facing a situation, one should act cautiously, plan carefully, and achieve success. Only when unavoidable should one respond—and even then, never by force" (DZJ 2.128).

> 物壯則老，是謂不道；不道，早已。
> When things reach their height, they grow old.
> This is called going against the Way.
> What goes against the Way comes to an early end.

董氏曰：「物壯極則老，兵強極則敗，皆非合道，宜早知止。」此章謂輔相以道，則人心愛戴，而用兵爭強，不足服人。
Mr. Dong said, "When things reach their extreme height, they grow old; when an army reaches its utmost strength, it is defeated. Both are not in accordance with the Way, so one must know early when to stop" (DZJ 2.130).

This chapter explains that when one assists others through the Way, people willingly serve him from the heart. But if one relies on military force and competes for dominance, it is not sufficient to earn the people's genuine submission.

右第三十三章，既盡治人之說，而兵亦有國之勢不能去者，故言用兵之道，宜果而不務強，且宜早知止。下章亦同。
The foregoing is Chapter 33. Having fully set forth the discussion of governing others, it recognizes that the use of arms is, given the conditions of the state, something that cannot be entirely dispensed with. Therefore, it speaks of the Way of employing arms: one should be resolute and not pursue forcefulness, and should also know to stop early. The following chapter is the same.

**Chapter 34 (DDJ 31)**

夫佳兵，不祥之器；物或惡之，故有道者不處。
A fine army is an inauspicious instrument; at times, things recoil from it.
Therefore, one who attains the Way does not dwell on it.

董氏曰：「佳兵者，用兵之善者也。兵終為凶器，惟以之濟難，而不以為常，故不處心於此也。」愚按：孟子曰：「善戰者，服上刑」，亦此意也。
Mr. Dong said, "'Fine army' refers to skillful use of the military. Yet an army ultimately becomes a tool of disaster, and it is employed only to resolve crises, not for ordinary affairs. Therefore, one should not dwell on it" (DZJ 2.133).

In my humble view, when Mengzi said, "The one who excels in war should receive the highest punishment" (4A14), he was expressing this idea.

君子居則貴左，用兵則貴右。
A noble person, when at home, esteems the left;
When employing the army, he esteems the right.

董氏曰：「左為陽，陽好生；右為陰，陰主殺。」
Mr. Dong said, "The left corresponds to yang, which favors giving life, while the right corresponds to yin, which governs destruction" (DZJ 2.135).

兵者，不祥之器，非君子之器，不得已而用之，恬淡為上。勝而不美。
The army is an inauspicious instrument, not a noble person's tool.
When its use is unavoidable, the best approach is calm and composed.
Even in victory, it is not to be glorified.

勝而不美，雖勝戰，而不以為美也。董氏曰：「惔，安也。好生惡殺，而無心於勝物也。」
"Even in victory, it is not to be glorified" means even when winning in war, it is not regarded to be beautified.

Mr. Dong said, "The term 'composed' means to be at ease. [The noble person] cherishes life and abhors killing, and harbors no intent to prevail over others" (DZJ 2.137).

> 而美之者，是樂殺人。夫樂殺人者，不可得志於天之下。
> One who glorifies it takes pleasure in killing.
> One who delights in killing cannot have his will fulfilled under heaven.

勝戰而以為美者，是嗜殺者也。孟子曰：「不嗜殺人者，能一之」，亦此意也。右第三十四章。
One who wins in war and glorifies it is someone who takes pleasure in killing. Mengzi said, "Only those who do not delight in killing can unify [the people]" (1A6), which conveys the same meaning.

The above is Chapter 34.

## Chapter 35 (DDJ 60)

> 以道莅天下，其鬼不神；非其鬼不神，其神不傷民；非其神不傷民，聖人亦不傷民。夫兩不相傷，故德交歸焉。
> When one governs all-under-heaven by means of the Way, the spirits lose their numinous potency; it is not that the spirits lack numinous potency, but that their potency does not harm the people. It is not only that their potency does not harm the people—the sage also does not harm the people. When the two do not harm one another, their virtue converges and returns.

聖人之治天下，人神各得其道，陰陽和而萬物理，無有邪氣干其間。故鬼神無眩怪之變，此謂其鬼不神也。豈有鬼怪傷民者乎？聖人之治，不傷於民。故人神胥悅，衆德交歸，如此。列子曰：「物無疵癘，鬼無靈響，是也。」朱子曰：「若是王道修明，則不正之氣，都消鑠了。」愚按：後世崇尚佛老，廣張淫祀，寺觀相望，必欲使其鬼有神，真此書之罪人也。治世者，既不能禁，又從而惑之，豈不悖哉？
When the sage governs all-under-heaven, both humans and spirits each attain their proper Way. Yin and yang are in harmony, and the myriad things follow principle, leaving no room for disruptive *qi* to intrude. Therefore, ghosts and spirits neither deceive nor cause strange disturbances—this is what is meant by "the spirits lose their numinous potency."

How could then the spirits possibly go astray and harm the people? The sage's governance does not harm the people, so humans and spirits rejoice together. Virtue circulates among all, returning to its ideal. As Liezi says, "Things have no calamities, and spirits do not respond with mysterious reverberations" (2.2). Master Zhu also notes, "If the kingly Way is cultivated and illumined well, all corrupt *qi* will disappear" (ZZQS 51.96).

My humble note: In later ages, people came to revere Buddhism and Daoism, and to spread illicit sacrifices far and wide, with temples and shrines facing one another everywhere, all intent on making their spirits numinous. These are truly the culprits against this text.[3] Those who govern the age, unable to prohibit such practices, instead go along and are deluded by them—how is this not perverse?

右第三十五章，言王道之效，至於人神各得其所。七章所謂嗇以治人者，其義止此。
The above is Chapter 35, which explains that the effect of the kingly Way is to ensure that both humans and spirit each attain their proper place. This corresponds to the full meaning of Chapter 7, which speaks of governing through cherishment, whose meaning stops here.

## Chapter 36 (DDJ 64; 63)

> 合抱之木，生於毫末；九層之臺，起於累土；千里之行，始於足下。
> A tree that can be embraced with two arms begins from the tiniest sprout.
> A nine-story tower rises from piles of earth.
> A journey of a thousand *li* starts beneath one's feet.

此設喻，言凡大事必始於微細也。.
This passage employs these metaphors to illustrate that every great undertaking must start from something small and subtle.

> 圖難於其易，為大於其細。天下之難事，必作於易；天下之大事，必作於細。
> One undertakes difficult tasks by starting with the easy,
> And accomplishes great tasks by beginning with the small.
> All difficult matters under heaven must be addressed through what is easy;
> All great matters under heaven must be carried out through what is small.

善惡皆由積漸而成。若以細事為微而忽之，以易事為無傷而不愼，則細必成大，易必成難，言當愼之於始，而慮其所終也。
Good and evil both arise and complete through gradual accumulation. If small matters are regarded as trivial and neglected, or easy tasks are assumed harmless and approached without caution, then the small will inevitably become large, and the easy will turn into the difficult. Therefore, one must be careful from the outset and consider how things will ultimately unfold.

> 夫輕諾必寡信，多易必多難。
> Making promises lightly surely leads to little trust;
> taking many things as easy surely leads to many difficulties.

---

[3] Here Yi I voices concern about certain later religious interpretations and popular practices that developed out of the DDJ and related Daoist teachings, especially where these were invoked to legitimate excessive ritualization, the veneration of ghosts, or other superstitious conduct. This critique is not directed at the DDJ itself but at the ways later generations misapplied and distorted its teachings.

不慎於始，則後必有悔。
If one is not careful from the start, regret will inevitably follow.

> 是以聖人猶難之，故終無難。
> For this reason, the sage treats it as difficult;
> Thus, in the end, there is no difficulty.

聖人於易事，猶難慎，故終無難濟之事也。
The sage treats even easy matters as difficult and proceeds with caution; thus, in the end, there is no task that proves difficult.

> 其安易持，其未兆易謀；其脆易破，其微易散。為之於未有，治之於未難。
> What is at ease is easy to hold; what has not yet shown signs is easy to plan for.
> What is fragile is easy to break; what is minute is easy to disperse.
> Act on it before it comes into being; bring it into order before it becomes difficult.

凡事慎始，則終必無患。在修己，則為不遠而復；在為國，則為迨天未雨，綢繆牖戶之意。
If one is cautious in all matters from the outset, there will ultimately be no trouble. Applied to self-cultivation, this is the meaning of "not straying far and returning" (*Yijing*, Hexagram Fu 復, 2). Applied to governing a country, it is like "repairing the eaves before the rain falls from the sky."[4]

右第三十六章，言慎始善終之意，以盡修己治人之道，蓋足其未足之義也。
This concludes Chapter 36. By stressing the importance of being cautious at the beginning and bringing matters to a proper close, it fully expresses the Way of self-cultivation and governing others. It also conveys the idea of completing what is yet incomplete.

## Chapter 37 (DDJ 73; 72)

> 勇於敢則殺，勇於不敢則活，此兩者或利或害。天之所惡，孰知其故？是以聖人猶難之。
> One who is bold in daring will be killed; one who is bold in not daring will live.
> Between these two, one may bring benefit or may bring harm.
> What heaven detests—who could know the reason?
> Therefore, the sage regards it as difficult.

剛強者，死之徒；柔弱者，生之徒，是常理也。或有時而反常，強利弱害，則天之所惡，難曉其故，聖人猶難言也。雖然要其終，則未始少失，故下文歷陳之。

[4] *Shijing*, *Guofeng* 國風, Binfeng 豳風, Chixiao 鴟鴞, 2; *Mengzi* 2A4.

The strong and unyielding are companions of death, while the soft and weak are companions of life (DDJ 76). This is the constant principle. Yet there are times when the reverse occurs: the strong bring benefit, and the weak incur harm. This stems from what heaven detests, and its reasons are difficult to fathom. Thus, the sage hesitates to offer a definitive explanation. Nevertheless, when one considers the ultimate outcome, those who proceed with caution from the start will seldom go astray. The passage that follows unfolds this point in detail.

> 天之道，不爭而善勝。
> The Way of heaven does not compete, yet it excels in prevailing.

溫公曰：「任物自然，而物莫能違。」
Honorable Wen remarked, "[The sage] entrusts all to the natural unfolding of self-so, such that nothing can go against the Way" (DZL 4.73,4).

> 不言而善應。
> [The Way of heaven] does not speak, yet it excels in responding.

董氏曰：「天何言哉？四時行焉，其於福善禍淫之應，信不差矣。」
Mr. Dong said, "What words does heaven speak? The four seasons take their turns, bringing blessings to the good and misfortune to the excessive. Truly, there is no deviation in this" (DZJ 4.126)

> 不召而自來。
> [The Way of heaven] does not call, yet it arrives on its own.

董氏曰：「神之格思，本無向背，如暑往則寒來，夫豈召而後至哉？」
Mr. Dong said, "'In the arrival of the spirit, there is originally no before or after.'[5] Just as winter comes after summer is gone, how could it come only after being called?"(DZJ 4.128).

> 天網恢恢，疏而不失。
> Heaven's net is vast and wide; though loose, nothing slips through.

董氏曰：「要終盡變然後，知其雖廣大，而微細不遺也。」
Mr. Dong said, "Only after considering the end and completing the changes does one realize that although the net of heaven is vast and wide, it misses nothing, even the smallest things" (DZJ 4.132).

> 民不畏威，則大威至。
> If the people do not fear authority, then greater authority will descend upon them.

---

[5] *Shijing*, *Daya*, Tangzhi shi 蕩之什, Yi 抑, 7.

民當畏威如疾，若不畏威，則必有可畏之大威至矣，不可以天道為無知也。
The people should fear authority as they would a disease. If they do not fear authority, then a greater, truly fearsome authority will surely arrive. One must not regard the Way of heaven as insensible.

右第三十七章，言天道福善禍淫之理，以為戒。下章同此。
This concludes Chapter 37. It explains the principle that the Way of heaven grants blessings to the good and brings calamity to the excessive, serving as a cautionary lesson. The following chapter continues this theme.

## Chapter 38 (DDJ 77; 79)

天之道，其猶張弓乎？高者抑之，下者舉之；有餘者損之，不足者與之。
天之道，損有餘而補不足。
The Way of heaven is like drawing a bow:
It presses down what is high and raises what is low,
Takes from what is in excess and gives to what is lacking.
The Way of heaven diminishes what has surplus and fills what is deficient.

董氏曰：「天道無私，常適乎中。故滿招損，謙受益，時乃天道。」
Mr. Dong said, "The Way of heaven harbors no selfishness and always accords with the balance. Thus, what is full invites loss, and what is humble receives gain—such is the Way of heaven in its timely workings" (DZJ 4.152).

天道無親，常與善人。
The Way of heaven shows no favoritism,
Yet it ever stands with those who are good.

書曰：「皇天無親，克敬惟親」，即此意也。
The *Shu* says, "August heaven shows no favoritism; it draws near only to those who are reverent."[6] This is precisely the meaning.

右第三十八章，與上章，皆言天道，而天道虧盈益謙而已，亦不出嗇之義也。
This concludes Chapter 38. Together with the previous chapter, it sets forth the Way of heaven. The Way of heaven diminishes what is full and increases what is humble, never departing from the principle of cherishing.

## Chapter 39 (DDJ 70)

吾言甚易知，甚易行，而天下莫能知，莫能行。

---

[6] This quotation above is a conflation of two distinct passages in the *Shujing*: the earlier part is from the Chapter "Cai Zhong zhi ming" 蔡仲之命, 2. "Heaven has no kin, it only aids virtue" 皇天無親，惟德是輔 and the latter part is from the "Tai Jia C" 太甲下, 8: "Heaven has no kin, it only reveres who is worthy" 惟天無親，克敬惟親.

My words are exceedingly easy to understand and easy to put into practice,
Yet under heaven, no one understands them or follows them.

性本固有，道不遠人。指此示人，宜若易知易行，而賢智過之，愚不肖不及，所以莫能知，莫能行也。
Human nature is originally inherent, and the Way is not far from people (*Zhongyong* 13). Pointing this out to others, it should seem easy to know and easy to practice; yet the wise may surpass it, and the foolish or unworthy may fall short. For this reason, no one understand it or put it into practice.

言有宗，事有君。
In speech, there is a root; in affairs, there is a ruler.

言以明道，事以行道；隨言隨事，各有天然自有之中，乃所謂至善而言之宗也，事之君也。
Speech is used to illuminate the Way; affair is used to practice the Way. In accordance with words and affairs, each has its own natural and inherent measure. This is what is called the ultimate goodness (*Daxue* 1)—serving as the root in speech and the ruler in affairs.

夫惟無知，是以不我知。
It is precisely because of their ignorance that they do not understand me.

眾人於道無識見，故終莫我知也。
Ordinary people lack the discernment of the Way. Thus, in the end, no one understands me.

知我者希，則我者貴。
Those who understand me are few;
those who take me as model are precious.

溫公曰：「道大，故知者鮮也。」
Honorable Wen said, "The Way is great, so those who understand it are few" (DZL 4.70,12).

是以聖人被褐懷玉。
For this reason, the sage wears coarse cloth while holding jade within.

內蘊至德，而不求人知，如被褐衣，而懷寶玉也。
The sage harbors supreme virtue within, yet seeks no recognition from others, like wearing coarse cloth while concealing precious jade inside.

右第三十九章，歎人之莫知，而悼道之難行，是終篇惓惓為人之意也。

The foregoing is Chapter 39. It laments that people do not understand, and mourns the difficulty of putting the Way into practice. This closes the text with a tone of deep concern for humanity.

**Chapter 40 (DDJ 53)**

大道甚夷，而民好徑。
The great Way is extremely level, yet the people favor shortcuts. (53)

道若大路，豈難知而難行哉？只是民情牽於私意，求捷徑而不遵大路耳。
The Way is like a great thoroughfare; how could it be difficult to know or difficult to follow? The problem lies only in human feelings being pulled by selfish intentions, so that people seek shortcuts instead of abiding by the broad road.

右第四十章，承上章，而言人之不能知、不能行者，由不知率性之道，而妄求捷徑故也。屈原曰：「夫惟捷徑而窘步」，亦此意也。
This concludes Chapter 40. Building on the previous chapter, it explains that people fail to understand or follow the Way because they do not recognize the path that accords with their true nature and instead pursue shortcuts in vain. As Qu Yuan (d. 278 BCE) said, "It is because I hastened my steps along the shortcut" (*Chuci*, Lisao, 2) which expresses this idea.

**Conclusion**

右醇言，凡四十章。首三章言道體，四章言心體，第五章總論治己治人之始終。第六章、七章，以損與嗇為治己治人之要旨，自第八章止十二章，皆推廣其義。第十三章因嗇字，而演出三寶之說，自十四章止十九章，申言其義。
The above comprises forty chapters of *Sunŏn*. The first three chapters discuss the essence of the Way, while Chapter 4 addresses the nature of the human heart-mind. Chapter 5 provides a comprehensive overview of the beginning and end of self-cultivation and governance. Chapters 6 and 7 highlight "unloading" and "cherishing" as central principles for governing oneself and others. Chapters 8 through 12 expand on these ideas, and Chapter 13, taking the character "cherishing" as its starting point, elaborates on the teaching of the three treasures. Chapters 14 through 19 continue to develop this teaching.

二十章言輕躁之失，二十一章言清靜之正。二十二章推言用功之要。二十三章、四章申言其全天之效，二十五章言體道之效，二十六章止三十五章言治人之道及其功效。三十六章言慎始慮終，防於未然之義。三十七章、八章言天道福善禍淫、虧盈益謙之理。三十九章、四十章歎人之莫能行道，以終之。
Chapter 20 addresses the errors that arise from frivolity and impatience, while Chapter 21 explains the uprightness in clarity and stillness. Chapter 22 examines the essential points of merits [of clarity and stillness]. Chapters 23 and 24 elaborate on the effects of fulfilling heaven's virtue, and Chapter 25 discusses the

impact of embodying the Way. Chapters 26 through 35 outline the Way of governance and its practical effects. Chapter 36 emphasizes the importance of caution from the outset, keeping the end in view, and guarding against what has not yet occurred. Chapters 37 and 38 explain the Way of heaven, which rewards goodness and restrains excess, showing how abundance is reduced while humility is increased. Finally, Chapters 39 and 40 lament that people fail to practice the Way, bringing the work to its conclusion.

大抵此書以無為為宗，而其用無不為，則亦非縈於虛無也。只是言多招詣，動稱聖人，論上達處多，論下學處少，宜接上根之士，而中人以下，則難於下手矣。但其言克己窒慾，靜重自守，謙虛自牧，慈簡臨民之義，皆親切有味，有益於學者，不可以為非聖人之書，而莫之省也。醇言終。

In general, this book (DDJ) takes non-action as its foundation. In practice, there is nothing that non-action cannot accomplish, so it is not a work that immerses readers in nihilism. It only means that the text often aims high, frequently invoking the sage; it contains much discussion for those advanced in understanding, but little for beginners. It is suitable for engaging men of superior capacity, but for those of average ability or lower, it is difficult to get started.

Yet its teachings on restraining oneself and curbing desire, on being calm, grave, and self-disciplined, on cultivating humility, and on ruling the people with kindness and simplicity—all are intimate and rich in meaning, beneficial for learners. It cannot be regarded as a book not by a sage, yet few reflect on it. Thus ends *Sunŏn*.

# Postscript

栗谷先生，嘗鈔老氏之近於吾道者二千九十有八言，為醇言一編，仍為之註解口訣。昔韓愈以荀氏為大醇而少疵，欲削其不合者，附於聖人之籍，曰：「亦孔子之志歟。」先生編書命名之意，或取於此耶。

The esteemed Master Yulgok once selected 2,098 words from the writings of Laozi that were close to our Way and compiled them into a work titled *Sunŏn*, providing his own annotations, glosses, and oral-reading marks. In earlier times, Han Yu (768–824) considered Xunzi's writings to be highly refined, though not without flaws; he excised the portions that did not accord with the Way, intending to incorporate the remainder into the texts of the sages, remarking, "This too was the intent of Confucius." Master Yulgok's purpose in compiling and naming this book may have been inspired by that precedent.

啓禧攷本文，蓋去其反經悖理者五之三爾，其取者，誠不害乎謂之醇也。去取如衡稱燭照，註解又明白亭當，必援而歸之於吾道。識者以為非先生知言之明，莫能為也。

I, Gyehŭi, upon closely examining the main text of this work, observed that the Master discarded nearly three out of every five passages that contradicted our classics or defied principle. What he retained is truly deserving of the name "purified." His process of selection and omission was as precise as weighing on a scale or inspecting by lamplight, and his annotations are clear, well-reasoned, and consistently return the reader to our Way. Discerning readers will recognize that, without the Master's exceptional clarity in understanding language, no one could have accomplished such a task.

異端之所以倍於吾道者，以其駁也。不駁者，固不無可取；去其駁，則醇矣。高明之士，墮落而不悟者，特見其醇而忘其駁也。苟無如先生之大公至明，惡而知其美，則醇駁相混，可用者，卒歸於不可用，而不可用者，或以為可用，其為害不貲。曷若區別醇駁，去其不可用，而存其可用哉？

The reason heterodox teachings deviate from our Way is their miscellaneity. Yet that which is not miscellaneous is not without value; remove the miscellaneous elements, and what remains is pure. A scholar of lofty understanding who falls into error and fails to perceive it often sees only the pure and forgets the miscellaneous. Truly, without the Master's great impartiality and supreme clarity, how could one discern its true merit? When the pure and the impure are mixed, what is usable eventually becomes unusable, and what is unusable may be mistaken for useful—resulting in incalculable harm. How, then, could one properly distinguish the pure from the impure, discard the unusable, and preserve what is usable?

當先生之編此也，龜峯宋先生止之曰：「非老子之本旨，有苟同之嫌。」其言亦直截可喜。而至若先生之範圍曲成，雖於異端外道，尚惜其可用者，混歸於不可用，必欲去其駁，而俾歸乎醇。百世之下，真可以見其心矣。於乎至哉！

When the Master was compiling this work, the esteemed Master Kubong Song [Ikp'il] cautioned him, saying, "This is not the original intent of Laozi; it risks awkwardly forcing agreement [with our Way]." His words were also straightforward and commendable. Yet within In the case of Master Yulgok, whose scope is refined and comprehensive, even when examining heretical or heterodox teachings, he still values what can be put to use. Yet these are often mingled with what is unusable; he insists on removing the impure so that what remains attains purity. Only after a hundred generations can one truly perceive the depth of his mind—truly a sublime achievement.

啓禧按：湖西巡過連山，偶得此編於慎齋金先生後孫，乃金先生手筆也。或恐泯沒，以活字印若干本，仍識其顛末如右云。

On an inspection tour of the Hosŏ region (present-day Ch'ungch'ŏng Province), I happened to pass through Yŏnsan (now the southeastern part of Nonsan, South Ch'ungch'ŏng Province). There, by chance, I came upon a copy of this compilation held by a descendant of Master Sindokjae Kim Chip. It is said that this copy was personally transcribed by Master Kim. Fearing that it might soon be lost, I had several copies printed in movable type and recorded the full account of its provenance, as noted above.

庚午正月上澣，後學洪啓禧謹書。

In the first ten days of the first lunar month, Kyŏng'o year (1750),
Respectfully written by the later scholar, Hong Gyehŭi.

# Part Two

# Han Wŏnjin's *Changja pyŏnhae*

# Translator's Introduction

## The Era of Han Wŏnjin: Chosŏn in the 17th–18th Centuries

The period from the late 17th to the mid-18th century, during which Han Wŏnjin 韓元震 (1682–1751) lived, was a transitional era in Chosŏn Korea, marked by efforts to recover from the devastation of wars and restore political and social stability. Although the dynasty attempted to rebuild following the Imjin War (1592-1598) and the Manchu Invasions (1636-1637), factional politics (*pungdang chŏngch'i* 朋黨政治) became increasingly entrenched, and royal authority remained unstable.[1] The periodic reversal of ruling factions (*hwanguk* 換局) during King Sukjong's (r. 1674–1720) and King Yŏngjo's reigns (r. 1724–1776), though attempting to loosen internal tensions, rather exacerbated conflicts among political forces, while the division of the Westerners (*sŏin* 西人) into two sub-factions, Noron and Soron, after the royal mourning ritual controversies (*yesong nonjaeng* 禮訟論爭)[2] in the late 17th century deepened party strife. King Yŏngjo promoted

---

[1] Factional politics in the Chosŏn dynasty refers to the ideological divisions and rivalries among scholar-officials of the *sarim* 士林 class, rooted in differing Neo-Confucian views and interpretations on state affairs. These factions claimed moral legitimacy and distinct philosophical lineages, clashing over appointments, foreign policy, and royal succession.

Factional politics in the Chosŏn dynasty emerged from ideological and policy disputes among Confucian scholar-officials after King Sŏngjong's death (r. 1469–1494). The first split appeared under King Yŏnsan'gun (r. 1495–1506) and formalized under King Chungjong (r. 1506–1544) into two major factions: the reformist Easterners (*tongin* 東人) and the conservative Westerners (*sŏin* 西人).

During King Sŏnjo's reign (r. 1567–1608), the Easterners divided into Southerners (*namin* 南人) and Northerners (*pugin* 北人) over issues of political rehabilitation and foreign policy toward the Ming and during the Imjin War. The moderate Southerners retained influence under King Hyŏnjong, while the radical Northerners soon declined.

The Westerners, dominant under King Injo, later split into the Old Doctrine (*noron* 老論) and Young Doctrine (*soron* 少論) factions. Their conflict centered on royal succession and political purges, with the Noron advocating strict orthodoxy and centralized control, and the Soron favoring moderation. The Noron ultimately dominated late Chosŏn politics under Kings Yŏngjo and Chŏngjo, though their dominance led to corruption and stagnation.

By the 19th century, royal authority weakened, and "government by powerful lineages" (*sedo* 勢道) replaced factional politics. Power shifted from ideological factions to a few aristocratic families, marking the end of the traditional factional system.

Han Wŏnjin, a staunch hardliner of Noron, a sub-faction of the Westerners reinforced the faction's conservative and hierarchical worldview by asserting the primacy of principle over *qi*. His reinterpretations sought to defend orthodox Neo-Confucianism against internal heterodoxy and external influences such as the Yangming school, Buddhism, and Daoism, thereby consolidating Noron ideological authority.

[2] The *Yesong* debates, or royal mourning ritual controversies, were two major disputes between the Westerners and Southerners during the reigns of Kings Hyŏnjong (r. 1649–1659) and

the policy of impartiality (*t'angp'yŏng ch'aek* 蕩平策) in an attempt to balance factions,[3] but in practice, it only served to solidify a Noron-centered political order.

During this time, Zhu Xi Neo-Confucianism was further entrenched as the sole ideological basis for governance and social control. Armed with Confucian orthodoxy, scholar-officials, who were both intellectuals and politicians, reinforced a culture that emphasized political legitimacy and moral justification. In this context, the debates over heresy within the Confucian tradition (*samun nanjŏk* 斯文亂賊; "rebels and traitors who disturb this culture [of ours]") went beyond academic disputes and became tools for political purges.[4] Neo-Confucianism grew increasingly dogmatic, widening the gap between theory and practice, while other schools of thought, such as Buddhism and Daoism, were denounced as heresies and subjected to persecution. Nevertheless, interest in practical knowledge, such as agriculture, medicine, astronomy, and geography, gradually spread, laying the foundation for the later rise of a new scholarly trend, later termed as "Practical Learning" (*sirhak* 實學).[5]

---

Sukjong. Ostensibly about the mourning period Queen Dowager Cho (1619-1674) should observe for King Hyojong (r. 1649-1659) and his consort, the debates in fact revealed deep ideological divisions. Rooted in differing interpretations of clan law (*chongbŏp* 宗法), they reflected broader struggles over Confucian orthodoxy and political legitimacy between the two factions.

[3] The policy of impartiality was a strategy under Kings Yŏngjo and Chŏngjo (r. 1776–1800) to curb factional strife by appointing officials from all factions regardless of affiliation. Aimed at harmony and merit-based governance, it in practice often sustained Noron dominance under the pretense of neutrality. Still, it brought relative stability and enabled administrative reform, though factional tensions persisted.

Han Wŏnjin, a hardline Noron, opposed the policy. Appointed royal lecturer in 1725, he initially won King Yŏngjo's favor but was soon dismissed after citing the *Mengzi*—"A minister regards his king as an enemy" (*sin si kun yŏ kusu* 臣視君如仇讐; 4B31)—to attack the Soron faction, an act seen as defying the policy's intent.

[4] *Samun nanjŏk* was a late Chosŏn term used to denounce those who interpreted the Confucian classics differently from Zhu Xi. A major 17th-century case was the dispute between Song Siyŏl of the conservative Noron faction and Yun Hyu 尹鑴 (1617–1680) of the Southerners. Song condemned Yun's alternative readings of texts like the *Zhouli* 周禮 as heretical threats to Neo-Confucian orthodoxy and political order. The conflict went beyond scholarship—Yun was executed, and the controversy strengthened Noron dominance by branding dissent as moral and political subversion.

[5] "Practical Learning," a conceptual construct formulated by twentieth-century scholars of Korean history, many of whom advanced nationalist interpretations of Chosŏn intellectual life as a form of indigenous modernization and reform movement distinct from the colonialism-imposed model, designates a broad intellectual current in late Chosŏn thought that sought to reorient Confucian inquiry toward empirical investigation, institutional reform, and concrete statecraft, placing greater emphasis on agriculture, commerce, technology, geography, and social policy than on purely metaphysical speculation. While its proponents did not reject Zhu Xi Neo-Confucianism itself, they criticized what they saw as the scholastic abstraction and moral formalism of orthodox Neo-Confucian discourses, calling instead for learning that yields tangible benefit in the ordering of society. For figures within the mainstream circle such as Han Wŏnjin, this emerging orientation in early 18th century posed a significant threat on both doctrinal and institutional grounds: doctrinally, it risked marginalizing the centrality of *li*

Socio-economically, there was a degree of recovery following the wars, but the class system grew more rigid. The traditional Neo-Confucian aristocrats called *yangban* expanded in number but also faced growing internal stratification and decline. Some members of the middle class attempted upward mobility through economic means, yet the Confucian social order and elite control restricted such social fluidity. Commerce and local markets developed, and monetary circulation increased, but agrarian values and status-based hierarchies limited the freedom of economic activity. This growing disconnect between lived reality and ideological values sparked emerging criticisms of Neo-Confucianism and a search for alternatives.[6]

Internationally, the fall of the Ming dynasty (1368–1644) and the rise of the Qing (1616–1912) brought major shifts to the East Asian order. After the Ming exhausted its strength during the Imjin War, the Jurchen-led Later Jin (1616–1636) rose to power and eventually conquered the Chinese mainland, renaming itself the Qing. Chosŏn, which viewed the Manchus as barbarians from the traditional Confucian worldview, found it difficult to accept diplomatic relations with this new regime. This tension culminated in the disastrous defeat of the Pyŏngja War, also known as Manchu Invasions. Though Chosŏn attempted a symbolic "Northern Expedition" to resist Qing dominance, practical limitations forced the kingdom to accept the new Qing-centered international order.

Culturally, elite efforts to restore Neo-Confucian order and hierarchy intensified, seen in the compilation of literary collections and genealogical records. At the same time, popular culture expanded due to the development of printing technology and market networks. Art forms such as *p'ansori* (a genre of musical storytelling performed by a singer and a drummer), vernacular fiction, and folk painting reflected the sentiments and desires of the common people, while court

based moral cultivation and the carefully elaborated metaphysics of principle and *qi*; institutionally, it challenged the authority of the established scholarly elite by redirecting intellectual legitimacy from classical exegesis to practical efficacy. In this sense, Practical Learning not only redefined the aims of learning but also destabilized the normative and social foundations upon which the orthodox Neo-Confucian order rested.

[6] For example, Western Learning (*Sŏhak* 西學), or Catholicism, was taken up primarily by Southerner factions who had been marginalized from central government from the mid- to late eighteenth century. Western Learning is better understood not simply as the introduction of foreign knowledge, but as a symptom of a deeper intellectual unsettling in late Chosŏn. By the mid-eighteenth century, the increasing popularity of Catholicism, along with new European scientific knowledge, exposed growing tensions within the established Neo-Confucian framework, regarding the adequacy of *li qi* metaphysics and the ritual foundations of social order. Thus, Western Learning signaled a shifting epistemic landscape in which the authority of the classical canon and its interpretive traditions could no longer remain unchallenged.

Although Han Wŏnjin died in 1751, before Western Learning emerged as an articulated threat to the society, his conservatism can be situated against this broader backdrop of incipient transformation. His commitment to orthodoxy, especially his insistence on the moral and metaphysical primacy of *li* over *qi* may be read as a response not only to internal debates within Neo-Confucianism but also to an intellectual climate already showing signs of strain.

music and ritual practices were systematized into refined formats. Thus, the late 17th to mid-18th century was a complex period marked by both the ruling class's efforts to reinforce traditional order and the gradual emergence of cultural and intellectual shifts at the grassroots level.

Han Wŏnjin lived in this period of rapid and significant transition when, externally, the Manchus long considered barbarians by the Han Chinese and Koreans had seized hegemony over East Asia and demanded Chosŏn's submission, while internally, signs of social fluidity and new alternative trends of thought, including Practical Learning, were gradually emerging. In response to these periodic shifts, Han took a staunch Noron position, absolutizing the legitimacy of Zhu Xi's Neo-Confucianism and its moral order. He offered an ideological framework of Confucian conservatism to resist the transformations of his age. By championing hierarchy and orthodox legitimacy, Han Wŏnjin viewed both social mobility and intellectual diversity as serious threats, working to preserve the Neo-Confucian world order and uphold the authority of the Noron establishment. In short, Han Wŏnjin was a quintessential figure of late Chosŏn conservatism, seeking to restore stability in a time of rupture through heightened moral rigor and the reassertion of orthodoxy.

## The Life and Thought of Han Wŏnjin: The Horak Debate[7]

Han Wŏnjin, courtesy name Tŏkso 德昭 (Virtue Shining) and pen name Namdang 南塘 (Southern Pond), was a member of the Ch'ŏngju Han lineage, a leading intellectual of the conservative Noron faction, and a student of Kwŏn

---

[7] The Horak Debate originated among the Eight Scholars of the Kangmun School (*Kangmun p'al haksa* 江門八學士), disciples of Kwŏn Sangha 權尙夏 (1641–1721). Its key figures, Yi Kan 李柬 (1677–1727) and Han Wŏnjin, debated whether the original natures of humans and nonhuman beings were identical or different. Kwŏn supported Han's view that "the natures of humans and things are different," giving Han the upper hand within the Noron faction of the Hosŏ region. However, since the discussion remained confined to Kwŏn's circle, it had not yet taken on the regional scope implied by the term "Horak Debate."

The debate became a regional controversy only when Noron scholars from Hanyang and Kyŏnggi, such as Pak P'ilju 朴弼周 (1665–1748), Ŏ Yubong 魚有鳳 (1672–1744), and Yi Chae 李縡 (1680–1746), joined the discussion. The full-fledged Horak Debate began in 1746 when Yi Chae criticized Han Wŏnjin's view of differing natures, prompting Han's rebuttal in 1747. Thereafter, the Hosŏ Noron (Horon) and the Hanyang–Kyŏnggi Noron (Nangron) became identified with opposing positions. The Nangron, siding with Yi Kan, accused the Horon of "blocking the path of people toward goodness" (*chŏ ch'ŏnha wi sŏn chi ro* 沮天下爲善之路), while Han Wŏnjin and Yun Ponggu 尹鳳九 (1681–1767) countered that the Nangron promoted a theory that made "no distinctions" (*mubun* 無分).

In this study, I use the term "Horak Debate" specifically for the early stage of the controversy between Han Wŏnjin and Yi Kan.

P. J. Ivanhoe has briefly introduced the main philosophical issues of the Horak Debate, as well as Han Wŏnjin's own position in it, to Western scholarship, focusing on the early exchange between Han Wŏnjin and Yi Kan. See Ivanhoe 2016, 90–100.

Sangha 權尙夏 (1641–1721), the foremost disciple of the 17th-century scholar and statesman Song Siyŏl. In 1717, during the reign of King Sukjong, Han was recommended for office due to his outstanding academic abilities. However, when the Noron faction fell from power after the Sinim Purge (*sinim sahwa* 辛壬士禍) following King Kyŏngjong's (r. 1720-1724) accession,[8] Han resigned from his post. He was later reinstated under King Yŏngjo and gained recognition as a royal lecturer, but was again removed from office for rejecting to work with the Soron faction and violating the spirit of the policy of impartiality.

Despite his political ups and downs, Han Wŏnjin's thought and scholarship became a central ideological foundation for the Noron regime of his time. His prolific writings and correspondence on Zhu Xi's Neo-Confucianism include the *Chusŏ tong'igo* 朱書同異考 (Examination of Agreement and Divergence in Zhu Xi's Writings), a systematic completion of Song Siyŏl's unfinished work, and the *Kyŏngŭi kimunnok* 經義記聞錄 (Record of Heard Teachings on the Classics), a comprehensive compilation of Kwŏn Sangha's teachings on the Confucian scriptures. These works are regarded as seminal texts in the interpretation and systematization of Neo-Confucian doctrine in late Chosŏn Korea.

Han Wŏnjin was the intellectual heir to the line of thought transmitted through Yi I, Song Siyŏl, and Kwŏn Sangha, representing the scholarly lineage of the Westerners and later the Noron faction. From a thoroughly orthodox Neo-Confucian standpoint, he constructed a systematic theoretical framework grounded in conservative interpretations. Han sought to rigorously clarify the conceptual relationship between principle and nature, systematizing it with meticulous precision in order to articulate the moral distinctions and essential differences not only between things and humans, but also among human beings.

At the same time, he firmly rejected and criticized doctrines he regarded as heterodox, such as Sŏn Buddhism and Yangming School, as well as the practical approaches of the Namin and the more open interpretations of Neo-Confucianism found in the Nangron tradition.[9] Rather than responding flexibly to the changing currents of his age, Han aimed to impose order through the reinforcement of doctrinal Neo-Confucian foundations. This stance made him a central figure in the increasing dogmatization of Neo-Confucianism and the tightening of ideological control in late Chosŏn Korea.

---

[8] The Sinim Purge is named after the years in which it occurred, Sinch'uk 辛丑 (1721) and Im'in 壬寅 (1722). This incident was a political purge in which the Soron faction seized power by accusing the Noron of treason during an intense factional struggle over the royal succession.

[9] Nangron scholars like Pak P'ilju and Yi Chae held that human and material natures are the same, that the unaroused mind is wholly good, and that sages and ordinary people share the identical substance. The Nangron generally viewed the heavenly principle as universal and undifferentiated, asserting that original nature—embodying this principle—is identical across all beings. Their theory of sameness, grounded in the principle-universalist (*rit'ong* 理通) stance, emphasized the inherent goodness of original nature.

Against this backdrop, Han Wŏnjin emerged as a national figure in the Horak Debate that shook the mainstream intellectual landscape of 18th-century Chosŏn. The debate originated within the scholarly lineage of his teacher, Kwŏn Sangha, and escalated into a sharp conflict between Han Wŏnjin's theory of the difference between human and non-human nature and Yi Kan's opposing view of their essential sameness. Han argued that the nature of humans and things is fundamentally different, claiming that only human beings possess a complete moral nature, and that non-human nature does not embody the full form of original human nature. In contrast, the Nangron school, following Yi Kan, argued that nature is the same for both humans and non-humans, and only the *qi* differs.

Han Wŏnjin's theory of the difference between human and non-human nature was rooted in his original formulation of the "three-tiered theory of nature" (*sŏng samch'ŭngsŏl* 性三層說) that the generation of all things in the universe unfolds through three stages: The first is the stage of transformation in *qi* (*kihwa* 氣化), where strong yang *qi* gives rise to masculine qualities and yielding yin *qi* produces feminine qualities. The second is the stage of material formation (*hyŏnghwa* 形化), in which the *qi* of yin and yang combine to generate the physical forms of all things. Finally, within these material forms, a third stage occurs, an ongoing process of transformation in *qi* embedded within material formation itself. Han applied this cosmological framework to his theory of mind and nature, thus articulating a distinctive metaphysical model in which nature is understood through this three-layered structure.

This three-tiered nature theory by Han posits that both humans and non-human beings possess nature that can be understood through three distinct levels: the nature that transcends the form-generating *qi* (*ch'o hyŏnggi-ji-sŏng* 超形氣之性), the nature that is based on material endowment (*in kijil-ji-sŏng* 因氣質之性), and the nature of mixed endowment (*chapgi-ji-sŏng* 雜氣之性). The nature that transcends the forming *qi* refers to a universal, transcendental nature that exists commonly in all things. It signifies the operation of *qi* beyond physical form, a kind of shared, supra-material basis. The nature that is based on material endowment is the nature that exists uniquely in human beings, shaped by their individual physical and emotional constitution, and manifests differently according to that constitution. Finally, the nature of mixed endowment refers to the specific and variable dispositions that arise from the mixed *qi* of individuals, explaining moral and psychological differences among people.

Han's theory first clarifies that both humans and non-human beings share the same universal, transcendental nature, but differ in their nature that is based on material endowment, a distinction that serves both as the basis for defining the essence of beings and as the origin of morality. He emphasizes that the nature of mixed endowment explains the individual differences among human beings and thus becomes the object of moral cultivation and ethical practice.

Building on Yi I's idea that nature can only be meaningfully discussed once principle is embedded within material endowment, Han Wŏnjin argued that human and non-human natures can be compared only at the level of this *qi*-based nature, leading to his central claim that they are fundamentally different. From this distinction, he affirmed the source of universal human morality, showing that humans possess a moral capacity unique to them and thereby demonstrating their existential value and inherent dignity as superior to other forms of existence.

In this understanding, Han further emphasized the necessity of unceasing self-cultivation in the pursuit of true benevolence. Using his three-tiered theory of nature as a framework, he argued that by refining one's temperament, the mind could be made sincere, enabling the moral transformation of one's material endowment and the full actualization of what it means to be human.

In the debate concerning the mind in its unactivated state (*mibal simch'e* 未發心體), Han departed from Yi Kan's view that the unmanifested mind is inherently good as a whole. Instead, Han argued that even in this unmanifest state, the mind contains the latent possibility of both good and evil, a view he termed "the theory that good and evil exist in the unactivated mind" (*mibal simch'e yu sŏnaksŏl* 未發心體有善惡說).[10] According to this view of Han, moral vigilance and inner tension are required at all times, since the potential for both virtue and vice is always present, even before the mind reacts. This position marks a clear departure from Yi Kan's assertion that the unaroused mind is wholly good.

While the Horak Debate may be dismissed as an impractical metaphysical exercise, like the earlier Four Seven Debate, it can also be understood as the conservative establishment's response to the moral collapse and social disorder of Chosŏn that followed the seventeenth century wars. Han's focus on the distinction between human and non-human nature aimed to restore moral autonomy and ethical clarity in the real world. Unlike Practical Learning scholars, who pursued actual economic and institutional reforms, Han sought to stabilize society by reinforcing orthodox Neo-Confucian principles. His Horon stance became both the conservative pinnacle of late Chosŏn Neo-Confucianism and a normative reference for later Confucian thought.

## *Changja pyŏnhae*

### Purpose of Composition

Han Wŏnjin's *Changja pyŏnhae* is not fully included in his *Namdang sŏnsaeng munjip* (*Munjip* hereafter). Only the preface written by Han himself appears there, in volume 31, folios 6b–7a, while the main text is not included at all. Among Han's independently authored works that are included in the *Munjip* are *Karye soŭi puch'ŏm* 家禮疏義付籤 (Supplementary Annotations and Indexed Commentary on the *Family Rites*), *Karye wŏllyu ŭirok* 家禮源流疑錄 (Record of Doubts on the Origins and Transmission of the *Family Rites*), *Kŏgwanrok* 居觀錄 (Record of

[10] See his "Insim tosim sŏl" 人心道心說 (*Munjip* 30.1a–7a); "Ponyŏn-ji-sŏng kijil-ji-sŏng sŏl" 本然之性氣質之性說 (*Munjip* 30.7a–10b).

Reflections in Seclusion), and *Hanssi puhun* 韓氏婦訓 (Instructions for Ladies of the Han Family). Even his most representative works, *Chusŏ tong'igo* and *Kyŏngŭi kimunnok* are included in the *Munjip* only in the form of prefaces. In this context, it is not unusual that only the preface to *Pyŏnhae* is preserved in the *Munjip*.[11]

The reason why *Pyŏnhae* was not included in the *Munjip* remains unclear. However, the preface by Han Wŏnjin, which does appear in the *Munjip* and is also placed at the very beginning of the Kyujanggak *Pyŏnhae* manuscript, serves as a crucial piece of primary evidence regarding the motivation and purpose behind the work. According to the preface,[12] the immediate impetus for Han Wŏnjin's writing of *Pyŏnhae* came in the winter of 1716, when he was asked by his friend Sŏng Kun'gak 成君覺 (dates unknown) to give lectures on the ZZ. Han says in the preface that he had been captivated by the elegant prose of the ZZ in his youth, but unable to grasp its deeper meaning, he had set the text aside for many years. In preparing for the lectures, however, he reread the work multiple times and came to the conclusion that although the ZZ's thought may superficially appear close to principle, it in fact distorts the true Way.

According to the preface, after the lectures concluded, Sŏng Kun'gak urged Han to preserve his teachings in writing. At first, Han adamantly refused, insisting that annotating the ZZ was not a task befitting a Confucian scholar. However, Sŏng countered that it was in fact the scholar's duty to correct the widespread harm caused by the ZZ, which had already circulated widely.[13] Persuaded by this argument, Han agreed and undertook the task of offering a critical and analytic interpretation of the text. This, as Han himself explains in the preface, was the motivation and purpose behind the composition of *Pyŏnhae*.

Interestingly, the writing and publication of the *P'yŏnhae* appear to have been prompted not solely by Han Wŏnjin's own initiative, but by the strong persuasion and encouragement of a friend named Sŏng Kun'gak. The exact identity of this "friend" (*uin* 友人) remains unclear. Given that Han's first wife came from the Sŏng family, it is possible that Sŏng Kun'gak was a relative by marriage,

---

[11] *Chusŏ tong'igo* and *Kyŏngŭi kimunnok* were added later when a more comprehensive version of the *Munjip* was reprinted in 1976, but even this newer edition still did not include *Changja pyŏnhae* in its entirety.

[12] To save space, citations from the original text are kept to a minimum in this Introduction. Readers are encouraged to refer to the corresponding passages in the translation below for a fuller reading.

[13] Kim Hangmok interprets Han Wŏnjin's publication of *Changja pyŏnhae* as a critical intervention aimed at the gradually rising trend among Chosŏn contemporary Zhu Xi scholars who were reading the ZZ in a favorable light. More specifically, Kim sees Han's work as a direct rebuttal to Pak Sedang 朴世堂 (1629–1703), who had composed a sympathetic commentary on the ZZ around 1680, titled *Namhwagyŏng chuhae sanbo*, which had by then gained wide circulation among Chosŏn Neo-Confucians. Han Wŏnjin's *P'yŏnhae* was both a Neo-Confucian critique of and a response to Pak Sedang's commentary. See Kim 2024, 65.

though no further details are known.[14] The preface also offers no explanation for why Sŏng selected the *Zhuangzi* in particular as the subject of Han's lecture, or how this choice related to Han's personal circumstances at the time.

There is, however, a document that offers an interesting clue as to why ZZ, rather than any other text, was selected. In 1730, when Han Wŏnjin was 49 years old, Kang Kyuhwan 姜奎煥 (1697–1731), his nephew and fellow disciple under Kwŏn Sangha, composed a sequel titled *Changja sok pyŏnhae* 莊子續辨解 (Supplement to Analytic Interpretation of the *Zhuangzi*). The preface to this work survives in volume 5 (folios 8b–9b) of the *Pisujae sŏnsaeng munjip* 賁需齋先生文集 (Collected Works of Master Pisujae Kang Kyuhwan), a compilation of Kang's writings edited by his student Kim Kŭnhaeng 金謹行 (b. 1712).[15] *Pisujae* was Kang Kyuhwan's pen name.

According to the preface, *Sok pyŏnhae* was composed in the autumn of 1730, when Kang was residing in Kŭmnŭng 金陵 (present-day Kimhae). During his stay, Kang taught his student Kim Kŭnhaeng the contents of Han Wŏnjin's *Pyŏnhae*, and added his own interpretations to form this supplementary volume. Unfortunately, the work itself has not survived, and only the preface remains. Therefore, we cannot know with certainty what views Kang added to Han's interpretation. Nonetheless, the preface is undoubtedly a fascinating and valuable document that offers indirect insight into how scholars of the Zhu Xi school during that time regarded Lao-Zhuang thought and how it was situated within the broader intellectual climate of the era.

Kang Kyuhwan was a contemporary of Han Wŏnjin, and as his nephew, colleague, and disciple, he was in a position to directly ask Han about any uncertainties or ambiguities surrounding the writing of the *Pyŏnhae*. Moreover, when Kang composed the *Sok pyŏnhae*, it is highly likely that Han Wŏnjin himself read this sequel written by his own nephew and his student. Therefore, it is unlikely that Kang would have misrepresented Han Wŏnjin's motivations for writing the *Pyŏnhae* in the preface to his own work. This suggests that Kang's preface holds interpretive and historical value equal to that of Han's own preface when it comes to understanding the origins of the *Pyŏnhae*.

In this preface of *Sok pyŏnhae*, Kang Kyuhwan points out that if Confucius represents yang, then Zhuangzi represents yin. Though yin and yang are opposites, neither can eliminate the other. Since it is impossible to eliminate one entirely, the most prudent and practical approach is to clearly distinguish between the two, so that Confucian scholars may be less susceptible to the influence of

---

14 In volumes 1 of *Munjip* and its *Supplement* (*sŭbyu* 拾遺), there are two poems Han Wŏnjin composed for Sŏng Kungak: one presented to him directly, entitled "Presented to Sŏng Kun'gak" 贈成君覺 (*Munjip* 1.13a), and the other written in response to a poetic rhyme by Sŏng, titled "Following Sŏng Kun'gak's Rhyme" 次成君覺韻 (*Munjip* 1.9b). These verses reveal that Sŏng Kungak was not merely a casual acquaintance but someone with whom Han shared a meaningful emotional and intellectual bond.

15 I include a full English translation of this preface of *Sok pyŏnhae* as an appendix to this book.

Zhuangzi's heterodox teachings. According to Kang, this was the very reason Han Wŏnjin composed his *Pyŏnhae.*

More specifically, Kang writes that Han chose the ZZ as the text of his critical engagement because he regarded it as the most prominent and insidious representative of heterodox thought in contrast to the Confucian Way. In his view, the world of learning had become increasingly vulnerable to confusion between orthodoxy and heterodoxy, particularly due to the rhetorical allure and philosophical vagueness of Zhuangzi's text. According to Kang, Han recognized that just as the cosmological opposition of yin and yang entails mutual presence, so too does the existence of the Confucian Way presuppose the persistent presence of its opposites. To properly affirm Confucian orthodoxy, then, one had to engage in the labor of differentiation, making explicit what must be followed and what must be rejected. The ZZ was not merely another alternative voice; it represented the yin in the cosmos, a mode of thought that, if left unchallenged, would blur the lines that Confucian sages had long worked to preserve.

Furthermore, Kang points out that, for Han, Zhuangzi's influence had already seeped deeply into certain trends within Confucianism itself in Chosŏn, particularly those that privileged *qi* or mind at the expense of *li.* Because of Zhuangzi's rhetorical brilliance and poetic indirection, earlier commentators had failed to confront the text with sufficient clarity or philosophical rigor. For Kang, Han thus undertook the *Changja pyŏnhae* not only to refute Zhuangzi's ideas, but also to secure the doctrinal clarity of the Confucian Way against the heterodoxy that had proven seductive to Confucians. In identifying Zhuangzi's relativism as a danger cloaked in charm, Han sought to restore the bright line between principle-based discernment and the formless ambiguity of Daoist thought, thereby making the distinction between Confucianism and heterodoxy as self-evident as the difference between the sun and the stars.

Kang Kyuhwan's remark that Han Wŏnjin was acutely aware of the harmful influence Zhuangzi was exerting on Chosŏn's Zhu Xi scholars is corroborated by another extant source on Han Wŏnjin, entitled *Namdang sŏnsaeng yŏnbo* 南塘先生年譜 (Chronological Record of Master Namtang; *Yŏnbo* hereafter).[16] While the exact date of the record's compilation is unknown, it likely dates from the reign of King Kojong (1863–1907), and the author remains unidentified. This *Yŏnbo* contains another fascinating testimony concerning Han Wŏnjin's relationship with the ZZ and the Neo-Confucian scholarly world of Chosŏn.

> In winter [of 1716], the Master [Han Wŏnjin] composed *Changja pyŏnhae.* Those in the world who enjoy reading ZZ are entirely unaware of the allegorical and metaphorical nature of his writing. As a result, their reading inevitably fell into

---

[16] This *Yŏnbo* is not included in the standard edition of *Munjip*, but only in the edition catalogued as 古 3428–758 and preserved at the Kyujanggak Institute for Korean Studies at Seoul National University. Here I used the version provided by the Digital Changsŏgak of the Academy of Korean Studies.

> the lamentable error of "a Yan person interpreting a Chu text" (i.e., forcibly attaching meanings or ideas that do not fit). Thus, the Master [Han] discerned where Zhuang Zhou's true intent lay, interpreted his meaning, examined his arguments, and clarified the harm in how [Zhuang Zhou] appeared to align with principle while in fact throwing the truth into confusion.[17] (26b)

The author of this *Yŏnbo* offers a concrete piece of information relevant to the social context surrounding the writing of the *Pyŏnhae*: despite the heretic status of the ZZ, it continued to be widely read among Chosŏn's Zhu Xi scholars. These scholars, the *Yŏnbo* states, failed to grasp the allegorical nature of the ZZ, and thus produced mistaken, likely sympathetic and positive, interpretations of it. Han Wŏnjin, in response, sought to interpret the ZZ more accurately, distinguish its distortions, and make clear the dangers of its teachings, which seemed superficially to resemble Neo-Confucian ones, but in truth undermined the Way. This implies that *Pyŏnhae* was composed not merely as a polemical rejection of the ZZ, but as a critical clarification aimed at his contemporaries and future Zhu Xi scholars who would be influenced by it.

However, the *Yŏnbo* does not mention Sŏng Kun'gak at all and instead attributes the work solely to Han Wŏnjin himself, stating that he wrote it for the benefit of scholars reading the ZZ. It also describes a contextual factor not specifically mentioned in Han's own preface, namely, that many scholars at the time were reading the ZZ, which connects the work more clearly to the intellectual climate of the period.

From both the preface and the *Yŏnbo,* we can indirectly gather that Han Wŏnjin's *Changja pyŏnhae* was part of a personal intellectual project intended to reinforce internal cohesion within the Chosŏn Zhu Xi school by offering a Neo-Confucian critique of the ZZ, which was considered for him as an archenemy to Confucius and his school. This then leads to a broader question: beyond these explicit records, how were Han Wŏnjin's life and times connected to the formation of the *Changja pyŏnhae*?

First, we should note that around the year 1716, when Han was composing the *Changja pyŏnhae*, he was engaged in prolific scholarly writing. As a young scholar within the Noron sub-faction, he was establishing and elaborating his own original positions on some of the most contested theoretical issues of the time, particularly those surrounding the concepts such as unactivated state of the mind (*mibal* 未發), human nature, and material endowment, issues that were central to the emerging factional disputes within the Chosŏn Zhu Xi learning.

The year before composing the *Pyŏnhae*, in 1715, Han completed the *Kyŏngŭi kimunnok*. That same winter, Han composed several pivotal essays, "Discussion on the Five Constants in the Unmanifest State" (*Mibal osang-byŏn* 未發五常辨), "Demonstration on the Nature Derived from Material Endowment" (*Kijil-ji sŏng*

17 冬著莊子辨解。世之好讀莊子者，全不知其寓言借事之意，而讀之實不免郢書燕說之歎。故先生的見，其莊周主意之所在，而解其義，而辨其說，而明其近理亂眞之獘也。

*pyŏnjŭng* 氣質之性辨證), and "Demonstration on the Nature of Humans and Non-Humans" (*Inmul-ji sŏng pyŏnjŭng* 人物之性辨證), which together form the theoretical core of his position in the Horak Debate over the sameness or difference between human and non-human nature. That is, while writing the *Pyŏnhae*, Han was actively participating in the Horak Debate and developing his philosophical arguments. From this, we may reasonably wonder whether Han's reading of the ZZ was in some way related to the debates. Indeed, some of Han's key points of criticism in the ZZ, such as those concerning the Way, human nature, and the mind, can plausibly be connected to issues he raised in the debates with Yi Kan and other advocates of the sameness view. We will examine this in detail later when we turn to his critique of the ZZ.

In other words, while the immediate cause for writing the *Pyŏnhae* was, as stated in the preface and the *Yŏnbo*, the urging of his friend Sŏng Kun'gak and the need to correct his contemporaries' misguided fascination with the ZZ, it is possible that Han's particular interest in the text at that moment had deeper roots. Namely, he may have seen in the ZZ a set of ideas that directly challenged the Neo-Confucian orthodoxy of the nature of humans and other beings that he was working to develop and defend. In this sense, his composition of the *Pyŏnhae* was not only a response to external cultural confusion caused by the ZZ readers but also a product of his own scholarly commitments during a time of controversy.

Secondly, it is worth noting that just one year after writing the *Changja pyŏnhae*, Han Wŏnjin authored the *Sŏnhak t'ongbyŏn* 禪學通辨 (General Refutation of Sŏn Learning) in 1717, in which he critiqued both Buddhism and the Learning of the Mind (*simhak* 心學) (i.e., Lu-Wang school 陸王學).[18] This context suggests that the period during which Han composed the *Changja pyŏnhae* was one in which he was particularly focused, as a staunch Neo-Confucian, on analyzing and critiquing other doctrinal traditions of the time, especially those regarded as heretical (*idan* 異端), such as Buddhism and Yangming learning.

This connection is further reinforced in the biography (*haengjang* 行狀) of Han Wŏnjin, written by his close friend Yun Ponggu 尹鳳九 (1683–1767), a fellow student under Kwŏn Sangha. Yun explicitly notes that Han's *Pyŏnhae* was part of his broader project of refuting heterodox teachings and that it shared the same overarching purpose as his *Sŏnhak t'ongbyŏn* and *Wang Yangmyŏng chipbyŏn*.

---

[18] In this text, Han points out that the theories of the mind proposed by Liu Jiuyuan 陸九淵 (1139-1192) and Wang Shouren closely resemble those of Buddhist thought. Twenty years later, in 1737 at the age of 56, he produced a more comprehensive critique of Wang Yangming's teachings from a Neo-Confucian perspective, entitled *Wang Yangmyŏng chipbyŏn* 王陽明集辨 (Collected Refutations of Wang Yangming). For reference, Korean translations of *Sŏnhak t'ongbyŏn* and *Wang Yangmyŏng chipbyŏn* are found in Yi 2009, 476–490 and 490–538.

> He had the *Changja pyŏnhae*, the *Sŏnhak t'ongbyŏn*, and *Wang Yangmyŏng chipbyŏn*, all of which carry on the legacy of safeguarding the Way and dispelling heterodoxies.[19] (*Pyŏnggye sŏnsaeng-jip* 59.24b)

Considering these circumstances, one might ask whether Han's simultaneous engagement, around 1716, in both establishing a Neo-Confucian theoretical position and critiquing heterodox teachings allowed him to consolidate and further develop his own distinct philosophical position within the Zhu Xi learning.

These two points outlined above suggest that the compilation of *Changja pyŏnhae* may have been tied not only to Han's personal intellectual trajectory but also to broader contexts of his time in Chosŏn. First, it is possible that in reading and annotating the ZZ, Han sought to examine and refine core issues such as the nature of *qi*, mind and nature, issues central to the ongoing debates on the sameness or difference between human and non-human nature, from a conservative Chosŏn Zhu Xi follower's standpoint.

Second, Han may have seen *Changja pyŏnhae* as a response to what he perceived as a growing threat posed by heterodox doctrines and an urgent call of the times to counter such teachings. Following the heterodoxy controversy (involving accusations of heresy and betrayal of the Confucian Way), orthodox Confucian scholars had become increasingly wary of unorthodox thought. As a result, there was growing need for Zhu Xi scholars to develop a more rigorous theories for distinguishing and refuting non-orthodox positions. Around 1716, Han Wŏnjin seems to have shared this sense of urgency and actively engaged in such tasks through concrete philosophical work.

Ultimately, *Changja pyŏnhae* can be understood as Han's attempt both to reinforce internal cohesion within the Chosŏn Neo-Confucian circle by offering a systematic critique of heterodoxy from a Zhu Xi perspective and to refine his position on core metaphysical questions through his critique of Zhuangzi.[20]

### Title and Structure

Regarding the title and structure of *Changja pyŏnhae*, Han Wŏnjin offers a succinct yet clear remarks in the preface. According to it, Han focused deliberately on the Inner Chapters of the ZZ, on the grounds that once one correctly understands and critiques the Inner Chapters, the rest will naturally follow.[21]

---

19 有莊子辨解，禪學通辨，陽明集辨。皆衛道闢異之遺意也。

20 Although Kim Tae-neon does not focus on Han Wŏnjin's critique of Zhuangzi or Buddhism, he meticulously examines how Han's criticisms of Yangming thought, T'oegye Yi Hwang, and the Nangron faction's interpretation of human-nature theory served to define a continuous line of transmission from Confucius to Mengzi, Zhu Xi, Yi I, Song Siyŏl, and Kwŏn Sangha, thereby constructing and elaborating a concept of "orthodox learning" (*chŏnghak* 正學). See Kim 2006.

21 Ever since Guo Xiang restructured the *Zhuangzi* into thirty-three chapters in the third century CE, scholars have widely accepted that the Inner Chapters preserve Master Zhuang's

As for why he titled his work *Changja pyŏnhae*, the *Yŏnbo* provides slightly more detailed information. Concerning the meaning of the title, it states, "Therefore, the Master [Han] discerned where Zhuang Zhou's true intent lay, interpreted his meaning, and analyzed his arguments…" 故先生的見，其莊周主意之所在，而解其義，而辨其說 (26b). Here, the term *pyŏnhae* in the title represents a pairing of two verbs: "to analyze/discern" and "to interpret/explain."

In terms of structure, *Changja pyŏnhae* follows the traditional format of earlier commentaries on the ZZ, adhering to the organization of the Inner Chapters. Before the commentary on the first chapter, Han Wŏnjin includes a preface in which he outlines the motivation and purpose for compiling the work. There is no postface at the end of the volume.

For each chapter, Han offers a general overview that captures the main idea of the chapter. He then divides the chapter into multiple segments based on core line, passage, or episodes, and provides his interpretations and critiques for each. Finally, at the end of each chapter, he summarizes his critiques of the chapter.

However, unlike standard commentaries, *Changja pyŏnhae* does not include the original text of the ZZ. It contains only Han Wŏnjin's commentary, which is a notable structural characteristic. Because the original text is omitted, it is often difficult to determine the precise meaning and context of Han's remarks without consulting the ZZ itself. Nevertheless, although it consists solely of commentary without the original text, Han's treatment is remarkably thorough, he engages closely with nearly every passage of the Inner Chapters, making *Pyŏnhae* a virtually complete commentary, at least on that portion of the text.

Another structural feature of Han Wŏnjin's *Pyŏnhae* is his distinctive redivision of the ZZ's Inner Chapters into basic interpretive units that he refers to as *tan* 段 (sections) or *chŏl* 節 (divisions). For example, in the "Free and Easy Wandering" (*Soyoyu* 逍遙遊) chapter, Han divides the text into three divisions, and further subdivides each into smaller paragraphs. In "On Treating All Things Equally" (*Chemullon* 齊物論), he classifies the content into thirty-five sections, discusses each section in turn, and then offers a comprehensive critique by grouping them into two halves—sections one through sixteen, and the remainder. Likewise, he divides "The Foundation of Nurturing Life" (*Yangsaengju* 養生主) into six sections, "Living Among People in the World" (*In'ganse* 人間世) into eighteen, "A Sign of Virtue Fulfilled" (*Tŏkch'ungbu* 德充符) into sixteen, "The Great Founding Master" (*Taejongsa* 大宗師) into twenty-two, and "Being in Accord with the Way of Emperor" (*Ŭngjewang* 應帝王) into fifteen.

Among the seven Inner Chapters, "Free and Easy Wandering" is unique in that Han uses the term "division" rather than "section" to divide the text, setting it apart from the other chapters. Furthermore, Han's use of "section" or "division" does not always correspond to conventional divisions, such as distinct stories or thematic essays typically used by other commentators. At times, he

more authentic ideas, in contrast to the Outer and Miscellaneous Chapters. Han Wŏnjin was almost certainly aware of this long held philological consensus.

considers a single sentence to constitute a *tan* (e.g., sections 3-6 of Chapter 2) while in other cases he groups two or more clearly separable episodes into a single section (e.g., section 16 of Chapter 4). This suggests a lack of consistency and structural coherence in his application of the *tan* concept. At present, it remains unclear what criteria Han Wŏnjin used to divide the ZZ text into these units.

Nonetheless, Han Wŏnjin regarded the seven Inner Chapters of the ZZ as forming a coherent and deliberate structure. At the beginning of each chapter, he briefly yet incisively explains how that particular chapter contributes to the internal organic unity among all seven chapters. For example, he views "Free and Easy Wandering" as the foundational essence of the Way, while "On Treating All Things Equally" follows as its function. Then, based on the principle of equalizing and harmonizing all things without harm, the question arises in "The Foundation of Nurturing Life" about how one might cultivate life. This cultivation of life leads to inward realization of the Way, which then extends outward in "Living Among People in the World" to the realization of the Way in the sociopolitical sphere. This inward cultivation and outward engagement represent the dual dimensions of personal self-actualization. Such a person becomes an integrated moral subject whose virtue is both inwardly complete and outwardly embodied ("A Sign of Virtue Fulfilled"). The achievement of such virtue leads to a deeper grounding in the root of the Way ("The Great Founding Master"), and once one has grasped this root, one becomes capable of ruling the world like a sage-king ("Being in Accord with the Way of Emperor").[22]

In short, chapters one and two represent the essence-function relationship of the Way, chapters three and four correspond to the inner-outer relationship in one's self-cultivation and governing others as the externalization of self-cultivation. Chapters five and six align the Way with virtue, and finally, chapter seven as the conclusion of cultivation correlates to governing the state and bringing peace to all-under-heaven, in contrast to the earlier focus on self-cultivation and conduct. Han thus believed that the structure of the ZZ Inner Chapters mirrors the eight-step structure of the Neo-Confucian classic, *Daxue*, moving from self-cultivation to governing the state and pacifying all-under-heaven.[23] This alignment implies that even the original thought of ZZ unfolds within a structural framework consistent with Confucian ideal.

---

22 This reading was earlier noted in Kŭm 2009, 127-28.

23 It refers to the following line in the *Daxue*: "When one fully investigates things, one's knowledge reaches its utmost. Once knowledge has reached its utmost, the will becomes sincere; when the will is sincere, the mind becomes upright; when the mind is upright, the body becomes cultivated. When the body is cultivated, the family becomes harmonious; when the family is harmonious, the state is well governed; and when the state is well governed, the world attains peace" 物格而後知至，知至而後意誠，意誠而後心正，心正而後身修，身修而後家齊，家齊而後國治，國治而後天下平。(2)

## Editions and Reception History

Until now, scholarly consensus has held that only a single manuscript of the *Changja pyŏnhae*, preserved in the Kyujanggak collection, exists. This view has gone largely unchallenged because scholars have not closely examined the fact that a text with the same title and content appears in volume 20.12a–34b of the *Yŏam chŏnsŏ* 旅菴全書 (Complete Works of Yŏam Sin Kyŏngjun).[24] Nor have they adequately explored the differences between this Yŏam edition and the Kyujanggak manuscript. When comparing the two versions bearing the same titles and contents, it becomes clear that another version, based on the Kyujanggak manuscript and intended to correct errors and typos, was circulating. This revised version was likely anonymous and not properly attributed to Han Wŏnjin.

Sin Kyŏngjun, courtesy name Sunmin 舜民 and pen name Yŏam 旅庵, was a leading late Chosŏn scholar exemplifying the practical turn in Neo-Confucianism. He is noted for his work in linguistics, including the *Hunmin chŏng'ŭm unhae* 訓民正音韻解 (Phonological Explanation of the Hunmin chŏng'ŭm) an eighteenth-century systematic study of Korean script and Sino-Korean phonology, and in geography, with works like the *San'gyŏngp'yo* 山經表 (Diagram of Mountain Lineages), a diagram tracing Korean mountain ranges via watershed lineages.[25]

The *Yŏam chŏnsŏ*, the most comprehensive collection of Sin Kyŏngjun's writings, including a version of the *Changja pyŏnhae*, was compiled in 1939–40 by his fifth-generation descendant Sin Chaehyu 申宰休, based on the 1910 woodblock edition of *Yŏam yugo* 旅菴遺稿 (Collected Posthumous Writings of Yŏam) printed by Sin Ikku 申益求, Sin's great-grandson.[26] Edited by two renowned historians, Chŏng Inbo 鄭寅普 (b. 1893) and Kim Ch'undong 金春東 (b. 1906), the edition added previously unpublished miscellaneous writings of Sin to the original compilation. In volume 20, a version of the *P'yŏnhae* basically the same as Han Wŏnjin's appears, likely included in error under Sin Kyŏngjun's name, as it lacks Han's preface. Since Han's preface had been published in the *Munjip* by the 1780s, it raises questions about how this work long attributed to Han came to appear under Sin's name in this twentieth-century edition.

Knowledge of Han Wŏnjin's authorship of the *Changja pyŏnhae* may not have been widespread, yet it is still puzzling that eminent scholars like Chŏng Inbo and Kim Ch'undong, editors of the *Yŏam chŏnsŏ*, overlooked it. A likely explanation is that a version of the *Pyŏnhae* lacking Han's preface circulated independently, and by the early twentieth century few knew its true provenance, making the misattribution more understandable.

---

[24] The *Yŏam chŏnsŏ* has not been digitized in the Comprehensive Database of Korean Classics (https://db.itkc.or.kr/) maintained by the Institute for the Translation of Korean Classics. The version used in this study is the scanned images of the original text provided by the National Library of Korea.

[25] Although there is still scholarly debate over the authorship of the *San'gyŏngp'yo*, it has traditionally been attributed to Sin Kyŏngjun.

[26] This *Yŏam yugo* is available online through Comprehensive Database of Korean Classics.

Why, then, did the editors attribute the work to Sin Kyŏngjun? A possible clue lies in a previously unknown partial commentary on the *Zhuangzi*, *Munjang Chunch'ik: Changja sŏn*, discovered and made public by Kim Namhyŏng in 2014, suggesting a potential connection between Sin and the ZZ (Kim 2014).

Strictly speaking, the *Changja sŏn* offers no explicit statement, unlike the *Pyŏnhae* preface, about its author or purpose. Kim Namhyŏng attributed it to Sin Kyŏngjun because a roughly 1,400-character commentary at the end of "On Treating All Things Equally" matches word-for-word an essay, *Sŏ Changja Chemullon hu* 書莊子齊物論後 (Essay Written after Reading Zhuangzi's "Qiwulun"), in volume 5 of *Yŏam yugo* (10b–13a) (Kim 2014, 14). However, this inference has limitations: if the *Changja Sŏn* simply copied the essay without attribution or acknowledgment, it may not have been Sin's work at all.

Second, if *Sŏ Changja Chemullon hu* in the *Yŏam yugo*—compiled some 130 years after Sin Kyŏngjun's death—was misattributed, then the case for identifying *Changja sŏn* as Sin's work collapses, too. Just as the *Changja pyŏnhae* in the *Yŏam chŏnsŏ* may have been wrongly credited to Sin, the essay could likewise reflect later misattribution by editors or descendants. Kim cites the frequent Daoist expressions and passages from the DDJ and ZZ in Sin's writings as evidence of his unusual engagement with Daoism (Kim 2014, 20). While this shows Sin's interest in Daoist classics, it cannot definitively prove he authored *Changja sŏn*.

Third, the general comment at the end of chapter two in *Changja sŏn* is not fully identical to the essay, containing two additional paragraphs—about 240 characters—not found in *Sŏ Changja Chemullon hu*. This difference suggests that these two texts are closely related rather than simple duplicates. This indicates shared textual transmission or editorial reuse and does not by itself establish common authorship.

Despite these uncertainties, however, I will provisionally follow Kim's attribution of *Changja sŏn* to Sin Kyŏngjun for the purposes of this discussion.[27] If Sin Kyŏngjun's deep engagement with the ZZ included writing his own commentary and consulting Han Wŏnjin's *Changja p'yŏnhae*, it helps explain, at least partially, how the *Pyŏnhae* may have been mistakenly attributed to him in the *Yŏam chŏnsŏ*. Later editors may have seen it as reasonable to include a work on the ZZ among Sin's posthumous writings.

However, important questions remain. Sin's stance toward the Zhuangzi, as seen in his essay *Sŏ Changja Chemullon hu*, is apparently appreciative, while Han's approach in the *Pyŏnhae* is highly critical. It is puzzling how the esteemed editors Chŏng Inbo and Kim Ch'undong could have overlooked this key difference.

---

27 In composing this work, Sin Kyŏngjun drew on Chinese commentators from Guo Xiang through Lu Xixing 陸西星 (1502–1606) and Yuan Hongdao 袁宏道 (1568–1610), as well as Korean scholars such as Pak Sedang and Han Wŏnjin, citing their writings in support of his own commentary. This demonstrates that Sin was consulting Han Wŏnjin's commentary while writing his own.

A more practical issue is that the *Pyŏnhae* in the *Yŏam chŏnsŏ* is textually inferior to the Kyujanggak manuscript. It lacks the preface, which alone notes Han Wŏnjin's authorship, and begins directly with chapter one, "Free and Easy Wandering," making it easy to misattribute the text to someone else.

An important characteristic of the Yŏam edition is that it clearly aims to revise an earlier manuscript, likely the Kyujanggak edition by clarifying ambiguous or obscure expressions.[28] It also corrects erroneous phrases.[29] Moreover, the Yŏam edition tends to simplify difficult or conceptually dense passages, making them easier to understand.[30] In this sense, the Yŏam edition of the *Pyŏnhae* appears, in essence, to function as a revised version of an earlier manuscript.

However, in the process of revision, the Yŏam edition exhibits numerous errors. These include the use of incorrect characters.[31] There are also signs that the editor lacked a deep understanding of the ZZ and other classical texts.[32] The

---

[28] For example, the Kyujanggak version's phrase "in the several paragraphs below" (*ch'a ha su tan* 此下數段; folio 11a[21], line 7) is rendered more precisely in the *Yŏam* edition as "the four paragraphs below" (*ch'a ha sa tan* 此下四段; folio 17a[129], line 2). Numbers in bracket [ ] indicate modern page numbers added by contemporary editors, as both editions—especially Kyujanggak—suffer from illegible original pagination due to scanning.

[29] For example, the Kyujanggak version glosses *po'gwang* or *baoguang* 葆光 in the "Qiwulun" as 斂莊其道 (folio 16a[32], line 1), while the *Yŏam* edition replaces 莊 with 藏 (18b[134], line 11). Since *po* 葆 means "to preserve," interpreting it as "to store" justifies the use of 藏.

[30] For example, both editions interpret the phrase "storing the world in the world" (*chang ch'ŏnha yŏ ch'ŏnha* 藏天下於天下) from the "Great Founding Master" chapter as *mul kak pu mul ya* 物各付物也—"each being is entrusted to each being." However, their explanations differ: the Kyujanggak version (33b[66], line 6–34a[67], line 8) provides a lengthy, detailed comment, while the *Yŏam* edition offers only a brief summary of it.

[31] For example, the Yŏam edition (31b[158], line 1) repeats the character *nae* 乃 three times, whereas the Kyujanggak version (38a[75], line 10) has it only once in *cha ki so i nae* 自其所以乃. In another instance, Kyujanggak's *cho sam mo sa, i yu si pi-ji sil* 朝三暮四， 以喻是非之實 (13a[25], lines 7–8) appears in *Yŏam* as 朝三暮四， 二喻是非之實 (18a[131], line 4), misreading 以 as 二. Similarly, *ch'ŏn* 天 in *kae Chu i ch'ŏnji mi saeng-ji-jŏn wi to* 盖周以天地未生之前謂道 (Kyujanggak 15a[29], line 10) is miswritten as *rae* 來 in *Yŏam* (19a[133], line 9), and 已 in 旣已以下復言 (15b[30], lines 9–10) is rendered as 曰.

While the Kyujanggak version contains occasional scribal errors, such mistakes are far more frequent in the *Yŏam* edition. These errors obscure the text's meaning and suggest that the editors did not thoroughly review it before printing.

[32] For example, in the "Qiwulun," the Kyujanggak version (8a[15], lines 6–7) interprets *ak ch'ul hŏ* 樂出虛 ("music arises from emptiness") as "emotion begins from stillness and proceeds to movement" (*chŏng chi si pal, yu chŏng ŏ tong* 情之始發　由靜而動). The Yŏam edition (15a[125], line 11) replaces *chŏng* 靜 with *chŏng* 情, reversing the relationship and misrepresenting Han Wŏnjin's view that emotion originates from emptiness and stillness. Similarly, in interpreting *chŭng sŏng kyun* 蒸成菌 ("steam produces mushrooms"), Yŏam changes 至 (to arrive) to 出 (to emerge), implying the self generates emotion rather than receiving it, contrary to Han's original framework. The editions also differ on *ujŏ yong* 寓諸庸 (lodged in the ordinary). Yŏam reads it as "balance in daily life, necessarily distinguishing right and wrong" (18a[131], line 3), whereas

original text of the ZZ is at times incorrectly quoted.[33] In some cases, an entire line of commentary is skipped altogether, and this occurs multiple times.[34]

It is unclear whether the numerous editorial errors in the Yŏam edition originated with its original editor or with Chŏng Inbo and Kim Ch'undong, who compiled and proofread the *Yŏam chŏnsŏ*, as no comparative text exists. Detailed examples of differences between the Yŏam and Kyujanggak versions are provided in the footnotes. Overall, the *Changja pyŏnhae* in the *Yŏam chŏnsŏ* appears to have been handled by someone unfamiliar with the *Zhuangzi*'s difficult prose, lacking knowledge of classical texts like the *Zhouyi* and *Zhongyong*, and without the classical Chinese reading skills or editorial expertise needed to accurately proofread Han Wŏnjin's complex sentences. If these errors did not originate with the compilers of the *Yŏam chŏnsŏ* but were already present in the copy they used, it is questionable why they regarded such a flawed and error-ridden text as an authentic work of Sin Kyŏngjun. Even so, the Yŏam edition shows that, based on the Kyujanggak version, at least one revised text was produced to clarify or simplify difficult passages. In this process, however, Han Wŏnjin's preface was removed, leading to later confusion about the authorship of the *Changja pyŏnhae*.

The significant textual differences between the Yŏam and Kyujanggak editions call for a more careful examination of the Yŏam edition's nature and its textual relationship to the Kyujanggak version. This translation is based primarily on the Kyujanggak manuscript, with corrections made through consultation of the Yŏam edition and the translator's judgment where errors or ambiguities occur; all such changes are marked editorially in the Chinese text.

---

Kyujanggak presents it as balanced harmony in daily life, not distinguishing right and wrong" (13a[25], line 5), aligning with Zhuangzi's idea of *chemul* 齊物.

Yŏam further misrepresents the metaphysics of the *Book of Changes*: it renders "still and yin" 靜而陰 as "moving and yin" 動而陰 and miswrites 已 (already) as 未 (not yet) in the phrase on the mind's activation (25a[49], lines 9–10). In all these cases, the Kyujanggak version preserves Han's intentions, while Yŏam introduces errors that distort his interpretations.

33 In the Yŏam edition, *ch'wi man pu tong* 吹萬不同 ("What is blown is not alike in myriad ways") is miswritten as *ch'wi man pullon* 吹萬不論 ("not argued in myriad ways") (14b[124], line 8), and *mak sa pok yang* 莫使復陽 ("none lets the yang return") appears as *yak sa pok yang* 若使復陽 ("if the yang were to return") (15a[125], line 7).

34 In the Yŏam edition, several lines from Han's commentary are missing, likely due to visual misreading of vertically formatted text. For example, folio 15a, line 7 omits *ikji sowi, pulga pok* 溺之所為，不可復… (What is done by drowning cannot return) (Kyujanggak 7b[14], lines 9–10), possibly because the Yŏam editor mistook it as a continuation of the preceding line. Similarly, in Chapter Six (Yŏam 28b[152], line 8; Kyujanggak 32b[64], lines 8–9), a line beginning *ko non to* 故論道 is skipped, and in Chapter Three (Yŏam 23a[141], line 5; Kyujanggak 22b[44], lines 1–2), a line on "to kill life is not to die, to generate life is not to live" 殺生不死，生生不生 is missing. In each case, these omitted lines align with the preceding or following line, suggesting unintentional skipping rather than deliberate editing.

## Han Wŏnjin on the *Zhuangzi*

Han Wŏnjin's *Changja pyŏnhae* differs from other ZZ commentaries in both form and content, most notably in its consistent Neo-Confucian critique. Aimed at Neo-Confucian readers, it was written to expose what Han viewed as the fantastical and false ideas concealed in the ZZ's allegories. Unlike most commentaries that approach the text with admiration, Han sought to refute it through Neo-Confucian reasoning.

Nevertheless, his annotations display exceptional rigor and fairness. He interprets the ZZ with clarity and precision. His commentary was even consulted by Sin Kyŏngjun, a more sympathetic reader of the text. This attests to the enduring value of *Pyŏnhae* as both a critical study and a testament to Han's scholarly integrity and confidence in Neo-Confucian thought.

### Praises

Despite his fundamentally critical stance, Han Wŏnjin praises the ZZ in several passages of *Changja pyŏnhae*, each time for a different reason. First, he points out that Zhuangzi had an accurate understanding of the intent of Confucius, the putative editor of the six classics, and of the vision of the Confucian sages presented in those texts. In the preface to the ZZ, he cites a passage from the chapter 33 "Under Heaven" of the ZZ (33.1), which outlines the core values of the six classics, and remarkably praises Zhuangzi as the person who, prior to the emergence of the Cheng brothers and Zhu Xi, most accurately understood the spirit of Confucius and the Confucian sage. Because Zhuangzi so thoroughly understood Confucius and offered a pointed critique, Han argues that an accurate and devastating critique of Zhuangzi is urgently needed to rescue the hearts of Neo-Confucian scholars who have fallen under Zhuangzi's spell and to restore the spirit of Confucius to its proper height.

Furthermore, Han Wŏnjin also states that Zhuangzi's conception of the Way does not differ in its utmost subtlety and vastness from that found in Confucian teachings.

> This section (i.e., Section 14; 6.3) elucidates the substance of the Way, exhausts its subtle mysteries, and extends to a vastness beyond even the [concept of] oneness. Its discourse is in accord with that of our Confucian tradition.[35]

In his commentary on the idea of the Way as it appears in the "Great Founding Master" chapter, Han states that Zhuangzi's Way, in terms of its

---

[35] 此一段，發明道體，盡其幽妙，極其廣大無一，言不同於吾儒矣。 Here, my translation proceeds on the judgment that the phrase *ŏn pu tong ŏ o yu ŭi* 言不同於吾儒矣 contains a scribal error in the character *pu* 不, which should be disregarded. This decision is based on a consideration of the overall meaning of the entire passage, including the sentence that follows.

ontological essence, its profound subtlety, and its all-encompassing vastness, does not differ from the Way spoken of in Confucian tradition.

To be sure, in the next sentence Han does point out the essential difference between Zhuangzi's and the Confucians' notion of the Way,[36] but at the very least, Han acknowledges that the breadth and depth with which Zhuangzi understood the concept of the Way matched that of Confucians. In this respect, Han evaluates Zhuangzi as having, albeit partially, approached the conception of the Way as expressed by the Confucian sages.

Another aspect of Zhuangzi that Han Wŏnjin praises is his literary talent and skill in textual composition (e.g., the last comment sections of Chapters 1, 2, and 7). Among early Chinese works, the ZZ stands out for its distinctive literary style. Beyond its philosophical content, it deeply influenced premodern East Asian literature through its creative use of allegory, vivid onomatopoeia, and daring imagery. Its repetition of words and phrases reinforces a relativistic logic, while its bold rejection of rigid classical conventions allows the author's own voice to emerge freely. These features earned the ZZ a lasting reputation as a brilliant, provocative, and imaginative masterpiece.

Han Wŏnjin's evaluation aligns closely with traditional praise for the ZZ's literary artistry. He notes Zhuangzi's eccentric diction, skillful composition, and subtle, elegant expression through allegory and metaphor. Han regards Zhuangzi's literary craftsmanship as that of a true master—so refined that ordinary readers struggle to grasp its depth. He further observes that this complexity led even seasoned commentators to miss the text's true intent. Yet, above all, Han consistently praises Zhuangzi's exceptional creative talent, which he saw as far beyond that of ordinary writers.

### Criticisms

These words of praise represent only a secondary aspect of Han Wŏnjin's view of the ZZ in the *Changja pyŏnhae*. In fact, most of Han's assessment is strongly critical. His stance toward the ZZ appears in the preface to the *Pyŏnhae* as follows:

> Specifically, in terms of being firmly grounded in the origin and ascending to mastery, there were aspects he failed to reach, yet he spoke presumptuously [as if he indeed mastered the Way]. As a result, those shortcomings eventually led him to heresy, and the harm he caused to the Way was profound.[37]

---

36 The sentence immediately following reads: "However, [for Zhuangzi,] what is called the Way is a single *yin* of emptiness and stillness that existed before heaven and earth came into being. Thus, from the very core—what serves as its brain—it is already different from our Confucians." 然所謂道者，乃指天地未生之前，一陰虛靜者，則其頭腦看起處，便自如吾儒不同矣。

37 特於其本源上達處，有所未及者而肆言之，故其弊遂至於爲異端，賊道之甚者矣。

Here, Han Wŏnjin adapts Confucius's phrase "Begin with lower learning and ascend to higher understanding" (*hahak i sangdal*; *xiaxue er shangda* 下學而上達; *Lunyu* 14.35) into "being firmly grounded in the origin and ascending to mastery" (*ponwŏn sangdal* 本源上達) to highlight Zhuangzi's key flaw. He argues that Zhuangzi, without truly reaching either the original ground or the higher realm of the sage, spoke as though he had, presumptuously claiming sagehood. This, Han contends, led Zhuangzi into heresy and misled those pursuing the Way. The question of what Han means by this "origin" and "higher realm" lies at the center of his critique of the ZZ and will be examined below.

Throughout the *Changja pyŏnhae*, the concept Han Wŏnjin critiques most extensively is Zhuangzi's notion of the Way. His first and most detailed discussion appears in his commentary on section twenty-three of "On Treating All Things Equally" (ZZ 2.7), where the Way is introduced. Han criticizes Zhuangzi for identifying the Way with "the state before the emergence of things," arguing that this reflects a fundamental misunderstanding of both the Way and of things themselves. Citing the *Xici* of the *Zhouyi*, Han explains that all things arise through the constant interaction of yin and yang—movement and stillness—which coexist without a separate point of origin. Zhuangzi, however, regards only movement and yang as constituting existence, mistaking the preceding stillness and yin state for the Way. Thus, Han concludes, Zhuangzi's Way is merely the realm of the form-generating *qi*, and fails to grasp the deeper meaning of the *Zhouyi* dictum: "Once yin, once yang, this is the Way" (*Xici* A.5).

At the same time, Zhuangzi describes the Way as "emptiness and stillness" (*hŏjŏng*; *xujing* 虛靜) or as primal undifferentiation (*hondon*; *hundun* 混沌), seeing it as the state prior to the opening of heaven and earth and before the birth of the myriad things. Han Wŏnjin, however, argues that this state is nothing more than one symbolic manifestation (*sang*; *xiang* 象) of yin, within which various vital energies are already latent. These energies later differentiate to generate heaven, earth, and all things, giving rise in turn to distinctions such as right and wrong, good and evil. Zhuangzi, by contrast, regards even these distinctions as encompassed within the Way and takes the "equal treatment of all things" (*manmul chedong* 萬物齊同) as the Way's very essence. As a result, Han contends, Zhuangzi's philosophy collapses into confusion and chaos, in which any type of man-made conceptual or societal distinction or difference is rejected and denied.

According to Han, Zhuangzi's conception of the Way as a state preceding the existence of all things places it not only prior to the creation of heaven and earth but even beyond the bounds of the cosmos itself. Han criticizes this as a misreading of the Way, arguing that to situate the Way outside heaven and earth and to devalue the cosmos is to fail entirely to grasp its true essence.

From a Confucian standpoint, the Way operates together with the order of heaven and earth, and human beings are to realize the Way within the framework of that cosmic order. The path to the Way lies in not departing from heaven and earth, but in fulfilling one's proper role within its structure. Han Wŏnjin's core claim is that the Way is not some external force that transcends heaven and earth, but an immanent principle that exists together with and within the very workings of the cosmos (e.g., his comment on the section one of Chapter 7).

Moreover, Han Wŏnjin sees Zhuangzi's conception of the Way as amounting to nothing other than non-being. In his commentary on "On Treating All Things Equally," (2.8), Han Wŏnjin claims that Zhuangzi regarded the state prior to the creation of heaven and earth as the Way. However, although this state corresponds to the yin state of *qi*, that is, to "something that exists," Zhuangzi, in tracing the chain of the generation of being infinitely backward, ultimately came to identify it with non-being. According to Han Wŏnjin, this stems from Zhuangzi's failure to understand that yin and yang, movement and stillness, are originally without beginning (*musi* 無始), and that a time in which no things existed is inconceivable. All things have always existed and simply come into being and pass away through the cyclical alternation of yin and yang. The Way, therefore, is a reality embedded within this ongoing process—not just a form of non-being, as Zhuangzi views.

According to Han, Zhuangzi claims that "suddenly there emerged non-being" (*a i yu mu* 俄而有無; 2.8) thereby suggesting that the Way transitions from non-being to being. In this, Zhuangzi treats the Way as something that originates in non-being. But Han sees this as a misinterpretation: being and non-being, that is, things and phenomena have always existed within the transformations of yin and yang. The Way does not precede or exist outside of being and non-being, but rather governs the myriad things from within their unfolding. In other words, Zhuangzi misunderstood the yin realm as non-being, and thus mistook the Way for something nonexistent, falling into a grave error.

The concept of the Supreme Ultimate, which, especially in Neo-Confucianism, is often treated interchangeably with the Way, also appears in the ZZ. But just as Zhuangzi's Way is ultimately non-being in Han Wŏnjin's view, so too is his Supreme Ultimate. For Zhuangzi, Non-Ultimate and Supreme Ultimate are the same in being identified with non-being. In Confucianism, however, Non-Ultimate and Supreme Ultimate are "the same yet different, and different yet the same." The tension between sameness and difference, essential to the Confucian understanding, is crucially absent in Zhuangzi's thought.

In his comment on ZZ 6.6, the section on Master Sanghu (Zi Sanghu 子桑戶), Han Wŏnjin criticizes Zhuangzi for repeatedly claiming that "the Way precedes the Supreme Ultimate," interpreting this as an attempt by Zhuangzi to speak about the Way from a place even higher than the Way itself. This, Han argues, is the attitude of someone who does not truly understand the Way, for it stems from a failure to recognize that the Way inherently consists of two tiers—upper and lower. Zhuangzi, following the logic of concepts he had constructed for himself, described the Way as the limit point of endlessly expansive formative *qi*-energy, but this, Han asserts, arises from a fundamental misunderstanding of the true nature of the Way.

Han especially questions whether Zhuangzi's use of Non-Ultimate truly refers to the Way at all, and he argues that Zhuangzi did not even properly grasp the meaning of the notion of Way. In Confucianism, the Way is both Non-Ultimate and Supreme Ultimate, the principle composed of these two levels that are distinct and yet unified. But Zhuangzi, unaware of this dual structure, instead understood the Way purely in terms of the *qi* that generates a form. As a result, Han concludes, Zhuangzi's thought is flawed at its root and lacks persuasiveness.

Han Wŏnjin understands Zhuangzi's Non-Ultimate as referring to a substantive, ontological origin: a kind of non-being as the root. For Han, Zhuangzi's world is a space that arises from non-being and ultimately returns to it. Thus, in Zhuangzi's framework, the Supreme Ultimate, the moment when form first appears through yin energy, can be easily replaced with the term Non-Ultimate, since both direct back to non-being. According to Han, this view is essentially identical to the doctrines of Buddhism.

However, Han Wŏnjin argues that in the Confucian tradition, neither Supreme Ultimate nor Non-Ultimate can be understood as a single static state of annihilated non-being or void. Rather, both are simultaneously existent and non-existent, absent yet present. There is no temporal or logical sequence between them. From this standpoint, Han maintains that Zhuangzi's Supreme Ultimate is essentially different from the Supreme Ultimate of Confucianism.

Furthermore, in the comments on the ZZ 6.3, Han criticizes this conception of the Way as ultimately reducing it to a yin-like (*ŭmjŏk* 陰的) entity—that is, a state of emptiness and stillness, a lone yin (*irŭm* 一陰) prior to the formation of heaven and earth. Zhuangzi describes the Way as having "something to feel" (*yujŏng* 有情), as having "something to trust in" (*yusin* 有信), and as being non-active and formless (*muwi muhyŏng* 無爲無形). It is said to be a being that becomes its own source and root (*chabon chagŭn* 自本自根), and to have existed prior to heaven and earth. Moreover, Zhuangzi explains the Way's generative function through divine beings, spirits and gods (*singwi* 神鬼; *chesin* 帝神), and employs the concepts of Supreme Ultimate and six ends (*yuggŭk* 六極) to articulate its spatial and temporal character. In Han's view, however, Zhuangzi ultimately identifies *qi* as the Way, which is why he attributes to the Way such notions as "something to feel" and "something to trust in." Because Zhuangzi regards this *qi* as the source of all things, he considers it the origin of all being. But this stands in stark contrast to the Confucian conception of the Way as the harmonious interplay of yin and yang, expressed in the phrase: "Once yin, once yang, this is called the Way." Therefore, Han Wŏnjin asserts that Zhuangzi's Way, though outwardly subtle and profound, is, when viewed from a Confucian perspective, deeply mistaken at its very core.

Ultimately, Han Wŏnjin's criticism is grounded in the view that Zhuangzi, failing to grasp the mutual interaction of yin and yang and the metaphysical basis of the Supreme Ultimate, misunderstood the true foundation of reality. He argues that Zhuangzi mistakenly took a static state of lone yin as the origin of all things, an error stemming from a complete failure to understand the Way. Han emphasizes that the Way is principle that precedes *qi*, while *qi* is a variable substance that contains both good and evil mixed together. Because Zhuangzi confined his understanding of the Way to the level of *qi*, he could not accept the Confucian doctrine of the original goodness of human nature, and thus ultimately fell into what Han calls heterodox learning. For Han, it is crucial that all students of Confucianism clearly recognize this and adhere to the correct Way.

From this perspective, Han Wŏnjin believes that Zhuangzi did not even properly understand *qi* itself. Zhuangzi, while asserting that the Way is without end, understood the Way to be a kind of a "vital force of emptiness and stillness" (*hŏjŏng-ji-qi* 虛靜之氣). He claimed that when a person is born, he receives this *qi*, thereby obtaining the Way; and when he dies, that *qi* returns to a dim and vast state of emptiness and stillness. Zhuangzi further asserted that from this same empty-still state, all things are generated anew, and that this cyclical process is what constitutes the Way's continuity. Supporting this claim, Zhuangzi offers the expression: "To kill life is not to die; to give birth to life is not to be born" (*salsaeng pulsa, saengsaeng pulsaeng*, 殺生不死， 生生不生; 6.4). Commenting on this proposition as it appears in the "Great Founding Master" chapter, Han Wŏnjin views Zhuangzi's conception of *qi* as the result of a failure to properly understand the actual nature of *qi*, namely, its inherent tendency to change, disperse, and vanish. When a person dies, *qi* is completely dispersed and ceases to exist; yet Zhuangzi mistakenly believed that *qi* continues to exist beyond death. According to Han, this reveals Zhuangzi's fundamental ignorance concerning both the Way and *qi*, and ultimately exposes the essential overlap between Zhuangzi's worldview and Buddhist doctrines.

Han points out that Buddhist teachings such as "Seeing one's nature and becoming the Buddha" (*kyŏnsŏng sŏngbul* 見性成佛) and "Transcending into nirvana" (*ch'owŏl myŏldo* 超越滅度) likewise originate from Lao-Zhuang thought, that is, from a mode of thinking centered on *qi* and on emptiness and stillness. In Han's judgment, Zhuangzi's metaphysical framework, in its emphasis on an enduring, returning *qi*, shares its foundation with Buddhist metaphysics.

## Mind and Self-Cultivation

Han Wŏnjin points out that Zhuangzi's ultimate philosophical aim is the recovery of or return to a state of primal undifferentiation that precedes the opening of heaven and earth. In Lao-Zhuang thought, all things originally emerge from the indistinct chaos, and to return to this undifferentiated state is considered the very path to attaining the Way. Accordingly, Zhuangzi treats all distinctions, between right and wrong, good and evil, order and disorder—as things already encompassed within the Way. His approach of refusing to make judgments of right and wrong, or good and evil, manifests as the practice of treating all things equally, which Zhuangzi considers the enactment of the Way.

In his comments on ZZ 7.7, however, Han argues that what Zhuangzi calls a state of undifferentiated chaos is in fact merely the residual tranquility of a single yin after the dissipation of yang. It is not the substance of the Way. In the Confucian tradition, the Way is identified with principle, and the path to recovering the nature of the Way lies in following good and eliminating evil. Zhuangzi, by contrast, equates the Way with *qi* and denies the very act of choosing between good and evil. Though both traditions speak of "the Way" and of "returning to the Way," their meanings differ as drastically as fragrant incense from rotten weeds, or ice from charcoal. At the core of Zhuangzi's worldview lies this concept of radical undifferentiation, an idea irreconcilable with the Confucian commitment to ethical distinctions and order, as Han emphasizes.

According to Han, there are two key aspects to Zhuangzi's method for attaining the Way. First is to empty the mind of all residues that cause one to see the world through the lens of distinctions, to purify the mind and forget the self-shaped by personal experiences in conjunction with unavoidable social structures. Second is that through this process, one comes to recognize the true nature of the world as one of absolute indistinction and treating all things equally. Only then can one be born and exist "spontaneously," roaming free and easy in a world of transformations governed by *qi*.

Let us now consider Han Wŏnjin's critique of Zhuangzi's notion of the mind. In one passage of the second chapter (ZZ 2.3), Zhuangzi likens the human body to a structure whose many joints each perform their role without any presuming to be the center. From this, he argues that even if many views exist, one should not cling to any single one. Zhuangzi calls the mind the "true lord" (*chin'gun* 真君), stating that the operations of the bones and organs neither benefit nor harm the truth of the mind. Here, the mind is treated as the locus of all judgment, yet it too is incapable of perceiving things impartially. Only the Way can do so. Thus, Zhuangzi concludes that the mind and the Way are ultimately one and the same. The Way is the true sovereign, and the mind is the true master.

In his comments on ZZ 2.9, Han Wŏnjin criticizes Zhuangzi's notion of the "true lord," arguing that it fundamentally differs from the Confucian conception of the same term. In Confucian thought, the true lord refers to the moral mind that encompasses both human nature and heaven's mandate; it is the ethical core of the person. But in Zhuangzi's usage, the true lord is nothing more than a kind of numinous awareness (*yŏnggak* 靈覺) devoid of moral discernment between good and evil. Han emphasizes that Zhuangzi's thought lacks the Confucian focus on moral cultivation and the inherent goodness of human nature.

Thus, Zhuangzi's understanding of the mind, as that which moves toward equalizing all things, amounts to a defense of the kind of mind that refuses to distinguish between good and evil. This stands in stark contrast to the Confucian tradition, where cultivating the mind means awakening to the moral substance of human nature, which is originally good. Because of this, Han Wŏnjin sees Zhuangzi's philosophy as heretical and morally confused.

Han then takes the critique further, arguing that Zhuangzi does not even see the mind as universally the same across individuals. In the "A Sign of Virtue Fulfilled" chapter, Zhuangzi uses the metaphor of "still water" or "a clear mirror" (5.1), claiming that a calm and steady mind reflects things clearly and enables correct judgment. That is, only when the mind is upright can it be bright, and only when it is bright can it properly evaluate situations. (ZZ 5.7). Han Wŏnjin partially affirms Zhuangzi's metaphors of "still water" and "a clear mirror" to describe the mind. He acknowledges that Zhuangzi was correct in recognizing that when the mind is calm and undisturbed, it can reflect and harmonize with the forms of things as they are. Such metaphors are also employed by Confucians, so Han concedes that Zhuangzi's insight into the mind is not entirely mistaken.

However, Han criticizes Zhuangzi for perceiving the mind but failing to grasp human nature. Because of this, the "water" or "mirror" that Zhuangzi envisions cannot serve as a reliable standard of judgment. Han points out that the clarity and stillness of the mind, as Zhuangzi describes it, function differently depending on one's *qi*—that is, one's inborn material endowment. No matter how calm or clear a person's mind may appear, the response to external things will differ depending on the purity or turbidity, balance or imbalance of that person's *qi*. Therefore, if one relies solely on *qi*, as Zhuangzi does, to reflect the external world, it will produce distortion and inconsistency in judgment.

This leads Han Wŏnjin to conclude that Zhuangzi's view of the mind ultimately lacks a dependable moral standard. The mind, as understood in the Confucian tradition, bears within it human nature and heaven's call, and cannot be reduced to a passive, receptive organ to be emptied, as Zhuangzi claims.

Following the critique, in his comments in section 12 (ZZ 4.2), Han Wŏnjin offers a critical analysis of Zhuangzi's notion of "fasting the mind" and his ideal of a mind that is "without mind and without traces." According to Zhuangzi, the ideal is to suppress the desires of the sensory organs, to commune inwardly with the Way, and to maintain a state in which the mind remains unmoved even in the face of moral distinctions such as good and evil. However, Han Wŏnjin argues that such an "unmoving mind" does not mean rejecting the very capacity for moral judgment, as Zhuangzi does, but rather maintaining moral discernment without being disturbed by external influences. In Han's view, Zhuangzi's position amounts to a rejection of the mind's capacity for judgment itself, ultimately leading to a confused and irrational extremism.

For Zhuangzi, even spirits and the transformations of the myriad things harmonize with this state of empty illumination and tranquil serenity (*kongmyŏng chŏngjŏk* 空明靜寂; ZZ 4.2), and he goes so far as to regard such inner emptiness as the generative source of all things. Han Wŏnjin, however, sees this as a fundamental error, mistaking an empty state of mind for the true source of creation and construing the Way on the basis of a void.

In addition, Han criticizes Zhuangzi's ideal of a mind without desire and without trace as ultimately amounting to a kind of strategic self-preservation, aimed at avoiding harm. Rather than embodying genuine conduct grounded in the Way, it represents a cunning use of wisdom to conceal one's actions by leaving no trace for others to follow.

Therefore, Han concludes that Zhuangzi's Way, despite its superficial appeals to non-action and simplicity, is in truth closer to the kind of manipulative know-how that the Confucians explicitly warned against—the "technical use of knowledge," rather than a true moral cultivation.

### "Treating All Things Equally"

Han Wŏnjin criticizes Zhuangzi's claim that, by emptying the mind, one can eliminate all internal biases and prejudices, thereby perceiving the world's true condition, namely, a reality of nondiscrimination and indistinction, in which all things appear to be undistinguishable and equal. This critique may well be understood as one of the most direct motivations behind Han's composition of the *Changja pyŏnhae*, particularly during the height of the Horak Debate, in which he was advocating the theory that human and non-human nature are distinct.[38]

For Zhuangzi, the sage is one who can regard all things, without distinction or discrimination, as equal, because that is the true nature of reality. All things arise from *qi*, return to *qi*, and undergo ceaseless transformation within *qi*. One may have a human form today, and tomorrow return to dust in the bosom of great nature. Therefore, there is no essential difference between how one treats a human being and how one treats a clod of earth. This impartiality toward all things is, for Zhuangzi, the mark of the sage.

In the beginning of the second chapter, Zhuangzi uses phrases such as "Blowing on the myriad things in a different way" (*ch'wi man pudong* 吹萬不同) and "who is it that rages?" (*noja ki su* 怒者其誰) to suggest that the diverse voices (i.e., opinions and discourses from people) of all things ultimately issue from a single source. This one source, to which all phenomena return, he names variously as the "Way of emptiness and non-being" (*hŏmu-ji-do* 虛無之道) or the "true lord." In other words, although the myriad things arise and differentiate themselves from this oneness, they ultimately return to it. The ultimate person (*chiin* 至人), having realized this truth, sees all things as equal and undivided.

Han Wŏnjin sees Zhuangzi as asserting, through the phrases "Blowing on the myriad things in a different way" and "who is it that rages?" that the diversity of all things ultimately originates from one root and returns to it. According to Zhuangzi, though human discussions, emotions, and modes of thought may differ, they all stem from a single origin, "heaven" or "the Way of emptiness and non-being," and thus all beings should be regarded as equal. On the premise that all things are fundamentally the same, Zhuangzi presents this transcendent and egalitarian view as the ideal state of knowing.

---

38 Mun Sŏgyun and Kim Wŏnil have interpreted the motivation behind Han's commentary from this perspective. See Mun 1993; Kim 2010.

However, Han Wŏnjin criticizes this logic from a Confucian standpoint, arguing that Zhuangzi's idea is a distorted view grounded solely in *qi* as the origin of all things. In Confucianism, both the root of all things and the principle of their differences are attributed to the operation of principle. Principle, which has goodness as its essential nature, provides a stable moral standard. By contrast, Zhuangzi's "oneness" is nothing more than the undifferentiated activity of *qi*, which cannot ensure moral purity. Since *qi* contains both good and evil, truth and falsehood, using it as the basis for equality among all beings undermines moral judgment and leads to a forced, superficial kind of egalitarianism.

This critique is closely linked to Han's consistent opposition to the theory of the sameness of human and non-human nature. Zhuangzi's doctrine of the equalization of all things supports this view at the ontological level, since it regards the nature of human and non-human beings as the same, both rooted in *qi*. But Han Wŏnjin, advocating instead the theory of difference, holds that humans and things have different natures: humans are inherently good by virtue of possessing principle as their inborn nature, while non-human things are not.[39]

---

[39] Han Wŏnjin's *qi*-monistic interpretation of the ZZ, which emphasizes the absolute indistinction and equality of all things, stands in sharp contrast to Guo Xiang's 郭象 (252–312) *duhua* 獨化 (self-transformation) reading of the text. For Guo Xiang, the representative commentator of the Western Jin (265–316), *duhua* signifies that each being arises and transforms of itself, without dependence on any external cause or transcendent Way. The Way, in his view, is not a prior unity but the immanent process of self-generation itself—the spontaneous realization of each being's own nature (*ziran* 自然). Thus, Guo redefines the ZZ as a philosophy of self-sufficient differentiation, where harmony arises from the coexistence of independent yet interrelated beings.

Han Wŏnjin, by contrast, interprets the ZZ as advancing a monistic Way grounded in the undifferentiated flow of *qi*. From his Neo-Confucian standpoint, this "unity of myriad things" 萬物一體 obliterates the distinctions between human and non-human, noble and base, right and wrong, by reducing them all to morally neutral *qi*. Such *qi*-monism, for Han, confuses *qi* with *li* and undermines the ethical hierarchy central to Confucian thought.

These opposing readings do not merely represent different exegetical preferences; they disclose two fundamentally incompatible metaphysical models of order. Guo Xiang's *duhua* articulates a pluralistic ontology in which differentiation is primary and irreducible. Because each being generates and fulfills its own nature without reliance on an external principle, value and order emerge immanently from the fittingness of each thing to its own allotment (*fen* 分). In this framework, the *Zhuangzi* becomes a defense of a world that is already complete in its diversity: the absence of a transcendent ground does not yield chaos but secures a dynamic harmony rooted in the mutual noninterference of self-realizing beings. Guo's reading therefore preserves distinctions without grounding them in a hierarchical metaphysics; difference is real, yet it does not entail conflict because each entity flourishes within its own sphere.

Han Wŏnjin's critique, however, exposes the ethical stakes of this metaphysical divergence. From his Neo-Confucian perspective, the collapse of distinctions into undifferentiated *qi* threatens the very conditions determined with principle and thus makes one's moral cultivation in his designated status hard to pursue. If all things are equally expressions of morally neutral *qi*, then the normative hierarchy that privileges human moral agency, ritual propriety, and sagely governance loses its ontological foundation. Han thus interprets the *Zhuangzi*'s unity

In the Confucian view, both the unity of origin (*irwŏn* 一源) and the myriad differences (*manch'a* 萬差) fall within the domain of principle, and thus remain consistent with goodness. Zhuangzi, on the other hand, situates these within the realm of *qi*, reducing everything to a chaotic, undifferentiated world where good and evil are mixed. Therefore, the equalization of all things that Zhuangzi promotes only leads to confusion, failing to achieve genuine equality due to its inability to transcend partiality and preserve moral discernment.

In Han Wŏnjin's view, both Zhuangzi and the theory of the sameness of human and non-human nature distort true equality and moral clarity, leading to a form of indiscriminate, *qi*-centered thinking. Treating humans and non-human things as ontologically or ethically identical undermines the distinction between principle and *qi,* and erodes the foundations of moral judgment.

Ultimately, Han Wŏnjin holds that while Zhuangzi's philosophy of equality may appear, on the surface, to treat all things fairly, it inevitably leads to moral confusion because it is grounded not in principle but in *qi*-based perception. He warns that this nihilistic doctrine of equality fails to realize true parity and instead obscures the proper standards of morality and judgment. Zhuangzi's theory of the myriad things aligns with the worldview of the sameness of human and non-human nature, which erases the essential difference between human nature and the nature of things, a position Han Wŏnjin sees as diametrically opposed to the Confucian understanding of humanity and the ethical order.

For Han, Zhuangzi's idea of "treating all things equally" reflects a view in which all beings forget their differences and proper places, merging indiscriminately into sameness. As noted above, Zhuangzi traces the origin of all things to non-being, arguing that distinctions such as life and death, or large and small, derive from non-being and are therefore not distinguishable in essence.

Zhuangzi underscores the essential unity of self and the myriad things with the phrase, "Heaven and earth and I were born together; all things and I are one." At first glance, this resembles the idea in Zhang Zai's *Ximing*. Han Wŏnjin, however, emphasizes a crucial difference: Zhang Zai begins with the unified oneness of principle and moves outward to encompass the diversity of things, whereas Zhuangzi denies such diversity, throwing the unity of principle into confusion. By positing that void and substance, being and non-being coexist simultaneously, Zhuangzi treats truth and falsehood, right and wrong, as equivalent.

Zhuangzi frequently uses the phrase *insi* 因是 (based on this), signaling a simultaneous following of both right and wrong, ultimately leveling moral

---

of the myriad things not as liberating but as destabilizing, since it blurs the boundary between differing status of beings. The disagreement with Guo is therefore not simply about whether the *Zhuangzi* affirms unity or multiplicity; it concerns whether the structure of reality itself supports ethical differentiation. Guo discovers a self-ordering cosmos that needs no transcendent moral anchor, whereas Han insists that without a distinction, the Zhuangzian metaphysical monism dissolves the grounds of moral judgment and practice.

distinctions. From a Confucian perspective, this is not insight but a confusion of discernment—a distortion of moral principle.

Han Wŏnjin's critique of Zhuangzi also targets contemporaneous proponents of the theory that human and non-human nature are fundamentally the same. Although these theorists did not claim, as Zhuangzi did, that humans and things are identical based on *qi*, they made a similar error by asserting that at the most fundamental level, there is no essential difference between beings. In doing so, they failed to recognize the unique purity and superiority of the principle inherent to humans. For Han, just as with Zhuangzi, their theory cannot explain why a human is ultimately human and not merely another animal.

## Theory on Nurturing Life

Han Wŏnjin understands Zhuangzi's approach to self-cultivation is oriented toward the nourishment and preservation of life. This concept of nurturing life, for Zhuangzi, is primarily concerned with the protection and extension of one's own life, and is not with any greater good involving others or the community. From the perspective of Han Wŏnjin's Confucian tradition, however, the true aim of life-nourishment should not be limited to preserving and prolonging one's individual life. Rather, it should be connected to the protection and extension of a life that is broader, greater, and more enduring, one that transcends the self.

In his comments on the opening passage of Chapter 3, Han Wŏnjin points out that when Zhuangzi speaks of quietly practicing the Way without revealing either good or evil, this may seem like a method for preserving one's life, but in reality, it is nothing more than a technique for using cunning in secret. For example, when Zhuangzi says "[the perfected one] commits evil but avoids punishment," it is, according to Han Wŏnjin, a clear indication of a petty person attempting to engage in wrongdoing while evading consequences in order to preserve his life by ignoble means. Such conduct is evidently flawed. Another expression of Zhuangzi, "to do good without seeking honor," although outwardly resembling the attitude of the Confucian noble person, in fact differs in substance. For the true noble person in the Confucian tradition, distinctions between public and private, good and evil, must be clearly maintained. One must fear that goodness may lack real substance if it does not bring about proper consequences, and only then can virtue truly be cultivated.

Han Wŏnjin also interprets the ZZ phrase "following the middle as the norm," by explaining that "spine" (*tok* 督) refers to the central meridian of the human body, the "governor vessel" (*tongmaek* 督脈), which symbolizes a guiding standard running straight through the center, like the seam of a garment. From this image, Han indirectly argues that the path Zhuangzi proposes, avoiding both extremes of good and evil, is a mechanical median that merely circumvents both poles. This, he claims, is fundamentally different from the Confucian balanced harmony in daily life, *chungyong* (*zhongyong*), which calls for "dynamic" moral discernment appropriate to the context. Though Zhuangzi's idea of "centeredness" may outwardly resemble the Confucian ideal, Han Wŏnjin asserts that its true aim is to destroy moral standards, thus contradicting the *chungyong* principle of making deliberate, appropriate ethical decisions, according to context.

Additionally, in his commentary on one passage in Chapter Three, Han Wŏnjin reiterates a common Confucian criticism of Daoist arts of nurturing life, namely, that they are ultimately selfish. Zhuangzi, he argues, fails to consider the principle of the cosmos that transcends the individual. Han Wŏnjin argues that in the Confucian tradition, true nourishing life goes beyond mere care for the body and must extend to the transmission of the Way. The physical body is finite and will inevitably perish, but the Way transcends time and space and is eternal; thus, to realize the Way is the ultimate purpose of life nourishment. What Confucianism means when it says "the Way has no end" refers to the shared principle of heaven and earth, which operates universally across all things in the cosmos and exists independently of any individual person. Still, the Way within an individual is not separate from the Way of heaven and earth, and for that reason, one can say "my Way also does not perish." However, this does not mean that one's own Way personally endures after death, but rather that it returns and is subsumed into the greater Way of the cosmos.

In contrast, when Zhuangzi says "the Way has no end," the meaning is different from the Confucian one. Zhuangzi understands the Way as a formless, quiet *qi*, such that birth is the moment when one receives this *qi*, and death is the return of this *qi* to a dark, formless void. In this view, all things are born from the void-like *qi* and endlessly return to it in a cyclical pattern. But Han Wŏnjin criticizes this perspective as lacking a proper understanding of the transformation and dissipation of *qi*: once a person dies and the *qi* dissipates, it ceases to exist. Zhuangzi, he argues, fails to recognize this. Han further notes the resemblance of Zhuangzi's view to Buddhist doctrines such as "seeing one's nature and becoming a Buddha" or the idea of entering nirvana. He interprets this as evidence that the teachings of Lao-Zhuang philosophy evolved into Buddhism.

Ultimately, Han Wŏnjin asserts that Zhuangzi's understanding of the Way is *qi*-centered, while Confucianism is rooted in the heavenly principle. From this difference arises a fundamental divergence between the two traditions. Han also critiques the Daoist concept of non-action, viewing it as nothing more than a defeatist doctrine. From his perspective, it serves only to excuse the sage from the responsibility he ought to bear toward the world.

To Han Wŏnjin, the Lao-Zhuang doctrine of non-action reveals an attitude characterized by refusal to engage with worldly affairs, fear of committing errors, and a preoccupation with avoiding misfortune. This disposition, he argues, resembles the fault of Xiang Yuan who is a morally hollow conformist whom Confucius and Mengzi criticized for outward respectability but inner lack of virtue (*Lunyu* 17.13; *Mengzi* 7B83). It is for this reason that Han considers Zhuangzi's orientation no different from the conduct of Xiang Yuan, the morally suspect type whom Confucius and Mengzi identified as the enemies of true virtue.

In sum, Han Wŏnjin argues that Zhuangzi's advocacy of nourishing life elevates the attitude of preserving one's physical body and avoiding harm as the highest goal. Such a posture, he contends, is in essence no different from the learning of Xiang Yuan, one who flatters the world and pursues only their own comfort. Zhuangzi's teaching, to be sure, displays depth and subtlety in its application, and its lofty, free-flowing rhetoric gives the impression of something elevated. However, Han insists that despite this refined appearance, Zhuangzi's learning is in truth base and overly preoccupied with self-preservation, which makes it difficult for ordinary readers to discern its flaws. For Han, the extent to which Zhuangzi distorts virtue through such language and phrasing is deeply serious, and the essential nature of his thought differs little from Xiang Yuan's evasive and self-serving posture. Therefore, Han Wŏnjin stresses that those who follow the Way of Confucius must clearly distinguish right from wrong and devote themselves to illuminating the truth.

## "Being So of Itself" or "Spontaneity"

According to Zhuangzi, the ideal sage regards all things equally, entrusting oneself to the flow of the world, living without conflict or selfish desire, and peacefully yielding to fate. Central to this ideal is "spontaneity" (*chayŏn*; *ziran* 自然), expressed in the phrase "following things as they are, and making no room for personal views" 順物自然而無容私 (7.3). In this state, the mind is emptied, still, and free of intention. Zhuangzi's notion of "not knowing" embodies following nature as it is, while the "undifferentiated chaos" refers to the Way as spontaneity.

Han Wŏnjin, however, contends that this surrender to nature, grounded in mindlessness and unknowing, conflicts with the Confucian cultivation of virtue through human nature and principle. What Zhuangzi calls natural spontaneity is, for Han, a realm of absolute equality where distinctions of right and wrong, good and evil, beauty and ugliness vanish, and even the sense of self dissolves. By contrast, Confucian "following principle" entails eliminating selfish desire to discern right from wrong, good from evil, and proper roles and statuses for each thing, then acting in accordance with this understanding.

From Han's perspective, Zhuangzi's world of nature is one of sameness and equality only, a partial and biased world lacking distinction and judgment. Even Zhuangzi's celebrated idea of transformation of things (*mulhwa*; *wuhua* 物化), which suggests embracing endless change, contradicts his own emphasis on dissolving the self and achieving a state of unwavering stillness or mindlessness.

Commenting on a passage from the "Great Founding Master" chapter (6.2), Han Wŏnjin explains the phrase "to hide the world in the world" (*chang ch'ŏnha ŏ ch'ŏnha* 藏天下於天下) as to mean entrusting each thing entirely to itself. When things are left in their proper places and entrusted to their own natural course, they follow their own position and flow, leaving no room for anything to escape. If the world were hidden within a single household, then—as in history, when the Qin lost the world to Han, and Han to Wei—it would imply that the world had somewhere to flee. But if the world is hidden within the world itself, even if it is lost, it will eventually be recovered by the people of the world, and thus the world has nowhere to escape.

Zhuangzi, observing the ceaseless transformation of all things, holds that when a person dies, they become something else, and that thing may become a person again—what he calls "ten thousand transformations without end." If one accepts this process with equanimity, the self is never truly lost; transformation is the continuous unfolding of the self rather than its disappearance. Han Wŏnjin, however, argues that Zhuangzi's sage, though yielding to things, still harbors personal desires and ignores the role of principle as understood in Confucianism. Without recognizing the need to relinquish the self fully, Zhuangzi's view of nature, grounded in following the transformations of *qi*, risks self-centeredness, whereas Confucianism emphasizes conforming to principle.

Thus, for Han Wŏnjin's understanding, the Lao-Zhuang concept of "being so of itself" is different from that of Confucianism. In the Confucian view, what is called "natural" refers to listening to and accepting the heavenly mandate, and this implies that both human beings and all things recover and return to the principle together along the path of humaneness and longevity. In contrast, Zhuangzi and Laozi understand "being so of itself" as surrendering oneself to the transformations of *qi*, the result of which is ultimately nothing more than a state of boundless and unrestrained self-indulgence.

This difference is not merely one of terminology but reveals a fundamental divergence in the understanding of the Way itself. Thus, a seemingly minor distinction in how "being so of itself" is interpreted leads, in reality, to a deviation as wide as a thousand leagues. Han Wŏnjin acknowledges that Zhuangzi's political philosophy takes "being so of itself" as its governing principle, but he criticizes it as deeply flawed, since it is not the heavenly principle, but merely the fluctuating movements of *qi*.

## Conclusion

In sum, Han Wŏnjin criticizes Zhuangzi's concept of the Way as fundamentally opposed to Neo-Confucian principle and *qi*. Zhuangzi treats the Way as empty stillness or undifferentiation, equating it with non-being, whereas Han sees the Way as an ever-present principle operating through yin and yang, with existence emerging from it, contrary to the idea that existence arises from non-existence, which undermines moral order. Han also faults Zhuangzi for reducing the Way to *qi* and for idealizing non-action, no-mind, and ignorance, arguing that the Way is both tranquil and luminous, inherently moral, and requires ethical engagement.

Han further condemns Zhuangzi's doctrine of treating all things equally as heterodox. By denying distinctions of right and wrong, good and evil, and high and low, Zhuangzi rejects the yin-yang order and the Confucian principle. Particularly, his view that all things arise from and return to non-being erases moral discernment and echoes Buddhist nirvana. Zhuangzi's portrayal of the Way as a transcendent entity outside heaven and earth is also criticized; for Confucians, the Way is immanent and realized through moral action within the cosmos.

As such, Han Wŏnjin sees Zhuangzi's philosophy as superficially profound but fundamentally at odds with Neo-Confucian transmission of the Way. Its *qi*-centered egalitarianism, collapse of moral distinctions, and misreading of the Way and the mind reduce human virtue to passive insensibility, diverging from Confucian aims of principle-*qi* harmony and moral cultivation.

After all, *Changja pyŏnhae* is more than a textual commentary; Han used it to diagnose and critique the philosophical and social crises of late 18th-century Chosŏn Korea. He viewed the fragmentation of principle and the rise of heterodox thought as symptomatic of a society in ethical flux. Against this backdrop, Han argued that true understanding of the world and human nature depends on principle, not *qi*. Zhuangzi's doctrine of equality, he contended, is nihilistic, eroding moral discernment, while Confucian principle preserves individuality within diversity and grounds both personal morality and social order. Han argues that the true whole must rest on principle; *qi*-based egalitarianism is illusory.

This principle-centered philosophy also underpins Han's critique of theories equating or blurring the distinction between human and non-human nature. He saw both Zhuangzi's understanding of the Way and mind, and Yi Kan's claim that human nature and thing-nature are identical, as misreadings that confuse *qi* with principle. Yi Kan's view, like Zhuangzi's, treats empty *qi* or the pure mind as the Way, forming a heretical stance that undermines Confucian foundations.

In conclusion, Han used his critique of Zhuangzi to underscore that the essence of Confucianism lies in following principle as ordained by heaven—upholding differentiation and moral discernment. In *Changja pyŏnhae*, he warned that conflating *qi* and principle erodes moral order and social structure. By advocating a strictly principle-based, conservative philosophy, Han sought to correct Zhuangzi's errors and defend Confucian orthodoxy in 18th-century Chosŏn.

# Author's Preface

余少也讀莊生書，雖喜其文章之古奇，亦不能深解其意，廢而不復觀者久矣。今年冬，友人成君覺請授是書，復取而讀之，反覆數遍，似有得其要領者，然後始見其為彌近理而大亂眞也。既而又取諸家註說而觀之，蓋皆郢書燕說耳，殆如余前日之於是書也。於是盡棄其說，更以吾說授之。

When I was young, I read the works of Zhuangzi. Although I admired the antiquated elegance and strangeness of his prose, I could not fully grasp its meaning, so I put the book aside and did not return to it for a long time. This past winter (1716), when my friend Sŏng Kun'gak (dates unknown) requested that I teach him this book, I picked it up again, read it repeatedly, and it seemed that I had come to understand its essential points. Only then did I realize that, although its messages seemed closer to principle, it greatly distorted the truth.

Soon after, I again gathered and examined various scholars' commentaries and theories on the book, but found that most of them merely misunderstood the original meaning.[1] Perhaps, they were the same as what I had previously held about the book. Thereupon, I discarded all of their explanations and proceeded to teach about the text using my own interpretations instead.

既卒業，君覺請錄其說。余曰：余雖力微，不能焚絕其書，顧何忍為箋註？雖甚不腆，亦何可甘心為周之所謂萬世一遇之聖人歟？ 君覺曰：不然。是書之行於天下久矣，今不可以焚絕。既不能焚絕，則無寧就其書而明辨之？使其詖淫邪遁之說，無所遁於天下後世，亦豈不為吾儒之一大快事也？余曰：然。誠若子言，庶幾免於君子譏乎！

After the classes ended, Kun'gak asked me to record my interpretations. I replied, "Although I am powerless to the extent that I cannot burn this book and make it disappear, how could I possibly bring myself to annotate it? Though I am quite shallow in learning, how could I ever acknowledge Zhuang Zhou as a so-called sage encountered only once in ten thousand generations?"[2]

Kun'gak replied, "That is not the case. This book has circulated under heaven for a long time, and we cannot simply burn it and make it disappear now. Since we cannot destroy it, there is no other way but rather to confront the book

---

[1] The phrase *Yŏngsŏ Yŏnsŏl* (*Yingshu Yanshuo* 郢書燕說), which literally means "A man from Ying writes a letter, and a man from Yan interprets it," originates from a story in which a man from Ying, a region of Chu, sends a letter to the chancellor of Yan. Due to a scribal mistake, an unintended phrase is included in the letter. The chancellor, unaware of the error, interprets the phrase in a completely different way. This expression has come to imply the tendency to completely misinterpret the original intent of a written text. This story appears in *Hanfeizi* 韓非子 32.47.

[2] The expression *manse ilu ji sŏng'in* (*wanshi yiwu zhi shengren*, 萬世一遇之聖人), meaning "a sage encountered only once in ten thousand generations," appears in ZZ 2.12.

and offer a clear analysis of its meaning. If we made those depraved, licentious, heretical, and escapist doctrines have no place to hide in the world of our future generations, wouldn't that also be a great achievement for us Confucians?"

I said, "Indeed. If things were truly as you said, perhaps we might avoid the ridicule of the noble person."

遂令執筆書之，盡內篇而止。蓋以內篇既明，餘不待解說而明矣。錄既成，名之曰《莊子辨解》。因略識其撰述之意，如右云。
丙申冬日，南塘散人識。
[Thereupon,] I finally took up the brush and began writing, but stopped after completing the Inner Chapters. In general, with the commentaries on the Inner Chapters, the message was already made sufficiently clear, and the rest naturally becomes self-evident without the need for further explanation. Having completed the record, I titled it *Changja pyŏnhae*. For this reason, I have briefly stated the purpose behind its composition as above.

Recorded in the winter of the year Pyŏngsin (1716) by the Recluse of Southern Pond (i.e., Han Wŏnjin).

> 又按莊生論六經之旨曰：詩以道性情，書以道政事，禮以道行，樂以道和，易以道陰陽，春秋以道名分。程朱未出之前，能以一言提其綱而論之，未有若是之明且盡者也。然則周之學，不可謂不深矣，其於聖人之意，亦不可謂不知也。特於其本源上達處，有所未及者而肆言之，故其弊遂至於為異端，賊道之甚者矣。學之不可不達本源也，又如此云。
> Upon further examination, I found that Zhuangzi spoke of the essential points of the six classics, saying: "With the *Shi* (Poetry) one speaks of human nature and emotions; with the *Shu* (Documents) one discusses government affairs; with the *Li* (Rituals) one addresses conducts; the *Yue* (Music), one expresses harmony; with the *Yi* (Changes), one explains the states of yin and yang; and with the *Chunqiu* (Spring and Autumn Annals), one clarifies names and their allotted status."[3]
>
> Before the emergence of Masters Cheng and Zhu, no statement that could capture the essence of the classics and discuss it in a single phrase had possessed such clarity and comprehensiveness as this. Therefore, one cannot say that Zhuang Zhou's learning lacked depth, nor that he did not know [about the messages of the sage].

---

[3] The passage Han Wŏnjin cites appears in *Zhuangzi* 33.1. However, the version he quotes differs slightly from the version currently most widely used, *Zhuangzi jishi*, by Guo Qingfan. The version in *Zhuangzi jishi* reads:

> With the *Shi*, one speaks of intent; with the *Shu*, one discusses human affairs; with the *Li*, one addresses conducts; with the *Yue*, one expresses harmony; with the *Yi* one explains the states of yin and yang; and with the *Chunqiu*, one clarifies names and their allotted status
> 詩以道志，書以道事，禮以道行，樂以道和，易以道陰陽，春秋以道名分。

[However,] at the point where one should ascend to the very source, there are aspects he fails to reach yet speaks of them freely, the resulting error ultimately goes so far as to become heterodox and profoundly injurious to the Way. Thus, in learning, one cannot but penetrate to the source—this is precisely what is meant here.[4]

[4] It appears to refer to the following statement in *Lunyu* 14.35: "One should learn from below and thereby reach what is above" 下學而上達.

# Chapter 1

# Free and Easy Wandering[1]

此篇大指，只是一大字：逍遥遊者。逍遥乎萬物之表也，廣大自得之貌。言至人之道，其大出乎萬物之表，而物無得與竝也。
The main message of this chapter lies solely in the single grand concept of "Free and Easy Wondering." It refers to leisurely roaming over the surface of myriad things, with an appearance characterized by vastness and self-sufficient contentment. It speaks of the Way of the ultimate person, and its greatness emerges from the surface of the myriad things.[2] Things cannot stand on equal footing with such a person.[3]

### Section 1 (ZZ 1.1; 2)[4]

> 北冥有魚，其名為鯤。鯤之大，不知其幾千里也。化而為鳥，其名為鵬。鵬之背，不知其幾千里也；怒而飛，其翼若垂天之雲。是鳥也，海運則將徙於南冥。南冥者，天池也。
> In the northern darkness, there is a fish called Kun. The size of the Kun is beyond reckoning, extending for thousands of *li*. When it transforms into a bird, it is called Peng. The span of the Peng's back is also beyond measure, stretching for thousands of *li*. When it rouses itself to fly, its wings spread like clouds that

---

[1] Han Wŏnjin, as he states in the concluding part of his commentary on this chapter, views this first chapter as consisting of three divisions and does not divide and arrange this chapter into clearly separated sections as he does with other chapters. The exact reason for Han Wŏnjin's distinctive approach to this first chapter, an approach not seen in his commentaries on other chapters, is currently unknown.

[2] The exact meaning of "its greatness emerges from the surface of the myriad things" is unclear. If the term "surface" (*p'yo* 表) is understood in contrast to "interior" (*ri* 裏) or "within" (*nae* 內), and considered in relation to concepts in later chapters such as "no-mind" (*musim* 無心) or the equal treatment of all things (*chemul* 齊物), then the phrase might be understood as describing the attitude of the ultimate person who does not intervene deeply into the inner workings of things but instead regards them all with detached equanimity.

[3] The term *mul* 物 is difficult to render consistently in modern language. In this translation, the translator has chosen two main renderings depending on the context:

1) When *mul* is contrasted with the subject or self, as an external object, it is rendered as "external thing."
2) When *mul* is used in a neutral, general sense, it is translated simply as "thing."

[4] In the main text of the first chapter of Han Wŏnjin's *Pyŏnhae*, there are no clearly numbered divisions. However, following Han Wŏnjin's own organizational scheme mentioned at the end of the chapter, the segments have been numbered for the convenience of readers.

hang across the sky. This bird, when the sea begins to move, sets forth toward the southern darkness. The southern darkness is the celestial lake.

齊諧者，志怪者也。諧之言曰：鵬之徙於南冥也，水擊三千里，摶扶搖而上者九萬里，去以六月息者也。
The *Qixie* is a work that records the marvelous. In it is written: "When the Peng journeys to the southern darkness, the waves it lashes rise three thousand *li*. Riding the whirl of the wind, it ascends ninety thousand *li* upward, borne aloft on a breath that lasts half a year."[5]

篇首鵾鵬之大，以喻至人之道大. 其下又引野馬、塵埃、蜩鳩、斥鷃之小，以見鵾鵬之至^大也。[6]
At the beginning of this chapter, with the immense size of the fish Kun and the bird Peng, he allegorizes the greatness of the Way of the ultimate person. Following that, drawing the insignificance of "haze," "dust," "the cicada and the dove" (ZZ 1.1), and "the quail" (1.2), he highlights the extraordinary greatness of Kun and Peng.

野馬也，塵埃也，生物之以息相吹也。
Wild vapors and drifting dust are the breaths of living beings, blown about as they exhale and inhale among one another.

野馬、塵埃，物之至小者也，以息相吹，氣之至微者也。野馬、塵埃爲氣息所動. 鵬之徙南溟，得大風而徙，盖借小以見大也。
"Wild vapors and drifting dust" are the tiniest of things; being stirred by the breath, they show the subtlest movement of *qi*. The wild vapors and dust are set in motion by the flow of breath. When the Peng travels to the southern darkness, it rides on a great wind. This is to use the small to reveal the great.

天之蒼蒼，其正色邪？其遠而無所至極邪？其視下也亦若是，則已矣。
The deep blueness of the sky, is that truly its own hue? Or is it simply that distance stretches endlessly, with no limit in sight? If one were to gaze downward from above and see it appearing the same, that would settle the matter.

---

[5] Han Wŏnjin's *Changja pyŏnhae* does not include the original *Zhuangzi* text, but for the reader's convenience and to facilitate a more accurate understanding of Han Wŏnjin's commentary, the full passages of the *Zhuangzi* text, often referred to as "sections" (*tan; duan* 段) by Han Wŏnjin, have been reconstructed from his commentary and provided in brackets at the beginning of each section. All English translations of the original *Zhuangzi* text are mine.

[6] A caret (^) indicates that the character before the mark is missing in the Yŏam edition. For example, in the Yŏam edition, the character *chi* 至 is absent in this phrase.

天之蒼蒼，其遠無窮[極]，[7] 承上九萬里字，說来言鵬程之遠也．與野馬、塵埃對說言，野馬、塵埃之小爲氣息所動者，其所遊亦至近．鵬之大得大風而徙者，其所遊亦至遠也。
"The sky's deep blueness" speaks of its limitless expanse. The phrase "ninety thousand *li*" follows upon this, describing the boundless distance of the Peng's flight. This is set in contrast to "wild vapors and drifting dust": being minute things moved by the faint breath of *qi*, the range of their movement is exceedingly near. The Peng, vast in form and borne by a mighty wind, journeys to remote distances, and the reach of its flight knows no bounds.

> 且夫水之積也不厚，則負大舟也無力。覆杯水於坳堂之上，則芥為之舟，置杯焉則膠，水淺而舟大也。風之積也不厚，則其負大翼也無力。故九萬里則風斯在下矣，而後乃今培風；背負青天而莫之夭閼者，而後乃今將圖南。蜩與學鳩笑之曰：我決起而飛，搶榆、枋，時則不至而控於地而已矣，奚以之九萬里而南為？
> And moreover, if the accumulation of water is not deep, it cannot support a large boat. If one pours a cup of water into a hollow on the floor, a mustard seed might serve as a boat, but if you place a cup on it, it will stick; the water is shallow and the vessel too large. Likewise, if the accumulation of wind is not sufficient, it cannot carry a great wing. Only when the wind reaches a depth of ninety thousand *li* does it lie beneath, and then one may summon the wind; only when one carries the blue sky on one's back without obstruction can one plan a journey south. The cicada and the young dove laugh at this, saying: "When we take off, we fly, grasping at elm and poplar; at times we fail to reach our mark and are forced back to the ground. How could we ever fly ninety thousand *li* to the south?"

且夫以下，再申野馬、塵埃、天之蒼蒼之意。盃水、芥舟，即野馬、塵埃之類。九萬里，風斯在下，即鵬之翱翔於蒼蒼至遠之中也。且夫二字，當諦看。纔說前段，將說後段，而中間下一且字，則可見前後段之一意，而反覆[復]申明也。故凡看文字，當看其更端處，起頭一字。
From the phrase "And moreover" onward, the passage reiterates the ideas expressed in "wild vapors and drifting dust" and "the sky's deep blueness." The "cup of water" and the "mustard-seed boat" correspond to the likes of "wild vapors and drifting dust." "Ninety thousand *li*, with the wind beneath" refers to the Peng soaring within that vast blueness, traversing the utmost distance.

The two words "and" and "moreover" must be carefully noted: they both conclude the preceding section and introduce what follows. The placement of the single word "and" in between reveals the continuity of thought between the two parts and shows how the earlier meaning is restated and expanded. Therefore, whenever one reads a text, one must pay attention to its turning points, especially the very first word that begins a new movement.

---

7 Variants in the Yŏam edition are added in brackets.

蜩與學鳩笑之曰：我決起而飛，槍榆枋，時則不至而控於地而已矣，奚以之九萬里而南為？適莽蒼者三湌而反，腹猶果然；適百里者宿舂糧；適千里者三月聚糧。之二蟲又何知！

The cicada and the fledgling dove laughed at this, saying: "When we leap up and fly, we reach the elm and the cassia; at times we fall short and land upon the ground. Why speak of flying ninety thousand *li* to the south?"

Those who travel only to the edge of the fields can go and return after three meals, their bellies still full. Those who journey a hundred *li* must pound their grain the night before; those who go a thousand *li* must store up provisions for three months. How could such two small creatures comprehend any of this?

適莽蒼[+者],[8] 以喻蜩鳩之飛。適千里，以喻大鵬之圖南。故以之二蟲又何知，結之。

"Those who travel only to the edge of the fields" serves as a metaphor for the flight of the cicada and the dove. "Those who go a thousand *li*" symbolizes the Peng's southward venture. Thus, the phrase "How could such two small creatures comprehend?" brings the passage to its conclusion.

小知不及大知，小年不及大年。奚以知其然也？朝菌不知晦朔，蟪蛄不知春秋，此小年也。楚之南有冥靈者，以五百歲為春，五百歲為秋；上古有大椿者，以八千歲為春，八千歲為秋。而彭祖乃今以久特聞，眾人匹之，不亦悲乎！湯之問棘也是已。窮髮之北，有冥海者，天池也。有魚焉，其廣數千里，未有知其脩者，其名為鯤。有鳥焉，其名為鵬，背若泰山，翼若垂天之雲，摶扶搖羊角而上者九萬里，絕雲氣，負青天，然後圖南，且適南冥也。

Small knowledge cannot compare with great knowledge, and a short lifespan cannot compare with a long one. How do we know this to be so? The morning mushroom does not know of the waxing and waning of the moon, and the cicada does not know the passing of the seasons. These are cases of a short lifespan.

In the south of Chu there is a mystical and numinous one that counts five hundred years as spring and five hundred years as autumn; in ancient times there was the great Chun tree, who counted eight thousand years as spring and eight thousand years as autumn. As for Peng Zhu, his longevity is renowned today, yet when ordinary people compare themselves to him, is it not pitiful?

These are the questions posed by Tang to Ji: In the desolate northern wastes lies the dark and boundless ocean, called the celestial lake. In it dwells a fish called Kun, several thousand *li* across, though no one knows how long it truly is. There is also a bird called Peng, with a back like Mount Tai and wings that hang like clouds across the sky. Riding the whirling currents shaped like a ram's horn, it soars ninety thousand *li*, piercing the clouds and bearing the blue sky upon its back. Only then does it turn southward, setting its course for the southern darkness.

---

8 [+字] indicates that in the Yŏam edition, the character inside the brackets has been added at this position.

斥鴳笑之曰：彼且奚適也？我騰躍而上，不過數仞而下，翱翔蓬蒿之間，此亦飛之至也。而彼且奚適也？此小大之辯也。
A quail laughed at this, saying, "Where could it possibly be going? When I leap into the air, I barely rise a few *zhang* before falling back, flitting among weeds and brush—that is the fullest extent of my flight. And yet, where is it headed?" This is the distinction between the small and the great.

小大之辨四字，是一篇關鍵處，所以結上文而起下文也。上文以物之大小對說，故結之曰小大之辨。下文又將說人之小大，故又以此起之，而下文之首又以故一字承之，其意明矣。雖以小大對說，其實借小以見大也。此篇大指之在一大字者，又可見矣。
The phrase "the distinction between the small and the great" mark a pivotal point of this chapter, serving both to conclude what precedes and to introduce what follows. The earlier section contrasts the small and the great among things, which is why it closes with this phrase. The next section will discuss the small and the great among people, so the same phrase opens the following discussion, reinforced by the word "therefore,"[9] making the connection clear. Though [this passage] treats small and great comparatively, using the small to highlight the great, it is evident that the focus of the chapter rests on the single notion of greatness.

### Section 2 (ZZ 1.3; 4; 5)

故夫知效一官，行比一鄉，德合一君而徵一國者，其自視也， 亦若此矣。而宋榮子猶然笑之。且舉世而譽之而不加勸，舉世而非之而不加沮，定乎內外之分，辯乎榮辱之竟，斯已矣。彼其於世，未數數然也。雖然，猶有未樹也。
Therefore, a man whose knowledge suffices for a single office, whose conduct matches that of a single village, whose virtue meets [the approval of] a single ruler and manifests over a state—such a man's seeing himself is much like this.

Rongzi of Song would still laugh at him. Though the whole world may praise him, he feels no impulse to excel; though the whole world may blame him, he feels no shame or discouragement. He discerns clearly what is internal and external, and distinguishes the boundaries of honor and disgrace. That was all. In his dealings with the world, he remains unmoved. Yet even so, he has not yet firmly rooted himself.

夫列子御風， 而行泠然善也，旬有五日而後反。彼於致福者，未數數然也。此雖免乎行，猶有所待者也。若夫乘天地之正，而御六氣之辯，以遊無窮者，彼且惡乎待哉！故曰：至人無己，神人無功，聖人無名。
Liezi could ride the wind and drift with a cool and effortless ease, returning to the ground only after fifteen days. In matters of fortune, he remained unmoved. Though freed from worldly exertion, he still relied on something. If he had

[9] This refers to the conjunction in "Therefore, a man whose knowledge suffices for a single office" (*ko pu chi hyo il kwan* 故夫知效一官; ZZ 1.3).

ridden the correctness of heaven and earth, and mastered the transformations of the six *qi*, he could have wandered the boundless. How then could he have relied on something?

Hence it is said: The ultimate person has no self; the spirit-like person claims no merit; the sage has no name.

徵一國，徵驗也，言德之著於一國也。[10] 如中庸久則徵之。徵宋榮子，不以毀譽而有所勸沮，明乎內外之辨，而定乎取舍之分也。然猶有未樹，則蓋求道而未至於道者也。

In the phrase "manifesting over a state," "to manifest" here means to test or to make evident. It refers to virtue being fully displayed throughout an entire nation. It is like the case that when practicing balanced harmony in daily life, [one's virtue] becomes manifest. In the case of Rongzi of Song, it means that he was not moved to greater effort by praise, nor disheartened by blame; he clearly distinguished what was internal and external, and determined what to accept and what to reject. The phrase, "But he has not yet firmly rooted himself," means that although he seeks the Way, he has not yet fully reached it.

列子御風，風ˆ喻道。御風而行，遵道而行也。冷然善，沛然無所碍也。旬有五日而後返，言旬日之後與道相違也。如顏子三月不違仁，而三月之後不能無違仁者也。雖免乎行ˆ，猶有所待，則盖至於道而未能與道爲一者ˆ也。乘天地之正，御六氣之辨，非但御風而已也。以遊無窮，非但旬日而已也。彼得其一端[其小者]而或息[+而]，此有其全體而不息也。

In the phrase "Liezi could command the wind," the wind metaphorizes the Way. "He commands the wind and drifts" means he follows the Way and proceeds. "[Drifting] with a cool and effortless ease" means that he moves swiftly without any obstruction. "After fifteen days, he returns" suggests that after ten days, there begins to be a divergence from the Way. This is similar to the case that Master Yan (i.e., Yan Hui) could go three months without straying from benevolence (*Lunyu* 6.7), but after three months, he was not able to have nothing from which to stray from benevolence. Although [Liezi] avoided [going against the Way] in his actions, it seemed as if he was still relying on something; thus, even though he had nearly reached the Way, he was not yet able to become one with it. "If he rode the correctness of heaven and earth, and mastered the transformations of the six *qi*" indicates that this person is not merely controlling the wind. "By doing so, he can wander the boundless" means that he does not do so for only ten days. When he gains even a single clue about something, he breathes at times. This is how he comes to possess the whole and thus no longer breathes.

---

[10] In the Yŏam edition, the final phrase appears as "His virtue suffers in a corner" (*ŏn tŏk chi ko ŏ il chu ya* 言德之苦於一周也). It seems likely that the scribe of the Yŏam edition mistook the characters 著 and 國 for the similar-looking characters 苦 and 周.

惡乎待，言身則道，道^則身，不復相待也。蓋與道為一者^也。知效一官，行比一鄉，德合一君，斥鷃之類也。宋榮子以下，大鵬之類也。然宋榮子不及列子，列子不及乘天地御六氣者。於大之中，又分小大。蓋自下推上，極言其[爲]大也。至人、神人、聖人，即乘天地御六氣者，當看一故字。
The phrase "how could then he have relied on [something]?" means that he himself has become the Way, and the Way becomes himself. There is no longer any reliance on anything else; he has become one with the Way. The phrase "A man whose knowledge suffices for a single office, whose conduct matches that of a single village, whose virtue meets [the approval of] a single ruler" refers to a type of person akin to a quail.

The passage beginning with "Rongzi of Song" refers to a type of person like the great Peng bird. However, Rongzi of Song does not reach the level of Liezi, and Liezi does not reach the level of one who rides heaven and earth, and controls the six *qi*. Even among great things, there again is a distinction between the smaller and the truly exceptional. Moving from the lowest to the highest, Zhuangzi extraordinarily speaks of what is truly great.

The "ultimate person," the "spirit-like person," and the "sage" are precisely those who ride heaven and earth and control the six *qi*; thus, one should see [at the end] the character "therefore."[11]

> 堯讓天下於許由，曰：日月出矣，而爝火不息，其於光也，不亦難乎！時雨降矣，而猶浸灌，其於澤也，不亦勞乎！夫子立而天下治，而我猶尸之，吾自視缺然，請致天下。許由曰：子治天下，天下既已治也。而我猶代子，吾將為名乎？名者，實之賓也，吾將為賓乎？鷦鷯巢於深林，不過一枝；偃鼠飲河，不過滿腹。歸休乎君！予無所用天下為。庖人雖不治庖，尸祝不越樽俎而代之矣。
> Yao wished to yield all-under-heaven to Xu You, saying, "The sun and moon have already risen, yet torches continue to burn—how laborious that light is! The seasonal rains fall, yet the fields are still soaked—how exhausting that nourishment is! If you were to take the realm, all-under-heaven would be well governed, while I remain merely to witness my own shortcomings. I humbly beg to hand the world over to you."
>
> Xu You replied, "You govern the world, and the world is already in order. If I were to take your place, would it be for a name? A name is but a guest of reality—shall I act as its guest? The tailorbird builds its nest deep in the forest using no more than a single branch. The mole drinks from the river, taking only enough to fill its belly. Return home and rest, my lord; I have no need for the rulership of the world. Even if the cook neglects his kitchen, the priest and the ritual officiant do not abandon their cups and sacrificial vessels to take his place."

---

[11] It refers to the following line in the original text: "Therefore it is said: the ultimate person has no self, the spirit-like person has no merits, the sage has no name." 故曰：至人無己，神人無功，聖人無名。(ZZ 1.3).

肩吾問於連叔曰：吾聞言於接輿，大而無當，往而不反。吾驚怖其言，猶河漢而無極也，大有逕庭，不近人情焉。連叔曰：其言謂何哉？曰：藐姑射之山，有神人居焉，肌膚若冰雪，淖約若處子，不食五穀，吸風飲露。乘雲氣，御飛龍，而遊乎四海之外。其神凝，使物不疵癘而年穀熟。吾以是狂而不信也。

Jian Wu asked Lian Shu, "I once heard words from Jie Yu: 'Vast and unbounded, it moves forward and does not return.' I was startled and terrified by what he said; it seemed as infinite as the milky way, vast and remote, beyond human emotions."

Lian Shu asked, "What exactly did he mean?"

Jian Wu replied, "On the distant Mount Gushe, a spirit-like person dwell. His skin is like ice and snow, its sinews firm as a virgin's body. He does not eat the five grains, but draws in the wind and drinks the dew. Riding on clouds and commanding flying dragons, he roams beyond the four seas. His spirit is so concentrated that no harm comes to living things, and the harvests ripen well every year. I dismissed this as madness and could not believe it."

連叔曰：然，瞽者無以與乎文章之觀，聾者無以與乎鍾鼓之聲。豈唯形骸有聾盲哉？夫知亦有之。是其言也，猶時女也。之人也，之德也，將旁礴萬物，以為一世蘄乎亂，孰弊弊焉以天下為事！之人也，物莫之傷，大浸稽天而不溺，大旱、金石流、土山焦而不熱。是其塵垢粃糠，將猶陶鑄堯、舜者也，孰肯以物為事！

Lian Shu said, "Indeed. The blind cannot appreciate the beauty of written words; the deaf cannot hear the sound of bells and drums. Is it only the body that can be blind or deaf? Knowledge too can be limited, as your words just now have shown. Such a person [like the spirit-like one on Mount Gushe], with such virtue, is about to embrace all things and regard them as one. Though the world longs for order amid chaos, who would exhaust themselves over worldly affairs? Such a person is unharmed by anything: floods reach to heaven yet do not drown him; droughts, molten stone, or scorched mountains do not harm him. Even the dust, dirt, and husks are like clay to be shaped, as if one were molding Yao and Shun—who would concern themselves with worldly things?

堯與許由、肩吾連叔問答二段，皆言至人之大，而許由又不及藐姑射之神人，亦前段之意也。[12]

The two sections (ZZ 1.4; 5), composed of the dialogues between "Yao and Xu You" and "Jian Wu and Yan Shu," both speak of the greatness of the ultimate person. However, Xu You also does not reach the level of the spirit-like person who dwells in a remote Mount Gushe, and thus the meaning is the same as that of the preceding section.

不食五穀，吸風飲露，喻不為世俗之所為也。乘雲御龍，遊乎四海之外，如上文乘天地，御六氣，遊於無窮之意也。神凝至年穀熟，言至人之德及於萬物，非但徼一

[12] In the Yŏam edition, this paragraph and the following one are not separated.

國也。不溺、不熱，言至人之無所動於貧賤、憂慽等外患也，非謂真。有入水不溺、入火不熱之事也。周之文大ˆ抵ˆ皆寓言。讀者當看其主意所在，不可直就言語文字而求之也。
The phrase "He does not eat the five grains, but draws in the wind and drinks the dew" is a metaphor indicating that he does not engage in the things of the secular world. The expression "Riding on clouds and commanding flying dragons, he roams beyond the four seas" conveys the same meaning as the earlier passage about "riding heaven and earth, controlling the six *qi*, and freely roaming in the realm of the boundless." From "focusing his spirit" to "the harvests ripen well every year," it means that the virtue of the ultimate person reaches all beings, not just manifesting one state. The phrases "not drowning" and "not be burned" signify that the ultimate person is unmoved by external afflictions such as poverty, low status, anxiety, or suffering, things that are said to be not aligned with what is truthful. He may enter water without drowning or fire without burning.

Zhuang Zhou's writing is, for the most part, composed in allegory, so the reader must attend to where the gist lies and must not try to extract it by clinging to the literal words and phrases

> 宋人資章甫而適諸越，越人斷髮文身，無所用之。
> A man from Song, carrying his ritual cap, once went to Yue; but the people of Yue, who cut their hair short and tattoo their bodies, had no use for it.

章甫喻至人之道滅，人喻世人之無知。[13] 盖與上文聾瞽之說相應。
"The ritual cap" is a metaphor for the disappearance of the Way of the ultimate person, while the "people" of [Yue] are a metaphor for the ignorance of people in the world. This corresponds to the story in the previous passage about the deaf and the blind.

> 堯治天下之民，平海內之政，往見四子藐姑射之山，汾水之陽，窅然喪其天下焉。 堯治天下之民，平海內之政，往見四子藐姑射之山，汾水之陽，窅然喪其天下焉。
> Yao governed the people under heaven and brought order to the affairs within the seas. When he went to visit the four masters on Mount Gushe, south of the Fen River, he became inwardly lost and forgot his dominion over the world.

堯治天下一段，總結知效[効]一官以下之意。
The section "Yao governed the world" brings to a conclusion all the meanings from the previous passages that start with the line "knowledge suffices for a single office."

---

13 In the Yŏam edition, the character *myŏl* 滅 is written as *wŏl* 越, in which case the sentence reads as follows: "The ritual cap of the Yin is a metaphor for the Way of the Ultimate Person, and the people of Yue are a metaphor for the ignorance of ordinary people" 章甫喻至人之道，越人喻世人之無知。

## Section 3 (ZZ 1.6; 7)

惠子謂莊子曰：魏王貽我大瓠之種，我樹之成而實五石，以盛水漿，其堅不能自舉也。剖之以為瓢，則瓠落無所容。非不呺然大也，吾為其無用而掊之。
Huizi said to Zhuangzi, "The King of Wei gave me seeds of a great gourd. I planted them, and when they grew, each fruit was large enough to hold five *shi*. I used it to hold water and drink, but it was so heavy and hard that I could not lift it. I split one open to make a dipper, yet it was so wide and ungainly that it could not hold anything. Though it was indeed vast, I found it useless, so I smashed it."

莊子曰：夫子固拙於用大矣。宋人有善為不龜手之藥者，世世以洴澼絖為事。客聞之，請買其方百金。聚族而謀曰：我世世為洴澼絖，不過數金；今一朝而鬻技百金，請與之。客得之，以說吳王。越有難，吳王使之將。冬，與越人水戰，大敗越人，裂地而封之。能不龜手一也，或以封，或不免於洴澼絖，則所用之異也。今子有五石之瓠，何不慮以為大樽而浮乎江湖，而憂其瓠落無所容？則夫子猶有蓬之心也夫！
Zhuangzi replied, "You, sir, are truly clumsy in making use of what is great. There was once a man in Song who knew how to make an ointment that kept hands from cracking. For generations, his family had used it to soften raw silk. A guest heard of it and offered a hundred pieces of gold for the formula. The family gathered to discuss it, saying, 'For generations, we have used this only for washing silk, earning but a few coins each year. Now, in one day, we can sell it for a hundred gold pieces. Let us sell it.' The guest then took the formula to the King of Wu. When Wu went to war with Yue and fought on the rivers in winter, the guest, using this ointment, led the navy to victory, and the king rewarded him with a fief. The salve that kept hands from cracking was the same, yet one man gained a fief while the other remained a humble washer of silk—the difference lay only in how it was used. Now you have a gourd that can hold five *shi*. Why not hollow it out to make a great vessel, float upon the rivers and lakes, and drift freely, instead of fretting that it is too wide and empty to contain anything? It would seem, sir, that you still harbor a cramped and confined mind."

惠子謂莊子曰：吾有大樹，人謂之樗。其大本擁腫而不中繩墨，其小枝卷曲而不中規矩，立之塗，匠者不顧。今子之言，大而無用，眾所同去也。
Huizi said to Zhuangzi, "I have a great tree that people call the ailanthus. Its large trunk is gnarled and swollen, unfit for the carpenter's line; its small branches are twisted and crooked, unfit for compass or square. It stands by the roadside, yet no craftsman will so much as glance at it. Your words are like this tree—vast, but useless, and thus shunned by all."

莊子曰：子獨不見狸狌乎？卑身而伏，以候敖者；東西跳梁，不避高下；中於機辟，死於罔罟。今夫斄牛，其大若垂天之雲。此能為大矣，而不能執鼠。今子有大樹，患其無用，何不樹之於無何有之鄉，廣莫之野，彷徨乎無為其側，逍遙乎寢臥其下？不夭斤斧，物無害者，無所可用，安所困苦哉！

> Zhuangzi said, "Have you never seen the wildcat or the weasel yourself? It crouches low, waiting for its prey; it darts east and west, leaping high and low, yet it ends up caught in traps and nets. Now take the yak—it is as huge as a cloud hanging in the sky. That, indeed, is greatness, yet it cannot catch a mouse. You, sir, have a great tree, and you worry that it is useless. Why not plant it in the wilderness of nowhere, in the broad plain of vast nothingness, where you may wander freely by its side or rest and sleep beneath its shade? It will never be cut down by axe or hatchet, and nothing will harm it. Having no use, what cause would it have for suffering?"

惠子莊子問答両段，承上文小大之辨，而皆言用大之術。盖讀此篇者，當知能與所能之辨。堯治天下以上，極言道之大，即所ˆ謂ˆ所能也。惠子以下，皆言用大之術，所謂能也。[14] 朱子以看花折柳喻能所，看折是能，[15] 花柳是所能也。

The two sections, composed of dialogues between Huizi and Zhuangzi (ZZ 1.6; 7), continue the theme from the previous passage concerning "the distinction between the small and the great," and both discuss the art of applying the great.

Readers of this section should recognize the distinction between "ability" and "object of ability."[16] The passages up to "Yao governed the world" (ZZ 1.5) fully explore the greatness of the Way; it is about what is called "object of ability." [In contrast,] the passages beginning with Huizi discuss the arts of applying that greatness; this is about what is called "ability." Master Zhu, using the example of "seeing flowers and picking willow branches," explains the difference between "ability" and "object of ability." [The act of] seeing and picking is "ability," while the flowers and willows are "the object of ability."[17]

---

14 In the Yŏam edition, the final phrase appears as *chŭk sowi sonŭng ya* 即所謂所能也. Based on the Yŏam edition's own distinction between *nŭng* 能 and *sonŭng* 所能, the second *so* 所 here seems to have been mistakenly inserted.

15 In the Yŏam edition, it is written as *yunŭng sonŭng kanjŏl siŭng* 有能所能，看折是能 (there is ability and the object of ability. Seeing and picking is ability).

16 In Buddhism, there is the concept of *nengsuo* 能所, where the active or subjective aspect of an action, behavior, perception, or event is referred to as *neng* 能, and the objective aspect is referred to as *suo* 所. This distinction can also be expressed in terms such as active and passive, subject and object, or agent and recipient. If the subject that perceives an object through conceptual engagement is called "the one who engages" (*nengyuan* 能緣) or "the one who knows" (*nengshi* 能識), then the object that is engaged with and perceived is called "the object of engagement" (*suoyuan* 所緣) or "the object of knowing" (*suoshi* 所識). Likewise, the one who sees is "the seeing subject" (*nengjian* 能見), and that which is seen is "the seen object" (*suojian* 所見). When such dualities or oppositions arise, one cannot enter into the true principle (*zhenli* 真理) of the absolute realm (*juedui jing* 絕對境), where all relativity is cut off. Therefore, in Buddhism, the aim is to transcend such dualistic oppositions.

17 In his "Da Lü Ziyue" 答呂子約, Zhu Xi wrote:

> There is a theory in Buddhist texts concerning "ability" and "the object of ability." "Ability" refers to what a person does, while "the object of ability" refers to that which a person acts upon. For instance, the Way corresponds to the object of ability while

## Concluding Remarks

篇當作三節。看自篇首至小大之辨，共為一大節，引物以明大小之分。知效[効]一官以下，至窅然喪天下，共為一大節，舉人以明大小之分。惠子謂莊子至終篇，共為一大節，承上小大之辨，以明用大之術。[+言即]下筆第一，言鵾鵬之大；終以用大結之，而中間極言小大之辨，借小喻大，而却出小大之辨四字，以該之第二節。以上只言大字，而近末方下一用字，首尾相應，展鋪有序，文章機軸，無不備矣。夫謂莊周之文無有倫序，而特其句語之奇而已者，可謂不知讀周之文矣。
This chapter is properly divided into three parts: From the beginning of the chapter up to "discerning the great and the small," it constitutes one large section, in which the distinction between the great and the small is clearly illustrated through references to [existing] things. From "knowledge suffices for a single office" to "forgetting [ruling] the world," it forms another large section, where the difference between the great and the small is clarified through examples of people. From "Huizi said to Zhuangzi" to the end of the chapter, it forms yet another major section, continuing from the earlier "discerning the great and the small" and elaborating on the art of employing greatness.

As the brush was set to the page, it began by discussing the vastness of Kun and Peng, and concluded this chapter with an explanation of the method of employing greatness. In the middle, it spoke exceptionally well about the distinction between the small and the great, using the small to enlighten the great, and it also emerges from the phrase of "distinction between the small and the great," all the discussions of which comprise the second section. In the earlier parts, it speaks only of the concept of "greatness," but as it nears the end, it consistently turns to write about the word "to use."

The beginning and end of this chapter correspond well with each other; the progression of the writing follows a clear order, and the composition of the sentences lacks nothing in structure and coherence. Generally, people say that Zhuang Zhou's writings have no order and that, particularly, his phrases and words are only bizarre, but such views reveal that they do not truly understand how to read Zhuang Zhou's prose.

---

learning corresponds to ability. To give an example: nowadays, when children compose paired phrases, they might say 'looking at flowers and picking willows.' Here, the acts of 'looking' and 'picking' are ability, and 'flowers' and 'willows' are the objects of ability. (*Huian xiansheng Zhu Wengong wenji* 48.19a)
佛書有能與所能之說。能謂人所做作，所能謂人所做作底事。如道則所能之謂，學卽所謂能也。如如今小兒屬對，看花折柳，看與折字是能，花與柳是所能。.

# Chapter 2

# On Treating All Things Equally

前篇言至人之道大，而至人之所以大者，在於齊萬物而為一，故齊物次之。齊，一也。物論猶言衆論也，言合衆論而為一也。
The previous chapter spoke of the greatness of the Way of the ultimate person. The reason the ultimate person is great lies in that they treat all things equally and regard them as one. Therefore, "treating all things equally" follows thereafter. "To treat equally" means "to make one" or "to regard as one." The term "discourses on things" is another way of saying "numerous opinions." [The title] refers to bringing together the various discussions and regarding them as one.

**Section 1 (ZZ 2.1)**

> 南郭子綦隱几而坐，仰天而嘘，嗒焉似喪其耦。顏成子游立侍乎前，曰：何居乎？形固可使如槁木，而心固可使如死灰乎？今之隱几者，非昔之隱几者也。子綦曰：偃，不亦善乎而問之也！今者吾喪我，汝知之乎？
> Ziqi of Southern Fortress was leaning on a table and sitting quietly, gazing up at heaven and exhaling slowly, lost in a state that seemed as though he had lost his companion. Ziyou of Yancheng stood before him in attendance and said, "Lord, what kind of state is this? Can the body indeed grow as still as withered wood, and the mind truly become like dead ashes? The one who reclines on the table now is not the same as the one who reclined before."
>
> Ziqi said, "Yan! What a fine question you ask! Just now, I have lost myself—do you understand what that means?"

第一段，喪我，言忘其身也。忘其身，則視天地萬物為一，不復知有彼我之分也。篇首即ˆ出喪我二字，以該一篇齊物之意，而與篇末物化二字相為終始。
The first section. The phrase "I have lost myself" means one's forgetting oneself. When one forgets oneself, he sees heaven, earth, and all things as one, no longer aware of any distinction between self and other. The chapter begins with the phrase "I have lost myself," which encapsulates the theme of treating all things equally, and corresponds to the closing words "transformation of things" (ZZ 2.14), forming the beginning and end [of the chapter].

## Section 2 (ZZ 2.1)

［子綦曰：］... 女聞人籟而未聞地籟，女聞地籟而未聞天籟夫！子游曰：敢問其方。子綦曰：夫大塊噫氣，其名為風。是唯无作，作則萬竅怒呺。而獨不聞之翏翏乎？山林之畏佳，大木百圍之竅穴，似鼻，似口，似耳，似枅，似圈，似臼，似洼者，似污者；激者，謞者，叱者，吸者，叫者，譹者，宎者，咬者，前者唱于而隨者唱喁。泠風則小和，飄風則大和，厲風濟則眾竅為虛。而獨不見之調調、之刁刁乎？子游曰：地籟則眾竅是已，人籟則比竹是已。敢問天籟。

[Ziqi continued,] "You have heard the piping of men, but not yet the piping of earth. You have heard the piping of earth, but not yet the piping of heaven!"

Ziyou asked, "May I ask by what means?"

Ziqi replied, "The great clod exhales its breath—this is what we call wind. When it does not stir, all is still; but once it stirs, all the myriad hollows give forth their cries. Have you not heard their long and resonant sounds? In the deep mountains and thick forests, among great trees a hundred spans around, there are hollows and cavities shaped like noses, mouths, ears, goblets, rings, mortars, and basins, some round, some uneven. When the wind passes through, some sounds strike sharply, others hiss, bellow, gasp, or whistle; those ahead begin the song, and those behind answer in harmony. When the breeze is gentle, the tones blend softly; when the gale is fierce, the chorus grows vast. But when the wind has passed, the openings fall silent again. Do you not see how their sounds rise and cease?"

Ziyou said, "The piping of earth, then, comes from all these hollows; the piping of men is what we make with bamboo flutes. May I ask, then, about the piping of heaven?"

第二段，人籟、地籟、天籟。籟聲[起]也。人籟，人之所吹也。比竹之聲[起]是也。地籟，地之所吹也。衆竅之聲[起]是也。天籟，天之所吹也。衆口之言是也。故下文以比竹言人籟，衆竅言地籟,[1] 吹萬言天籟,[2] 吹萬，即衆口之言，而所謂物論也。天以真宰，言衆口之言，莫非真宰之所吹，故以物論為天籟。

The second section. In the phrase, "the piping of men, the piping of earth, the piping of heaven," the word "piping" means its sound. The "the piping of men" refers to that which is blown by humans, namely, the sound of a bamboo flute. The "piping of earth" refers to that which is blown by the earth, that is, the sounds that arise from all the holes on the ground. The "piping of heaven" refers

---

[1] In the Yŏam edition, *chiroe* 地籟 appears as *illoe* 人籟. Since Han Wŏnjin has already defined the *chiroe* just above as "the sound of the earth's blowing, the sounds of many apertures" 地籟，地之所吹也。衆竅之聲, the *illoe* in the Yŏam edition is a scribal error for *chiroe*.

[2] In the Yŏam edition, this entire sentence starting from this phrase is omitted. Unlike the Kyujanggak edition, which reiterates and elaborates on the concepts of *illoe*, *chiroe*, and *ch'ŏlloe* in this sentence, the Yŏam edition interprets the sentence solely in relation to *illoe* and derives the concept of discourses on things from this idea of *illoe*. However, as will be seen later, Han Wŏnjin understands the discourses on things not as stemming from *illoe*, but from *ch'ŏlloe*.

to that which is blown by heaven, namely, the words spoken from countless mouths. Thus, in the following passage, the bamboo flute is used to explain the "piping of men"; the various holes on the earth are used to describe the "piping of earth"; and the mouths where numerous [words] are uttered are used to describe the "piping of heaven." That "ten thousand kinds of words are uttered" refers to the words that come from the mouths of countless people; this is called "discourses on things."

Heaven, through the concept of the "true sovereign,"[3] speaks through the words that come from the mouths of countless people. No single utterance among them in which the true sovereign does not make. Therefore, [Zhuang Zhou] regards discourses on things as the piping of heaven.

盖比竹之聲[起]不同，而同出[大]於人之所吹；衆竅之聲[起]不同，而同出[大]於地之所吹；衆口之言不同，而同出[大]於真宰之所吹。異者本同，三者皆然也。然人籟易聞，而地籟難聞；地籟易聞，而天籟難聞。故先言人籟，次言地籟，次言天籟。借人籟以喻地籟，借地籟以喻天籟。從粗說入精，從浅說入深。使人易曉人籟，人所已聞；地籟，人所未聞。故下文不復言人籟，只言地籟，而天籟尢人之所未聞。故待其問，而言之。大塊，地也。畏住[隹]，崔崔也。從者作畏。

The sound of bamboo flutes is not all the same, yet what they have in common comes from being blown by human beings. The sound of the various holes upon the earth is not all the same, yet what they have in common comes from being blown by the earth. The words uttered from countless mouths are not all the same, yet what they have in common comes from being blown by the true sovereign. The differences are originally from the same origin. This is the case in all three instances.

However, the "piping of men" is easy to hear, while the "piping of earth" is more difficult to hear; and the "piping of earth" is easy to hear, while the "piping of heaven" is more difficult to hear. This is why [Zhuangzi] speaks first of the "piping of men," then of the "piping of earth," and only afterward of the "piping of heaven."

By using the "piping of men" to illuminate the "piping of earth," and using the "piping of earth" to illuminate the "piping of heaven" he describes a progression from the coarse to the refined, and from the shallow to the profound. It allows people to easily understand that the "piping of men" is something they have already heard, whereas the "piping of earth" is something they have not yet heard. Therefore, in the following passage, the "piping of men" is no longer discussed; only the "piping of earth" is mentioned, while it is further emphasized that the "piping of heaven" is something people have yet to hear. And thus, [Zhuangzi] waits for another question,[4] and then goes on to explain that the great clod is the earth itself.

---

[3] This concept first appears in section 8 below as well as in ZZ 2.3.

[4] This refers to the line in the original text, "Ziyou said, 'May I ask by what means?'" 子游曰：敢問其方。

As for the phrase ["the mountains and thickets are] "awe-inspiring and still,"[5] the phrase means "twisting and lofty." [Later] followers have rendered it as awe-inspiring.

[+佳]隆起茂盛之貌,[6] 大塊噫氣，萬竅怒號，言一[人]氣所動，衆聲紛挐，盖如程先生隙中日光之喻。然程先生以理言，周以氣言；程先生以物性言，周以物論言。此其不同也。厲風濟，則衆竅為虛，言衆聲生於無，而ˆ復歸於無也。盖此一段已包括齊物之意。

[The phrase "awe-inspiring and still"] refers to the appearance of the earth rising and the thickets growing densely. The phrases "The great clod breathes *qi* out" and "the hollows of all things begin to cry out" describe the movement of a single *qi*, producing a cacophony of all kinds of sounds. This is like Master Cheng's metaphor of "sunlight entering through a crack."[7] Master Cheng spoke

---

[5] These two characters appear in the phrase *sallim-ji oe ch'oe* 山林之畏佳 in the original text.

[6] In the Yŏam edition, this paragraph is not separated from the previous one, unlike the Kyujanggak edition. This arrangement allows these sentences to be interpreted as flowing more smoothly, without interruption. The editing and structure found in the Yŏam edition appear to correct an error present in the Kyujanggak edition.

[7] "The sunlight shining through a crack" (*kyŏkjung ilgwang-ji ron* 隙中日光之論) is a philosophical metaphor. It expresses that when sunlight passes through even the smallest crevice, it does not appear as a fragmented or diminished part, but rather as a manifestation of the entire sun. This illustrates that even the tiniest thing reveals the fullness of its essence and function. The wholeness of the whole is reflected in the part (the microcosm reflecting the macrocosm), suggesting that principle or the Way is fully present everywhere. Zhu Xi writes as follows:

> In the section "What is called nature is that which is born with" [from *Mengzi* 6A3], Mengzi discusses the difference between the nature of human beings and the nature of things. Truly, what is received from *qi* is not the same, and if we seek the reason for this, it lies in the fact that the quality and distribution of *qi* are not identical, and the principle endowed is likewise truly different. This is why Mengzi distinguishes between the nature of a dog, the nature of an ox, and the nature of a human being, yet does not speak of differences in the *qi* of dogs, oxen, and humans. The same reasoning applies to the section where he speaks of how humans differ from birds and beasts (*Mengzi* 4B47).
> 生之謂性一章，論人與物性之異。固由氣稟之不同，但究其所以然者，却是因其氣稟之不同，而所賦之理固亦有異。所以孟子分別犬之性、牛之性、人之性有不同者，而未嘗言犬之氣、牛之氣、人之氣不同也。人之所以異於禽獸一章，亦是如此。

If the previously mentioned view that the nature of humans and the nature of things are the same were correct, then Mengzi' words would be improper, and instead, it would be Gaozi's view that all whites—whether of snow, feathers, or jade—are indistinguishable, that would become the more valid argument.

On this point, Master Cheng offered the illuminating "sunlight through a crack" analogy. It is an exceptionally kind and lucid explanation, showing how to perceive difference within sameness, and sameness within difference. One must carefully reflect on this. Once that is done, and one revisits the words of the sages repeatedly, there is no contradiction among them whatsoever.

in terms of principle, while Zhuang Zhou spoke in terms of *qi*; Master Cheng discussed the nature of things, whereas Zhuang Zhou spoke through discourses about things. These are their differences.

The phrase "once the great wind passes, the hollows fall silent again" expresses that all sounds arise from non-being and return again to non-being. This single passage already contains the meaning of "treating all things equally."

## Section 3 (ZZ 2.1)

> 子綦曰：夫吹萬不同，而使其自已也，咸其自取，怒者其誰邪！
> Ziqi said, "Blowing on the myriad things in a different way, so that each can be itself, all take what they want for themselves, but who is it that stirs it all up?"

第三段，此以下至終篇，即釋[敍]天籟也。吹萬不同，怒者其誰，借上萬字怒字，而言吹萬不同，言衆論之不同也。怒者其誰，言使之有是衆論者一也。一者，即所謂真宰之天也，即周所謂虛無之道也。前段大塊噫氣，萬竅怒號，一本之散為萬殊也。此段吹萬不同[論]，怒者其誰，萬殊之歸於一本也。萬物出於一，而復歸於一。故至人^之^[+今]體是道者，必齊萬物而為一也。

The third section. From this paragraph to the end of the chapter, the text offers an interpretation of the "piping of heaven." The expressions "blowing on the myriad things in a different way" and "who is it that stirs it all up?" borrow the previous terms "myriad" and "anger" to explain the meaning of the phrase "blowing on the myriad things in a different way," namely that all human discourses are not the same. And "who is it that stirs it all up?" expresses that what allows for the existence of all such discourses is one and the same.

That "one" is what is referred to as "the true sovereign," which is heaven itself. What Zhuang Zhou calls the Way of emptiness and non-being. The previous paragraph's phrase, "the great clod exhales *qi*, and ten thousand holes roar in anger," describes how one root source becomes manifested into myriad differences. [In contrast,] this section's "blowing on the myriad things in a different way" and "who does the sounding" convey how those myriad differences return to one root. Myriad things are born from the one and return to the one. Therefore, for the ultimate person to realize this Way means necessarily treating all things equally and regarding them as one.

---

However, if one clings to a single-sided view and each side insists on its own reasoning, they end up evading each other, contradicting and diverging, and for the rest of their lives, there will never be a moment when they can reconcile and unify their understandings. (*Huian ji* 61.115)

若如所論，則孟子之言為不當，而告子白雪、白羽、白玉之白更無差別，反為至論矣。程先生有一處有隙中日光之論，最為親切，更須詳味於同中識其所異，異中見其所同。然後聖賢之言反覆，都不相礙。若只據一偏，各說道理，則互相逃閃，終身間隔，無復會通之時矣。

然在吾儒見處，則ˆ一本萬殊，皆理也。在周之見處，則一本萬殊，皆氣也。理一於善，氣雜於善惡。故以理齊之，則事事物物之上，一循天，則無一毫私意之間隔，而萬物真得其齊矣。以氣[+言]齊之，則事事物物之間，真妄是非，錯雜混淆，其所以齊之者，不過以私意強之，而萬物終不得其齊矣。此朱子所謂彌近理，而大亂真者也。自此至第七段，皆言物論之不同，盖廣說十六段彼是之意。
However, from our Confucian perspective, both the one origin and the ten thousand manifestations fall within [the domain of] principle. From Zhuang Zhou's perspective, both the one origin and the ten thousand manifestations fall within [the domain of] *qi*. Principle is consistently aligned with the good, while *qi* is a mixture of good and evil. Therefore, if one treats things equally through principle, then in all situations and matters, one follows heaven consistently, leaving not even the slightest space for selfish intentions, and allowing all things to truly become equal. But if one treats things equally through *qi*, then in all situations and matters, truth and delusion, right and wrong become chaotically mixed. [As a result,] this attempt at making all things equal fails to transcend personal intent and is forcibly imposed, and in the end, all things fail to attain true equal status. This is what Master Zhu referred to when he said, "It comes close to principle, but greatly confuses what is truthful."[8]

From this point up to the seventh section, they speak entirely about the non-uniformity of "discourses on things." Broadly speaking, it also addresses the theme of distinguishing *this* and *that* discussed in the sixteenth section.

## Section 4 (ZZ 2.2)

> 大知閑閑，小知閒閒；大言炎炎，小言詹詹。
> Great knowledge is expansive and unhurried; small knowledge is confined and restless. Great words are calm and lucid; small words are sharp and contentious.

第四段，知，知ˆ識也。言，言ˆ議也。知識、言ˆ議ˆ即所謂物論也。大、小即物[+之]論之有不同也，承上文吹萬不同而言也。
The fourth section. "Knowledge" refers to understanding, and "words" refers to discourse. Understanding and discourse are what is called "discourses on things." The notions of "great" and "small" indicate the inconsistency or non-uniformity in these discourses on things. This continues the meaning of the phrase "blowing on the myriad things in a different way" from the previous passage.

## Section 5 (ZZ 2.2)

> 其寐也魂交，其覺也形開，與接為構，日以心鬬。
> In sleep, the soul goes wandering; in waking hours, the body scurries about. With everything one encounters, they (i.e., soul and body) become entangled, day after day, exhausting the mind in conflict.

[8] See Zhu Xi, "Preface" 序, *Zhongyong zhangju* 中庸章句, 3.

第五段，言ˆ事物之日接於心，物論之所由生也。
The fifth section. [This line] conveys that when every affair or object touches the mind daily, it is where discourses on things arise

**Section 6 (ZZ 2.2)**

> 縵者、窖者、密者。小恐惴惴，大恐縵縵。
> Those who are vain, devious, or narrow-minded—when faced with small fears, they grow jittery and uneasy; when faced with great fears, they become numb and overwhelmed.

第六段，縵者、窖者、密者，言人品之不同。小恐、大恐，言接物感動之不同，物論之ˆ所以有不同也。此二段承上文大知一段，而詳言之。
The sixth section. "Those who are vain, devious, or narrow-minded" refer to the differences in human character. The terms "small fears" and "great fears" express how emotional movements vary when [the mind] comes into contact with things, and this is why discourses on things have differences. These two sections elaborate further on the preceding passage about "great knowledge."

**Section 7 (ZZ 2.2)**

> 其發若機栝，其司是非之謂也；其留如詛盟，其守勝之謂也；其殺如秋冬，以言其日消也；其溺之所為之，不可使復之也；其厭也如緘，以言其老洫也；近死之心，莫使復陽也。喜怒哀樂，慮嘆變慹，姚佚啟態；樂出虛，蒸成菌。
> Its (i.e., the mind's) sudden stirring is like the snapping of a bowstring—this refers to its constant judgment of right and wrong. Its persistence is like that of one bound by an oath—this refers to its clinging to victory. Its withering is like [the alternation of] autumn and winter—this speaks of its daily decline. When it sinks and is lost, it cannot be brought back again. Its weariness is like a sealed envelope—this speaks of its stagnation in old age. When the mind approaches death, nothing can make it revive again.
>
> Joy and anger, sorrow and delight, reflection and sighing, change and stagnation, modesty, defiance, bluntness, arrogance. From emptiness comes pleasure, and from the gathering of vapors, mushrooms take form.

第七段，其發若機栝，心感於物，發之甚急也。其留如詛盟，物主於心，滯而不化也。其殺如秋冬，言本心之日亡也。溺之所為，不可復，言心之溺於事物，而不可復返也。[9] 其厭如緘，言溺之固結，不可復解也。近死之心，莫[若]使復陽，言心

---

[9] The Yŏam edition completely omits the line: 溺之所為，不可復，言心之溺於事物，而不可復返也。 Comparing it with the Kyujanggak edition (page 7b(14), lines 9-10), it is clear that the Yŏam editor, working from the Kyujanggak edition as a base, attempted to correct redundancies and errors in the "discourses of things" section but mistakenly skipped this entire line between the sentence ending with 言本心之日亡也 on line 8-9 and the next sentence starting at line 10. Visually, the endings of these two sentences, 之日亡也 and 可復返也, align in the

之不活，不可復生也。盖言心ˆ之接物也。發之甚躁，故為物所動，而留而不化，客心為主於內，故本心日亡。本心日亡於外，故溺而不返。
The seventh section. The phrase "Its sudden stirring is like the snapping of a bowstring" means that the mind, affected by external things, reacts and expresses its feelings very quickly. "Its persistence is like that of one bound by an oath" means that when the external things are grounded in the mind, they are stuck and do not change. "Its withering is like [the alternation of] autumn and winter" means that the original mind gradually disappears day by day. "When it sinks and is lost, it cannot be brought back again" means that the mind becomes obsessed with some matter or external thing and cannot turn back. "Its weariness is like a sealed envelope" means that the state of indulgence is so tightly sealed that it cannot be undone. "When the mind approaches death, nothing can make it revive again" indicates that when the mind is no longer alive, it cannot be revived.

In general, when the mind encounters external things and expresses itself too hastily, it becomes stirred by external stimuli. [What has been stirred] then settles and no longer changes, so that the guest mind, [which comes from the outside,] becomes the master within. As a result, the original mind perishes day by day. Because the original mind is daily lost by external things, once one becomes indulgent, there is no way to return.

溺者，亡之致。厭者，溺之甚。死者，厭之驗也。喜怒哀樂以下，言情之有萬變也。慮，謀慮也。歎，憂歎也。變，不一也。慹，固滯也。
The word "to sink" refers to a state where the loss [of the original mind] has already reached. The word "weariness" indicates that this condition of being lost has deepened. The word "death" then represents the outcome or consequence of such deep entanglement. The phrase of "joy and anger, sorrow and delight" that follows illustrates that human emotions are subject to countless variations and changes. The word "reflection" refers to scheming or deliberation. "Sighing" expresses anxiety; "change" shows that things do not remain the same; and "stagnation" conveys a state in which [the mind] is hardened and blocked.

姚[妖]佚啟態，逐物異態也。樂出虛，情之始發由静[情]，而動自無而有，如樂聲之出虛也。蒸成菌，情之滯累，由意至[出]我，我復生意，如氣蒸之成菌也。
The phrase "modesty, defiance, bluntness, arrogance" describes various different attitudes that follow external things. The expression "from emptiness comes pleasure" means that the initial emergence of emotion comes from stillness, where [the mind] begins to move from non-being, just as music sounds emerge from emptiness. The phrase "from the gathering of vapors, mushrooms take form" illustrates that emotions, when blocked and accumulated, arise from the

same position, so when moving from one line to the next, the editor likely accidentally omitted the whole line. This kind of mistake is common when reading vertically written texts but also indirectly reveals the insufficient rigor of the Yŏam editor's compilation. Moreover, it stands as evidence that the Yŏam edition is a later version based on the Kyujanggak edition.

faculty of thought and reach the self, which in turn generates further thoughts; [this] is likened to the situation that gathered vapors generate mushrooms.

物論至紛，而不過是非两端。是非之興，又不過原於七情之感應。故此段始舉是非二字，以該物論之衆，下復詳言七情，以明是非之所由起。自第三段至此，皆言物論之不同，而人之自溺於物論不ˆ同ˆ之中，不知所以齊之者，皆不足以與於道也。
Discourses on things are varied, but they do not go beyond the two poles of right and wrong, and the emergence of right and wrong originates only from the responses of the seven emotions. Therefore, this section begins by mentioning the two characters for right and wrong in order to frame the issue of the variety of discourses on things, and then proceeds below to explain in detail, clarifying that the origin of right and wrong lies in the seven emotions.

From the third section up to this point, it is all about how discourses on things are not the same, but people themselves indulge in this variety of those discourses; those who do not understand how to treat all such discourses equally are not sufficient to follow the Way.

**Section 8 (ZZ 2.2; 3)**

> 日夜相代乎前，而莫知其所萌。已乎已乎！旦暮得此，其所由以生乎！非彼無我，非我無所取。是亦近矣，而不知其所為使。若有真宰，而特不得其眹。可行已信，而不見其形，有情而無形。
> Day and night take turns before us, yet no one knows where their arising begins. Enough, enough! From dawn to dusk we gain this—by what comes through it are we made to live! Without that, I would not exist; without me, there would be no one to take it. This understanding comes close to the truth, yet we still do not know what makes it so. It is as though there were a true sovereign, but we cannot glimpse his trace. His workings can be trusted, yet his form cannot be seen. He has what is felt, yet no form.

第八段，日夜相代乎前，言日夜相代，而是非之感無窮也。莫知所萌，言是非相争，莫知其所由起也。所由起即道也。若知所由起之處，則便知是非皆生於道，而不復事於分爭矣。已乎已乎，歎辭，如往者不可諫之意。
The eighth section. The phrase "Day and night take turns before us" expresses that while day and night continually replace each other, our sense of right and wrong remains inexhaustible. The line "no one knows where their arising begins" points out that although people dispute over what is right and wrong, no one truly knows the origin from which such disputes arise. That very origin is the Way. If one were to know where such arising begins, then understanding of right and wrong would all stem from the Way, and thus, there would be no more division or contention. The exclamation "Enough, enough" serves as an interjection, much like expressing that there is little more to be said about something or someone that has already passed.

朝暮得此，所由以生，如来者可追之意也。得此之此字，亦指道也，言朝暮得此道，即所以為生也。生字與上段陽字相應。彼之近死者不可復生，而此之[言]得道者猶可復陽也。非彼無我，非我無所取，是知彼我之不可相無，故曰近。近者，近於道也。

The phrase "From dawn to dusk we gain this—by what comes through it are we made to live" means like that someone who has come can be traced back. The word "this" in "gaining this" refers to the Way. Thus, to gain this Way from dawn to dusk means one comes to life through it. The word "life" corresponds to the character yang in the previous paragraph. The one who is "close to death" [in that earlier passage] cannot come back to life, the one who attains the Way here can once again return to the state of yang. The phrase "Without that, I would not exist; without me, there would be no one to take it" means that [the Way] and I are mutually indispensable. Therefore, it is said to be "close," meaning close to the Way.

然猶不知彼我之皆出於道之所使，則亦未為至矣。所ˆ為ˆ使，即指真宰之道也。彼我之間，道無不包，故曰不得其眹。眹，分際也。自此漸說合物論ˆ之異，直說到十五段，方生之說而ˆ極，即推明十六段，彼是莫得其偶之意。

However, not knowing that [the distinction between] that thing and I stems from what the Way itself causes, and thus, it also indicates that one has not yet reached the ultimate realization [of the Way]. The phrase "that which causes it to be so" refers to the true sovereign, the Way itself. There is nothing between that thing and I that the Way does not encompass. Hence, it is said that "one can find no trace of him."

Here, the notion of trace refers to the dividing boundary or distinction. From this point, [Zhuangzi] gradually discusses the differences among discourses on things. This discussion continues directly up to Section 15, where the theory of things arising simultaneously side by side is thoroughly examined. In Section 16, [this theory] is further clarified, conveying that neither "that" nor "this" can find a perfect pair or match.

已信，甚實也。有情，主宰也。言真宰之道，至實能宰，而無形也。信情若皆作實，両句意疊矣。與大宗師篇，道有情有信，無為無形之語同。

The phrase "[his workings] can be trusted in" implies that it is profoundly substantial or real. "he (i.e., true sovereign) has what is felt" means that there is something that preside over, speaks of the Way of true sovereign, who is extremely substantial and has the capacity to rule, even though it possesses no physical form. Attributing both trust and feeling effectively ascribes substance to it (i.e., the Way); thus, the meanings of these two phrases overlap. This is the same as what is stated in the chapter [six] "The Great Founding Master": "In the Way, there is what is felt and what is trusted, yet without action and without form" (ZZ 6.3).

**Section 9 (ZZ 2.3)**

> 百骸、九竅、六藏，賅而存焉，吾誰與為親？汝皆說之乎？其有私焉？如是皆有，為臣妾乎。其臣妾不足以相治乎。其遞相為君臣乎。其有真君存焉。如求得其情與不得，無益損乎其真。
> The hundred bones, nine orifices, and six viscera— all are contained within me. With which of them should I be most intimate? Should you delight in them all alike? Does each have a private element. If that is so, are they all servants and concubine? But if they are servants and concubines, are they insufficient to govern each other? Or should they take turns ruling and serving? It seems there must be a true lord dwelling among them. Yet whether I seek or fail to grasp what is felt [from it], that neither increases nor diminishes his authenticity.

第九段，一身之中百骸皆備，而莫得有所私焉，以喻一世之間，衆論咸備，而不可有所偏向也。真君即心也。求得與不得，無益損乎其真，言百骸、九竅，各有所求，而得與不得，俱無損益於心君之真也。百骸不能相治，而惟心治之；衆論不能自齊，而惟道齊之。在萬物則道為真宰，在一身則心為真君。心與道一也。邵子所謂心為太極者也。
The ninth section. Within the human body, though all one hundred bones are fully present, none of them claims personal or preferential status. This is intended to illuminate the idea that, in this one life, though countless discourses may all be present, none should be given biased favor.

The "true lord" refers to the mind. The statement that "whether I seek or fail to grasp what is felt [from it], that neither increases nor diminishes his authenticity" means that while the hundred bones and nine orifices each have their own pursuits, whether they attain them or not does not in any way add to or subtract from the authenticity of the mind, which is the lord.

The hundred bones cannot govern each other, but the mind alone governs all discourses. Yet even the mind cannot treat all opinions equally by itself; only the Way can regard them impartially. Thus, among all things, the Way is the "true sovereign," while within the body, the mind is the "true lord." The mind and the Way are one and the same. This corresponds to what Shao Yong called "The mind becomes the Supreme Ultimate" (*Zhuzi yulei* 100.31).

然吾儒所謂真君之心，包性命，而言莊周所謂真君之心，指靈覺，而言性命一於善，靈覺無分於善惡。此所以語同，而實不同也。前段出真宰字，此段又出真君字，暗說齊物之意。
However, what we Confucians call the "true lord" refers to the mind that encompasses both [innate] nature and [heavenly] mandate. In contrast, what Zhuang Zhou calls "true lord" refers to a numinous perception. Nature and mandate are consistently aligned with goodness, whereas numinous perception makes no distinction between good and evil. Although the terms used are the same, the underlying substances differ.

In the previous section, the phrase "true sovereign" appeared, and in this paragraph, the phrase "true lord" appears again. This subtly suggests the idea of treating all things equally.

**Section 10 (ZZ 2.3)**

> 一受其成形，不亡以待盡。與物相刃相靡，其行盡如馳，而莫之能止，不亦悲乎！終身役役而不見其成功，苶然疲役而不知其所歸，可不哀邪！人謂之不死，奚益？其形化，其心與之然，可不謂大哀乎？人之生也，固若是芒乎！其我獨芒，而人亦有不芒者乎！
> Once one has taken on a formed body, it does not perish until its complete exhaustion. In encountering things, it [i.e., body] cuts and is cut, wears and is worn; its movement rushes on like a galloping horse, and none can halt it—is this not sorrowful? Through a whole life of toil and striving, one never beholds the completion of one's work; weary and worn, one knows not where one's return lies—how can this not be lamentable? People call this "not yet dead," but what gain is there in that? The body changes, and the mind changes with it—can this not be called the great grief? Is human life not indeed this bewildered? Could it be that I alone am lost in confusion, while others are not?

第十段，一受成形，言人之受形而生也。不亡以待盡，言不死以待盡，盖指未死之前。與物相刃相靡，即所謂與接為搆，日以心鬬者也。行盡如馳，莫之能止，言以此行之盡其平生[日]，如馬馳驟，不知所止也。終身役役，薾然疲役，言形之所以化也。形化固哀[芒]，而心之與化，尤可哀。故前只言哀，而此言大哀，下語極有權衡。其我獨芒，人亦有不芒者，言人與我皆芒，歎世人之無不然也。此一[二]段，承上両段，言其不能齊物之患。
The tenth section. The phrase "Once one has taken on a formed body" refers to a person receiving a physical form and being born. "It does not perish until its complete exhaustion" means not yet dead while waiting for the end, referring to the time before death. "In encountering things, it cuts and is cut, wears and is worn" describes becoming entangled and in contact with other things, causing the mind to be in conflict day by day. "Its movement rushes on like a galloping horse, and none can halt it" means that, living by this, one spends one's entire life rushing about like a galloping horse, never knowing where to stop. "Through a whole life of toil and striving" refers to the reason why the body undergoes transformation. The transformation is truly sorrowful, but since it is the mind that brings about this change, it is all the more sorrowful. Thus, the earlier passage merely spoke of sorrow, whereas this passage speaks of great sorrow. The following sentence presents a profound weighing and balance. "Could it be that I alone am lost in confusion, while others are not?" expresses that both others and I are lost in darkness, and laments there is no one in the world who is truly free from it.

This one section connects the previous two sections and speaks of the distress that arises from being unable to view all things equally.

## Section 11 (ZZ 2.4)

> 夫隨其成心而師之，誰獨且無師乎？奚必知代而心自取者有之？愚者與有焉。未成乎心而有是非，是今日適越而昔至也。是以無有為有。無有為有，雖有神禹，且不能知，吾獨且柰何哉！
> To follow one's complete mind and take it as one's teacher—who, then, is without a teacher? Why must one insist on knowing the alternation [of things], and that the mind seizes what it takes for itself? Even the foolish, too, have [such a teacher] within. When right and wrong arise before the mind has been made complete, it is like setting out for Yue today and having arrived there yesterday. Thus, what is not becomes what is. When what is not becomes what is, then even a god-like [Emperor] Yu could not comprehend it—how, then, could I alone deal with it?

第十一段，成心之心，即所謂真君之心也。成之者，存而成之也。師心云者，張^子^所謂以己心為嚴師。釋氏所謂即心即佛也。然所謂心者，在莊釋則同，而在吾儒則不同於彼矣。知代，賢者之知代變者也。
The eleventh section. The notion of the mind in the phrase "complete mind" refers to the so-called mind of the "true lord."[10] "To complete [the mind]" means to preserve and perfect it. The phrase "to take the mind as a teacher" refers to Master Zhang's (i.e., Zhang Zai) saying that "one should take one's own mind as a stern teacher."[11] It is also akin to the Buddha's saying, "the mind is the Buddha."

However, though this so-called "mind" is the same for both Zhuangzi and the Buddha, in our Confucian tradition, it is not viewed in the same way. The term "knowing alternation [of things]" means that the worthy understand that [all things and affairs] alternate and change.

心自取，心自得也。奚必知代，愚者與有，如孟子所謂非獨賢者，有是心也。人皆有之者也。未成乎心云云，言未存此心，而妄有是非，猶今日適越，而自謂昔至，言無是理也。神禹不知吾獨奈何，甚絶之之辭也。
The phrase "What the mind takes for itself" means that the mind awakens or realizes itself. "Why must one insist on knowing the alternation [of things] ... Even the foolish, too, have [such a teacher] within" is like what Mengzi's says, "It is not only the wise who have this mind; all humans possess it" (6A10). The phrase "before the mind has been made complete…" means that although this mind does not yet exist, it is absurd to claim that it has notions of right and

---

[10] The concept of "complete mind" (*sŏngsim*; *chengxin* 成心) has historically been interpreted in both positive and negative ways in the tradition of interpreting the *Zhuangzi*. Those who view it positively interpret it as "to complete or perfect the mind," while those who take a negative view understand it as an already-formed, fixed mindset. Here, Han Wŏnjin takes a positive view of the concept.

[11] The exact sentence is as follows: "The beginning of rectifying the mind must be to take one's own mind as a stern teacher" 正心之始當以己心為嚴師 (*Zhangzi quanshu* 6.65).

wrong, like someone who has just left for Yue today but says to have arrived yesterday. This indicates that is unreasonable.

Finally, "even a god-like [Emperor] Yu could not comprehend it—how, then, could I alone deal with it?" is a strong expression of refusal to answer.

## Section 12 (ZZ 2.4)

> 夫言非吹也。言者有言，其所言者特未定也。果有言邪？其未嘗有言邪？其以為異於鷇音，亦有辯乎，其無辯乎？
> Speech is not mere breath. When one speaks, there are words—but what those words refer to has yet to be fixed. Is there then truly such a thing as speech? Or has there never been speech? If one thinks it differs from the cries of fledglings, then is there a distinction—or is there none?

第十二段，非吹之吹字，徼上文吹萬之吹字，而言即指真宰之道也。言衆論之言，雖出於真宰之所使，然又不可直以衆論為真宰也，猶萬竅怒號，雖風之所使，而不可直以萬竅怒號為風也。
The twelfth section. In the phrase "not mere breath," the word "breath" comes back from the one in the previous paragraph's "blowing on the myriad things in a different way." It refers to the "true sovereign" as the Way. It means that all kinds of spoken discourses arise from what the "true sovereign" commands, but one cannot directly consider all the discourses themselves as the "true sovereign." It is like the sound of a thousand holes angrily shouting. Although it is caused by the wind, the angry shouting of the thousand holes itself cannot be directly called the wind.

言者，雖自有言，所謂以言者，實真宰之所吹，而真宰之吹者，又未有常形，故曰特未定。言果待於真宰之吹，而非出於自已，則人之有言，果不可謂有言。而無以異於鷇音之無知矣。此二段，言是非之本於心，言議之本於道，而人之不能齊物者，在於不能成心與知道也。
[Similarly,] when one speaks, although he has words [to use], what is called 'by using words' is in fact the blowing of the true sovereign. What the true sovereign blows does not yet have a constant form, so it is said "not determined yet." Speech indeed awaits the blowing of the "true sovereign"; it does not originate from oneself. Thus, when a person has words, in truth, we cannot really say he has them. Yet, to regard [human speech] as no different from the cries of fledglings is ignorant, [too]. These two sections convey that: Right and wrong are rooted in the mind, while speech and discourse are based in the Way. But the reason humans cannot treat all things equally is because they fail to complete the mind and thereby realize the Way.

## Section 13 (ZZ 2.4)

> 道惡乎隱而有真偽？言惡乎隱而有是非？道惡乎往而不存？言惡乎存而不可？道隱於小成，言隱於榮華。故有儒、墨之是非，以是其所非，而非其所是。欲是其所非而非其所是，則莫若以明。
> Where could the Way be hidden, such that truth and falsity arise? Where could speech be hidden, such that right and wrong appear? How could the Way depart and yet not be present? How could speech remain and yet be impossible to utter? The Way is obscured by partial achievements; speech is obscured by ornate embellishment. Thus, the Confucians and Moists contend over right and wrong—affirming what the other denies, and denying what the other affirms. If one wishes to affirm what they deny and deny what they affirm, nothing is like to use illumination.

第十三段，言道與言之隱在乎是非之相爭，與其是非相爭，呶呶於辨詰不若，両忘而明之也。明字與隱字相應。上文固已包說道字，而猶未明ˆ言。道字至此，始出道字，指示其本。而此下數[四]段，極言是非之無分，直說到道樞而止。
The thirteenth section. [This section] states that the Way and speech are concealed within the conflict between right and wrong. To participate in the disputes between right and wrong, and to endlessly dispute and press arguments is not as good as forgetting both sides and illuminating them. The notion of illumination corresponds to that of concealment.

Although the previous paragraph already provided a broad explanation of the concept of the Way, it had not yet been explicitly mentioned. [The specific reference to] the character for the Way first appears here, pointing to its root.

In the few paragraphs that follow, [Zhuang Zhou] pushes to the extreme the idea that there is no distinction between right and wrong. It speaks directly about the concept of "the Way as the pivotal hinge" and ends [the paragraphs].

## Section 14 (ZZ 2.5)

> 物無非彼，物無非是。自彼則不見，自知則知之。故曰：彼出於是，是亦因彼。
> There is nothing that is not *that*, and nothing that is not *this*. Seen from [the standpoint of] *that*, one does not perceive it; known from [the standpoint of] *this*, one understands it. Therefore, it is said: "*That* arises from *this*, and *this* in turn depends on *that*."

第十四段，物無非彼，言自此觀彼，則固已彼為彼，而自彼觀此，則又以此為彼矣。物無非是，言自此觀此，則固以此為是，而自彼觀彼，則又以彼為是矣。故曰物無非彼，物無非是，自彼不見，自知則知。言自彼觀之ˆ，固不見其此之為此，而自我視之，則ˆ皆知此之為此也。
The fourteenth section. The phrase "There is no thing that is not *that*" means that if one looks at *that* from the standpoint of *this*, then *that* truly becomes *that*.

And, if one looks at *this* from the standpoint of *that*, then one comes to regard *this* as *that*.

The phrase "nothing that is not *this*" means that if one looks at *this* from the standpoint of *this*, one truly regards *this* as *this*, and if one looks at *that* from the standpoint of *that*, then one again ends up regarding *that* as *that*.[12] Therefore, it is said: "There is no thing that is not *that*, and no thing that is not *this*. Seen from [the standpoint of] *that*, one does not perceive it; known from [the standpoint of] *this*, one understands it." This means: when viewing from the standpoint of *that*, one cannot see that *this* is *this*; but when viewing from oneself, one comes to fully know that *this* is *this*.

物無非彼，物無非是，而自彼觀之，則物皆為彼；自我視之，則物皆為此。彼是本無定分，而有言是，[+是]故彼之名立，有言彼。故[所]是之名立，[+彼]彼是之名，相因而生，故曰彼出於是，是亦因彼。
There is nothing that is not *that*, and nothing that is not *this*, which means, from the standpoint of *that*, all things become *that*; from the standpoint of the self, all things become *this*. *That* and *this* originally have no fixed distinction, yet when one speaks of *this*, the name of *that* is established; when one speaks of *that*, the name of *this* is established. Their names arise in dependence on one another, which is why it is said: "*That* arises from *this*, and *this* in turn depends on *that*."

盖自本言之，則彼是即為一。自分言之，則彼是，實相因此。彼是之不可偏廢，而萬物之當齊也。彼是字與是非字不同，彼是猶言彼此也。據下文，彼亦一是非，此亦一是非，可見。
From the standpoint of the origin, *that* and *this* form a single whole; from the standpoint of differentiation, there come *that* and *this*. Their actual forms are based on this. Neither *that* nor *this* can be set aside, but the myriad things must accordingly be treated equally. [Moreover,] the notions of *that* and *this* differ from the notions of right and wrong; *that* and *this* is like saying "each and the other." As the text later shows, *that* itself is a right-and-wrong, and *this* itself is a right-and-wrong, too, as can be seen.

## Section 15 (ZZ 2.5)

> 彼是，方生之說也。雖然，方生方死，方死方生；方可方不可，方不可方可；因是因非，因非因是。是以聖人不由，而照之于天，亦因是也。
> [The example of] *that* and *this* are [for] an explanation of mutual arising. Even so, where there is birth, there is death; where there is death, there is birth. Where there is possibility, there is impossibility; where there is impossibility, there is possibility. Based on right, wrong arises; based on wrong, right arises. Therefore,

---

[12] In the original text, it reads 以彼為是 ("to regard that as this"), but in terms of meaning it is more appropriate to understand it as 以彼為彼 ("to regard that as that"). Accordingly, the translator has emended the original text and translated it on that basis.

the sage does not perceive by his own initiative, yet illumines all things in light of heaven, and thereby aligns with what is.

第十五段，彼是，方生之說，言彼是各自私己，猶方生者，自私其生，而諱惡其死也。故下文以雖然二字反其意，而言之以明死生可否皆相因，而不可相無，則是非亦當各因其分，而不可廢一也。聖人不由，照之於天，言聖人不由去非取是，一偏之術，而照之以天道也。所謂天道，亦因ˆ其是非，不求去取也。此以上皆言物論之末異而本同。
The fifteenth section. The phrase, "[The example of] *that* and *this* are [for] an explanation of mutual arising" means that *that* and *this* [arises] one private, individual self, and that "mutual arising" is born out of private partiality, which seeks to avoid and detest death. Therefore, the following phrase "even so" is used to turn the meaning back, clarifying that death and life, permission and prohibition all depend upon each other, and cannot exist without each other. Thus, right and wrong, too, each originate from their respective allotments, and cannot be entirely abolished or eliminated.

The phrase "therefore, the sage does not perceive by his own initiative, yet illumines all things in light of heaven" means that the sage does not follow a single-sided method of rejecting the wrong and choosing the right, but instead illumines things in accordance with the Way of heaven. This so-called Way of heaven serves as the ultimate basis for distinguishing right and wrong, but it does not seek to choose one or eliminate the other.

In this way, the above discussion expresses that although all discourses end in difference, they are the same at the root.

## Section 16 (ZZ 2.5)

是亦彼也，彼亦是也。彼亦一是非，此亦一是非。果且有彼是乎哉？果且無彼是乎哉？彼是莫得其偶，謂之道樞。樞始得其環中，以應無窮。是亦一無窮，非亦一無窮也。故曰莫若以明。
A *this* is also *that*, a *that* is also *this*. A *that* contains both right and wrong; a *this* also contains both right and wrong. So then, now, should there be a *this* and *that*, or should there not be a *this* and *that*? A state in which *this* and *that* no longer stand in opposition is called the pivotal hinge of the Way. When the hinge is properly set in the middle of the ring, it responds without end. Its right is an endless unfolding, and its wrong is also an endless unfolding. Therefore, it is said "Nothing is the same as to use illumination."

第十六段，此一段正居一篇中間，包括上下文意，一段之中，又自具一篇體段了。此一段，可以讀此篇矣。自彼是相對，約之以至於莫得其偶，而爲道樞之一。自道樞之一，得之以是，環中應物，而齊是非之無窮。上一半以物論，言包括上文之意；下一半以齊物，言包括下文之意。盖道樞二字爲一段之樞紐，此一段爲一篇之樞紐。
The sixteenth section. This section is positioned precisely at the center of the chapter and encompasses the messages of both the preceding and following

paragraphs. At its core, it also forms a self-contained segment. By reading this single paragraph, one can grasp the entire chapter.

[This paragraph] begins with the idea that *this* and *that* are relative and proceeds to connect them, culminating in the assertion that "none of [these relative things] can find their [true] counterpart," and [ultimately,] that they must become one through "the Way as the pivotal hinge." By attaining oneness through ["the Way as the pivot,"] one can respond to external things and treating all their rights and wrongs equally without an end.

The first half [of this paragraph], based on discourses on things, encompasses the message of the preceding paragraph, while the latter half, based on the concept of treating all things equally, encompasses the message of the following paragraph. The notion of "the Way as the pivotal hinge" serve as the pivot of this one section, and this one section becomes the pivot of the entire chapter.

又見得莫若以明一句，爲篇内關鍵之語。前段言莫若以明，承上是非相爭之隱道，而[以]反之以言，道之當明，盖啓明之之端。此言莫若以明，承上明之之端，而極言是非無分之爲道，以示明之之地頭。後段言，此之謂以明，承上明之之地頭，極言是非之齊，以著明之之實。
One also finds [in this section] the phrase "nothing is as good as to use illumination," which becomes a keyword within this chapter.

An earlier section (Section 13; ZZ 2.4) mentions [the same phrase] "Nothing is as good as to use illumination" is mentioned. There, it is linked to the idea that contention over right and wrong obscures the Way, and that in contrast, the Way ought to be expressed through illumination, which opens up the beginning of illumination. Here, [however,] the phrase "nothing is as good as to use illumination," building on the earlier notion of the beginning of illumination, pushes to an extreme the idea that the Way is the recognition that there is no distinction between right and wrong, and in doing so, it defines the boundaries of the concept of illumination.

In the later paragraph (i.e., this section), this is again referred to simply as "to use illumination," which likewise continues the earlier boundary of illumination [namely, the insight that there is no separation between right and wrong,] and asserts, in an extreme manner, to treat right and wrong equally and by doing so, reveal it is the substance of the illumination.

## Section 17 (ZZ 2.6)

> 以指喻指之非指，不若以非指喻指之非指也；以馬喻馬之非馬，不若以非馬喻馬之非馬也。天地一指也；萬物一馬也。
> To use pointing to illustrate that pointing is not really pointing is not as good as to use non-pointing to illustrate that pointing is not really pointing. To use a horse to show that a horse is not a horse is not as good as to use a non-horse to show that a horse is not a horse. Heaven and earth are one pointing; all things are one horse.

第十七段，指馬之喻，言以是觀非，以非觀是，不若以是觀是，以非觀非[是]，而兩忘之也。天地萬物，極其齊而言也。此以下，皆言齊物之事。
The seventeenth section. The metaphor of pointing and a horse illustrates that using the right to judge the wrong or the wrong to judge the right is inferior to using the right to judge the right and the wrong to judge the wrong, and then forgetting both perspectives.

The phrases "heaven and earth [are one pointing]" and "all things [are one horse]" means to equalize [all things] in an extreme manner. All that follows this speaks to the process of treating all things equally.

### Section 18 (ZZ 2.6)

> 可乎可，不可乎不可。道行之而成，物謂之而然。惡乎然？然於然。惡乎不然？不然於不然。物固有所然，物固有所可。無物不然，無物不可。
> [One says] "possible" for "what is possible," and "impossible" for "what is impossible." The Way is completed as one practices, and things are so as they are called so. Why are they so? They are so because they are [perceived] so. Why are they not so? They are not so because they are [perceived] not so. A thing indeed has what it is. A thing indeed has what it can be. Nothing is [inherently] not what it is, nothing is [inherently] not what it can be.[13]

### Section 19 (ZZ 2.6)

> 故為是舉莛與楹，厲與西施，恢恑憰怪，道通為一。
> Therefore, whether a tiny stalk or a towering pillar, a leper or the [legendary] beauty Xi Shi, something vast and expansive or strange and grotesque, the Way unites them all as one.

第十九段，恢恑，廣大踈濶之貌。憰怪，偏狹狡詰之貌。二者，正相反也。
The nineteenth section. "Vast and expansive" refers to a state of wide openness. "Strange and grotesque" refers to a narrow-mindedness and slyness. These two stand in direct opposition to each other.

### Section 20 (ZZ 2.6)

> 其分也，成也；其成也，毀也。凡物無成與毀，復通為一。
> In their differentiation, things take form; in their formation, they are to be destroyed. All things, having no fixed completion or destruction, return to and unify as one.

---

13 In both the Kyujanggak edition and the Yŏam edition, there is no mention of Section 18. It is unclear whether the author simply skipped the Section Eighteen by mistake and proceeded directly to Section 19, or even whether Han Wŏnjin originally provided commentary on this portion or not. As will be seen below, there are a few additional places in this work where sections appear to be missing, and it is difficult to explain why they are currently missing.

第二十段，自指馬之喩至此，復推廣道樞之義。
The twentieth section. From the metaphor of pointing and a horse up to this point, the meaning of "the Way as the pivot" has been further expanded.

**Section 21 (ZZ 2.6)**

> 唯達者知通為一，為是不用而寓諸庸。庸也者，用也；用也者，通也；通也者，得也。適得而幾矣。因是已。已而不知其然，謂之道。
> Only one who has mastered [the Way] knows that [all things] unify as one and are not used for right [and wrong] while entrusting themselves to the ordinary. The ordinary is the useful; the useful is the penetrable; the penetrable is the attainable; and fitting into the attainable, that is it. [The one with the Way] is based on this, and stops there, not knowing he is so. This is called the Way.

第二十一段，為是不用，而寓諸庸，言不主一偏而寓諸中庸也。是即是非之是也，庸即中庸也，所謂道樞也。寓諸庸即環中以應無窮也。此所謂中庸，乃不[必]分是非，遂物流循者，即政[正]如胡廣、柳宗元之中庸，而小人無忌憚之甚者也。
The twenty-first section. The phrase, "[for one who has mastered the Way, all things unified as one] are not used for right [and wrong] while entrusting themselves to the ordinary" expresses that one does not cling to one side but instead entrusts himself to the virtue of balanced harmony in daily life (*chungyong*; *zhongyong*). Here, the word "right" refers to the right of "right and wrong"; and "ordinary" refers to the balanced harmony in daily life, which is the so-called "the Way as the pivot." "Entrusting to the ordinary" means to stand at the very center of the pivot, thus being able to respond to anything without an end.

[For Zhuangzi,] this so-called balanced harmony in daily life is precisely the state of not distinguishing right from wrong but simply following external things like flowing water. It corresponds exactly to the balanced harmony in daily life advocated by Hu Guang (91-172) and Liu Zhongyuan (773-819). How deeply such petty-minded men are unashamed![14]

[14] Hu Guang was known for not correcting the abuses of corrupt officials or powerful ministers, in order to preserve his own position. This selfish and opportunistic attitude was justified by interpreting it as the virtue of *zhong*. Thus, Hu Guang's *zhong* refers to acting in a self-centered and opportunistic way, to justify oneself. By contrast, Liu Zhongyuan understood virtue of *zhong* as placing great emphasis on the timeliness in one's moral judgments and actions. For Liu, the significance of timing outweighed the importance of human subjectivity in moral judgment and action. As a result, his thought is seen as emphasizing the absoluteness of what is inevitable or beyond human control in ethical decision-making, thereby losing the balance that ancient Confucians sought to maintain between human agency and contextual conditions in the practice of balanced harmony. Here, Han Wŏnjin claims that Zhuangzi's concept of *zhongyong* resembles Hu Guang's opportunism or Liu Zhongyuan's fatalism.

## Section 22 (ZZ 2.6)

勞神明為一，而不知其同也，謂之朝三。何謂朝三？曰狙公賦芧，曰：朝三而莫四。眾狙皆怒。曰：然則朝四而莫三。眾狙皆悅。名實未虧，而喜怒為用，亦因是也。是以聖人和之以是非，而休乎天鈞，是之謂兩行。

To exhaust spirit-like illumination to [forcefully] unify [all things] without knowing that they are already the same, this is what is meant by "three in the morning." What is "three in the morning"? When a monkey trainer was distributing acorns, he said, "You get three in the morning and four in the evening." The monkeys were all enraged. So, he said, "If so, then you get four in the morning and three in the evening." The monkeys were all overjoyed. [There] what was said and what was actually [given] were not mismatched, yet joy and anger arose from there. It is also a "based on *this* (i.e. partiality)." Therefore, the sage harmonizes with both right and wrong and rests in heavenly evenness. This is called walking both paths.

第二十二段，朝三暮四，以[二]喻是非之實本同，而是非之用有異也。故齊物者，合其異，而返其同也。

The twenty-second section. Using the phrase "three in the morning and four in the evening," [Zhuangzi] illustrates that the essence of right and wrong is originally the same, but their functions give rise to differences. Therefore, to treat all things equally is to reconcile those differences and return to their underlying sameness.

## Section 23 (ZZ 2.6)

古之人，其知有所至矣。惡乎至？有以為未始有物者，至矣盡矣，不可以加矣。其次以為有物矣，而未始有封也。其次以為有封焉，而未始有是非也。是非之彰也，道之所以虧也。道之所以虧，愛之所以成。果且有成與虧乎哉？果且無成與虧乎哉？

The people of the past, their knowing reached far. How far did it reach? So far to the point that they regarded there was not yet the beginning of things, it was the ultimate and the complete, to which nothing more could be added. Next, they regarded that there was a thing, but there was not yet the beginning of boundary among them. And then, they regarded that there is boundary, but there was not yet the beginning of right and wrong among them. Once right and wrong become prominent, the Way is damaged. And once the Way is damaged, favoritism becomes to be formed. But do such things as completion and demolition exist indeed, or do they not?

第二十三段，未始有物，即周之所謂道也。有物，即氣也。有封，即天地也。有是非，即事物之紛羅者也。自道而爲氣，自氣而爲天地，自天地而爲事物。有事物則是非彰，是非彰則道虧，道虧則愛成。愛成者，自私之謂也。

The twenty-third section. The phrase "there was not yet the beginning of things" refers to what Zhuang Zhou means by the Way. The phrase "there is a thing" refers to *qi*. The phrase "there is boundary" refers to heaven and earth. The phrase "there is right and wrong" signifies the entangled and chaotic intertwining of affairs and things.

From the Way arises *qi*; from *qi*, heaven and earth are formed; from heaven and earth, affairs and things are created; and when affairs and things come to be, right and wrong become clearly distinguished. When right and wrong are made distinct, the Way becomes distorted; and when the Way is distorted, favoritism arises. The arising of favoritism refers to the emergence of private self.

有成，故有虧。無成，則[故]無虧矣。有成與虧，末流之分也。無成與虧，本源之一也。聖人之齊物，所以復其道之本一也。此周之意也。
Where there is formation, distortion follows; where there is no formation, there is no distortion. The existence of formation and distortion arises only at the end of the current of differentiation, while their nonexistence reveals their original oneness at the source.

The sage treats all things equally, precisely because he returns to this root unity of the Way. This is what Zhuangzi meant.

然周以未始有物爲道，則全不識道字，又不識物字。盖動靜無端，陰陽無始。陽爲事物，而陽前有陰，則陰亦事物也。動爲事物，而動前有靜，則靜亦事物也。夫豈有無物之時哉。既無無物之時，則所謂道者，亦在乎ˆ事物之中，而爲此事物之主也。今謂有無物之時，則是只知有動而陽之物，而不知此陽之前，又有靜[動]而陰之物也。以未始有物爲道，則是只以動而陽者爲物，而却認其靜而陰者爲道也。
However, Zhuang Zhou regarded "the time before things began to exist" as the Way. If so, then he did not fully understand the concept of the Way, nor did he fully grasp the concept of thing.

Generally, movement and stillness have no beginning, and yin and yang have no first moment. Yang is a state and a thing, but before yang, there was yin; therefore, yin too was a state and a thing. Movement becomes a state and a thing, but before movement, there was stillness; therefore, stillness also is a state and a thing. How then can there be a time when a thing does not exist at all? Since there is no time without a thing, the so-called Way also exists among affairs and things and is the master of these affairs and things.

Now, [Zhuangzi] says there is a time without a thing, and this means he only knows a thing that is moving and yang, but does not know, before this yang, there is also a thing that is still and yin. Since he regards "the time before a thing began to exist" as the Way, this means he only regards the moving and yang aspect as a thing and mistakenly recognizes the still and yin aspect as the Way.

然則周之所謂道者，即不過形氣之粗者，而不知此上面[而]，更有所謂一陰一陽之道也。故周之語道，一則曰虛靜，二[一]則曰混沌。

If this is so, then what Zhuang Zhou called "the Way" is nothing more than the crude *qi* that gives form, and he did not realize that there is a further dimension, which is what is called [in the *Zhouyi*,] "once yin, once yang, that is called the Way" (*Xici* A 5). Thus, what Zhuangzi terms the Way is, first, "emptiness and stillness" (cf. ZZ 13.1) and, second, "primal undifferentiation" (cf. ZZ 7.7; 11.4; 12.11).[15]

虛靜ˆ、混ˆ沌ˆ，皆是天地未闢，萬物未生之時，一陰之象也。一陰之中，輕淸重濁，剛柔燥濕之氣，無不備焉。分而爲天地萬物，高下散殊，而事物之是非善惡，亦皆由此而生。故周便以是非善惡爲皆道之當有，而其所以求道者，專以齊物爲宗，故其學遂陷於猖狂妄行之域。所見一差，其害至此，可不懼哉。
Both "emptiness and stillness" and "primal undifferentiation" describe a time when heaven and earth had not yet opened, and all things had not yet been born. This is [just] the image of a single yin. Within this singular yin, which is the light and pure, the heavy and turbid, the strong and weak, the dry and moist *qi*, there is nothing that is not already contained. [This *qi*] divides and creates heaven and earth and all things. Rising upward and sinking downward, dispersing and becoming diverse, they give rise to the right and wrong, good and evil, of all events and things from this.

Therefore, Zhuang Zhou came to regard right and wrong, good and evil, all as things that the Way must inherently include. Hence, to seek the Way means, for him, nothing other than esteeming the equal treatment of all things as the foundation. As a result, his learning ultimately falls into the domain of crazy thinking and deluded conduct.

When his perception deviates even slightly, the harm that follows can reach this extent—how could one not be afraid?

## Section 24 (ZZ 2.7)

有成與虧，故昭氏之鼓琴也；無成與虧，故昭氏之不鼓琴也。昭文之鼓琴也，師曠之枝策也，惠子之據梧也，三子之知幾乎！皆其盛者也，故載之末年。唯其好之也，以異於彼，其好之也，欲以明之彼。非所明而明之，故以堅白之昧終。
There are accomplishment and failure. So, Master Zhao playing the lute is an example. There is also such a thing as no accomplishment and no failure. So, Master Zhao not playing the lute is an example. Zhao Wen played the lute, Music Master Kuang waved his baton, and Huizi leaned on his desk. The knowledge of these three was close to perfections. All were flourishing, and so their names were passed down through the ages. Yet in what they liked, they differed from the [sage]. What they liked, they wanted to make it clear. What is not clear, they tried to make it clear, and so they ended up entangled in the foolishness of "hard" and "white."

---

[15] In this commentary, Han Wonjin consistently writes *hundun* as 混沌, though the original *Zhuangzi* text writes it as 渾沌.

> 而其子又以文之綸終，終身無成。若是而可謂成乎，雖我亦成也。若是而不可謂成乎，物與我無成也。是故滑疑之耀，聖人之所圖也。為是不用而寓諸庸，此之謂以明。
>
> Their sons, too, devoted their lives to [their fathers'] teachings, yet to the end they never attained accomplishment. If this is so, can such men be said to have achieved completion? If so, then so have we all. If not, then neither we nor anything else has ever achieved it. Therefore, the dazzling brilliance of doubt and uncertainty is precisely what the sage contemplates. [The sage] does not employ right [or wrong] but entrusts [all things] to the ordinary. This is what it means to use illumination.

第二十四段，昭氏之ˆ鼓琴、不鼓琴，言昭氏能鼓琴，而他人不能，則是昭氏有成，而他人有虧也。昭氏若不鼓琴ˆ，則是昭氏無成，而他人亦無虧也。此盖以昭氏與他人對說，以證其成虧。

The twenty-fourth section. The phrase "Master Zhao playing the lute and not playing the lute" means that if Master Zhao knows how to play the lute, but others do not, then this implies that Master Zhao accomplishes, while others fail. However, if Master Zhao does not play the lute, then this means that there is nothing accomplished by him, and likewise, nothing is ruined by others. This uses Master Zhao in contrast to others in order to demonstrate the notions of "accomplishment and failure."

以上文愛之所以成，下文其子無成，物與我無成，觀之則可見矣。終身無成，言昭氏能鼓琴，而其子學之無成，此所謂有成與虧也。可謂成、不可謂成，言以人之各有所能，而謂之成，則我之有一能者，亦可謂成也。以人之不能兼他人之能謂之無成，則物與我不能相兼者，皆可謂無成也。

By referring to the phrase "the reason favoritism arises" from the previous section, one can understand the meaning of the phrases in the subsequent lines, "his son accomplished nothing" and "things and I have accomplished nothing." The phrase, "to the end they never attained accomplishment" means that although Master Zhao knew how to play the lute, his son, despite learning it, was unable to achieve anything. This illustrates what is called "there is accomplishment and failure."

What may be called 'accomplished' and what may not be called 'accomplished': if one speaks of accomplishment on the basis that each person has his own particular ability, then even my possessing a single ability could also be called 'accomplished.' If, on the basis that a person cannot combine the abilities of others, one calls it 'no accomplishment,' then wherever things and I cannot mutually encompass one another, all may likewise be called 'no accomplishment.'

以此言之，則無物不成，無物不虧，此其不可是此非彼，而當兩忘而齊之也。滑疑，不分明也。耀，明也。滑疑之耀，不明之明也。不明之明，所以齊是非，而明此道者，故曰聖人之所圖也。

To put it this way: there is nothing that is not accomplished, and there is nothing that is not failed. This is, one cannot declare, "this is right, and that is wrong," so one must forget both and treat them equally.

The term "doubt and uncertainty" means unclear or uncertain, and "dazzling brilliance" means illumination. Thus, the phrase "the dazzling brilliance of doubt and uncertainty" means "an uncertain brightness." An uncertain brightness refers to treating right and wrong equally and thereby illuminating the Way. Therefore, [Zhuangzi] says: "This is what the sage contemplates."

為是不用，以下皆引前段之語，而結之。文字照應，血脈貫通，此可見矣。自達者以下至此，皆釋環中之意。
The phrase "[The sage] does not employ right [or wrong] and what follows all draw upon the earlier section to form a conclusion. One can see that the characters correspond to one another, and that the flow of the text is coherent throughout.

From "one who has mastered" (ZZ 2.6) onward, everything serves to interpret the meaning of "the very center of the ring."

**Section 25 (ZZ 2.8)**

> 今且有言於此，不知其與是類乎？其與是不類乎？類與不類，相與為類，則與彼無以異矣。
> Now let me make another statement on this. Does one not know whether this is of the same kind or not of the same kind? This which is of a kind and this which is not of a kind together become of a kind, and then this is no different from that.

第二十五段，類與不類，相與爲類，即前段彼是相因之意也。
The twenty-fifth section. "This which is of a kind and this which is not of a kind together become of a kind" expresses the same meaning as the earlier passage "*That* and *this* become the basis for each other" (ZZ 2.5).

**Section 26 (ZZ 2.8)**

> 雖然，請嘗言之。有始也者，有未始有始也者，有未始有夫未始有始也者。有有也者，有無也者，有未始有無也者，有未始有夫未始有無也者。俄而有無矣，而未知有無之果孰有孰無也。今我則已有謂矣，而未知吾所謂之其果有謂乎，其果無謂乎？
> Even so, let me [again] say it. There is that which was called beginning. There is the time that there was not yet having a beginning. There is the time that "there was not yet having a beginning" itself had not yet begun. There is that which is called being. There is that which is called non-being. There is the time that there was not yet having non-being. There is the time that "there was not yet having non-being" itself had not yet begun. And then suddenly there are being and non-being. But about the result of being and non-being, one does

not [really] know what being is and what non-being is. Now I have just mentioned "being," but I don't yet know whether what I have said has really said something or has said nothing.

第二十六段，始也者，氣也。未始有始也者，道也。未始有夫未始有始也者，道之本於無也。有也者，事物也。無也者，道也。再言未始有無，言道之極於無也。蓋周以天[來]地未生之前謂道，而不知此爲陰之物。故便以道爲無。若知動靜無端，陰陽無始，而本無無物之時，則亦不敢以道把作無矣。俄而有無，言有道也。此承上段彼是之說，推言事物之本於無。俄而以下，又言自無而適有也。
The twenty-sixth section. The phrase "That which was called beginning," meaning is *qi*. "There was not yet having a beginning" is the Way. "That 'there was not yet having a beginning' itself had not yet begun" means that the Way is rooted in non-being. "That which is called being" refers to an affair or a thing. "That which is called non-being" is the Way. In other words, "there was not yet having non-being" indicates that the ultimate limit of the Way lies in non-being.

In general, Zhuang Zhou referred to the time before heaven and earth had arisen as the Way. But he did not realize that [what he was calling the Way] was a thing of yin. Therefore, he took the Way to be non-being. If one understands that movement and stillness have no beginning, that yin and yang have no origin, and that there was never a time when a thing did not exist, then one would also not dare to call the Way "non-being."

The phrase "and then suddenly there is non-being" means that the Way has come into existence. This continues the previous section's explanation of *this* and *that*, inferring that an affair or a thing is originally grounded in non-being. From the phrase "and then suddenly" onward, it once again indicates a transition from non-being to being.

## Section 27 (ZZ 2.9)

天下莫大於秋豪之末，而大山為小；莫壽乎殤子，而彭祖為夭。天地與我並生，而萬物與我為一。既已為一矣，且得有言乎？既已謂之一矣，且得無言乎？一與言為二，二與一為三。自此以往，巧歷不能得，而況其凡乎！故自無適有，以至於三，而況自有適有乎！無適焉，因是已。
Under heaven, nothing is greater than the tip of an autumn hair, and Mount Tai is smaller. No one has lived longer than a dead child, and Pengzu died younger. Heaven and earth were born with me at the same time, and all things become one with me. Since all have already become one, can one say anything more about it? Since one has already said "to become one," can I have nothing more to say? The one and the word I spoke about it make two, and two together with the original one make three. If one goes on like this, even a skilled mathematician cannot tell where it will end. Then what about ordinary people? Therefore, if by going from non-being to being, one arrives at three, how much further will we go by going from being to being? Better not to go at all, it is based on this.

第二十七段，言事物本，皆自無中出，故推其本之無，則大小、壽夭，無可分別者也。天地與我並生，萬物與我為一，與張子西銘之意同。此盖周之見處，高於世俗一層者也。然西銘據ˆ理一而推分殊。周之齊物，廢分殊，而亂理一，所見有虛實故也。秋豪、泰山至此，言萬物之出於一，旣已[曰]以下復言，一之散爲萬。因是字，凡五六出，而因是者，因其是非兩行之謂也。到底結之，以齊之之意也。
The twenty-seventh section. [This section] states that any affairs and things fundamentally all arise from non-being. Therefore, if one traces back to that fundamental non-being, there is no basis for distinguishing between large and small, long life and early death.

The phrase, "heaven and earth were born together with me, and all things become one with me" conveys the same message as Master Zhang's in *Ximing*.[16]

In this way, what Zhuang Zhou gazes toward lies a level above the mundane world. However, while [Zhang Zai's] *Ximing* proceeds from the unity of principle and develops through its diversification, Zhuang Zhou's "treating all things equally" discards this diversification and confounds the unity of principle, because in his view, both emptiness and substance coexist.

[In the original text] from the mention of "a tip of autumn hair" to "Mount Tai," it expresses that all things emerge from the one. From that point onward, it states that this one disperses and becomes the manifold.

The phrase "based on this" appears five or six times. This phrase means that [one should] base himself on both right and wrong and walk both paths at the same time. Having arrived here, the conclusion is to treat them equally.

## Section 28 (ZZ 2.10)

> 夫道未始有封，言未始有常，為是而有畛也。請言其畛：有左，有右，有倫，有義，有分，有辯，有競，有爭，此之謂八德。
> In the Way, there is no boundary yet; in words, there is no constancy. But because one makes something *this*, there came to be a demarcation. Let me tell you more about the demarcations. When there is left, there is right; when there are relationships, there is morality; when there are divisions, there are discriminations; when there are competitions, and there are battles. These are called the eight virtues.

---

[16] In *Ximing*, Zhang Zai writes the following lines, which Han Wŏnjin sees as expressing the same idea as Zhuangzi's idea of treating all things equally:

> Heaven is called father, and earth is called mother. I, this small being, dwell mixed and centered among them. Therefore, the fullness of heaven and earth is my body, and the guidance of heaven and earth is my nature. The people are my siblings, and the creatures are my companions. (1-2)
> 乾稱父，坤稱母。予茲藐焉，乃混然中處。故天地之塞，吾其體。天地之帥，吾其性。民吾同胞，物吾與也。

第二十八段，此一段，又言道之一者，分爲物論之不同。自今且以下至此，反復言萬殊之出於一本，一本之散爲萬殊，知其一，則知其當齊故也。此下二段，專言齊之之意[+也]。堯舜問答一段，又引聖人，以證其說，猶孟子道性善，而稱堯舜以證之者也。

The twenty-eighth section. This section explains again that the Way as a single entity becomes differentiated, leading to differing discourses on things. From the phrase "now also" (ZZ 2.8) up to this point, it repeatedly states that the myriad particularities arise from this one fundamental source, and that this one source disperses to become the myriad particularities. Therefore, by knowing the one, one comes to understand that all the various things should be treated equally.

The two sections following this focus solely on the meaning of treating everything equally. One section (i.e., Section 31; ZZ 2.10) concerning the dialogue between Yao and Shun brings in the sages to validate [Zhuang Zhou's] argument, just as Mengzi, in discussing the goodness of human nature, invoked Yao and Shun as examples to prove his point.[17]

## Section 29 (ZZ 2.10)

> 六合之外，聖人存而不論；六合之內，聖人論而不議。春秋經世，先王之志，聖人議而不辯。故分也者，有不分也；辯也者，有不辯也。曰：何也？聖人懷之，衆人辯之以相示也。故曰：辯也者，有不見也。夫大道不稱，大辯不言，大仁不仁，大廉不嗛，大勇不忮。道昭而不道，言辯而不及，仁常而不成，廉清而不信，勇忮而不成。五者园而幾向方矣。故知止其所不知，至矣。孰知不言之辯，不道之道？
>
> Beyond the six realms, the sage exists but does not engage in discussion. Within the six realms, he discusses but does not debate. Concerning the chronicles of ruling the world or the records of the former kings, the sage debates but does not discriminate. Thus, one who divides fails to divide; one who discriminates fails to discriminate. One may ask: What does this mean? The sage embraces things, but ordinary people discriminate among them and thereby parade their discriminations to one another. Thus, it is said: one who discriminates fails to see. The great Way is not termed; great discrimination is not spoken; great benevolence is not benevolent; great modesty is not humble; great courage does not harm. If the Way is made clear, it is not the Way. If discriminations are put into words, they do not suffice. If benevolence has a fixed form, it cannot be complete. If modesty is punctilious, it cannot be trusted. If courage harms, it cannot be complete. These five are all round, but they tend toward the square. Therefore, understanding that rests in what it does not understand is the finest. Who can comprehend discriminations that are not spoken, the Way that is not uttered?

---

17 This refers to the following line in the *Mengzi* 3A1: "When Mengzi spoke of human nature being good, he always referred to Yao and Shun" 孟子道性善，言必稱堯舜。

第二十九段，六合之外，周之前未有言者，而周始言之。周之見處，亦自遠大非淺，夫之所可方也。存而不論之說，亦可謂知聖人之意矣。此段及下段，皆以ˆ不辨結之不辨，即齊物之意也。

The twenty-ninth section. The phrase "beyond the six realms" refers to "not-yet-being," which Zhuang Zhou previously mentioned (see Section 23; ZZ 2.6; and Section 26; ZZ 2.7). [This marks] the first time Zhuang Zhou concretely states the realm he envisions. This realm, too, is vast in itself but not base. It is a place where he may rightfully reside. The view that something exists but is not spoken of can also be said to reflect the intention of the sage.

This section, along with the one that follows, both use [the ideal of] non-discrimination to conclude the discussion of non-discrimination, which expresses the idea of treating all created things equally.

### Section 30 (ZZ 2.10)

> 若有能知，此之謂天府。注焉而不滿，酌焉而不竭，而不知其所由來，此之謂葆光。
>
> If there is one who can understand this, such a person may call it the heavenly storehouse. One pours into it and it is never full; one draws from it and it never runs dry, yet it does not know from where it comes. This is what is called preserved light.

第三十段，天府，道之所存、主處也。葆光，斂莊[藏]其道，而不露也。葆光字[存]，與上文滑疑，下文愚芚，一意，皆天地未生前，一陰虛靜之象也。

The thirtieth section. The notion of "heavenly storehouse" refers to the place where the Way exists, its principal dwelling. "Preserved light" means to gather in the Way, to store it, and not to reveal it outwardly. The concept of the preserved light corresponds in meaning to the term "doubt and uncertainty" from the earlier passage (Section 24; ZZ 2.7), and to "the foolish" in the passage below (Section 31; ZZ 2.12). All of these express the same idea: a single image of empty and tranquil yin before heaven and earth have yet come into being.

### Section 31 (ZZ 2.10)

> 故昔者堯問於舜曰：我欲伐宗、膾、胥敖，南面而不釋然。其故何也？舜曰：夫三子者，猶存乎蓬艾之間。若不釋然，何哉？昔者十日並出，萬物皆照，而況德之進乎日者乎！
>
> Therefore, long ago, Yao said to Shun, "I wish to attack the rulers of Zong, Kuai, and Xu Ao. Even as I face south (i.e., sit on the throne), this thought continues to trouble me. Why is that?" Shun answered, "The three rulers are but petty dwellers in the weeds and brush. If you are not untroubled, what is the reason? Long ago, ten suns rose at once, myriad things were all shone brightly. And how much greater is virtue than those suns!"

第三十一段，堯之不容三子，不能齊物者也；舜之所稱十日并出，萬物皆照，齊物之意也。

The thirty-first section. Yao's refusal to accept the three men (i.e., the rulers of Zong, Kuai, and Xu Ao) indicates that he was unable to treat all things equally. In contrast, Shun's statement that ten suns rose all at once and illuminated myriad things means that he was able to treat all things with equality.

## Section 32 (ZZ 2.11)[18]

> 齧缺問乎王倪曰：子知物之所同是乎？曰：吾惡乎知之！子知子之所不知邪？曰：吾惡乎知之！然則物無知邪？曰：吾惡乎知之！雖然，嘗試言之。庸詎知吾所謂知之非不知邪？庸詎知吾所謂不知之非知邪？且吾嘗試問乎女：民溼寢則腰疾偏死，鰌然乎哉？木處則惴慄恂懼，猨猴然乎哉？三者孰知正處？民食芻豢，麋鹿食薦，蝍且甘帶，鴟鴉耆鼠，四者孰知正味？猨，猵狙以為雌，麋與鹿交，鰌與魚游。毛嬙、麗姬，人之所美也，魚見之深入，鳥見之高飛，麋鹿見之决驟。四者孰知天下之正色哉？自我觀之，仁義之端，是非之塗，樊然殽亂，吾惡能知其辯！
>
> Toothless asked Wang Ni, "Do you know that by which things are deemed alike in their affirmations?"
>
> Wang Ni replied, "How would I know that?"
>
> [Toothless said] "Then do you know that you do not know it?"
>
> [Wang Ni] said, "How would I know that?"
>
> [Toothless said] "Then you know nothing about things?"
>
> [Wang Ni] said, "How would I know that either? Even so, let me say something. How could I possibly know that what I call knowing is not actually not knowing? How could I possibly know that what I call not knowing is not actually knowing? Now let me ask you something. If a person sleeps in a damp place, their back aches and they end up half paralyzed, but is that true for a loach? If a person lives in a tree, they are terrified and shake with fear, but is that true for a monkey? Of these three, then, who knows the right dwelling place? Humans eat the meat of grass-fed and grain-fed animals; deer eat grass; centipedes enjoy snakes; hawks and falcons prefer mice. Of these four, who knows the right taste? Monkeys pair with monkeys, deer roam with deer, and fish swim with fish. Humans declare that Mao Qiang and Lady Li were beautiful, but if fish saw them, they would dive deep into the stream; if birds saw them, they would fly off; if deer saw them, they would bolt away. Of these four, who knows the right beauty? When I see it from my own perspective, the beginnings of benevolence and righteousness, the paths of right and wrong, all are tangled and confused. So how could I possibly know anything about such discriminations?"

---

[18] From this section to the end of this chapter, Han Wŏnjin does not make separate sectional divisions, though the reason for this is unclear. For the sake of consistency and the reader's convenience, I have added numbered sections even where Han did not distinguish them.

齧缺曰：子不知利害，則至人固不知利害乎？王倪曰：至人神矣：大澤焚而不能熱，河、漢沍而不能寒，疾雷破山、風振海而不能驚。若然者，乘雲氣，騎日月，而遊乎四海之外。死生无變於己，而況利害之端乎！
Toothless asked, “If you do not know what is beneficial or harmful, then does the ultimate person likewise know nothing of such things?”

Wang Ni replied, “The ultimate person is mystical. Even if the great marshes catch fire, he does not burn; even if the great rivers freeze, he does not chill; even if lightning splits the mountains and gale winds shake the sea, he is not frightened. Such a person rides upon the clouds and mist, straddles the sun and moon, and wanders beyond the four seas. Death and life bring no change to himself, how much less the matters of gain and loss!”

齧缺、王倪問答，承上不辨之言，言齊物之道，在於無知。無ˆ知則不辨矣。無知者，不辨之本，而不辨者，無知之用也。自用而推其本[去]也。孰知正處，孰知正味，孰知正色，言道之無分於彼此，皆齊物之意。死生無變於已[己]，齊物之極也。死生亦大矣，而能一死生，則其爲齊物至矣。
The dialogue between Toothless and Wang Ni continues the message of “not discriminating” from above, explaining that the Way of treating all things equally exists within the absence of knowing. When in a state of the absence of knowing, one ceases to discriminate. The absence of knowing is the root of non-discrimination, and non-discrimination is the functioning of the absence of knowing. [Zhuangzi] moves from the functioning back to the root.

The phrases ““Who knows the right dwelling place?” “Who knows the right taste?” and “Who knows the right beauty?” express that within the Way there is no distinction between *this* and *that*, so all things must be treated equally. “Death and life bring no change to oneself” represents the ultimate in treating all things equally. Death and life are serious matters, but if one can regard them as one, then the treatment of all things as equal has reached its highest.

## Section 33 (ZZ 2.12)

瞿鵲子問乎長梧子曰：吾聞諸夫子，聖人不從事於務，不就利，不違害，不喜求，不緣道，无謂有謂，有謂无謂，而遊乎塵垢之外。夫子以為孟浪之言，而我以為妙道之行也。吾子以為奚若？
Frightened Magpie said to Long-living Paulownia, “I’ve heard Confucius say that the sage does not strive, does not seek gain, does not avoid harm, does not delight in pursuing, does not cling to the Way, says nothing yet speaks, speaks yet says nothing, and wanders beyond dust and grime. Confucius himself dismissed this as wild and careless talk, but I believe it expresses the working of the mysterious Way. What do you make of it?”

長梧子曰：是黃帝之所聽熒也，而丘也何足以知之！且女亦大早計，見卵而求時夜，見彈而求鴞炙。予嘗為女妄言之，女以妄聽之，奚？旁日月，挾宇宙，為其脗合，置其滑涽，以隸相尊。眾人役役，聖人愚芚，參萬歲而一成純。萬物盡然，而以是相蘊。予惡乎知說生之非惑邪！予惡乎知惡死之非弱喪而不知歸者邪！麗之姬，艾封人之子也。晉國之始得之也，涕泣沾襟；及其至於王所，與王同筐床，食芻豢，而後悔其泣也。

Long-living Paulownia said, "Even the Yellow Emperor would be perplexed by such words, how could you expect Confucius to understand them? And as for you, you're far too quick to pass judgment. You see an egg and demand a crowing rooster; you see a crossbow pellet and expect a roasted dove. Let me try saying something reckless, and I hope you'll listen with equal recklessness. How about that? [The sage] leans on the sun and moon, cradles the universe under one arm, merges with things, leaves the confusion just as it is, and honors what others look down on. Where ordinary men struggle and strain, the sage is dull and blank. He flows through ten thousand generations yet rests in the simplicity of oneness. For him, all things are completely as they are, and so they enfold and complete each other. How do I know that loving life isn't a delusion? How do I know that hating death isn't like a man who forgot his way home after leaving it in his youth? Lady Li was once the daughter of the border guard of Ai. When first taken captive and brought to Jin, she wept until her robe was soaked with tears. Later, living in the ruler's palace, sharing his bed, eating his rich food, she later regretted that she had wept.

予惡乎知夫死者不悔其始之蘄生乎！夢飲酒者，旦而哭泣；夢哭泣者，旦而田獵。方其夢也，不知其夢也。夢之中又占其夢焉，覺而後知其夢也。且有大覺而後知此其大夢也，而愚者自以為覺，竊竊然知之。君乎，牧乎，固哉！丘也，與女皆夢也；予謂女夢，亦夢也。

[Long-living Paulownia continued:] "How would I know that the dead do not look back on life and wonder why they longed for it? A man who dreams of drinking wine may wake in tears; a man who dreams of weeping may rise and go hunting at dawn. While dreaming, he does not know it's a dream, some even dream of interpreting dreams. Only upon waking do they know it was a dream. And someday will come a great awakening, then we will know this has all been one great dream. Yet the fools think they're awake, confident they grasp the truth. They call one man ruler, another herdsman, how dense! You and Confucius are both dreaming. And when I say you're dreaming, I'm dreaming too."

是其言也，其名為弔詭。萬世之後，而一遇大聖知其解者，是旦暮遇之也。既使我與若辯矣，若勝我，我不若勝，若果是也？我果非也邪？我勝若，若不吾勝，我果是也？而果非也邪？其或是也，其或非也邪？其俱是也，其俱非也邪？我與若不能相知也，則人固受其黮闇。

"Words like these will be called the supreme swindle. But ten thousand generations from now, a great sage may appear who understands their meaning, and even then, it will be as if he came in the blink of an eye. Suppose you and I have had an argument. If you have beaten me instead of me beating you, does that necessarily mean you are right and I am wrong? If I have beaten you instead of you beating me, does that necessarily mean I am right and you are wrong? Is one of us right and the other wrong? Or are both of us right, or both wrong?

If neither you nor I know the answer, then surely others are even more uncertain."

吾誰使正之？使同乎若者正之，既與若同矣，惡能正之！使同乎我者正之，既同乎我矣，惡能正之！使異乎我與若者正之，既異乎我與若矣，惡能正之！使同乎我與若者正之，既同乎我與若矣，惡能正之！然則我與若與人俱不能相知也，而待彼也邪？何化聲之相待，若其不相待。和之以天倪，因之以曼衍，所以窮年也。
"So, whom should we ask to decide what is right? Should we ask someone who agrees with you? But if they already agree with you, how can they decide fairly? Should we ask someone who agrees with me? But if they already agree with me, how can they decide? Should we ask someone who disagrees with both of us? But if they already disagree with both of us, how can they decide? Should we ask someone who agrees with both of us? But if they already agree with both of us, how can they decide? Clearly, then, neither you, nor I, nor anyone else can know the answer. Should we wait for yet another person? But to wait for one shifting voice to pass judgment on another is no different from waiting for none at all. Harmonize them all with heavenly equality, let them follow their endless transformations, and live out your years accordingly."

謂和之以天倪？曰：是不是，然不然。是若果是也，則是之異乎不是也亦無辯；然若果然也，則然之異乎不然也亦無辯。忘年忘義，振於無竟，故寓諸無竟。
"What do I mean by harmonizing with heavenly equality? Right is not truly right; so is not truly so. If right were truly right, it would stand apart so clearly from not-right that no debate would be necessary. If it were truly so, it would stand apart so clearly from not-so that no dispute would arise. Forget the passage of years; forget righteousness. Leap into the boundless and make it your dwelling!"

瞿鵲、長梧問答，承上不知之語，言此不知爲妙道之行，知之者爲大覺，而必遇聖人，而後知此之知也。不從事以下，皆愚芚、不知之貌。與天道篇，虛靜恬淡[惔]，寂寞無為之語，相表裏；彼以虛靜寂寞爲萬物之本，此以愚芚、不知爲妙道之行。周之見處，盡於是矣。
The dialogue between Frightened Magpie and Long-living Paulownia continues the words of 'not knowing' found earlier (Section 31; ZZ 2.11), explaining that 'not knowing' becomes the practice of the wondrous Way. One who knows this attains great awakening and necessarily encounters a sage, though only later comes to understand this.[19]

---

19 In Han Wŏnjin's phrase, "[he] later comes to understand this" (*hu chi ch'a chi chi ya* 後知此之知也), the referent of this (*ch'a* 此) is somewhat unclear. In context, it seems reasonable to interpret this *ch'a* as referring to 'having already attained great awakening through not knowing.' The passage in this chapter that most closely parallels this is in meaning: "Only after a great

From "does not engage in affairs" onward, all refer to the appearance of the [sage as] 'dull and blank' and 'not knowing.' In the 'Way of heaven' chapter, there are expressions such as 'emptiness, stillness, serenity, and clarity' (ZZ 13.1) and 'silence, solitude, and non-action' (ZZ 13.1). These two are complementary, and in that context, 'emptiness and stillness' are regarded as the root of myriad things. This is to take 'dull and blank' and 'not knowing' as a practice of the wondrous Way. What Zhuang Zhou envisions here lies in this.

然虛靜寂寞，即一陰之靜，而此陰之本於前陽，則安得爲萬物之本也。愚芚、不知，即善惡之混，而天理常屈於人慾，則安得爲妙道之行也。
However, 'emptiness and stillness,' 'silence and solitude' are just the tranquility of a single yin, and this yin's root is the prior yang, how then could [one single yin] be the root of all things? 'Dull and blank' and 'not knowing' contain both good and evil mixed together. If the principle of heaven always yields to human desire, how could they be the practice of the wondrous Way?

所謂道者，至虛之中至實者存，至靜之中至動者具。渾然而至善，粲然而至昭，則虛靜寂寞、愚芚、無知者，豈所以語道者哉。妄言、妄聽，言道在不知，則固不可以言語傳受。而今予與汝欲以言辨，則是妄也。將言道妙，而先自咎，其言之妄者，還以明。夫道在不知也。
What is called the 'Way' is supremely empty yet supremely substantive; it exists in the midst of supreme stillness yet possesses supreme movement. Though mixed, it is supremely good; though pure, it is supremely bright. How then can one speak of the Way by means of emptiness, stillness, dull-wittedness, or the absence of knowing?

The phrases "reckless speech" and "reckless hearing" signify that the Way is found in 'not knowing,' so it cannot truly be conveyed or given through language. If you and I now try to discriminate by words, this is only futile. It is stated that the Way is wondrous, but humans first carry their own faults, and they return the futility of words with clarity. Therefore, the Way lies in not knowing.

嘗，嘗試也。奚，何也。猶言何則也ˆ。萬物盡然，以是相蘊，言愚芚之道，萬物盡然，而聖人却，又以是愚芚之道，包之也。蘊，包也。萬世一遇大聖，是朝暮遇者，可見，周之自信之篤。俟後之遠，而不蘄[鄿]知於一世也。彼世人之ˆ有小知，一能便蘄見於一世，而不見知，則又怨者。
The word "to try" means "to test." "How" is the same as what, asking "What kind of principle is this?" The phrase "all things are completely as they are, and so they enfold and complete each other" means that the Way of dull-wittedness leaves all things in the state that they really are, and the sage also uses this Way of dull-wittedness to embrace all things. "To enfold" means to embrace.

---

awakening does one realize that this has been a great dream" (*ch'a yu taegak i huji ch'a ki taemong ya* 且有大覺而後知此其大夢也; 2.12), where 'this' refers to life itself.

The phrase "If in ten thousand generations one meets a great sage, it is as if meeting him morning and evening" shows Zhuang Zhou's deep faith in himself, indicating that though one waits for a distant future, one does not seek knowledge limited to a single generation. People in this world have small knowledge and can only seek what is visible within one generation, thus failing to see great wisdom, and so they end up complaining.

其視周爲何如哉。盖周之見處，亦高矣。其文，亦奇矣。然自有周書以來，註家非一，而未有能識其見處。解其文字者，則周之自期於萬世者，亦可謂不誣矣。然雖有大聖人者出，亦必不以周之知爲知矣。然則周終無所遇矣。
What is the 'viewing' that Zhuang Zhou does like? Generally, the place where Zhuang Zhou looks is also lofty. His writing is likewise extraordinary. Yet ever since Zhuang Zhou's book came into being, the commentators have all differed, and no one has yet truly recognized the place that Zhuang Zhou was looking toward. If one [accurately] interprets his words, Zhuang Zhou is someone who envisions ten thousand generations, and even that cannot be said to be a mere exaggeration. However, even if a great sage were to appear in the world, it still does not necessarily follow that what Zhuang Zhou knew would thereby become true knowing. Thus, in the end, Zhuang Zhou had no one he could meet.

既使我與若辯，承上妄言、妄聽，而言妄言、妄聽，即所謂與辨也，而待彼也。彼指萬世之聖人也。言我與若辨此道，而世人未有能定其是非者，則將待於萬世之聖人也。盖歎世人之不知道，而齊物之意，亦寓其中。
The phrase "If you and I were to argue" follows the earlier phrases of "reckless speech" and "reckless hearing." These reckless speech and reckless hearing refer to the so-called act of making discriminations together, and it implies waiting for 'that person,' 'That [person]' is the sage awaited across ten thousand generations. If I were to distinguish this Way with you, and the people of the world still could not determine what is right or wrong, then it means one must wait for the sage of ten thousand generations. Though the people of the world do not know the Way, the meaning of treating all things equally is already embedded within it.

化聲相待，言是非待言語而辨也。若其不待，言與其待言語而辨是非，何如。其與ˆ兩忘，而不相待也。和[化]之天倪，因之曼衍，忘年忘義，振於無竟，即上環中以應無窮之意也。自今且至此，皆釋環中以應無窮之意也。
"All voices wait for one another" means that right and wrong await language in order to be distinguished. "As if they do not wait" asks: What is it like to distinguish right and wrong by waiting for language? It means forgetting both sides, and then not waiting on each other at all.

"Harmonize by the heavenly equality, and follow the vast and far" and "forget age and forget righteousness, and rise within the limitless" express the idea of responding to things without end by holding to the very center of the ring.

From the phrase beginning "now also" (ZZ 2.8) up to this point, all these passages interpret the idea of responding to things without an end by being like the ring's very center.

## Section 34 (ZZ 2.13)

> 罔兩問景曰：曩子行，今子止，曩子坐，今子起，何其無特操與？景曰：吾有待而然者邪！吾所待又有待而然者邪！吾待蛇蚹、蜩翼邪！惡識所以然？惡識所以不然？
>
> Shadow Doubt asked the Shade, saying: "Formerly you moved, and now you are still; formerly you sat, and now you rise—how is it that you have no constant way of conduct?"
>
> The Shade replied: "Am I as I am because I depend on something? And does that on which I depend also depend on something else? Do I depend on the snake's slough or the cicada's wing? How would I know why it is so? How would I know why it is not so?"

罔兩問景，言萬物之皆出於道也。吾有待而然，景之待於形也，所待又有待形之，又待於真宰之道也。言萬物之是非成毀相因而生，而又皆同歸於道，則可見其自私者之為遠於道，而齊之者之ˆ為合於道也。

The passage where Shadow Doubt questions Shade expresses that all things arise from the Way.

The phrase "Am I as I am because I depend on something?" means that Shade depends on a physical form, which in turn depends on another form it can lean on, and ultimately, all relies upon the true sovereign, the Way. It states that the right and wrong of all things, their completion and failure, arise by depending on each other, and all equally return to the Way as one. Therefore, what is personal or partial is distant from the Way, and treating all things equally is what accords with the Way.

## Section 35 (ZZ 2.14)

> 昔者莊周夢為胡蝶，栩栩然胡蝶也，自喻適志與！不知周也。俄然覺，則蘧蘧然周也。不知周之夢為胡蝶與，胡蝶之夢為周與？周與胡蝶，則必有分矣。此之謂物化。
>
> Once, Zhuang Zhou dreamed he was a butterfly—fluttering about, fully a butterfly, feeling at ease and pleased with himself, unaware that he was Zhou. Suddenly he awoke, and there he was unmistakably Zhou. He did not know whether it was Zhou who had dreamed of being a butterfly, or a butterfly dreaming of being Zhou.
>
> Between Zhou and the butterfly there should have been some distinction. This is called the transformation of things.

莊周夢蝴蝶,[20] 言萬物之為一體也。比上罔兩問景，又是密一密，栩栩然蝴蝶，周之夢為[而]蝴蝶也。蘧蘧然周，蝴蝶之夢為周也。自物觀之，則周與蝴蝶有辨，而自道觀之，則周與蝴蝶，即一也。故曰物化。此一段，總結一篇齊物之意。與上文風竅之說，相為表裡。物化二字，又結一段之意，而與篇首喪我二字相應。喪我者，齊物之謂也。物化者，物齊之謂也。

The passage where Zhuang Zhou dreams of being a butterfly speaks to the oneness of all things. Compared to the earlier passage where Shadow Doubt questioned Shade, this one is even more profound and yet secretive.

The phrase "fluttering about, fully a butterfly" means that Zhou became a butterfly in his dream. And "he was unmistakably Zhou" means that the butterfly, in the dream, became Zhuang Zhou.

From the perspective of thing, there is a distinction between Zhuang Zhou and the butterfly. But from the perspective of the Way, Zhuang Zhou and the butterfly are one and the same. Hence the term "the transformation of things."

This single passage encapsulates the entire message of this chapter on treating all things equally. It forms a complementary pair with the discussion of wind and the hollows in the earlier passages (Sections 2 and 3; ZZ 2.1).

The phrase "transformation of things" also concludes the message of this section. It corresponds to the phrase "lose oneself" that appears at the very beginning of the chapter (Section 1; ZZ 2.1). "Lose oneself" refers to treating all things equally, while transformation of things refers to all things becoming equal.

## Concluding Remarks

此篇篇[之]首，即擧喪我二字，以示齊物之方。篇末復出物化二字，以證物齊之實；中間又說道樞二字，以指齊物之本。大塊噫氣一段，言一本之散為萬殊，以啓齊物之端。罔兩問景一段，言萬物之復為一體，以會齊物之極。中間方詳說齊物之意，而吹萬不同以下，言物論之末異而ˆ本同。

At the beginning of this chapter, [Zhuangzi] mentions the phrase "lose oneself," and in doing so, he shows the method of treating all things equally. And at the end of the chapter, the notion of "transformation of things" appears again, thereby proving the actuality of the equality among all things. In the middle, he speaks of the concept of the pivot of the Way, by which he points to the foundation of treating all things equally.

The passage "The great clod breathes *qi* out" (section 2; ZZ 2.1) discusses that the one root disperses and generates ten thousand particularities, thereby opening the clue to treating all beings equally.

The passage "Shadow Doubt asks Shade" (section 34; ZZ 2.13) speaks of the myriad things returning to one body, and through this, reveals the highest realization of treating all beings equally. In the middle part, the meaning of "treating all things equally" is explained in detail.

---

20 In the Kyujanggak edition, this 'Butterfly Dream' passage is separated as a distinct section, but in the Yŏam version, it is not separated.

Beginning with the phrase "Blowing on the myriad things in a different way" (section 3; ZZ 2.1), it is spoken that although the conclusions of discourses on things differ, their root is the same.

結歸都在十六段，是非、莫得其偶一句上，以示道樞之所在。指馬之喩以下，反覆[復]言齊之之意，皆自十六段「環中以應無窮」一句上推出來，以示道樞之爲用。此道樞二字，爲一篇之樞紐者也。

All of this leads to a single line in section 16 (ZZ 2.5), which says that "neither side can find its proper match" in terms of right and wrong. With this, [Zhuangzi] reveals the place where the "pivot of the Way" is found. From the metaphor of "pointing and the horse" (section 17; ZZ 2.7) onward, [he] repeatedly expounds the meaning of "treating all things equally."

[Zhuangzi] traces everything back to the single phrase in section 16 (ZZ 2.5): "from the center of the ring, it responds to the infinite," and through this, he shows that this is the functioning of the Way as a pivot. The notion of the pivot of the Way thus becomes the central pivot of this entire chapter.

十六段以上，雖非無齊之之意，而大意以物論為主，故其說齊之者略矣。十六段以下，固皆兼說物論，而大意以齊之為主，故每段必以齊之之意結之。蓋此為一篇[片]文字，故上下所言互相出入，雖若不可分段，大意所分，則又自不亂正，如《大學》之八條目、《中庸》之四大節。

Above section sixteen, the meaning of "treating things equally" is not absent, but the main focus lies in the "discourses on things." Therefore, any explanation of "equal treatment [of things]" [in those parts] remains brief.

However, below section 16, while the discussions still encompass the "discourses on things," the central focus shifts to "treating things equally." As such, every section [from section sixteen onward], without exception, concludes with the meaning of "equal treatment [of things.]" Thus, this becomes the key concept of the entire chapter.

Therefore, what is said above and below [section sixteen] connects and responds to one another. If the text is not divided by formality but rather by its underlying meaning, it would remain coherent and not confused. It would resemble the eight articles in the *Daxue* (2)[21] or the four major divisions in the *Zhongyong*.[22]

---

[21] The eight articles of the "Daxue" are: 1) the investigation of things (*gewu* 格物); 2) the extension of understanding (*zhizhi* 致知); 3) the authentication of intention (*chengyi* 誠意); 4) the rectification of the heart-mind (*zhengxin* 正心); 5) the cultivation of the self (*xiushen* 修身); 6) the regulation of the family (*qijia* 齊家); 7) the governance of the state (*zhiguo* 治國); and 8) the pacification of the world (*ping tianxia* 平天下).

[22] The four major divisions (*sa taejŏl* 四大節) of *Zhongyong* refer to an interpretive approach proposed by Zhu Xi in his later years. With this concept, he claims that the current text of *Zhongyong* is understood as divided into four large sections, each organized around a distinct theme. The four themes are: 1) the philosophical exploration of the concept of *zhongyong* 中

雖略[若]分箇節次先後，而大體相關，故語意不得無時相攙入。讀此篇者，以此意推之，則亦或知此解之不妄矣。
Although [this chapter is] loosely divided into individual sections and arranged in a certain order, they are, on the whole, interrelated. Therefore, at no point are the meanings of words not deeply interconnected. If readers of this chapter reflect on this intention, some will come to see that this kind of interpretation is not without substance.

此篇蓋周之文用，意最深者，故始合而分，至中而復合。既合而分，至末而復合。假寓言而談實相語。雖幻而意獨至，苟非得意而忘言者，難乎讀是書矣。若論其文字之體，則句句神，字字奇，熟讀可見，今不暇論也。
In this chapter, Zhuang Zhou's use of writing reaches its deepest level of meaning. Thus, in the beginning, the meaning comes together and then divides; in the middle, it comes together again, and once joined, it divides once more; at the end, it comes together yet again. He borrowed the form of allegorical speech to speak of what is real. Though it may seem strange, its meaning is uniquely profound.

Unless one grasps the purport and forgets the words, it will be difficult indeed to read this book. As for the style of its writing, every sentence is inspired, every character marvelous—this becomes clear upon careful reading, and I shall not discuss it here.

---

庸 (sections 1–11); 2) the balance between what is manifest and what is hidden, embracing both the subtle and the great (sections 12–20); 3) the Way of Heaven and the Way of humans (sections 21–32); and 4) the essential message of the entire work: a summation of *Zhongyong* text (section 33). In short, for Zhu Xi, the Four Great Sections represent an attempt to understand the present form of *Zhongyong* which may appear somewhat textually disordered, in a more systematic way by dividing it into four major thematic blocks.

In Chosŏn, numerous scholars devoted themselves to various creative interpretive efforts to understand the structure of *Zhongyong* text in a more consistent and systematic way. These efforts were based on Zhu Xi's structural interpretation of the text using the concept of "major divisions," by which he divided the text into sections. See Choi 2010.

Han Wŏnjin regarded Zhu Xi's theory of six major divisions as an early-stage theory and viewed the theory of four essential points as Zhu Xi's final position. Accordingly, he discarded the six-division theory, renamed the four-point theory as the "four major divisions," and formalized it as Zhu Xi's orthodox view. Han Wŏnjin's interpretation became the mainstream position within the Kiho school of thought to which he belonged from the eighteenth century onward. See Choi 2007, 271-303.

# Chapter 3

# The Foundation of Nurturing Life

前篇言齊物：齊物則物無害已，而可以養生。故養生次之。主，猶言本也，言養生之本也。

The previous chapter discussed the equal treatment of all things. When one treats things equally, nothing can harm him, and thereby life can be nurtured. Hence, the topic of nurturing life follows. The term "foundation" in the chapter title is akin to "root," indicating the fundamental basis for nurturing life.

**Section 1 (ZZ 3.1)**

> 吾生也有涯，而知也无涯。以有涯隨无涯，殆已；已而為知者，殆而已矣。為善无近名，為惡无近刑。緣督以為經，可以保身，可以全生，可以養親，可以盡年。
>
> My life has an end, but knowledge has no end. To pursue the endless with what has an end, this is nothing but perilous. To know this and still pursue knowledge is perilous upon peril. When one does good, one should not draw near to fame; when one does evil, one should not draw near to punishment. By following the thread of the mean as one's constant rule, one can preserve the body, keep life whole, care for one's parents, and complete one's allotted years.

首段有涯，有限也；無涯，無限也。言以有限之生，役於無限之知，則精神內弊，患害外至。知者，即危身之道，而非養生之方，故曰殆已。承前篇以不知齊物之意而言，故下筆第一言，便打到「知」之一字，以起下文，無近名，無近刑之意。

In the opening section, "Having an end" means "having limit" or "being finite," while "having no end" means "having no limit" or "being infinite." It says that when one uses a finite life in pursuit of infinite knowledge, the vital essence and spirit are worn away from within, and anxiety and harm arise from without. [This pursuit of] knowledge thus becomes a path that endangers the body, and it is not a method for nurturing life. Therefore, it is said to be "nothing but perilous."

Continuing from the previous chapter, [this one] discusses the meaning of not knowing how to treat all things equally. Therefore, the first thing mentioned in the writing was the single word "knowledge," and by doing so, it gives rise to the meanings of the later sentences: "not drawing near to fame" and "not drawing near to punishment."

蓋爲善爲惡，皆就暗暗地，做不使人覺知者，即所以不用知者，而爲養生之本也。然爲善，不敢[能]做大爲惡，亦不敢[能]做大巧，爲避患者，可見，其用知之深密也。
Whether one does good or evil, it must be done quietly and without drawing attention, so that others are unaware [of one's actions]. In this way, not using knowledge becomes the foundation for nurturing life. However, by doing good while not daring or being able to commit great evil, and by not daring or being able to engage in great contrivance, one thereby avoids calamity. From this it can be seen how deeply concealed and subtle is the proper use of knowledge.

爲惡無近刑者，內不絶爲惡之事，而外不被爲惡之禍，小人之尤者也。其說之非，不待多辨而明矣。至於爲善，無近名者，其語有似乎君子。爲己之學，則尙絅者，亦或有取[斯]矣。然實有公私邪正之辨。君子不要近名，懼善之未實也。此之不要近名，懼善之爲禍也。一懼於不實，則爲之益力，而以至於善日積ˆ矣。一懼於爲禍，則爲之不敢，而必至於善一[日]喪矣。學者正當於此，似是處痛加明辨也。
"When one does evil, one should not draw near to punishment" means that although one does not completely stop doing evil deeds inwardly, one does not suffer the calamity of doing evils externally. This refers to the failings of a petty person. It is clear that the error of this view requires no further analysis.

When it comes to doing good, the phrase "not drawing near to fame" resembles [the conduct of] a noble person. Learning for oneself is like wearing a thin and simple garment over fine clothes.[1] Some may find guidance in this.

However, in reality, there is a distinction between the public and the private, and between evil and righteousness. A noble person must not draw near to fame and should fear whether the good [he practices] lacks substance. This means that one should avoid pursuing fame and should fear that goodness might become a source of harm. Once one begins to fear the lack of substance in one's good deeds, one will strive even more to practice them sincerely. In doing so, one's closeness to true goodness will accumulate day by day. Once one comes to fear that [goodness] may become a source of harm, one may dare to do what should not be done, and then one's attainment of goodness is sure to be ruined all at once. Those who pursue learning must be correct and upright on this point. This is similar to locating a sore spot and applying clear and precise discernment to the pain.

緣督以為經，言曰緣善惡之中，以爲常也。督者，督脉也。人之脊脉謂之督脉。督脉在背之中。故衣後中縫，亦謂之督。
The phrase, "By following the thread of the mean as one's constant rule," means to regard that which arises from the balance between good and evil as the

[1] The original phrase "simple garment over fine clothes" (*sanggyŏng* 尙絅) means to add a thin layer over fine silk clothes, so as not to display the finery outwardly. This symbolizes how a gentleman, though possessing praiseworthy virtue, does not show it openly to others.

constant [standard]. The thread of the mean here refers to the governor vessel.[2] The blood vessel that runs along the ridge of a person's back is also called the governor vessel. Since the governor vessel lies at the very center of the back, the seam that runs down the center of the back of a garment after it is made is also called the "the thread of the mean."

## Section 2 (ZZ 3.2)

庖丁為文惠君解牛，手之所觸，肩之所倚，足之所履，膝之所踦，砉然嚮然，奏刀騞然，莫不中音。合於桑林之舞，乃中經首之會。文惠君曰：譆！善哉！技蓋至此乎？庖丁釋刀對曰：臣之所好者道也，進乎技矣。始臣之解牛之時，所見无非牛者。三年之後，未嘗見全牛也。方今之時，臣以神遇，而不以目視，官知止而神欲行。依乎天理，批大郤，導大窾，因其固然。技經肯綮之未嘗，而況大軱乎！

Cook Ding was cutting up an ox for Lord Wenhui. Wherever his hands touched, his shoulders leaned, his feet stepped, or his knees pressed, there came a sound—*whack! whish!*—and the rhythm of the knife was in perfect accord, as though with the dance of the Mulberry Grove and the harmony of the music [for the Emperor Shun].

Lord Wenhui said, "Ah! Excellent! Can such skill truly reach this height?"

Cook Ding laid down his knife and replied, "What I care for is the Way, which goes beyond mere skill. When I first began cutting up oxen, all I could see was the whole ox. After three years, I no longer saw the ox as a whole. Now I meet it with my spirit rather than look at it with my eyes. My bodily senses rest, and my spirit acts as it wills. Following the natural patterns, I strike through the great gaps, guide the blade through the great openings, and respond to the ox as it is. The edge of my blade has never encountered even the smallest joint or tendon—how much less the great bones!"

良庖歲更刀，割也；族庖月更刀，折也。今臣之刀十九年矣，所解數千牛矣，而刀刃若新發於硎。彼節者有間，而刀刃者无厚，以无厚入有間，恢恢乎其於遊刃必有餘地矣，是以十九年而刀刃若新發於硎。雖然，每至於族，吾見其難為，怵然為戒，視為止，行為遲。動刀甚微，謋然已解，如土委地。提刀而立，為之四顧，為之躊躇滿志，善刀而藏之。文惠君曰：善哉！吾聞庖丁之言，得養生焉。

[Ding continued] "A good cook changes his knife once a year, for he cuts. An ordinary cook changes his knife every month, for he hacks. Now I have used this knife for nineteen years, and in cutting up several thousand oxen, its edge is as if it had just come from the whetstone. For the joints have spaces between them, while the blade has no thickness. To let what has no thickness pass through what has space between—how easy and ample the movement of the

[2] The governing vessel refers to one of the eight extraordinary meridians, which begins at the perineum, runs upward along the center of the back along the spine, passes through the nape of the neck, over the crown of the head, and ends at the upper gums.

> blade! Thus, after nineteen years, the edge of my knife is still as if freshly sharpened. Even so, whenever I come to a complex structure, I see that it is difficult, and I take warning. I keep my gaze fixed, move the blade with care, and act slowly. Then, with the slightest motion of the knife—*whish!*—the whole thing comes apart, falling to the ground like a clod of earth. Afterward, I lift the knife, stand upright, look around in satisfaction, and, pleased with myself, carefully put the blade away."
>
> Lord Wenhui said, "Excellent! From the words of Cook Ding, I have learned how to nurture life."

庖丁解牛一段，借丁之解牛，以喻緣督為經之意。彼節有間。數語形容庖丁解牛，入妙處，極妙，而ˆ又以此喻之於緣督為經之意，尤妙。彼節有間，即善惡之有間也。以刀刄之無厚入於彼節之有間，即以身行於善惡之間也。恢恢遊刃，即身之行於善惡之間者，恢恢然，無左右觸禍之患也。
This one section about the story of Cook Ding dismembering the ox uses the case of Cook Ding's cutting up the ox to reveal that the meaning of "following the thread of the mean as the constant rule" lies in the empty gaps between the joints of the ox. Various expressions in this section vividly describe how Cook Ding's dismemberment of the ox reaches a subtle and extremely skillful level, and through this, they also illuminate the even more profound meaning of "following the thread of the mean as the constant rule." The fact that each joint of the ox has a gap means that there is a space between good and evil. Using a blade without thickness to insert into those joint gaps means acting between good and evil. The phrase "how easy and ample the movement of the blade" means that one's actions between good and evil are so wide and broad that there is neither left nor right, thus there is no concern about encountering trouble.

## Section 3 (ZZ 3.3)

> 公文軒見右師而驚曰：是何人也？惡乎介也？天與，其人與？曰：天也，非人也。天之生是使獨也，人之貌有與也。以是知其天也，非人也。
> When an officer of the Documents Office saw the Commander of the Right, he was startled and said, "What sort of person are you? How did you come to be one-footed? Was it heaven, or was it man?" "It was heaven, not man," replied [the Commander]. "When heaven gave me life, I was made to be one-legged. My human appearance is something granted to me. From this I know that it was heaven, not man."

公文軒一段，承上文，言養生者，固蘄免於患禍[害]，然患禍之來，[+來]或出於天之所使，而人之所ˆ不能免者，故隨其所遇，安之若命，不以憂畏自傷，亦養生之道也。有與之與字，語助辭，與天與、人與之與，同。言人之貌有，是獨也歟。人之ˆ貌，本無是獨，而斯人也獨，則知其天也云爾。
The section about an officer of the Documents Office continues from the previous passage, explaining that nurturing life truly means seeking to avoid worries

and calamities. However, worries and calamities sometimes arise because heaven wills it so, and humans cannot avoid it. Therefore, one should accept what one encounters, calmly embrace it as fate, and by doing so, not harm oneself through anxiety or fear. This, too, is a way of nurturing life.

In the phrase "is it there?" the character *yŏ* is a particle, the same as the *yŏ* in "Was it heaven or man?" It speaks whether, among the [natural] human form, there is one-leggedness or not. It is said that, among the human form, there is originally no such one-leggedness, but this person is one-legged, and from this, one knows that it was [because of] heaven.

## Section 4 (ZZ 3.4)

> 澤雉十步一啄，百步一飲，不蘄畜乎樊中。神雖王，不善也。
> The marsh pheasant walks ten paces for one peck and a hundred paces for one drink, yet it does not wish to be kept in a cage. Even if you treat it like a king, its spirit will not be content.

澤雉一段，[3] 承上段，而言患害之來，多由[有]於榮利之拘係，故養生者，必去而不處也。

This one section about the marsh pheasant continues from the previous section, explaining that worry and harm often arise from entangling relationships driven by the pursuit of self-interest. Therefore, one who nurtures life must eliminate [such pursuits] and avoid placing themselves in such situations.

## Section 5 (ZZ 3.5)

> 老聃死，秦失弔之，三號而出。弟子曰：非夫子之友邪？曰：然。然則弔焉若此，可乎？曰：然。始也，吾以為其人也，而今非也。向吾入而弔焉，有老者哭之，如哭其子；少者哭之，如哭其母。彼其所以會之，必有不蘄言而言，不蘄哭而哭者。是遁天倍情，忘其所受，古者謂之遁天之刑。適來，夫子時也；適去，夫子順也。安時而處順，哀樂不能入也，古者謂是帝之縣解。
> When Lao Dan died, Qin Shi went to mourn him, but after giving three cries, he turned and left the room.
>
> "Weren't you a friend of the Master?" a disciple asked.
>
> "I was," [Qin Shi] replied.
>
> "And you think it's appropriate to mourn him like that?"
>
> "Yes," said Qin Shi. "At first, I believed he was the very one, but now I see he was not. When I went in to mourn, I saw old men weeping for him as if he were their son, and young men weeping as if he were their mother. To gather people like that, he must have done something to make them speak of him, though he did not ask to be spoken of, or to make them weep, though he did not ask to be mourned. That is to hide from heaven, to turn away from the true

[3] In the Yŏam edition, this section is not separated from the preceding one.

condition, and to forget what one is born with. In ancient times, this was called the crime of hiding from heaven. Your master came because the time called for it, and he left because he followed the course. If you are content with the time and willing to go along with things, then grief and joy have no way to enter. In the old days, this was called being free from the bonds of heaven."

老聃一^段[數]，言人有生，則必有死。死者，人之所不可諱。雖養生者不得免焉，故視死如生[徃]，不以哀樂動其心，亦養生之道也。
This one section concerning Lao Dan explains that when a human is born, he is bound to die. Death is something one cannot escape. Even those who nurture their lives well cannot escape it. Therefore, viewing death as equal to birth, and thereby not moving one's heart/mind with sorrow and joy, it is also the Way of nurturing life.

**Section 6 (ZZ 3.6)**

指窮於為薪，火傳也，不知其盡也。
One may point out that although the firewood is exhausted, the fire is transmitted on, and no one knows its end.

末端，指，指意也。就養生主，主字翻作指字，言養生之指意也。薪，喻物。火，喻道。薪窮火傳，言物有窮而道無盡也。窮於為薪一句，與篇首吾生有涯一句，相應，言善養生者，養其形而傳其道。有涯之生，雖有時盡，而所得之道，即[其]無時而盡也。此養生之指意云也。
In the final section, the character for "to point out" means the main point. In terms of the title, "the foundation of nurturing life," the notion of "foundation" can be replaced with this notion of "main point,", which will refer to the "main point of nurturing life."

The "firewood" represents a thing, and the "fire" the Way. The phrase "the firewood runs out, but the fire is passed on" means that while things come to an end, the Way has no end. The phrase "although the firewood is exhausted" corresponds to the phrase "my life has an end" found at the very beginning of this chapter. It says, one who nurtures life well is someone who not only cares for the body but also transmits the Way. The finite life eventually comes to an end with time, but attaining the Way does not perish with time. This is said to be the main purpose of nurturing life.

**Concluding Remarks**

物有盡而道無盡者，亦吾儒之所言也。然吾儒所謂道無盡者，即[而]指天地公共[共公]之理也。吾^身^之^理^，雖與吾身而存亡，天地公共[共公]之理，卻不以吾身之存亡而存亡也。此所謂道無盡也。然吾身之理，即與天地公共[共公]之理，非有二理，則雖謂[爲]吾身之道不亡，亦可也。非謂吾身所具[有]之理，雖其死後，團聚不亡，寄寓在天地中間，身死之後，猶認以爲已[己]物也。

Things have an end, while the Way has no end; this is also what we Confucians say. However, when we Confucians say "the Way has no end," we are referring to the universal principle of heaven and earth. The personal principle that belongs to me may exist and perish along with me, but the universal principle of heaven and earth does not come into being or cease to exist based on whether I exist or not. This is [what we Confucians mean by] "the Way has no end."

However, my personal principle and the universal principle of heaven and earth are not two [separate] principles. That is, it is also possible to say that even my own Way does not perish. [But] it is not to say that the principle inherent in my body, even after death, does not perish but still gathers as a whole, residing between heaven and earth, and after the body dies, one regards it as one's own.

周之所謂道無盡，其指異於是．周盖認氣之虛靜者爲[而]道，故以人之得是氣，而生者爲得道， 而生以人死， 而其氣歸於冥漠者爲道之復返於虛靜， 而又自虛靜復[後]爲人物， 萬古相傳也． 後篇所謂殺生不死， 生生不生者， 皆指此耳．[4] 殊不知氣化流行，徃過來續，人死而氣散者久，則必無也．此其無見於道．故亦無見於氣也．釋氏之見其源，亦出於老莊，故其言見性成佛，超越滅度者，其指亦如此．
What Zhuang Zhou means by "the Way has no end" differs in its main point from this. In general, Zhuang Zhou regards the Way as an empty and tranquil *qi*. Therefore, when a person is born by obtaining this *qi*, being born is considered the attainment of the Way; and when a person lives and dies, and that *qi* returns to a dark and vast state, it is seen as the Way returning to its original empty and tranquil state.

Moreover, from that empty and tranquil state, all people and all things are once again brought forth, this is what continues through all ages and generations. The passage in the later chapter, namely, the so-called "To kill life is not to die; to give life is not to be born" (ZZ 6.4), merely points to this idea. [Thus,] in particular, [Zhuangzi] fails to recognize that *qi* undergoes transformation and flow, that it departs, passes, returns, and continues, and that when a person dies and their *qi* has long since dispersed, [the *qi*] will inevitably cease to exist. This shows that he did not truly grasp the Way, and did not understand *qi* either.

The origins of Śākyamuni's view (i.e., transmigration) also stem from Laozi and Zhuangzi. Therefore, the [Sŏn Buddhist] teaching such as "seeing one's nature to become a Buddha" and "transcending to nirvana" share the same message as this (i.e., Zhuangzi's *qi*-centric theory).

---

[4] In the Yŏam edition, this entire sentence is missing. As in the earlier case from the Chapter Two, it seems a line was accidentally skipped by the copyist or editor.

# Chapter 4

# Living Among People in the World

前篇言養生，養生則得道於己，而可以行世，故人間世ˆ次之。
The previous chapter spoke of nurturing life. By nurturing life, one attains the Way within oneself, and through this, one can engage with the world. Hence, the chapter on "Living Among People in the World" comes next.

## Section 1 (ZZ 4.1)

顏回見仲尼請行。曰：奚之？曰：將之衛。曰：奚為焉？曰：回聞衛君，其年壯，其行獨，輕用其國，而不見其過，輕用民死，死者以國量乎澤，若蕉，民其无如矣。回嘗聞之夫子曰：治國去之，亂國就之，醫門多疾。願以所聞思其則，庶幾其國有瘳乎！
Yan Hui, seeing Zhongni (i.e., Confucius), asked to go on a journey. He said, "Where are you going?"

[Yan Hui] replied, "I am going to the state of Wei."

[Zhongni] asked, "What will you do there?"

[Yan Hui] said, "I have heard of the ruler of Wei: in his prime, he acts independently, lightly administering his state without noticing his own faults; lightly using his people even to the point of death. The dead are counted by the swampful, like so much grass. His people have nowhere to turn. I once heard you say, Master: 'Leave the well-governed state and go to the one in chaos. At the doctor's gate are many sick men.' I wish to reflect on what I have heard in order to consider proper principles—perhaps then the state may be restored!"[1]

## Section 2 (ZZ 4.1)

仲尼曰：譆！若殆往而刑耳！夫道不欲雜，雜則多，多則擾，擾則憂，憂而不救。古之至人，先存諸己，而後存諸人。所存於己者未定，何暇至於暴人之所行！
Zhongni said, "Alas! You are going forth only to meet with punishment! The Way does not tolerate mixture. When it is mixed, it becomes manifold; when manifold, it becomes confused; when confused, it brings anxiety; and anxiety cannot be rescued. The ultimate persons of old first established [the Way] within themselves, and only afterward established it in others. If what you

[1] In both the Kyujanggak and the Yŏam editions, the first section is missing. The reason for this absence is unclear.

would establish in yourself is not yet settled, how could you have leisure to correct the conduct of the violent man (i.e., the ruler)?

且若亦知夫德之所蕩，而知之所為出乎哉？德蕩乎名，知出乎爭。名也者，相軋也；知也者，爭之器也。二者凶器，非所以盡行也。且德厚信矼，未達人氣；名聞不爭，未達人心。而彊以仁義繩墨之言術暴人之前者，是以人惡有其美也，命之曰菑人。菑人者，人必反菑之，若殆為人菑夫！
Moreover, do you even understand whence virtue becomes dissipated, and from where knowledge arises? Virtue is dissipated through fame; knowledge arises from contention. Fame means mutual contention; knowledge is the instrument of contention. These two are baleful instruments, not the means by which one can fully practice [the Way]. When one's virtue is deep and one's trust is solid, it still does not yet reach the *qi* of others; when one's name is renowned yet without contention, it still does not yet touch their minds. But if one forcibly takes the verbal arts of benevolence and righteousness, along with the measuring cords and ink lines of moral standards, and brandishes them before the violent man, this is precisely why people come to detest those who possess such excellence. Such a person is called a calamity-bringer. As for the calamity-bringer—people are sure to bring calamity upon him. You are indeed about to become a calamity to others!"

第二段，道不欲雜，雜字包下文名字、知字，而言名與知，道之所以雜也。此段與第八段相反，而正相應八段一宅，即道之不雜也。無感其名，無門無毒，即去名與知之謂也。
The second section. In the phrase "The Way does not tolerate mixture," the word "mixture" encompasses the meanings of the notions such as "fame" and "knowledge" that appear in the section below. Fame and knowledge refer to elements that cause the Way to become mixed or impure.

This section and the eighth one stand in contrast to each other,[2] but the phrase "dwelling in oneness" (ZZ 4.2) in section eight directly corresponds to the idea that "the Way does not tolerate mixture" in this section. The expressions [in section 8], "to feel nothing for fame" and "having no gate and no obstruction" refer to the elimination of fame and knowledge.

[2] Here Han Wŏnjin does not clarify exactly in what way they are opposed, so it is difficult to determine the precise nature of the contrast. However, it seems to relate to Confucius' stance on Yan Hui's decision to go to the state of Wei. In the section two, Confucius is skeptical, suggesting that Yan Hui will only face punishment if he goes to Wei. Yet in the section 8, Confucius advises acting with composure and clarity and knowing when to advance or retreat without being swayed by fame. So, in section 8, Confucius does not see Yan Hui's political engagement in Wei entirely negatively, as he did in section 2. Thus, the contradiction that Han sees here is likely the difference in Confucius's stance regarding Yan Hui's entry into politics.

## Section 3 (ZZ 4.1)

> 且苟為悅賢而惡不肖，惡用而求有以異？若唯无詔，王公必將乘人而鬭其捷。而目將熒之，而色將平之，口將營之，容將形之，心且成之。是以火救火，以水救水，名之曰益多，順始無窮。
>
> [Zhongni continued] "Moreover, if he (i.e., the ruler of Wei) took pleasure in the worthy and despised the unworthy, why would he employ you to seek something different? You must not instruct anything. The rulers and nobles would surely ride upon others and contend for advantage. Then your eyes would dazzle them, your complexion would pacify them, your mouth would scheme for them, your bearing would give them form, and your mind would complete it all. Thus, you use fire to counter fire and water to counter water. This is called "ever increasing," and by following the initial course, you proceed without end."

第三段，惡用而言，彼若悅賢而惡不肖，則用賢已[己]多矣，又何事於用汝也。求有以異言，若用汝，必求其有異於他人之賢者也。若唯無詔，詔，告也。言汝則無有以異於人者，告之則彼必以王公之勢[勞]，乘人之不及而鬭其捷也。自苟爲悅賢，至順始無窮爲一意。若殆以不信，以下又爲一意。言無詔，則無救於彼，而反益其惡；厚言，則逆彼之心，而徒救[彼教]吾身也。

The third section. The phrase "why would [he] employ [you]?" means: If that person took pleasure in the worthy and despised the unworthy, then he would have already appointed many, and why would he make another effort to appoint you now? The phrase "seeking something different" implies: If he were to appoint you, it is because he must be looking for something in you that is different from other worthies. In "you must not instruct anything," the word "to instruct" means "to state or report something." It means that you should have nothing by which to differ from others; if you instruct him, he will surely rely on his power, take advantage of others' shortcomings and contend for victory [against you]. [Therefore,] from the phrase "If he took pleasure in the worthy" to "by following the initial course, you proceed without end," there is only one meaning.[3]

From [the next section that begins from] "you will be endangered and thus not be trusted" onward,[4] there is also only one message here: If one has no instruction, there will be no remedy for him; on the contrary, it only deepens his faults. But if one speaks with earnest advice, it runs counter to his mind and merely serves to preserve my own life (rather than instruct him).

---

[3] The meaning is that one should not differentiate yourself from others before the ruler to save yourself in politics.

[4] This passage was probably meant to be included in the commentary of the following section. It seems to have been placed in the present section by a copyist's or editor's mistake.

## Section 4 (ZZ 4.1)

若殆以不信，厚言，必死於暴人之前矣。且昔者桀殺關龍逢，紂殺王子比干，是皆脩其身， 以下傴拊人之民，以下拂其上者也，故其君因其脩以擠之。是好名者也。昔者堯攻叢枝、胥敖，禹攻有扈，國為虛厲，身為刑戮，其用兵不止，其求實无已。是皆求名、實者也，而獨不聞之乎，名、實者，聖人之所不能勝也，而況若乎！雖然，若必有以也，嘗以語我來！

[Zhongni continued,] "If you are on the verge of being disbelieved, and you speak with earnest advice, you will surely die before the violent man. In the past, King Jie put Guan Longfeng to death, and King Zhow executed Prince Bi Gan. Both were upright in their conduct, devoted themselves to helping the people, and used their positions as ministers to oppose their superiors. That is why their lords used their integrity to ensnare them, for they loved a good reputation. In ancient times, [emperor] Yao attacked Congzhi and Xu'ao, and [emperor] Yu attacked Youhu, leaving their lands empty and their people's bodies slain. They never stopped deploying their armies and never stopped pursuing some gain. All of them were seekers of fame or gain. Have you never heard that fame and gain are things even sages could not prevail over, much less someone like you? Still, you must have something [in mind]. Tell me about it."

第四段，承前段，必死暴人之語，以終第二段之意。此以上言[定]，處世之道，不可先人後已，而輕犯暴人也。

The fourth section. [This section] continues from the previous one. The phrase "You will surely die before the violent man" concludes the message of the second section.[5] This section emphasizes that the Way of conduct in the world is never to place oneself above others or to provoke the violent ruler, even slightly.

## Section 5 (ZZ 4.1)

顏回曰：端而虛，勉而一，則可乎？曰：惡！惡可？夫以陽為充孔， 揚采色不定，常人之所不違，因案人之所感，以求容與其心。名之曰日漸之德不成，而況大德乎！將執而不化，外合而內不訾，其庸詎可乎！

Yan Hui said, "What if I am upright yet empty, diligent and single-minded—would that suffice?"

[Confucius] said, "How? How could that suffice? When you use yang-energy to fill the apertures and displays changing colors, following what ordinary people do not resist and responding to what moves them, you will seek to please him and align with his mind. This is called the virtue of gradual daily progress, which does not reach completion—let alone great virtue! To grasp without transforming, to harmonize outwardly while remaining inwardly unyielding—how could such a thing ever suffice?"

---

[5] The second section states that the Way does not mix with desires such as fame or knowledge.

第五段，端而虛，端，正直也。虛，忘身也。勉而一，勉，力[身]也；一，不變也。直道忘身勉力不變，即忠信事君之事也。周以忠信事君爲取禍之道，故以ˆ爲不可。
The fifth section. In the phrase, "upright yet open-minded," "upright" means being honest, and "empty" means to forget oneself. In "diligent and single-minded," "diligent" means to make an effort, and "single-minded" means to remain unchanged. That is, to be directly oriented toward the Way, to forget oneself, and to devote oneself fully without changing, this describes being loyal and trustworthy in serving a ruler. However, Zhuang Zhou regards serving the ruler with loyalty and trustworthiness as a path that invites disaster, and therefore as that which could not suffice.

## Section 6 (ZZ 4.1)

> 然則我內直而外曲，成而上比。內直者，與天為徒。與天為徒者，知天子之與己皆天之所子，而獨以己言蘄乎而人善之，蘄乎而人不善之邪？若然者，人謂之童子，是之謂與天為徒。外曲者，與人之為徒也。擎、跽、曲拳，人臣之禮也，人皆為之，吾敢不為邪！為人之所為者，人亦无疵焉，是之謂與人為徒。成而上比者，與古為徒。其言雖教讁之實也。古之有也，非吾有也。若然者，雖直不為病，是之謂與古為徒。若是，則可乎？仲尼曰：惡！惡可？大多政法而不諜，雖固，亦无罪。雖然，止是耳矣，夫胡可以及化！猶師心者也。
> [Yan Hui said,] "Then suppose I am straight within but outwardly flexible, and complete [duties] by comparing with what has been done before. Being straight within makes one a companion of heaven. One who takes heaven as his companion knows that the son of heaven and himself are both children of heaven. Why, then, should he alone seek that his words be approved by others, or seek that his words be disapproved by others? If one were like this, people would call him a "child." This is what is called taking heaven as one's companion.
>
> Being outwardly flexible makes one a companion of men. Holding the tablet, kneeling, bowing, or crouching—these are the proper conducts of a minister. Everyone observes them, so why should I not? Acting as others act leaves no room for fault—this is what it means to be a companion of men.
>
> Completing [duties] by comparing with what has been done before makes one a companion of antiquity. Though those words may be the substance of teaching or reproaching, they belong to the ancients, not to myself. In this way, even if I may be straightforward, I will not be distressed—this is what it means to be a companion of antiquity. If I act in these ways, could that suffice?
>
> Zhongni said, "Alas! How could that suffice? You rely on too many administrative methods and regulations, yet these do not end. Although they are fixed, they are innocent. Even if so, that is all. How could you hope to bring real transformation to him? You are still letting the mind be your teacher!"

第六段，內直，內無所必也。外曲，外徇[憎]於人也。成而上比，引古爲言[定]已，不自當也。內無所必，外徇於人，引古爲言已，不自當，即智術御人之事也。周以智術御人，可以免罪。[6] 而猶不免於心跡之露，被人覺知，故又以爲不可。太多政法而不諜。政法，方便智謀也ˆ. 不ˆ渫ˆ，不用言語之渫渫[諜諜]也。政法，指內直、外曲、上比三說而[之]言也。不渫，以教非吾有[儒]言也。

The sixth section. "Straight within" means that there is nothing one must do inwardly. "Outwardly flexible" refers to being manipulated or controlled by others from the outside. "Complete [duties] by comparing with what has been done before" means bringing in past examples to speak, but in doing so, failing to be valid in and of itself.

When one has no necessary reason internally, is subject to others' manipulation from without, and relies on past examples in speech that are not valid in themselves, this becomes a matter of a knowledge technique used to control others. Zhuang Zhou holds that even though one might escape blame through such a technique of knowledge used to control others, the traces of the mind of the one using the technique are revealed, perceived, and known by others. Therefore, he also considers this unacceptable.

In the phrase, "You rely on too many administrative methods and regulations, yet these do not end," the "administrative methods and regulations" refers to expedient strategies or clever schemes, and "not ending" means that he does not rely on the incessant flow of words. Here, the "administrative methods and regulations" refers to the three explanations mentioned earlier: being upright within, outwardly flexible, and comparing to ancient precedents. And "not ending" indicates instructing [the ruler] through examples that are not my own.

## Section 7 (ZZ 4.2)

顏回曰：吾无以進矣，敢問其方。仲尼曰：齋，吾將語若！有而為之，其易邪？易之者，皞天不宜。顏回曰：回之家貧，唯不飲酒、不茹葷者數月矣。若此，則可以為齋乎？曰：是祭祀之齋，非心齋也。回曰：敢問心齋。仲尼曰：若一志，无聽之以耳而聽之以心，无聽之以心而聽之以氣。聽止於耳，心止於符。氣也者，虛而待物者也。唯道集虛。虛者，心齋也。

Yan Hui said, "I have nothing more to advance; may I ask about the way [I move forward]?"

Zhongni said, "It is fasting—let me tell you how. If you possess [much] and [attempt to] fast, would it be easy? Those who think it is easy are not fitting to the bright heaven."

Yan Hui said, "My family is poor. For several months I have neither drunk wine nor eaten meat. Doing this way, would it count as fasting?"

Zhongni said, "That is fasting in ritual and sacrifice, but not the fasting of the mind [that I mean]."

Yan Hui said, "May I then ask about the fasting of the mind?"

---

[6] In the Yŏam edition, the character *ka* 可 is written as *pul* 不. This means that the Kyujanggak edition and the Yŏam edition interpret the meaning in completely opposite ways. The interpretation in the Kyujanggak edition appears to be the correct one.

Zhongni said, "You should unify your intent: do not hear with the ears but hear with the mind; do not hear with the mind but hear with *qi*. If hearing stops at the ears, the mind stops at the sign [of cognition]. *Qi* is empty and waits upon things. The Way reaches when [the mind is] emptied. Emptying is the fasting of the mind."

第七段，無聽之以心[氣]，聽之以氣。此言心如吾儒所謂意也。此言氣如吾儒所謂心也。符，應也。止於符，止於應，其所接之事也。虛中無偏主也。虛而待物，言中無偏主，而待事物無窮之來也。唯[無]道集虛，虛則道存。故謂之集虛。蓋周之意，則ˆ直以氣之虛者爲道，非若吾儒之言，心虛而道具也。
The seventh section. In the phrase "Do not hear with the mind but hear with *qi*," this "mind" referred to here is what we Confucians call "intent," and this *qi* referred to here is comparable to what we Confucians refer to as the mind.

The notion of "sign" means "to correspond" or "to resonate." The phrase "to stop at the sign" means that [the mind] rests in resonance with what it encounters.

In emptiness, nothing is biased or central. The phrase "[the *qi* is] empty and awaits things" means that in emptiness, there is nothing biased or central, but one awaits things and affairs that endlessly approach to him. "The Way reaches when [the mind is] emptied" means that because [the mind] is empty, the Way can be present; thus, it is said "[the Way] reaches in emptiness."

Zhuang Zhou's intent is to identify the emptiness of *qi* directly with the Way. This is not the same as our Confucian idea that the mind is empty, and then the Way becomes present there.

## Section 8 (ZZ 4.2)

顏回曰：回之未始得使，實自回也；得使之也，未始有回也。可謂虛乎？夫子曰：盡矣。吾語若！若能入遊其樊而无感其名，入則鳴，不入則止。 無門無毒，一宅而寓於不得已，則幾矣。
Yan Hui said, "Before I was ever put to use, it was truly from myself; once I was put to use, there was no longer any self of mine. Can this be called empty?"

The Master said, "That is complete. Let me tell you: if you can enter and roam within its enclosure without being moved by fame—singing when entering and stopping when not—having neither gate nor obstruction, dwelling in oneness while lodging in what cannot be helped, then you are near it."

第八段，無門無毒，不入則止，是無門也。入則不拒，是無毒也。如來者不拒，往者不追之意。一宅而ˆ寓於不得已，一，純也。宅，心齋也。純於心齋也ˆ。言虛而待物迫，而後應也。此一句爲一篇宗指。此一段言，應世之當以無心也。
The eighth section. The phrase "having neither gate nor obstruction" means that if something cannot enter, it stops, because there is no gate. If it does enter, it is not blocked because there is no obstruction. This is like saying: "One does not block what comes, nor chase after what goes."

In "dwelling in oneness while lodging in what cannot be helped," the word "oneness" means being pure or being wholly devoted to, and "to dwell" refers to the fasting of the mind. [Thus, this phrase expresses] a state of being pure in or being wholly devoted to the mind's fasting. It speaks of [the mind] being empty, awaiting the approach of external things, and only then responding to them. This single phrase represents the fundamental message of this chapter.

This section speaks of the idea that, in responding to the world, one must do with no mind.

## Section 9 (ZZ 4.2)

> 絕迹易， 無行地難。為人使，易以偽；為天使，難以偽。
> To leave no trace is easy, but walking without touching the ground is difficult. When worked by others, it is easy [to act] with deceit; but when worked by heaven, it is difficult [to act] with deceit.

第九段，絕迹易，無行地難，言[定]不行猶易，行而無跡爲難。爲人使，行之以人道也，爲天使，行之以天道也。人道有跡，故易人[當入]於僞。天道無跡，故無所容僞矣。此段[孤]言，行世之當以無跡也。
The ninth section. The phrase "To leave no trace is easy, but walking without touching the ground is difficult" means that not walking at all is rather easy, but walking without leaving any trace is difficult.

When worked by others, one should act according to the human Way; when worked by heaven, one should act according to the Way of heaven. The human Way leaves traces, and thus it is easy for humans to fall into falsity. The Way of heaven, however, leaves no traces, so there is nothing for falsity to take hold of.

This section teaches that in engaging with the world, one must act in such a way that leaves no trace.

## Section 10 (ZZ 4.2)

> 聞以有翼飛者矣，未聞以无翼飛者也；聞以有知知者矣，未聞以无知知者也。
> You have heard of those who fly with wings, but never of those who fly without them. You have heard of those who know through knowledge, but never of those who know without it.

第十段，有翼飛者，有迹之行也。無翼飛者，無迹之行也。有知知ˆ者，有心之應也。無知知ˆ者，無心之應也。聞不聞者，言有跡[迹]有心者，舉世皆然，而無跡無心者，世無其人。此并無跡無心而言。
The tenth section. "Flying with wings" is a movement that leaves traces, whereas "flying without wings" is a movement without traces. "To know with knowledge" involves the mind that responds, while "to know without knowledge" is a response with no mind.

As for whether one has heard of such things or not: having traces and having the mind is common to all people in the world, but having no traces and no mind refers to the fact that there is no such person in the world. This likewise conveys that one must be without traces and without mind.

## Section 11 (ZZ 4.2)

> 瞻彼闋者，虛室生白，吉祥止止。夫且不止，是之謂坐馳。
> One who contemplates that closed chamber finds that within an empty room brightness arises, and that auspiciousness comes to rest in stillness. But if one is not at rest, this is what is called "sitting while galloping."

第十一段，虛室生白，虛室喻心。生白，生明也。言心虛，則明也。吉祥止止，言虛明之地，萬善所止也。上止字以吉祥言，下止字以虛明言。止則虛明也。言吉祥止於虛明也。或曰兩止字，皆以吉祥言，止而又止，言多也。義亦通。[7] 周以虛而待物。虛室生白，言心其於心體所見，可謂無異於吾儒矣。然周之學陷於遥蕩恣睢者，何也。其失，專在於吉祥止止一句。

The eleventh section. In the phrase "within an empty room brightness arises," "empty room" is a metaphor for the mind, and "brightness arises" means that illumination emerges. It states that when the mind is empty, it illuminates.

"Auspiciousness comes to rest in stillness" expresses that a place that is empty and bright is where all goodness dwells. The first *chi* that means "come to rest" is for auspiciousness, while the second *chi* is for the emptiness and illumination. When [the mind] comes to rest, it is empty and bright. [Thus,] it says, auspiciousness comes to rest at emptiness and illumination. Some say that both instances of *chi* are for auspiciousness, understanding it as '[auspiciousness] rests and is still,' a repetition of the word, and this interpretation is also valid.

Zhuang Zhou awaits external things with emptiness. The phrase "within an empty room brightness arises" speaks of how the mind perceives its own essence, and one can say it is no different from our Confucian stance. However, Zhuang Zhou's learning falls into the pit of remoteness, indulgence, arrogance, and fierceness. Why is that? What he has lost lies entirely in the single phrase, "Auspiciousness comes to rest at stillness."

盖以虛明爲吉祥之本，而不知虛明即氣也。旣是氣，則虛明之中，煞有淸濁粹駁之雜，而不祥不吉者，亦本於此也。循是氣質而行者，安得不有吉祥。[8] 凶咎之相雜，而爲遥蕩恣睢也。

[Zhou] regards emptiness and illumination as the root of auspiciousness, but he does not know that emptiness and illumination are just *qi*. That they are *qi*, within emptiness and illumination, are deeply mixed clarity and turbidity, purity and

[7] In the Yŏam edition, the passage from *hok wal* 或曰 to *ŭi yŏk t'ong* 義亦通 is entirely omitted.

[8] In terms of the sentence's meaning, the character *pul* 不 here appears to be a mistake of the character *p'il* 必.

variegation, and are neither blessed nor auspicious also stems from this. If one follows this material endowment and acts upon it, how could one's action necessarily be auspicious? [There,] misfortune and flaws are intermingled. That is why [Zhuangzi] ends up being so remote, unrestrained, arrogant, and fierce.

盖心之未發，萬事未萌，即[爲]天地未闢之前，一陰之靜也。心之已[未]發，萬事出焉，即天地旣闢之後，一陽之動也。性之具於未發，而行乎已發，即道之行乎一陰一陽者也。性道純善，而氣質有雜。性純善，故未發而具[有]於氣之虛靜，不爲氣所昏，則爲大本之立[主]。已發而行乎氣之淸和，不爲氣所掩[搖]，則爲達道之行。氣有雜。故未發之前，善惡未形而粹駁，則在已發之際，粹駁用事而善惡斯分。此吾儒之學，所以以理御氣，不以氣御理也。
The state where the mind has not yet been activated, and all affairs have not yet begun to sprout, this is before heaven and earth have opened, and [this state] is the tranquility of a single yin. When the mind has already been activated and all affairs have emerged in the mind, this is after heaven and earth have already opened, and [this state] is the movement of a single yang.

The original human nature is equipped with in what has not yet been activated, and is put into action in what has already been activated. Thus, the Way operates in [the alternation of] once yin and once yang. Nature and the Way are purely good, but material endowment is a mixture [of good and not good]. Because nature is purely good, it remains unaroused and is contained within the emptiness and stillness of *qi*. If it is not darkened by *qi*, it can be established as the great root [of all virtues]. Even after it is activated, if it acts within the clarity and harmony of *qi* and is not obscured by it, one still can act, with it, in a way that is in accord with the Way.

[However,] since *qi* contains mixtures, before activation, good and evil have not yet taken form, and it is both pure and mixed. Thus, in the process of activation, the pure and the mixed employ external conditions, and good and evil become differentiated. This is why we Confucians learn to control *qi* with principle but not to control principle with *qi*.

乃周之見，則以天地未闢之前，一陰虛靜者，爲萬物之本，故亦以人心未發之前，其虛靜明者，爲萬善之本。此其所見，頭顱一錯，無言不錯也。
[However,] what Zhuang Zhou sees [as the Way] is the state before heaven and earth have opened. [For him,] what is the emptiness and stillness of the single yin becomes the root of the myriad things. Therefore, he also takes the state before the human mind has been activated as emptiness and stillness, and sees that it becomes the root of all good. This is what he views, and it is consistently mistaken from the beginning; there is nothing that can be said to be not wrong in it.

或曰先儒有言，澹一氣之本，又有言，氣之初，亦無不善。然則天地未闢之前，人心未發之時，氣之虛靜、虛明者，乃氣之本體[則]，以虛靜、虛明爲[而]萬善之本者，有何不可。此蓋執言，迷旨自誤，誤人之甚者也。盖以澹一爲氣之本者，對攻取[故斯]而言也。以氣之太初湛[澹]一淸虛爲善者，對糟粕煨燼之氣而言也。
Some may say that among earlier Confucians, there was one who stated, "Clarity and unity are the root of *qi*."[9] There was also one who said, "Even at its beginning, *qi* is not without goodness."[10] If so, then the state before heaven and earth had opened, and before the human mind had been aroused. *Qi* in emptiness and stillness, and in emptiness and illumination, is taken as the original essence of *qi*. [We Confucians, too,] regarded this emptiness, stillness, and illumination as the root of all goodness, so what fault could there be in that? [However,] this stems from clinging to [the superficial resemblance of] Zhuangzi's words, and falling into error through a confused understanding. It has seriously led others to misunderstandings. [Zhang Zai's view that] clarity and unity are the root of *qi* was stated in contrast to [the tendency of *qi*, such as] attack and seizure. And [Cheng Yi's view that] the original state of *qi*, i.e., clear, unified, pure, and empty, is good was spoken in contrast to *qi* as sediment or leftover residue.

豈爲澹一淸虛之中，更無淸濁粹駁之雜，而有[至]善無惡，與性道無別耶。豈如以陽明，對陰濁而言，則陽明爲善而陰濁爲惡也。豈謂陽明之中，更無毫髮邪惡之雜耶。
How could it be that within the clarity, unity, purity, and emptiness, there is no mixture of clarity and turbidity, simplicity and complexity, that there is goodness but no evil, and that [*qi*] is thus indistinguishable from nature or the Way? How could it be that when speaking of yang's brightness in contrast to yin's turbidity, yang's brightness is considered good while yin's turbidity is considered evil? Could it mean that within yang's brightness itself there is not even the slightest admixture of evil?

且以澹一淸虛爲氣之本者，姑亦就此，天地萬物未生之前而言也。若自一陰一陽之道說來，則澹一淸虛者，即前陽既滅之餘太極之靜而生陰者也。前陽爲此陰之本，而此陰又ˆ爲後陽之本。陰爲陽之母，陽爲陰之父，互爲其本，而太極又爲陰陽全體之本，則安得以一陰爲氣之本哉。
Moreover, if we briefly explore the idea of taking clarity, unity, purity, and emptiness as the root of *qi*, it refers to the state before heaven, earth, and the myriad things have come into being.

If we speak of [the *Zhouyi*'s theory] that "once yin, once yang, this is the Way" (*Xici* A.5), then what is called clarity, unity, purity, and emptiness is precisely the yin that emerges after the previous yang has already receded, having fully embodied the stillness of the Supreme Ultimate. The previous yang becomes the root of this yin, and this yin, in turn, becomes the root of the next

[9] This refers to Zhang Zai. See his *Zhangzi quanshu* 2.124. In the work, the character *tam* 澹 appears as *cham* 湛. The full original sentence is as follows: "Clarity and unity are the root of *qi*, while attack and seizure are the desires of *qi*." 湛一氣之本，攻取氣之欲。
[10] This refers to Cheng Yi. See Zhu Xi, *Zhuzi yulei* 59.19.

yang. Yin is the mother of yang, and yang is the father of yin; they are mutually foundational. The Supreme Ultimate is, in turn, the root of both yin and yang as a whole. How, then, can one claim that a single yin is the root of *qi*?

動靜勢均，陰陽位敵，固未有善惡之偏，而以陰陽，對太極而言，則太極理也，陰陽氣也。理一而氣殊，則又安得以一陰爲純善者哉。周之見乎氣者，盖限於今天地已闢之後，而僅能就此，推其未生者，而謂之道實不知。
The forces of movement and stillness are balanced, and the positions of yin and yang are matched; indeed, there is not yet any predominance of good or evil. If one speaks of the Supreme Ultimate in relation to yin and yang, then the Supreme Ultimate is principle, and yin and yang are *qi*. Principle is one, and *qi* is many. How then could one claim that yin alone is purely good?

Zhuang Zhou's view of *qi* is limited to what exists after heaven and earth have already taken form; he could only proceed from that point. When it comes to considering what lies before their creation, one can say that [Zhou] does not actually know what the Way is.

其此天地未生之前，即是一陰之靜，而此陰之前，又是陽動。動靜無端，陰陽無始，而動靜陰陽之上，更有所謂太極之道也。故其論人心，亦指未發虛明，而謂之道，謂之吉祥之本，而不知有所謂性善之理。然則論道論性，而近於周之說者，不可謂知性知天，而易以陷於異端之學矣。學者，可不審所擇焉。
Before heaven and earth had come into existence, there was the stillness of a singular yin, and prior to this yin, yang was already in motion. [Thus,] movement and stillness have no beginning, and yin and yang have no point of origin. Above both movement-stillness and yin-yang, there exists something that is called the Supreme Ultimate as the Way. Therefore, when considered in terms of the human mind, it refers to a state that has not yet been activated but is empty and illuminating. This is called the Way and the root of auspiciousness, but he does not understand the principle of the inherently good nature.

If this is so, speaking of the Way and of nature in this manner may align closely with the views of Zhuang Zhou, but his account can neither be said to acknowledge nature nor to grasp heaven, and it is prone to fall into heterodox learning. Those who learn must discern what they choose [to learn].

### Section 12 (ZZ 4.2)

> 夫徇耳目內通而外於心知，鬼神將來舍，而況人乎！是萬物之化也，禹、舜之所紐也，伏戲、几蘧之所行終，而況散焉者乎！
> Take control of the ears and eyes to communicate internally and be apart from the mind's knowing. Then even ghosts and spirits will come to dwell, how much more so with humans! This is the transformation of all things, the bond between Yu and Shun, the constant practice of Fu Xi and Ji Qu. how much more with those who are scattered?

第十二段，徇ˆ耳ˆ目ˆ，謂ˆ徇耳目之所欲也。內通[道]謂其道內通於心也。外於心知，言耳目之所徇，雖通於內，而亦不以此動其心也。然徇耳目，則不擇善惡矣。內通則善惡皆由心所使也。然則所謂不動心者，亦以其善惡之間，無所容心於揀擇去取[擇揀去斯]，爲無所繫累而不動也。此其爲猖狂妄行之甚者也。
The twelfth section. The phrase "to take control of the ears and eyes" refers to having the desires of the ears and eyes submitted. "To communicate internally" means that the Way communicates inwardly with the mind. "To be apart from the mind's knowing" signifies that although the ears and eyes are brought into submission, and there is inward connection, even then, such things do not move the mind. If so, when the ears and eyes are subdued, one cannot distinguish between good and evil.

When there is an inward connection, then both good and evil arise from the command of the mind itself. In this sense, the so-called "unmoved mind" means that, in the process of distinguishing, choosing, rejecting, or accepting between good and evil, the mind admits nothing and becomes entangled with nothing; it remains unmoved. This indicates that [Zhang Zhou's] deluded and irrational behavior has reached an extreme.

鬼神來舍，萬物之化，言鬼神亦合於此心之虛明，而萬事皆從此虛明中，造化也。亦其所謂虛靜寂寞，爲萬物之本者也。
The phrases "ghosts and spirits come to dwell" and "the transformation of all things" refer to the idea that ghosts and spirits are also in harmony with the mind in the empty and illuminating state, and that all affairs arise and transform from the emptiness and illumination. It is the creation and transformation. This, too, expresses the notion that what is called emptiness, stillness, silence, and solitude is the foundation of all things.

自心齋至此，言處世之道，當以無心無跡[迹]，廹[迫]而後應也。前段以知術御人爲不可，而此以無心無跡爲可，則似乎非用知術者。然所謂無心無跡者，實要以全身遠害，而又沒其痕跡，不使人覺知[正]，則乃其用智術之深者也。
From "the fasting of mind" to this point, [Zhuang Zhou] speaks of the Way of conducting oneself in the world that one must respond, without mind, without traces, after having diminished [the previous self]. The previous passage holds that using the skills of knowledge to control others is impermissible, while this one regards having no mind and leaving no trace as permissible, which seems to imply the no-use of such techniques.

However, what is called being no mind and no trace ultimately centers on preserving the body and avoiding harm. It also involves leaving no trace so that others are unaware of one's actions, and this is the profound use of the technique of knowledge.

## Section 13 (ZZ 4.3)

葉公子高將使於齊，問於仲尼曰：王使諸梁也甚重，齊之待使者，蓋將甚敬而不急。匹夫猶未可動，而況諸侯乎！吾甚慄之。子常語諸梁也，曰：凡事若小若大，寡不道以懽成。事若不成，則必有人道之患；事若成，則必有陰陽之患。若成若不成而後無患者，唯有德者能之。吾食也，執粗而不臧，爨無欲清之人。今吾朝受命而夕飲冰，我其內熱與！吾未至乎事之情，而既有陰陽之患矣；事若不成，必有人道之患。是兩也，為人臣者不足以任之，子其有以語我來！

Zigao the Lord She, was about to be sent as an envoy to Qi. He asked Zhongni, "When the king sends me [as envoy], the matter is treated with great seriousness. Surely Qi will receive the envoy with utmost respect but without haste. Even a commoner is not easily moved—how much more, then, a ruler of a state! I am greatly apprehensive. You often speak to me, saying: 'Whether the matter is small or great, the few cannot complete it by their own means. If it fails, there will surely be trouble from others; if it succeeds, there will surely be trouble from [hidden] yin and yang. Only the virtuous can accomplish it without danger, whether it succeeds or fails.' In my meals, I grasp the coarse without refinement, and at the stove there is no one who cares for cleanliness. Now, if I receive my orders in the morning and by evening drink ice, how could I not feel heat within! I have not yet fully attended to the reality of affairs, and already there is the trouble of yin and yang. And if a matter fails, there will surely be trouble from others. These are two sides of the same issue: as a minister, I am not sufficient to carry out this mission. You must have some way to instruct me!"

仲尼曰：天下有大戒二：其一，命也；其一，義也。子之愛親，命也，不可解於心；臣之事君，義也，無適而非君也，無所逃於天地之間。是之謂大戒。是以夫事其親者，不擇地而安之，孝之至也；夫事其君者，不擇事而安之，忠之盛也；自事其心者，哀樂不易施乎前，知其不可奈何而安之若命，德之至也。為人臣子者，固有所不得已，行事之情而忘其身，何暇至於悅生而惡死！夫子其行可矣！

Zhongni said, "Under heaven, there are two great imperatives: one is fate, and the other is moral duty. Children's affection for their parents, that is fate; it cannot be unraveled by the mind. A minister's service to his ruler is the moral duty; there is no action toward which the ruler is not proper, and nowhere to escape between heaven and earth. These are called the great imperatives. Therefore, one who serves one's parents does not choose the place in which to be at ease—this is the perfection of filial piety; one who serves one's ruler does not choose the tasks by which to be at ease—this is the fullness of loyalty. One who governs his own mind does not easily display sorrow or joy before others; understanding that things cannot be helped, he accepts them as fate—this is the perfection of virtue. One who is a minister or a son inevitably faces constraints; acting according to the realities of affairs while forgetting the self, how could he have leisure to delight in life and detest death! If you acted this way, you would be all right.

丘請復以所聞：凡交，近則必相靡以信，遠則必忠之以言，言必或傳之。夫傳兩喜兩怒之言，天下之難者也。夫兩喜必多溢美之言，兩怒必多溢惡之言。凡溢之類妄，妄則其信之也莫，莫則傳言者殃。故法言曰：傳其常情，無傳其溢言，則幾乎全。

[Zhongni continued,] "I, Qiu, want to tell you again what I have heard: in all relationships, with those near, one must rely on mutual trust; with those far, one must remain loyal in speech, and words must be conveyed by someone. But conveying words that are pleasing or infuriating to both parties is the difficulty of the world. Words of joy for both parties inevitably overflow with praise; words of anger for both inevitably overflow with blame. Anything that overflows is false; when it is false, trust is lost, and when trust is lost, the one who transmits the words suffers calamity. Thus, the model saying goes: "Convey one's common feelings, but do not convey words that overflows; then you will be almost complete.

且以巧鬥力者，始乎陽，常卒乎陰，大至則多奇巧；以禮飲酒者，始乎治，常卒乎亂，大至則多奇樂。凡事亦然。始乎諒，常卒乎鄙；其作始也簡，其將畢也必巨。

[He went on saying,] "Likewise, those who rely on skills to contend with strength begin with brightness but end with shadow; at great scale they exhibit much cleverness. Those who drink in accordance with ritual propriety begin with order but always end in disorder; at great scale they indulge in much extravagance. The same holds for all affairs: beginning with sincerity, they always end in baseness; what starts simply will, when completed, inevitably become excessive.

夫言者，風波也；行者，實喪也。風波易以動，實喪易以危。故忿設無由，巧言偏辭。獸死不擇音，氣息茀然，於是並生心厲。剋核大至，則必有不肖之心應之，而不知其然也。苟為不知其然也，孰知其所終！

"Speech is like wind and waves; conduct is the loss of substance. Wind and waves are easily stirred, and the loss of substance is easily endangered. Thus, anger arises without cause, and clever words take biased sides. When a beast dies, it makes no choice of sound, and its breath is agitated; from this, harsh feelings arise together in the mind. When the pressure and strain grow great, there will inevitably be unworthy thoughts responding, yet one does not realize it. If one does not realize it, who can know how it will end?

故法言曰：無遷令，無勸成。過度，益也。遷令、勸成殆事，美成在久，惡成不及改，可不慎與！且夫乘物以遊心，託不得已以養中，至矣。何作為報也！莫若為致命。此其難者。

"Therefore, a model saying says: 'Do not alter what has been decreed; do not urge things to completion.' To go beyond the proper measure is excess. Altering decrees and urging completion endanger affairs. When what is good is brought to fulfillment, it endures; when what is evil is fulfilled, there is no time to amend it. How could one not be cautious! Moreover, to ride upon things and let the mind wander, to entrust oneself to the unavoidable and thereby nourish the balance—this is the utmost. What further response or recompense could there be? Nothing is better than fulfilling one's allotted fate. This is what is most difficult."

葉公子高問答，第一段，言處世之道ˆ，安其所遇，而不可妄生，計較趍避之心也。第二段言，言之當愼。第三段言，言行之當愼。第四段言，言行之當，[+愼]隨物應之，無所容心，廹[迫]而後應也。託不得已以養中，與上文一宅寓於不得已ˆ意同。此盖莊周處世之秘法[密]也。
[The passage of] questions and answers with Zigao the Lord She. The first part speaks of the Way of conducting oneself in the world: one should be at peace with whatever one encounters, but must not recklessly endanger one's life. This is the mind that carefully examines [fate] and runs away from and avoids unnecessary harm. The second part speaks of that one's speech must be cautious. The third part discusses that both speech and action should be carried out with care. The fourth part explains that one's words and actions must respond to external things accordingly, without clinging to personal preferences, and only after self-restraint has been achieved.

The phrase, "to entrust oneself to the unavoidable to cultivate the balance," carries the same meaning as the earlier line "to dwell in oneness and entrust oneself to the unavoidable." This is the secret method behind Zhuangzi's Way of conducting in the world.

**Section 14 (ZZ 4.4)**

顏闔將傅衛靈公大子，而問於蘧伯玉曰：有人於此，其德天殺。與之為無方，則危吾國；與之為有方，則危吾身。其知適足以知人之過，而不知其所以過。若然者，吾奈之何？
Yan He was about to become tutor to the crown prince of Duke Ling of Wei, and he asked Qu Boyu, saying: "There is a man here whose virtue is lacking by nature. If I treat him without any principle, he will endanger my state; if I treat him with a certain principle, he will endanger my life. His intelligence is just enough to see others' faults, yet he does not know the reason for his own faults. What should I do with such a man?"

蘧伯玉曰：善哉問乎！戒之慎之，正汝身也哉！形莫若就，心莫若和。雖然，之二者有患。就不欲入，和不欲出。形就而入，且為顛為滅，為崩為蹶。心和而出，且為聲為名，為妖為孽。彼且為嬰兒，亦與之為嬰兒；彼且為無町畦，亦與之為無町畦；彼且為無崖，亦與之為無崖。達之，入於無疵。
Qu Boyu said, "A fine question indeed! Be cautious and vigilant. Make yourself upright. For the body, nothing is better than to follow along; for mind, nothing is better than to be in harmony. Yet both of these have their dangers. Though you follow along, do not allow yourself to be drawn into his affairs; though you harmonize, do not let yourself be drawn out too far. If your body follows along

and is drawn inward with him, you will be overthrown, destroyed, collapsed, and brought low. If your mind harmonizes and is drawn outward, you will become the object of talk and reputation, of delusion and blame. If he wishes to be like a child, then be a child with him; if he chooses erratic ways, follow him in those ways; if he acts recklessly, be reckless along with him. Grasp his mind completely and guide him to a point where no fault remains.

汝不知夫螳蜋乎？怒其臂以當車轍，不知其不勝任也，是其才之美者也。戒之慎之！積伐而美者以犯之，幾矣。汝不知夫養虎者乎？不敢以生物與之，為其殺之之怒也；不敢以全物與之，為其決之之怒也。時其飢飽，達其怒心。虎之與人異類而媚養己者，順也；故其殺者，逆也。
[Qu Boyu continued:] "Do you not know the mantis that raises its arms in rage to block the wheel of a carriage, unaware that it cannot withstand it—yet that is precisely the excellence of its nature. Beware and be cautious! To confront someone by relying on your own accumulated abilities and strengths—that is perilous."

"Do you not know the man who raises a tiger? He does not dare feed it living creatures, for fear of arousing its fury in the kill; nor does he dare feed it whole ones, for fear of provoking its rage in the tearing apart. Regulate its hunger and fullness, and understand the stirrings of its anger. Though the tiger is a different kind of creature from man, it submits to the one who feeds it—this is compliance; yet when it kills him, that is rebellion."

夫愛馬者，以筐盛矢，以蜄盛溺。適有蚉虻僕緣，而拊之不時，則缺銜、毀首、碎胸。意有所至，而愛有所亡，可不慎邪！
"One who loves his horse keeps its dung in baskets and its urine in jars; but if, when a gadfly lands on it, he strokes it at the wrong moment, the horse may break its bit, smash its head, or crush its chest. When one's intention goes too far, love is lost—how can one not be cautious!"

顏闔問答，言處世之道，當徇[循]人之情，與物無違也。
[The section of] questions and answers with Yan He states that the Way of conducting oneself in the world should be to bring one's emotions under control and have nothing to go against [the natures of] external things in the relationships with them.

## Section 15 (ZZ 4.5)

匠石之齊，至乎曲轅，見櫟社樹。其大蔽數千牛，絜之百圍，其高臨山十仞而後有枝，其可以為舟者旁十數。觀者如市，匠伯不顧，遂行不輟。弟子厭觀之，走及匠石，曰：自吾執斧斤以隨夫子，未嘗見材如此其美也。先生不肯視，行不輟，何邪？
When Carpenter Shi went to Qi and arrived at Quyuan, he saw an oak tree at the shrine. Its size could shade several thousand oxen; its girth measured a hundred spans. It rose ten *ren* up the mountain before it even began to branch, and

the branches that could make boats were more than ten in number. People gathered to look at it as though at a marketplace. But the carpenter did not so much as glance at it—he kept walking without stopping. A disciple, weary of looking, ran to catch up with Carpenter Shi and said, "Since I first took up axe and adze to follow you, I have never seen timber so magnificent as this! Yet, Master, you would not even look at it, and you walked on without stopping—why is that?"

曰：已矣，勿言之矣！散木也，以為舟則沈，以為棺槨則速腐，以為器則速毀，以為門戶則液樠，以為柱則蠹。是不材之木也，無所可用，故能若是之壽。
[Shi] replied, "Enough! Say no more! That is a useless tree. If made into a boat, it would sink; if made into an outer shell of coffin, it would rot quickly; if made into a vessel, it would soon break; if made into a door or window, it would ooze sap; if made into a pillar, it would be eaten by worms. It is a useless tree, and precisely because it is useless, it has been able to live out its years as it does."

匠石歸，櫟社見夢曰：女將惡乎比予哉？若將比予於文木邪？夫柤、梨、橘、柚、果、蓏之屬，實熟則剝，剝則辱，大枝折，小枝泄。此以其能苦其生者也，故不終其天年而中道夭，自掊擊於世俗者也。物莫不若是。且予求無所可用久矣，幾死，乃今得之，為予大用。使予也而有用，且得有此大也邪？且也，若與予也皆物也，奈何哉其相物也？而幾死之散人，又惡知散木！
When Carpenter Shi returned, the oak at the shrine appeared to him in a dream, saying: "How could you compare yourself to me? Were you trying to measure yourself against a timber like me? As for the likes of catalpa, pear, orange, pomelo, fruits, and young shoots—when their fruit ripens, it splits; when it splits, it is disgraced; large branches break, small branches droop. This is because they cannot endure the hardships of life, and so they do not complete their natural years, dying prematurely in the middle, striking themselves against the world. Among things, nothing is not like this. Moreover, I have long sought to be timber that is of no use. Now, near death, I have attained that state, and it is of great use to me. If one uses me and finds me useful, is it not because of this greatness? Moreover, you and I are both but things, and how could you compare me to you as thing? Yet an useless person who are near death [like me]—how could you understand me being a useless tree!"

匠石覺而診其夢。弟子曰：趣取無用，則為社何邪？曰：密！若無言！彼亦直寄焉，以為不知己者詬厲也。不為社者，且幾有翦乎！且也，彼其所保，與眾異，以義譽之，不亦遠乎！
When Carpenter Shi awoke, he examined his dream. A disciple asked, "If it has become useless, then what purpose does it serve to be at the shrine?"

Shi replied, "Hush. Say no more. That tree simply lodged itself there as it was, assuming that those who failed to understand it would reproach and mistreat it. Had it not been at the shrine, it would almost certainly have been cut down. Moreover, what it preserves is unlike that of others. To commend it under the rubric of righteousness only sets it further apart, does it not?

櫟社第一段，幾死，乃今得之，言予之求，無所可用，久矣，而世人未必知。予知無用，故予幾不免於死矣，乃今遇汝而明予之爲無所ˆ用，則予之久於求無所可用者，於今乃得之，而爲予[余]之大用也。下幾死，亦同此。
In the section of the oak tree at shrine, the phrase "near death, now I have found it" expresses [the same meaning of] that "I have sought that I have no use for a long time," but since the people of the world did not truly understand the uselessness I understand, I nearly could not avoid death [many times], and now, meeting you clearly reveals that I have [truly] become useless, [the state] which I have long wished to be, and now, at last, I have achieved that, and that becomes my great use. The passage below the phrase "near death" carries [the same meaning] with this.

## Section 16 (ZZ 4.6)

南伯子綦遊乎商之丘，見大木焉有異，結駟千乘，隱將芘其所藾。子綦曰：此何木也哉？此必有異材夫！仰而視其細枝，則拳曲而不可以為棟梁；俯而見其大根，則軸解而不可為棺槨；咶其葉，則口爛而為傷；嗅之，則使人狂酲三日而不已。子綦曰：此果不材之木也，以至於此其大也。嗟乎！神人以此不材！
Ziqi the Count of the South was roaming on the hills of Shang when he saw a great tree that was extraordinary. He harnessed four teams of a thousand chariots and concealed his carriage near its roots. Ziqi said, "What kind of tree is this? It must be a timber of exceptional quality!"

Looking up at its fine branches, he saw that they were twisted and knotted, unfit to serve as beams. Looking down at its massive roots, he saw that the trunk split and could not serve as an outer shell of coffin. Biting its leaves caused the mouth to rot and become injured; smelling them drove one into a three-day delirium that would not cease.

Ziqi said, "This is indeed a tree of no use, yet it has grown to such a size. Alas! Only a spirit-like person could endure its uselessness!"

宋有荊氏者，宜楸、柏、桑。其拱把而上者，求狙猴之杙者斬之；三圍四圍，求高名之麗者斬之；七圍八圍，貴人富商之家求樿傍者斬之。故未終其天年，而中道已夭於斧斤，此材之患也。故解之以牛之白顙者，與豚之亢鼻者，與人有痔病者，不可以適河。此皆巫祝以知之矣，所以為不祥也，此乃神人之所以為大祥也。
In Song, there was a man of Jing clan, who raised catalpa, cypress, and mulberry. Those branches that arched upward were cut by those seeking stakes for monkeys; those with three or four spans of girth were cut by those seeking elegant timber for fame; those with seven or eight spans were cut by the homes of nobles and wealthy merchants seeking nearby logs. Thus, before completing its

> natural years, it is cut down in the middle of its growth by axe and adze—this is the calamity of timber. Likewise, a white-foreheaded ox, a pig with a raised snout, or a person with hemorrhoids cannot be made to cross a river [for the ritual purpose]. All of these are known to be inauspicious by shamans and diviners. Yet this is precisely why the spirit-like person considers them highly auspicious.

自櫟社至支離疏，皆言處世免禍之道，莫過於不材無用。
From the passage about the oak tree at shrine to the [next] passage about Crippled Shu (ZZ 4.7), it is said that in the Way of conduct in the world and avoiding misfortune, nothing is better than failing to be a good asset and becoming useless.

### Section 17 (ZZ 4.7)

> 支離疏者，頤隱於臍，肩高於頂，會撮指天，五管在上，兩髀為脅。挫鍼治繲，足以餬口；鼓筴播精，足以食十人。上徵武士，則支離攘臂而遊於其間；上有大役，則支離以有常疾不受功；上與病者粟，則受三鐘與十束薪。夫支離其形者，猶足以養其身，終其天年，又況支離其德者乎！
> A man known as Crippled Shu, with his chin pressed into his navel, shoulders towering above his head, a pigtail pointing skyward, his five organs elevated, and two thighs pressed against his ribs. Through sewing and washing, he earns just enough to sustain himself; by winnowing and sifting out grain, he can provide food for ten people. When the authorities muster the soldiers, he waves his arms and wanders freely among them. When a large labor project is organized, he is excused because of a chronic ailment. And when grain is distributed to the sick, he receives three large measures and ten bundles of firewood. Even with a crippled body, he manages to care for himself and live out the years heaven granted him. How much more may they do so, whose deformity is that of their virtue!

支離疏。鼓筴播精，鼓筴，如鼓琴之類。播精，言播聲音之精者也。言鼓筴播精，取其直足以食十人也。
The man called "Crippled Shu": in the phrase "winnowing and sifting out grain," the action of handling the winnow is like playing a musical instrument, similar to a zither. "Sifting out grain" refers to the subtlety and precision of the sound as the grain is sorted. The expression "handling a winnow and sifting out grain" is used to convey directly that he produces enough to feed ten people.

### Section 18 (ZZ 4.8)

> 孔子適楚，楚狂接輿遊其門曰：鳳兮鳳兮，何如德之衰也！來世不可待，往世不可追也。天下有道，聖人成焉；天下無道，聖人生焉。方今之時，僅免刑焉。福輕乎羽，莫之知載；禍重乎地，莫之知避。

When Confucius went to Chu, Jie Yu, the madman of Chu, roamed by his gate and cried out: "Phoenix, phoenix, how virtue has waned! The future cannot be awaited; the past cannot be reclaimed. When the world follows the Way, sagehood is accomplished; when the world lacks the Way, sagehood simply survives. In the present time, barely escaping punishment is all one can hope for. Fortune is as light as a feather, yet no one knows how to bear it; misfortune is as heavy as the earth, yet no one knows how to avoid it.

已乎已乎，臨人以德！殆乎殆乎，畫地而趨！迷陽迷陽，無傷吾行！吾行卻曲，無傷吾足！山木自寇也，膏火自煎也。桂可食，故伐之；漆可用，故割之。人皆知有用之用，而莫知無用之用也。
Enough, enough—imposing virtue on others! Dangerous, dangerous—marking the ground and rushing about! Foolish, foolish—do not obstruct my path! I walk a winding way; do not injure my feet. Mountain trees harm themselves; the oil in the lamp consumes itself. Cinnamon can be eaten, so it is cut; lacquer can be used, so it is chopped. All know the use of the useful; none know the use of the useless."

接輿一段，言無道之世，不可出也。
This section concerning Jie Yu states that in the Wayless world, one should not seek to rise in the world.

## Concluding Remarks

此篇首言，暴人之國，不可[正於]往，終言無道之世，不可出。此盖處世之大要，而其文首尾，亦自相應也。中間以無心無跡[迹]，與物無違。不材無用爲處世之秘法，而又以不得已三字，爲秘法中秘法。
At the beginning of this chapter, it states that one must not go to a country ruled by a violent sovereign, and at the end, it asserts that in the world devoid of the Way, one should not seek to rise. This is the essence of engaging with the world, and the opening and closing of the chapter correspond with each other. The middle part regards having no mind or trace, being in harmony with external things without going against them, and being useless by not becoming fine material, as the secret method of worldly engagement. Moreover, the concept of being inevitable is considered the secret within the secret of this method.

盖此篇專以全身遠害，爲至人之能事，則周之學，盖無異於鄉愿之媚世取[求]容者，而其用意深微，托言高抗[抗]，使人莫覺其爲私邪鄙陋之學，則其爲亂德之深[甚]，視鄉愿又不啻九萬里矣。爲孔子之學者，可不明辨，而深闢之哉。
This chapter regards preserving one's body intact and avoiding harm as the utmost task of an ultimate person. In that sense, Zhuang Zhou's learning is no different from that of Xiang Yuan (*Lunyu* 17.13; *Mengzi* 7B83), who flatters the world and seeks only his own comfort. However, [Zhuangzi's] application of such ideas was deep and subtle; he relied on lofty and playful language, making

it difficult for people to realize that he had engaged in a base and self-serving kind of learning. As such, his distortion of virtue was severe. Indeed, not far removed from what we see in the case of Xiang Yuan. Those who follow Confucius's teachings must clearly discern right from wrong and thoroughly reveal the truth.

# Chapter 5

# A Sign of Virtue Fulfilled

前篇，言養生處世。既能養生，又能處世，則德之充實於內者，符驗於外矣。故德充符，次之。充，充實也。符，符驗也。
The previous chapter spoke of nurturing life and conducting oneself in the world. Now that we could understand how to nurture life and how to conduct ourselves, it follows that a person whose virtue is fully realized inside will naturally exhibit an outward sign that testifies to its effect. Therefore, [the chapter titled] "A Sign of Virtue Fulfilled" comes next. [Here,] the word "fulfilled" means "fully realized" and "a sign" that which proves or demonstrates an effect.

**Section 1 (ZZ 5.1)**

> 魯有兀者王駘，從之遊者，與仲尼相若。常季問於仲尼曰：王駘，兀者也，從之遊者，與夫子中分魯。立不教，坐不議，虛而往，實而歸。固有不言之教，無形而心成者邪？是何人也？仲尼曰：夫子，聖人也。丘也，直後而未往耳。丘將以為師， 而況不如丘者乎！奚假魯國！丘將引天下而與從之。常季曰：彼兀者也，而王先生，其與庸亦遠矣。若然者，其用心也，獨若之何？
> In Lu, there was a cripple named Wang Tai. Those who followed him were as numerous as those who followed Zhongni.
>
> Chang Ji asked Zhongni, saying, "Wang Tai is a cripple, yet those who follow him are as many as those who follow you. Standing, he gives no teaching; sitting, he engages in no discussion. They go to him empty, and return full. Does he truly have a teaching without words, and a forming of the mind without visible form? What manner of man is he?"
>
> Zhongni said, "That man—he is a sage. I myself merely lag behind and have not yet attained his level. I, Qiu, would take him as my teacher—how much more so should those beneath me! Why speak only of the state of Lu? I would lead the whole world to follow him."
>
> Chang Ji said, "But he is a cripple, and yet he is called Master Wang! How far apart this is from what is ordinary. If this is so, what sort of mind is it that he employs?"

王駘第一段，擧用心二字，做題目，其下所言，即其用心之方[力]也。死生不變，用心之極致也。死生亦大，而不與之變，則其餘可知矣。
The first section concerning Wang Tai deals with the notion of "using the mind," and what is discussed under the chapter title is precisely the method of using the mind. The ultimate state of using the mind is remaining unchanged amid life and

death. Though life and death are of great importance, if one can remain unshaken by them, then all other matters can also be understood.

**Section 2 (ZZ 5.1)**

> 仲尼曰：死生亦大矣，而不得與之變，雖天地覆墜，亦將不與之遺。審乎無假，而不與物遷，命物之化，而守其宗也。
> Zhongni said, "Life and death are indeed great matters, yet he remains unchanged through them. Even if heaven overturns and earth collapses, he would not be left behind with them. He is lucid in what is without falseness, and does not shift along with things. He commands the transformations of things, yet holds fast to their origin."

第二段，遺，亡ˆ失[近]也。天地覆墜，不與之亡失ˆ，即死生不變之意也。無假者，實也。審乎無假，審乎道德之實也。不與物遷，不變不遺之意也。命物之化，言萬物變化，由我命之也。宗，始也，主也，即道德之實者也。不與物遷，故命物之化，審乎無假，故能守其宗也。

The second section. The word "to be left behind" means "to be lost." The phrase "heaven overturns and earth collapses" implies that [he] is not lost along with them, but he remains unchanged even amid life and death. "Without falseness" means to be genuine or real. And "to be lucid in what is without falseness" refers to examining the actual state of the Way and virtue. "He does not shift along with things" means that it is neither changed nor lost. "To command the transformations of things" means that the transformations of all beings are commanded by me.

The notion of "origin" means the beginning or the foundation, which refers to the actuality of the Way and virtue. Because he does not shift with external things, one is able to command their transformations, and because he is lucid in what is without falseness, he can preserve the origin.

**Section 3 (ZZ 5.1)**

> 常季曰：何謂也？仲尼曰：自其異者視之，肝膽楚越也；自其同者視之，萬物皆一也。
> Chang Ji said, "What do you mean by that?"
>
> Zhongni said, "Viewed from the side of their difference, the liver and the gall are as far apart as Chu and Yue; but viewed from the side of their sameness, myriad things are all one."

第三段，異者，承上段物字而言；同者，承上段宗字而言。言物則異而道則同也。

The third section. The term "different" follows from the earlier use of the word *things*, and "same" follows from the earlier use of the word *origin*. When speaking of things, they differ; but with respect to the Way, they are the same.

### Section 4 (ZZ 5.1)

> 夫若然者，且不知耳目之所宜，而游心於德之和。
> If one is like this, he does not concern himself with what suits the ears and eyes, but lets his mind wander freely in the harmony of virtue.

第四段，不知耳目所宜，承上段異者而言；遊心乎德之和，承上段同者而言。言忘其異而循其同也。遊心字與上文用心字相應。
The fourth section. The phrase "to not concern himself with what suits the ears and eyes" continues the notion of difference from the previous section. The phrase "to let his mind wander freely in the harmony of virtue" continues the notion of sameness from the previous section.

[This section] speaks of forgetting the differences and following the sameness. The term "let the mind wander" corresponds to the term "using the mind" in the earlier section 1 (ZZ 5.1).

### Section 5 (ZZ 5.1)

> 物視其所一，而不見其所喪，視喪其足，猶遺土也。
> He looks at things from the standpoint of their oneness and does not see what they have lost. Seeing the loss of his own foot is to him like losing a clod of earth.

第五段，視其所一，承上遊心德和，而言不見所喪。承上不ˆ知ˆ耳目，而言遊心乎德之和，故視其所一矣。不知耳目所宜，故不見其所喪也。視喪其足，猶ˆ遺土，視其喪足，猶土芥也。土，作士字誤也。
The fifth section. The phrase "to looks at things from the standpoint of their oneness" continues from the previous paragraph's "wandering the mind in the harmony of virtue." But when [this section] speaks of the notion of "not seeing what they have lost," it continues what the previous section means "to not concern himself with what suits the ears and eyes," and "to let his mind wander freely in the harmony of virtue," and so he can "see [things] from their oneness." Since "he does not know what the ears and eyes find suitable," it follows that "he does not see what has been lost." The phrase "to see the loss of his own foot as like losing a clod of earth" means that he regards the loss of his foot as something as insignificant as a mustard seed in the soil. Here, the word "earth" is likely a scribal error for "scholar-official."

### Section 6 (ZZ 5.1)

> 常季曰：彼為己，以其知得其心，以其心得其常心，物何為最之哉？
> Chang Ji said, "He acts for himself; because he knows how to attain [the state of] his mind and, having attained it, abides in his constant mind, what thing should be considered superior to him?"

第六段，言爲，已以其有[意]知覺，得其知覺之心[志學之心]，以其得本心。常心即本心也。物何爲最之，言至人之ˆ得其常心，物何爲ˆ貴之哉。最之，猶言貴之也。

The sixth section states: in acting for himself, by means of his conscious awareness, he attains the mind of awareness, and through this, he recovers his original mind. The phrase "constant mind" refers precisely to the original mind. The phrase "what thing should be considered superior to him?" states that since the ultimate person has attained the constant mind, why should anything be considered more precious? Here, "superior to him" means to be regarded as [more] precious.

## Section 7 (ZZ 5.1)

> 仲尼曰：人莫鑑於流水，而鑑於止水，唯止能止眾止。
> Zhongni said, "People do not see their reflection in running water—they see it in still water. Only what is still can still the many that are still."

第七段，承上何最之問，而釋爲最之義。止水鑑[終]形，喻常心之鑑裁萬物[事物]也ˆ。[1] 唯止能止衆止，言心正，故明。明，故能鑑裁事物,[2] 使各止其所止也。此以止水，喻心。應帝王篇，又以明鏡，喻心。

The seventh section continues the question in the previous section, "what thing should be considered superior to him?" and goes on to explain the meaning of "being superior."

The notion that still water reflects an outer form means that a constant mind reflects and shapes all things. The phrase "Only what is still can still the many that are still" means that because the mind is upright, it is illuminating; and because it is illuminating, it can reflect and shape affairs and things—enabling each to come to rest in its proper place. This uses the image of "still water" as a metaphor for the mind. In the [seventh] Chapter of "Being in Accord with the

---

[1] In the Yŏam edition, "all things" (*manmul* 萬物) appears as "affairs and things" (*samul* 事物), and the character *ya* 也 is missing. The likely reason for the substitution of *manmul* with *samul* in the Yŏam edition is that the scribe may have skipped a line and moved to the next, which happened to begin with a very similar phrase, "to discern and judge affairs" (*kamjae samul* 鑑裁事物), thus causing the confusion. This can be easily confirmed by comparing it with the Kyujanggak edition. See the line 10 of folio 29b (modern page number 58) and line 1 of folio 30a (59) in the Kyujanggak edition.

[2] In the Yŏam edition, the entire portion from the end of the previous sentence, "to discern and judge all things" (*kamjae manmul ya* 鑑裁萬物也) to "therefore it can…" (*ko nŭng* 故能) at the beginning of the next sentence is omitted. As mentioned in the previous foot note, this likely occurred because the scribe accidentally skipped the final line of the page and moved directly to the first line of the following page. Coincidentally, the first phrase on the next page, "to discern and judge affairs" (*kamjae samul* 鑑裁事物), was very similar to the final phrase of the sentence that should have continued, "to discern and judge all things" 鑑裁萬物也, which likely caused the error.

Way of the Emperor," [Zhang Zhou,] again to the image of a clear mirror, likens the mind (ZZ 7.6).

明鏡、止水之喻，吾儒亦用之。周之於心，不可謂無見也。唯其有見於心，無見於性，故所謂水、所謂鏡，無所準[准]，則或有時，不得其監，照之正也。盖鏡雖同明，鐵之精粗不同，水雖同止，潭之大小不同。鏡之照物粗者，或有所差，水之鑑形小者，或有所遺[失]。此即心雖同ˆ靜，亦雖同明，其氣質之偏全粹駁，亦自有不同者，而應物之際，專任是氣者，不能無所差矣。
The metaphors of the clear mirror and still water are also used in our own Confucian tradition, so it cannot be said that Zhuang Zhou's understanding of the mind was entirely mistaken. While he may have seen something about the mind, he understood nothing about human nature. Therefore, what he refers to as "water" or "mirror" cannot serve as a reliable standard [of perception or judgment]. So, there are times when one cannot determine whether what is reflected is correct. Even if all mirrors are equally illuminating, the fineness or coarseness of the metal from which they are made varies. [Likewise,] even if all water is equally still, the size of the pond [in which it sits] is not the same. When a mirror reflects external things coarsely, [some images] are reflected with less precision. When water reflects external forms only on a small scale, it means some portions [of the reflection] are missing. This means that even if the mind is equally still and equally illuminating, due to the material endowment, such as its imbalance or wholeness, its purity or mixture, there are still differences in the [reflected images] themselves. Thus, in the [mind's] response to external things, when one entirely entrusts himself to the material endowment, there can be no but differences [in consequence].

**Section 8 (ZZ 5.1)**

> 受命於地，唯松柏獨也在，冬夏青青；受命於天，唯舜獨也正，幸能正生，以正衆生。
> Of those that receive life from the earth, only the pine and cypress are unsurpassed; they remain ever green through both winter and summer. Of those that receive life from heaven, only [Yao and] Shun stand supreme, fortunate to have kept their own lives upright and thereby to have set others right as well.

第八段，引松柏之冬夏不變，以證聖人之死生不變。正生，正其所生，而不變也。以正衆生，謂爲ˆ衆生之所宗主也。
The eighth section draws on the fact that pine and cypress trees do not change whether in winter or summer, and uses this to demonstrate that the sage remains unchanged even amid life and death.

"Keeping one's life upright" means to make what is born upright and not subject to change. "By doing so, he set others' lives upright" that he becomes the foundation of all living beings.

## Section 9 (ZZ 5.1)

> 夫保始之徵，不懼之實。勇士一人，雄入於九軍。
> Now, the sign of preserving the beginning lies in the reality of being without fear. A single brave man can charge boldly into nine armies.

第九段，保始即上文守宗之謂也。不懼即上文死生不變之意也。言勇士之求名者，猶能不變其始，不懼其死，況如下文所言聖人者乎。
The ninth section. The phrase "preserving the beginning" refers to the previous paragraph's "to hold fast to the origin." (section 2) "Being without fear" corresponds to the idea in the previous paragraph that "one does not change amid life and death" (section 2). The statement "a single brave man seeking honor" means that he can avoid altering his beginning and face death without fear; then, how much more so for someone like the sage spoken of in the next paragraph?

## Section 10 (ZZ 5.1)

> 將求名而能自要者，而猶若此，而況官天地，府萬物，直寓六骸，象耳目，一知之所知，而心未嘗死者乎！
> One who is about to seek fame yet are able to restrain themselves are already like this—how much more so one who serves heaven and earth, who stores ten thousand things, who merely lodges within his six bodily parts, treats his ears and eyes as mere adornments, and unifies what he knows within what he should know, and his mind has never known death.

第十段，官，主也。府，藏也。主宰天地，容藏萬物，言道之大，如此也。直，特也，但也。寓六骸，象耳目，言特ˆ寓之[+之]於六骸，象之以耳目也。言以至大之道，假人形，而寄[寓]之也。一知之所知，言所知有萬，而合之爲一也。心未嘗死，言心常虛明主宰，而不滯於物也。此心字，即結上文用心之心字。
The tenth section. The notion of "to serve as the steward" means to preside or supervise, and "to store" means to embrace or contain. To preside over heaven and earth and to embrace all things indicates that the Way is as great as this. [The character that originally means] "directly" here stands for "merely" or "just." The phrase "to lodge within six bodily parts and to treats the ears and eyes as mere adornments" means that [the Way] particularly dwells on the six parts of the human body and represents itself through the ears and eyes. This conveys that the supremely great Way [merely] borrows the human form and depends upon it. "To unify what one knows within what one should know" means that although knowledge is vast and manifold, it is all combined into one unity. "The mind has never known death" means that the mind is constantly empty, illuminating, and presides over, but is not obstructed by [external] things. This concept of the "mind" concludes the discussion of how to use the mind from the preceding section [1].

## Section 11 (ZZ 5.1)

彼且擇日而登假，人則從是也。彼且何肯以物為事乎！
He will soon choose a day and ascend. People then follow this person. How would he be willing to regard a thing as an [important] matter?

第十一段， 登假猶《中庸》所謂奏假也。且擇日而登假[+乎]，言豈擇日而登假乎。[3] 言無時而不進假於道也。人則從是，結篇首從遊ˆ二字。
The eleventh section. The phrase "to ascend" is the same as the phrase "advance and arrive" in the *Zhongyong* (33).[4] Also, the phrase "to choose a day and ascend" indicates how one should choose any day to ascend off. It states that one does not advance toward the Way just at any time.[5] The phrase "people then follow this person" (i.e., Wang Tai) serves to conclude the notion of "to follow and roam" at the very beginning of this section.

## Section 12 (ZZ 5.2)

申徒嘉，兀者也，而與鄭子產同師於伯昏無人。子產謂申徒嘉曰：我先出，則子止；子先出，則我止。其明日，又與合堂同席而坐。子產謂申徒嘉曰：我先出，則子止；子先出，則我止。今我將出，子可以止乎，其未邪？且子見執政而不違，子齊執政乎？申徒嘉曰：先生之門，固有執政焉如此哉？子而說子之執政而後人者也！聞之曰：鑑明則塵垢不止，止則不明也。久與賢人處，則無過。今子之所取大者，先生也，而猶出言若是，不亦過乎！子產曰：子既若是矣，猶與堯爭善，計子之德不足以自反邪？
Shentu Jia was a cripple who studied together with Zichan of Zheng under Master No-Person of First Darkness. Zichan said to Shentu Jia, "If I go out first, you stay; if you go out first, I will stay."

The next day, they sat together in the same hall, side by side on the same mat. Zichan said to Shentu Jia again, "If I go out first, you stay; if you go out first, I will stay. Now I am about to go out—can you stay behind, or not yet? Moreover, when you see those in power, you do not avoid them; are you perhaps equal to those in power?"

Shentu Jia said, "In our Master's gate, are there truly such things as those in power? You speak of 'those in power' and already reveal yourself as one who delights in them! I have heard it said, 'When a mirror is too clear, dust and dirt do not remain upon it; but if it allows them to remain, it is no longer clear.

---

[3] In the Yŏam edition, the phrase *ŏn kae t'aek il i tŭng kyŏk* 言豈擇日， 而登假 is entirely omitted from this sentence. This omission was likely due to an editorial error in the Yŏam edition, where the editor appears to have confused the position of the three characters *i tŭng kyŏk* 而登假, which appear twice in the same form on line 10 of folio 30b (60), and inadvertently skipped ahead to the later occurrence of the phrase.
[4] It refers to the following sentence: "[I] advance and arrive, [the ancestral spirit] responds in silence; at such a time, there is no contention" 奏假無言，時靡有爭。
[5] This seems to mean that such a person does it at the appropriate moment.

When one stays long among worthy men, one commits no fault.' Now the great thing you have taken from our Master is his teaching—yet you still speak in such a way. Is that not itself a fault?"

Zichan said, "[Although] you are [a cripple] as you are, do you still contend in goodness with Yao? Is it that your virtue is not sufficient to reflect upon yourself?"

申徒嘉曰：自狀其過以不當亡者眾，不狀其過以不當存者寡。知不可奈何而安之若命，惟有德者能之。遊於羿之彀中，中央者，中地也，然而不中者，命也。人以其全足笑吾不全足者多矣。我怫然而怒，而適先生之所，則廢然而反。不知先生之洗我以善邪！吾與夫子遊十九年矣，而未嘗知吾兀者也。今子與我遊於形骸之內，而子索我於形骸之外，不亦過乎！子產蹴然改容更貌曰：子無乃稱！

Shentu Jia said, "Many there are who confess their faults though they do not deserve to perish; few there are who conceal their faults though they do not deserve to live. To know that nothing can be done and to accept it as fate—only those of virtue can do so. When one moves within the range of Yi's bow, to stand at the very center is to stand on level ground, yet whether one is struck or not depends on fate. Many with whole feet laugh at me for having none. I become indignant, but when I go to see the Master and return, my anger has entirely melted away. I do not know whether it is that the Master has washed me clean with his goodness! I have associated with the Master for nineteen years, yet I have never once felt myself to be a cripple. But now you and I dwell within the bounds of form and body, and yet you seek me beyond form and body—is that not excessive?"

Zichan started in surprise, his expression changing, and said, "Nothing further to say!"

申徒嘉，第[+十]二段,[6] 狀，貌也。貌者，人之文[能]於外者也。言人之自文其過，以爲不當亡[已]者衆，不文其過，以爲不當存者寡，而知其不可奈何而安之若命，又進於不文其過矣。故曰，惟有德者能之。盖申徒嘉引以自處，嘉之不自知其爲兀[凡]者，即知其不可奈何而安之者也。

The twelfth section on Shentu Jia. The term "appearance" refers to a person's outward form or physical looks, which means the patterns or marks a person reveals externally. It speaks of people who acknowledge and adorn their faults—there are many who think they ought not to perish; but those who conceal their faults and think they ought not to survive are few. And "to know that nothing can be done and to accept it as destiny" goes even further than not concealing one's faults. Therefore, it is said, "Only those of virtue can do this."

Shentu Jia, through his own circumstances, became unaware of why he became one-legged. That is, he is the one who knows how to "come to peace with

[6] The character *sip* 十 is missing in both the Kyujanggak and Yŏam editions. Since the correct sequence is Section 12, the character 十 has been inserted.

what cannot be helped."

形骸之內，德也。內字與形骸字，有辨。形骸之外，即形骸之在外者，外字與形骸者，無辨。無乃稱，言無得以稱也， 猶《論語》所謂民無得以稱焉者也。
The phrase "inside the physical form" refers to virtue. Between "inside" and "form/body," there is a distinction. The phrase "outside the physical form" refers to things external to the external form, and between outside and physical form, there is no such distinction. The phrase "nothing further to say" means there is nothing more to be said; it is the same as in the *Lunyu,* where it says: "The people had nothing more to say about it" (8.1).

**Section 13 (ZZ 5.3)**

魯有兀者叔山無趾，踵見仲尼。仲尼曰：子不謹，前既犯患若是矣。雖今來，何及矣？無趾曰：吾唯不知務而輕用吾身，吾是以亡足。今吾來也，猶有尊足者存，吾是以務全之也。夫天無不覆，地無不載，吾以夫子為天地，安知夫子之猶若是也！孔子曰 ： 丘則陋矣。夫子胡不入乎？請講以所聞！無趾出。
In Lu, there was a cripple called Toeless of Mount Shu, who had lost his toes. He walked on his heels to visit Zhongni. Zhongni said, "You were not careful—before, you brought such misfortune upon yourself. Even though you come now, what can it avail you?"

Toeless said, "It was only because I did not know how to conduct myself and carelessly misused my body that I lost my toes. Now that I have come, I still have what remains of my body to honor and preserve—therefore I make it my business to keep it whole. heaven covers all without exception, and earth bears all without exception. I take you, Master, as my heaven and earth—how can I know that you are still like this?"

Confucius said, "I am indeed narrow-minded. Why do you not come in? Pray, teach me what you have heard."

Toeless then went away.

孔子曰：弟子勉之！夫無趾，兀者也，猶務學以復補前行之惡，而況全德之人乎！無趾語老聃曰：孔丘之於至人，其未邪！彼何賓賓以學子為？彼且蘄以諔詭幻怪之名聞，不知至人之以是為己桎梏邪？老聃曰：胡不直使彼以死生為一條，以可不可為一貫者，解其桎梏，其可乎？無趾曰：天刑之，安可解？
Confucius said, "Disciples, take heed! Toeless is a cripple, yet he still devotes himself to learning in order to make up for the faults of his former conduct. How much more, then, should one whose virtue is whole!"

Toeless spoke to Lao Dan, saying, "As for Kong Qiu (i.e., Confucius), his understanding of the ultimate person is still far from complete! Why does he behave so ceremoniously, teaching others as though he were a master? He seeks to make a name for himself by means of eccentric and strange talk. Does he not know that, for the ultimate person, such things are but shackles to the self?"

Lao Dan said, "Why not simply enable him to see life and death as a single thread, and right and wrong as one continuous strand—thus freeing him from his shackles? Would that not suffice?"

Toeless said, "He is punished by heaven—how could he be freed?"

叔山無趾第一段，尊足，尊於足者。德，性也。在周所見，則氣之虛靜也。賓賓，多儀[儒]貌。幼恠，幼，少[山]也。自少而習於恠也。或疑幻字之誤。
In the first section on the Toeless of Mount Shu. The phrase "worth more than a foot" means "that which is more precious than the feet." [In the phrase "a person who has completed virtue"], the term virtue here refers to nature [in our Confucian tradition]. From Zhuangzi's perspective, it means the emptiness and stillness of *qi*. The word "ceremoniously" describes a repeated perfunctory manner. In the phrase "childish and strange,"[7] the word "childish" means young, suggesting that the person had been practicing strange things since childhood. Some suspect that this character may be a scribal error for the one for "to be deluded or illusionary."

**Section 14 (ZZ 5.4)**

魯哀公問於仲尼曰：衛有惡人焉，曰哀駘它。丈夫與之處者，思而不能去也。婦人見之，請於父母曰與為人妻，寧為夫子妾者，十數而未止也。未嘗有聞其唱者也，常和而已矣。無君人之位以濟乎人之死，無聚祿以望人之腹。又以惡駭天下，和而不唱，知不出乎四域，且而雌雄合乎前。是必有異乎人者也。
Duke Ai of Lu asked Zhongni, saying, "In Wei, there is a hideous man named Ai Tai Tuo. When men dwell with him, they long for him and cannot bear to leave. When women see him, they beg their parents, saying, 'Rather than be another man's wife, let me be his concubine'—and there are dozens who say so without end. Yet no one has ever heard him raise his voice in song; he only ever joins in harmony with others. He holds no position of ruler to save men from death, nor possesses wealth to fill others' bellies. And still, though his ugliness startles the world, he harmonizes without leading, and his knowledge is not beyond the four borders—yet even so, the male and female unite before him. Surely, he must be different from other men!"

寡人召而觀之，果以惡駭天下。與寡人處，不至以月數，而寡人有意乎其為人也；不至乎期年，而寡人信之。國無宰，寡人傳國焉。悶然而後應，氾而若辭。寡人醜乎，卒授之國。無幾何也，去寡人而行，寡人卹焉若有亡也，若無與樂是國也。是何人者也？
(Duke Ai continued:) "[So,] I have summoned him to see for myself, and indeed,

[7] As Han Wŏnjin points out above, in the current Guo Qingfan's standard edition of the ZZ, the character *yu* 幼 is written as *hwan* 幻.

his ugliness startles the world. Yet when he was with me—not even a month had passed before I began to feel an affection for him as a person; not even a full year before I came to trust him completely. When the state had no chief minister, I entrusted the government to him. He responded slowly and hesitantly, as though declining the offer. I was ashamed of myself, yet in the end, I handed the state over to him. Not long after, he left me and went away, and I felt as grieved as if I had lost something dear—there seemed to be no more joy for me in ruling this state. What kind of man could he be?"

仲尼曰：丘也，嘗使於楚矣，適見㹠子食於其死母者，少焉眴若，皆棄之而走。不見己焉爾，不得類焉爾。所愛其母者，非愛其形也，愛使其形者也。戰而死者，其人之葬也，不以翣資。刖者之屨，無為愛之，皆無其本矣。為天子之諸御，不爪翦，不穿耳；娶妻者止於外，不得復使。形全猶足以為爾，而況全德之人乎！今哀駘它未言而信，無功而親，使人授己國，唯恐其不受也，是必才全而德不形者也。

Zhongni said, "I, Qiu, once went on a mission to Chu. On the way, I saw piglets eating the flesh of its dead mother. After a short while, their eyes flickered, and it suddenly threw it away what and fled. [They felt that the mother] did not see them, and that she was no longer like herself. What they loved in their mother was not her form, but that which gave life to her form. When a man dies in battle, no one uses banners or fans in his burial [for they are useless to him]. When a man has lost his feet, he no longer cherishes his shoes—for in both cases, the root is gone. When women are chosen to be consorts of the son of heaven, their nails are left uncut, and their ears are not pierced. Having taken a new wife, he stops at the external [form], and is no longer made to serve [the internal] again. If so, much care is taken to preserve the body, how much more for a man whose virtue is intact? Now Ai Tai Tuo had not yet spoken, yet he was trusted; he had done no service, yet he was treated with intimacy. The ruler even entrusted him with the state and only feared that he might refuse. This [man, Ai Tai Tuo] must be one whose abilities are complete and whose virtue does not manifest outwardly."

哀公曰：何謂才全？仲尼曰：死生存亡，窮達貧富，賢與不肖，毀譽、饑渴、寒暑，是事之變，命之行也；日夜相代乎前，而知不能規乎其始者也。故不足以滑和，不可入於靈府。使之和豫通而不失於兌，使日夜無郤而與物為春，是接而生時於心者也。是之謂才全。何謂德不形？曰：平者，水停之盛也。其可以為法也，內保之而外不蕩也。德者，成和之修也。德不形者，物不能離也。

Duke Ai of Lu said, "What is meant by foundation being complete?"

Zhongni replied, "Life and death, preservation and destruction, constraint and success, poverty and wealth, worthiness and unworthiness, blame and praise, hunger and thirst, cold and heat these are the transformations of affairs and the operations of mandate. Day and night alternate before us, and knowledge cannot regulate their beginnings. Therefore, they are insufficient to facilitate harmony and cannot enter the numinous treasury. To let them be harmonized, at ease, and unobstructedly communicating without losing openness, and to let day and night have no blockage and be spring together with things this is to come into contact with them and give rise to timeliness within the mind. This is what is meant by foundation being complete."

[Duke Ai] said, "What is meant by virtue that does not take form?"

[Zhongni] said, "Levelness is the fullness of water at rest. It is something that can serve as a model. One preserves it within, and the exterior is not set in motion. Virtue is what one cultivates through which harmony is completed. When virtue does not take form, things cannot separate from it."

哀公異日以告閔子曰：始也，吾以南面而君天下，執民之紀，而憂其死，吾自以為至通矣。今吾聞至人之言， 恐吾無其實， 輕用吾身而亡其國。吾與孔丘，非君臣也，德友而已矣。
On another day, Duke Ai reported this to Lord Min, saying, "At first, I thought that, by facing south and ruling all-under-heaven, grasping the ordering threads of the people, and worrying over their [life and] death, I myself had reached the utmost penetration [in ruling]. Now I have heard the words of the ultimate person, and I fear that I lack the substance, that I lightly employ my own person and thereby lose the state. As for my relation with Confucius, it is not one of ruler and minister. We are simply friends in virtue."

魯哀公第一段，卹焉，卹，憂[急]也。第二段，止於外，不得復使，言取妻者，止決於外貌，而不待[得]復使，以試其才也。
In the first passage on Duke Ai of Lu, the word "to care for" means to worry about. In the second passage, the phrase "[Having taken a new wife, he] stops at the external, and is no longer made to serve [the internal] again" means that one who has taken a new wife ceases making judgments based on outer appearance and is no longer swayed by it. By doing so, he puts his foundation to the test.

## Section 15 (ZZ 5.5)

闉跂支離無脤說衛靈公， 靈公說之， 而視全人， 其脰肩肩。甕盎大癭說齊桓公， 桓公說之， 而視全人， 其脰肩肩。故德有所長， 而形有所忘， 人不忘其所忘， 而忘其所不忘， 此謂誠忘。故聖人有所遊， 而知為孽， 約為膠， 德為接， 工為商。
[The crippled man] lame, hunchbacked, and cleft-lipped, spoke with Duke Ling of Wei. Duke Ling was delighted with him, and afterward, whenever he looked at men with normal bodies, he found their necks and shoulders absurdly thin. Likewise, the man with the great swelling on his neck, spoke with Duke Huan of Qi. The duke too was delighted, and when he saw ordinary men, he thought their necks and shoulders were also too lean.

Thus, when one's virtue reaches its height, the body is forgotten. People often fail to forget what ought to be forgotten, and instead forget what ought to be remembered—this is what may truly be called genuine forgetting. Hence the sage roams freely; for him, knowledge becomes a burden, promises a binding glue, virtue a form of entanglement, and skill a merchant's trade.

聖人不謀，惡用知？不斵，惡用膠？無喪，惡用德？不貨，惡用商？四者，天鬻也。天鬻者，天食也。既受食於天，又惡用人？有人之形，無人之情。有人之形，故群於人；無人之情，故是非不得於身。眇乎小哉！所以屬於人也。謷乎大哉！獨成其天。

Since the sage makes no plans, why would he need knowledge? Since he does not carve, why rely on glue? Since he suffers no loss, why depend on virtue? Since he has nothing to sell, why act like a merchant? These four are the nourishment by heaven. To live on heaven's food, what need then has he for human aid? He has a human form but not human feelings. Because he bears the form of a man, he moves among men; because he lacks human feelings, judgments of right and wrong cannot cling to him. How minute and small he is. He belongs to the human. How vast and great he is. Alone he completes the heavenly.

闉跂第二段，德，得也。德爲接，以得爲接也。無喪，惡用德，言無失，惡用得乎。

In the second passage of [this section] concerning the man who is lame, the character that stands for "virtue" is here for "to obtain." Thus, the phrase "virtue becomes a form of entanglement" implies to regard obtaining something as making a connection. The phrase "There is no loss, so how could virtue be used?" means that since there is nothing lost, what would there be to obtain.

## Section 16 (ZZ 5.6)

惠子謂莊子曰：人故無情乎？莊子曰：然。惠子曰：人而無情，何以謂之人？莊子曰：道與之貌，天與之形，惡得不謂之人？惠子曰：既謂之人，惡得無情？莊子曰：是非吾所謂情也。吾所謂無情者，言人之不以好惡內傷其身，常因自然而不益生也。惠子曰：不益生，何以有其身？莊子曰：道與之貌，天與之形，無以好惡內傷其身。今子外乎子之神，勞乎子之精，倚樹而吟，據槁梧而瞑。天選子之形，子以堅白鳴！

Huizi said to Zhuangzi, "Can a person truly be without feeling?"

Zhuangzi said, "Yes."

Huizi said, "If a person has no feelings, how can he still be called a person?"

Zhuangzi said, "The Way gives him his appearance, and heaven gives him his form. How could he not be called a person?"

Huizi said, "Since he is called a person, how could he be without feelings?"

Zhuangzi said, "That is not what I mean by 'being without feelings.' What I mean is that one does not let likes and dislikes wound one's inner self, but always follows what is natural and does not add anything to life."

Huizi said, "If he does not add anything to life, how does he keep possessing a body?"

Zhuangzi said, "The Way gives him his appearance, and heaven gives him his form; he does not let likes and dislikes wound his inner self. But now you,

> going outside your spirit and exhausting your essence, lean against a tree and chant, or prop yourself against a withered log and doze off. Heaven has fashioned your form, yet you make a clamor over hardness and whiteness!"

末段，有人之形，與人爲群也。無人之情，與天爲徒也。惠子之以堅白鳴，是不能無人情，而與天爲徒也。上文皆引形毁之人，以明德之充符，不在於形，故此段又出形字，極言外形骸之道而結之。
The last section states that if one possesses human form, one joins in fellowship with others; but if one lacks feelings, one joins in fellowship with heaven. Huizi made a clamor over the issue of hardness and whiteness, but this cannot lead to having no feelings or to forming fellowship with heaven.

In the preceding paragraphs, [Zhuang Zhou] drew examples of people whose physical forms were damaged to illustrate a sign of fulfilled virtue and to emphasize that virtue does not reside in external appearance. Therefore, in this section, the notion of form appears [a lot], and the text speaks in extreme terms about distancing oneself from the Way of the physical form and bringing the discussion to a conclusion.

## Concluding Remarks

篇內皆人ˆ形毁貌，醜之人爲言，言德之充實符驗，不在於形之全否，貌之妍醜也。亦言外形骸而一道德也。王駘之徒衆，皆悅之德之，符驗於外也。其一死生，忘形骸者，德之充實於中也。篇末，無人情[恃]，即一死生，忘形骸之本也。其文首尾布置，亦有序。一死生，外形骸，即所以齊萬物，而一道德者也ˆ。盖周之學，以虛無爲道，以齊物爲宗，故七篇之中，無非此意。
This chapter presents stories on people whose physical forms are damaged and whose appearances are unattractive, in order to show that the signs of fulfilled virtue do not lie in whether the body is intact or the appearance is beautiful or ugly. It also teaches that one should distance oneself from the physical form and body, and unite with the Way and with virtue.

The group around Wang Tai all rejoiced in virtue and demonstrated it outwardly. They regarded life and death as one and forgot about their physical bodies; thus, their virtue can be said to be in full accord with balance.

At the end of this chapter, it is stated that the absence of feeling is the very root of viewing life and death as one and of forgetting physical appearance.

The sections before and after are expansive in scope, and they correspond to and follow each other in order: first, viewing life and death as one; then, distancing oneself from the physical form and body; and then, through that, treating all things equally and uniting the Way with virtue.

Zhuang Zhou's learning takes emptiness and non-being as the Way, and treating all things equally as the foundation. Thus, among the seven [Inner] Chapters, there is none that does not express this message.

# Chapter 6

# The Great Founding Master

大宗師者，道也。前篇言成德之至。成德者，以道爲本。故繼之以大宗師，以示大本之所在。

The Great Founding Master is none other than the Way. The previous chapter spoke of the utmost attainment in the completion of virtue. One who has completed virtue regards the Way as fundamental. Thus, by continuing with the notion of the Great Founding Master, this chapter reveals where that great foundation is.

### Section 1 (ZZ 6.1)

> 知天之所為，知人之所為者，至矣。知天之所為者，天而生也；知人之所為者，以其知之所知，以養其知之所不知，終其天年而不中道夭者，是知之盛也。雖然，有患。夫知有所待而後當，其所待者特未定也。庸詎知吾所謂天之非人乎？所謂人之非天乎？且有真人，而後有真知。
>
> To know what belongs to heaven's doing and what belongs to human doing—this is the utmost [knowing]. To know what belongs to heaven's doing is to live in accord with heaven. To know what belongs to human doing is to take what one knows and use it to nourish what one does not know; to complete one's allotted years without perishing midway is the consummation of knowledge. Even so, there is a concern. For knowing depends on something before it can be right, yet what it depends on is never fixed. How could one ever be sure that what I call heaven is not human, or what I call human is not heaven? Only when there is a true person can there be true knowing.

第一段，天之所為，天道之自然也。人之所為，人事之當然也。但所謂天道人事，不同於吾儒之指也。天而生者，如《中庸》所謂生知也。以其所知，養其不知，如《中庸》所謂學知也。[1] 不中道夭，言不半道而廢也。知有所待而後當，必待生知、學知之人，而後當知此也。所謂有真人而後有真知也。

The first section. The phrase "what belongs to heaven's doing" refers to the Way of heaven, which is that which occurs of itself. The phrase "what belongs to human doing" refers to what human affairs must naturally be so. However, what [Zhuang Zhou] means by the Way of heaven and the [workings of] human affairs are not the same as what we Confucians mean by those terms.

The phrase "to live in accord with heaven" is the same as what the *Zhongyong*

---

[1] The Yŏam edition omits the sentence that runs from 以其所知 to 學知也.

calls "knowing from birth."[2] The phrase "to take what one knows and use it to nourish what one does not know" corresponds to what the *Zhongyong* calls "knowing through learning." The phrase "without perishing midway" means not giving up halfway along the path.

The phrase "knowing depends on something before it can be right" means that one must first wait for those who are born knowing and those who come to know through learning, and only afterward can this knowledge be attained. This corresponds to the line: "Only when there is a true person can there be true knowing."

所待未定，言生知、學知之人，未可必得，故曰特未定。庸詎知天之非人，人之非天，言天道人事無二，致及其知之則一也。道莫先於知之，故論道第一語，則下知之一字。而道非人，人所可知,[3] 故終又曰，有真人，而後有真知。
The phrase "what it depends on is never fixed" means that even those who are born knowing or those who come to know through learning are not necessarily guaranteed to attain such knowledge. Thus, [Zhuangzi] says: "What it depends on is never fixed. How could one ever be sure that what I call heaven is not human, or what I call human is not heaven?" This expresses that the Way of heaven and the affairs of humans are not two separate things, and that when one arrives at this realization, [he knows] that they are only one.

There is nothing that precedes the Way in priority over knowing it; therefore, the discussion about the Way is the very first concept, and the notion of "to know" follows. The Way is not human, yet it is something that can be known by humans, and so, at the end, he states: "Only when there is a true person can there be true knowing."

**Section 2 (ZZ 6.1)**

> 何謂真人？古之真人，不逆寡，不雄成，不謨士。若然者，過而弗悔，當而不自得也。若然者，登高不慄，入水不濡，入火不熱。是知之能登假於道也若此。
> What is meant by the true person? The true person of old did not forcibly go against what was unfavorable or lacking, did not take pride in success, and did not scheme for affairs. Such a one, when erring, felt no regret; when acting rightly, took no self-importance. Such a one could climb to great heights without fear, enter water without getting wet, and enter fire without being burnt—this is how one's knowing can rest upon and rely on the Way. It was like this.

[2] It refers to the first phrase of the following line in the *Zhongyong*: "Some are born knowing it, some come to know it through learning, and some come to know it through hardship. But once they know it, it is one and the same" 或生而知之, 或學而知之, 或困而知之, 及其知之, 一也 (20).

[3] In the Yŏam edition, the sentence from *ko non to* 故論道 to *in so ka chi* 人所可知 is missing.

第二段，承上段末句先釋眞人之德，而結之曰：知之能登假於道，即所謂有真人而後有真知者也。
The second section follows the final phrase of the preceding paragraph and interprets it in terms of the virtue of the true person. It then concludes by stating: "this is how one's knowing can rest upon and rely on the Way," which is precisely what is meant by the phrase "Only when there is a true person can there be true knowing."

## Section 3 (ZZ 6.1)

古之真人，其寢不夢，其覺無憂，其食不甘，其息深深。真人之息以踵，眾人之息以喉。屈服者，其嗌言若哇。其耆欲深者，其天機淺。古之真人，不知說生，不知惡死；其出不訢，其入不距；翛然而往，翛然而來而已矣。
The true person of old, in sleep, did not dream; when awake, he had no worries; in eating, he had no taste; and in breathing, he breathed deeply and fully. The true person breathes from the heels, while the common people breathe from the throat. Those who are bent and constrained, their words choke as though they vomit. Those whose likes and desires run deep, their natural mechanism is shallow. The true person of old did not know to delight in life, nor to hate death. In going out, he did not rejoice; in coming in, he did not resist—light and free, he went and came, that was all.[4]

## Section 4 (ZZ 6.1)

不忘其所始，不求其所終；受而喜之，忘而復之。是之謂不以心捐道，不以人助天。是之謂真人。
[The true person of old] did not forget where it begins, nor seek to know where it ends. What he received, he accepted with joy; what he lost, he let go without regret. This is called not abandoning the Way through the mind, and not assisting heaven through human effort. This is what is called the true person.

第四段，不以心捐道，言不以有心捐道也。周以虛無爲道，故亦以無心道爲得道也。
The fourth section. The phrase "not abandoning the Way through the mind" means that, though something arises within the mind, [the true person of old] did not forsake the Way. Since Zhuang Zhou regards emptiness and non-being as the Way, he also sees "no mind" as the state in which the Way is realized.

## Section 5 (ZZ 6.1)

若然者，其心志，其容寂，其顙頯，淒然似秋，煖然似春，喜怒通四時，與物有宜，而莫知其極。

[4] Section 3 is missing in both Kyujanggak and Yŏam editions.

For such a one, in this way, the mind rests where the will is set; the countenance is still; the brow is open and broad. He looks melancholic like autumn and warm like spring. His joy and anger correspond to the four seasons; he is in harmony with all things, yet none can discern his limits.

第五段，其心志，志者，心之所之也。言隨其心而所之，無所矯拂也。
The fifth section. In the phrase "the mind rests where the will is set," the will refers to the direction or aim of the mind. It means that even when following wherever the mind goes, there is nothing that needs correcting or discarding.

## Sections 6 and 7 (ZZ 6.1)

故聖人之用兵也，亡國而不失人心；利澤施於萬物，不為愛人。故樂通物，非聖人也；有親，非仁也；天時，非賢也；利害不通，非君子也；行名失己，非士也；亡身不真，非役人也。若狐不偕、務光、伯夷、叔齊、箕子、胥餘、紀他、申徒狄，是役人之役，適人之適，而不自適其適者也。
Therefore, when the sage employs the army, he may bring a state to ruin yet never lose the hearts of the people. His benefits and blessings extend to myriad things, yet he does not do so out of love for his people. Thus, to find joy in completely controlling things—such a one is not a sage; to have favoritism—such a one is not benevolent; to time with heaven—such a one is not worthy; to fail to move freely through gain and loss—such a one is not a noble person; to pursue fame and lose oneself—such a one is not a scholar-official; to ruin oneself without authenticity—such a one is not one who truly serves others.

As for Hu Buxie, Wu Guang, Bo Yi, Shu Qi, Qizi, Xu Yu, Ji Ta, and Shentu Di—they were those who served the service of others, sought the fulfillment of others, and did not themselves find fulfillment in their own fulfillment.

古之真人，其狀義而不朋，若不足而不承，與乎其觚而不堅也，張乎其虛而不華也，邴邴乎其似喜乎！崔乎其不得已乎！滀乎進我色也，與乎止我德也，厲乎其似世乎！警乎其未可制也，連乎其似好閉也，悗乎忘其言也。
The true person of old was upright in conduct but not partisan. He seemed incomplete yet did not try to make himself complete. He was firm in principle yet not unyielding, expansive in emptiness yet not ostentatious. He appeared calm, as if quietly pleased; lofty, as if compelled by what could not be avoided; restrained, as if only his expression advanced; composed, as if his virtue held him still. He seemed severe, as if resembling the world; ungovernable, as if beyond control; self-contained, as if fond of closing himself off; and forgetful, as if he had lost his own words.[5]

## Section 8 (ZZ 6.1)

以刑為體，以禮為翼，以知為時，以德為循。以刑為體者，綽乎其殺也；以

[5] Sections 6 and 7 are contained neither in the Kyujanggak edition nor in the Yŏam edition.

禮為翼者，所以行於世也。

[The true person] takes punishment as the substance, ritual as the wings, knowing as what is timely, and virtue as the natural course. To take punishment as the substance means to be firm when something must be ended, and to take ritual as the wings means to conduct oneself properly in the world.

第八段，以刑為體，以禮為翼。刑者，陰之屬；禮者，陽之屬。言陰為體，陽為用也。

The eighth section. The phrase "[The true person] takes punishment as the substance, and ritual as the wings" means that punishment belongs to the yin aspect, while ritual belongs to the yang aspect. In other words, yin serves as the essence, and yang functions as the application.

### Section 9 (ZZ 6.1)

以知為時者，不得已於事也；以德為循者，言其與有足者至於丘也，而人真以為勤行者也。故其好之也一，其弗好之也一。其一也一，其不一也一。其一，與天為徒；其不一，與人為徒。天與人不相勝也，是之謂真人。

To take knowing as what is timely is to do anything inevitably in any affairs. To take virtue as the natural course means the one whose self-satisfaction reaches [the level of] Confucius, but who people genuinely regard is arduously practicing [the Way]. Therefore, what he likes is one, and what he does not like was also one. His being one is one; his not being one is also one. In being one, he is on the same side with heaven. In not being one, he is on the same side with humans. When heaven and humans do not contend to overcome one another, such a one is called a true person.

第九段，自第二段至此，皆釋有真人而後有真知之意，而備述無心無知之事。無心無知，即有所以眞知道也。第三段以下，雖不言知字，以第二段推之可見，其言知志也。

The ninth section. From Section 2 up to this point, all the discussion has been an interpretation of the meaning of the [previous] phrase "Only when there is a true person can there be true knowing." It thoroughly sets forth the necessity of "no mind" and "non-knowing," because these two are the way how one gets the true knowing. Although from Section 3 onward the notion of to know or knowing is no longer explicitly mentioned, one can see, through reference to Section 2, that [those subsequent sections ultimately] speak about it.

### Section 10 (ZZ 6.2)

死生，命也，其有夜旦之常，天也。人之有所不得與，皆物之情也。彼特以天為父，而身猶愛之，而況其卓乎！人特以有君為愈乎己，而身猶死之，而況其真乎！

Life and death are of fate. Constant as the coming of night and dawn is of heaven. What humans cannot obtain or bestow is the nature of things. If they regard heaven as the father and love it of their own accord, then how much more should they love what is superior? If people regard the ruler as above themselves and die for him of their own accord, then how much more should they do for what is true?

第十段，所謂卓，所謂眞，皆指大宗師之道。而言承上眞人眞知，始提出道體，而言此一段包下文四段之意。
The tenth section. What is called "superior" and what is called "true" both point to the Way of the Great Founding Master, and they continue from the previous phrase "true person, true knowledge" and begin to speak of the essence of the Way. This indicates that this single section encompasses the meaning of the four sections that follow.

### Section 11 (ZZ 6.2)

泉涸，魚相與處於陸，相呴以溼，相濡以沫，不如相忘於江湖。與其譽堯而非桀，不如兩忘而化其道。
When the spring dries up, the fish are left together on land. They moisten each other with their breath and wet each other with their foam, but it would be better for them to forget each other in rivers and lakes. Rather than praising Yao and condemning Jie, it would be better to forget them both and transform their ways.

第十一段，言是非兩忘之爲道。
The eleventh section speaks of how forgetting both right and wrong is the Way.

### Section 12 (ZZ 6.2)

夫大塊載我以形，勞我以生，佚我以老，息我以死。故善吾生者，乃所以善吾死也。
The great clod bears me with form, toils me with life, lets me rest with age, and gives me repose with death. Therefore, to care well for my life is precisely to care well for my death.

第十二段，言死生一視之爲道。
The twelfth section teaches that to regard life and death as one and the same is the Way.

### Section 13 (ZZ 6.2)

夫藏舟於壑，藏山於澤，謂之固矣。然而夜半有力者負之而走，昧者不知也。藏大小有宜，猶有所遯。若夫藏天下於天下，而不得所遯，是恆物之大情也。

To hide a boat in a ravine or a mountain in a marsh may be called secure. Yet in the middle of the night, a strong man may carry them away, and the ignorant will not know. There is a proper place to hide the large and the small, yet both can still be taken. But to hide the world within the world, leaving no place for it to be taken away—this is always the great nature of all things.

特犯人之形而猶喜之，若人之形者，萬化而未始有極也，其為樂可勝計邪！故聖人將遊於物之所不得遯而皆存。善妖善老，善始善終，人猶效之，又況萬物之所係，而一化之所待乎！
One takes particularly the human form, yet he still delights in it. As for what pertains to the human form, its transformations are myriad and have no ultimate limit—how could the joy he affords ever be fully reckoned? Therefore, the sage wanders in that from which things cannot escape, and in all of them he abides. He is at ease with dying young and with growing old alike, good in beginning and good in ending. If such a one can serve as a model for humanity, how much more so for that to which myriad things are bound, and upon which the unity and transformation depend?

第十三段，言物各付物之爲道。釋上第十段：死生之命，夜旦息之天，人之不得與之意。下文又釋卓、眞之道。藏小大：小，舟也；大，山也。藏舟於壑，藏山於澤，是不能物各付物也。不能物各付物，則莊小大,[6] 雖有宜，猶有所遯矣。[7] 藏天下於天下，物各付物也。物各付物，則隨物隨在物，不得其所遯矣。如藏天下於一家，則秦失之漢，漢失之魏，而天下有所遯矣。藏天下於天下，則天下之人失之，天下之人得之，而天下無所遯矣。
The thirteenth section states that entrusting each thing to the thing itself is the Way. It interprets the phrase from Section 10, "Life and death are of fate, night and dawn are of heaven, and [these are] what humans cannot obtain or bestow."

The passage below also offers an interpretation of the Way as "superior" and "true" [in Section 10]. In the phrase "to hide the small and the great," "the small" refers to a boat, and "the great" refers to a mountain. "A boat is hidden in a ravine; a mountain is hidden in a marsh" means that each thing could not be entrusted to the thing itself. If each thing cannot be entrusted to itself, then when there is a proper place to hide the large and the small, yet both can still be taken.

"To hide the world in the world" means entrusting each thing entirely to the thing itself. When each thing is entrusted to itself in this way, one follows the thing and the place where the thing is, and so "there is no place for it to be taken away" If the world were hidden within a single household, then when Qin lost the world to Han and Han to Wei, it would mean that the world had a place from which it could be taken. [But] if one hides the world within the world itself, then even if the people of the world lose it, it is still the people of the world who

---

[6] In the original text of the *Zhuangzi*, the character *chang* 莊 appears as *chang* 藏. The character *Chang* 莊 found in both the Kyujanggak and Yŏam editions is a miswriting of *Chang* 藏.
[7] In the Yŏam edition, the sentence from 藏舟於壑 up to 猶有所遯矣 is missing.

regain it, and thus the world has nowhere from which it can be taken away.

蓋以喻人死為物，物復化為人，萬化未始有極，而能安於所化，不以死生累其心，則其為人為物，莫能遯我，而我未嘗亡也。所謂遊於物之所不得遯而皆存者也。然吾聖人之物各付物，生順死安，真能不以死生累其心矣。周之物各付物，要以遊於物之所不得遯，而形雖萬化，我欲常存也，不惟不知無此理，其自私自利，不肯舍我甚矣。是豈真能不以死生累其心，與吾聖人同哉？其公私邪正之分，學者不可不知也。[8]

Based on this, [Zhuangzi] teaches that a person dies and becomes another thing, and that thing again becomes a person, [and thus says,] "[a thing] endlessly transforms without ever having a limit." When one can find peace within that ceaseless transformation, and life and death no longer weary the mind, then whether one becomes a human being or another thing, nothing can escape from what I call "me," and this "me" has never, in fact, escaped or departed. It is what [the main text] says, "[the sage] freely wanders where the things cannot be taken away and all remain present."

However, the sage in our [Confucian] tradition entrusts each thing to itself, follows life, rests peacefully in death, and is truly able not to let life and death weary the mind. Zhuang Zhou's [sage, too,] entrusts each thing to itself and, in doing so, seeks to freely wander in the place where nothing can be taken away, but [in such a place], though the physical form may undergo all kinds of transformation, the desires of the self still persist. [In such a state of Zhuangzi's sage,] not only does he fail to realize that there is no such principle; his selfish pursuit of private advantage and his refusal to relinquish the self are extreme indeed. How, then, could this truly be a case where life and death do not weary the mind? How could it be the same as the sage in our tradition? Those who study the distinctions between what is public and private, what is evil and what is right, cannot fail to recognize this.

善妖善老，善始善終，即安命順天，人不得與，而物各付物也。聖人如此人，猶效之，況於道乎？萬物所係，一化所待，即所謂大宗師之道也。猶未說出道字，下文始言之。

"[The sage] is at ease with dying young and with growing old alike, good in beginning and good in ending" means to be at peace with fate and to follow heaven; it is what humans cannot attain or grant [at will], and the state where each thing

[8] In the Yŏam edition, the long and detailed commentary by Han Wŏnjin on the *Zhuangzi* original phrase "hiding the world in the world" (*chang ch'ŏnha ŏ ch'ŏnha* 藏天下於天下) found in the Kyujanggak edition, from the phrase *mul kak pu mul* 物各付物 up to *hakja pul ka pu chi ya* 學者不可不知也, is replaced by a much shorter and simpler sentence as follows: "[The original sentence] means entrusting right and wrong to right and wrong, and entrusting life and death to life and death. 'Not able to flee' means that right and wrong cannot flee from right and wrong, and life and death cannot flee from life and death" 言付是非於是非，付死生於死生也。不得所遯，是非不得遯其是非，死生不得遯其死生也。

is entrusted to what it is in itself. The sage is like such a person, and [people] models themselves upon him. How much more so when it comes to the Way?

"To which myriad things are bound, and upon which the unity and transformations depend" refers precisely to the Way as the Great Founding Master. The "Way" itself has not yet appeared; it is only in the following passage that it is first addressed.

**Section 14 (ZZ 6.3)**

> 夫道，有情有信，無為無形；可傳而不可受，可得而不可見；自本自根，未有天地，自古以固存；神鬼神帝，生天生地；在太極之先而不為高，在六極之下而不為深；先天地生而不為久，長於上古而不為老。
>
> In the Way, there is what is felt and what is trusted, yet without action and without form. It can be transmitted, yet not received; attained, yet unseen. It is grounded in itself and rooted in itself. Before heaven and earth came into being, it had already existed of itself from the most ancient times. It brings forth the numinosity of spirits and Lord on High, and gives birth to heaven and earth. It existed before the Supreme Ultimate yet does not deem itself high; it lies beneath the six ends yet does not deem itself deep. It was born before heaven and earth, yet does not consider itself long-lived; it surpasses high antiquity, yet does not consider itself old.
>
> 豨韋氏得之，以挈天地；伏犧氏得之，以襲氣母；維斗得之，終古不忒；日月得之，終古不息；堪坏得之，以襲崑崙；馮夷得之，以遊大川；肩吾得之，以處太山；黃帝得之，以登雲天；顓頊得之，以處玄宮；禺強得之，立乎北極；西王母得之，坐乎少廣，莫知其始，莫知其終；彭祖得之，上及有虞，下及五伯；傅說得之，以相武丁，奄有天下，乘東維，騎箕尾，而比於列星。
>
> Xiwei attained it and thereby upheld heaven and earth. Fuxi attained it and continued the breath of the primordial mother. The Dipper attained it and has never erred through the ages. The sun and moon attained it and have never ceased their course. Kan Huai attained it and reached Kunlun. Feng Yi attained it and roamed the great rivers. Jianwu attained it and dwelled upon Mount Tai. The Yellow Emperor attained it and ascended to the cloudy heavens. Zhuanxu attained it and resided in the dark palace. Yuqiang attained it and stood at the northern pole. The Queen Mother of the West attained it and sat in the place of Shaoguang—none know her beginning or her end. Pengzu attained it and lived from the age of Yao and Shun to the five lords. Fu Yue attained it and served as minister to King Wuding, who ruled over the world; he then rose to the eastern governor, rode between the Dipper's Winnowing Basket and Tail, and took his place among the stars.

第十四段，此段論道最詳，有情以其主宰而言也，有信以其至實而言也。主宰而又無所作爲[而]，至實而又無有形體，故曰無為無形。

The fourteenth section discusses the Way in the most detailed manner. The phrase "[In the Way,] there is what is felt" describes [the Way] viewed from the aspect of its [anthropomorphic] presider. The phrase "[In the Way,] there is what is trusted" describes [the Way] viewed from the utterly substantial aspect. It is presiding, yet it does nothing by way of deliberate action; it is utterly substantial, yet it has no physical form. Thus, [Zhuangzi] says "without action, without form."

周之論道，可爲[謂]幾矣。然道上不得着情字，着此一字亦可見。周之認氣爲道也。有情有信，故可傳而可得；無爲無形，故不可受而亦不可見。自本自根，自爲萬化之本，而自[化]則無所本；自爲萬物之根，而自[此]則無所根也。未有天地，自古以存，即所謂自本自根也。

Zhuang Zhou's discussion of the Way [in this manner] can be a framework. However, to the concept of the Way, the notion of feeling cannot rightly be attached, and yet here again we find it attached. This is because Zhuang Zhou regarded *qi* as the Way. Since it has something to be felt and trusted, it can be transmitted and obtained. And because it is without action and form, it cannot be received, nor can it be seen. The phrase "to be grounded in itself and rooted in itself" means that [the Way] is the source of all transformations in itself, and it exists as it is in and of itself, and there is nothing else upon which it bases its foundation or root. It is the foundation of all things by itself and the root of all things by itself. It does not take anything else as its foundation or root. The phrase "before heaven and earth came into being, it had already existed of itself from the most ancient times" expresses precisely what is meant by the phrase "to be grounded in itself and rooted in itself."

神鬼神帝，生天生地，即其爲萬化，萬物之根本也。鬼帝以造化，而言天地該事物，而言太極，指天地有形之極處，而言非如孔子所謂太極也。六極，亦言天地有形，上下四方之極也。上二句以位言，言在有形之上，而不爲高。在有形之下，而不爲深也。下二句以時言，言推之於前，則先天地生，而不爲久。引之於後，則恒[亘]古今存，而不爲老。高而能深，故不爲高；深而能高，故不爲深；見在，故不久；日新，故不老。此以上，言道之體。

The phrase "[the Way] brings forth the numinosity of spirits and Lord on High, and gives birth to heaven and earth" means that [the Way] undergoes myriad transformations and becomes the root and foundation of all things. It brings about transformations through ghosts and Lord on High, whereby heaven and earth come to be endowed with all affairs and things. [Then, Zhuangzi] speaks of the Supreme Ultimate, which here refers to the furthest limit after heaven and earth have already taken form. However, this is not the same as the Supreme Ultimate spoken of by Confucius.[9]

---

[9] The concept of Supreme Ultimate in the *Xici* of the *Zhouyi* refers to the Way as the one beyond the form: "That which is above form is called the Way, and that which is below form is called a vessel" 形而上者謂之道, 形而下者謂之器 (A.12). Han Wŏnjin here argues that Zhuangzi's concept of Supreme Ultimate is of below form, that is, not metaphysical.

The phrase "six ends" also refers to the furthest ends of the six directions, i.e., above, below, and the four cardinal directions, after heaven and earth have taken on form. With these two lines above, [Zhuang Zhou] speaks about the position of the Way: though it is above things with form, it does not regard itself as higher than them; though it is below things with form, it does not consider itself as deeper than them. He also uses these two lines below to discuss the temporality of the Way: if one pushes it forward in time, it is "born before heaven and earth," yet it does not regard itself as long; if one pulls it backward, it has existed from time immemorial to the present, and yet it does not consider itself as old.

[The Way] is both high and can be deep, and so it is said: "it does not regard itself as high." It is deep and can be high, and so it is sad: "it does not regard itself as deep." It is present here and now, and so it does not regard itself as long. It is ever-renewing, and so it is said: "it does not regard itself old." Up to this point, Zhuangzi has been speaking about the substance of the Way.

豨韋氏以下，言天地、日月、山川、人物，皆得道而生，是說道之用。此一段，發明道體，盡其幽妙，極其廣大無一，言不同於吾儒矣。[10] 然所謂道者，乃指天地未生之前，一陰虛靜者，則其頭腦看起處，便自如吾儒不同矣。程子嘗論老佛之言曰：言言是句句同，然而不同。正謂此矣。

From the passage beginning with "Xiwei," [Zhuangzi] speaks of how heaven and earth, the sun and moon, mountains and rivers, human beings and things—all of these come into being through attaining the Way. This explains the function of the Way.

This section elucidates the substance of the Way, exhausts its subtle mysteries, and extends to a vastness beyond even the [concept of] oneness. Its discourse is in accord with that of our Confucian tradition.

However, [for Zhuangzi,] what is called the Way is a single yin of emptiness and stillness that existed before heaven and earth came into being. Thus, from the very core that serves as its brain, it is already different from our Confucians'. Master Cheng once discussed Laozi and the Buddha, saying: "Every word seems right, every passage appears similar, yet they are not the same."[11] This is precisely what he meant.

## Section 15 (ZZ 6.4)

南伯子葵問乎女偊曰：子之年長矣，而色若孺子，何也？曰：吾聞道矣。南

[10] In both the Kyujanggak and Yŏam editions, the phrase 言不同於吾儒矣 retains the negation marker *pul* 不. However, given the contrast in meaning between this and the following sentences, the negation marker should be removed. I have thus eliminated it here for the sake of clearer and more accurate meaning.

[11] The exact source for this quotation has not been located, but a similar remark appears in the *Zhuzi yulei* 101.48.

伯子葵曰：道可得學邪？曰：惡！惡可！子非其人也。夫卜梁倚有聖人之才，而無聖人之道，我有聖人之道，而無聖人之才，吾欲以教之，庶幾其果為聖人乎！不然，以聖人之道告聖人之才，亦易矣。

Zikui the Count of the South asked a hunched woman, "You are of great age, yet your complexion is like that of a child. How is this so?"

She replied, "Because I have understood the Way."

Zikui the Count of the South said, "Can the Way be learned?"

She said, "No, no—how could it! You are not the kind of person for it. Buliang Yi had the talent of a sage but not the Way of a sage; I have the Way of a sage but not the talent of a sage. I wished to teach him, hoping that perhaps he might truly become a sage. If not, then to speak of the Way of the sage to one who has the talent of the sage—how easy that would have been!

吾猶守而告之，參日而後能外天下；已外天下矣，吾又守之，七日而後能外物；已外物矣，吾又守之，九日而後能外生；已外生矣，而後能朝徹；朝徹，而後能見獨；見獨，而後能無古今；無古今，而後能入於不死不生。

[She continued] "Yet I persisted in guiding him. After three days, he was able to cast the world aside. When he had set the world aside, I continued to guide him, and after seven days he was able to cast things aside. When he had set things aside, I again continued to guide him, and after nine days he was able to cast life aside. When he had cast life aside, then he was able to perceive through the dawn; when he perceived through the dawn, he was able to behold the Alone; when he beheld the Alone, he was able to be without past and present; and when he was without past and present, he was able to enter into that which neither dies nor is born.

殺生者不死，生生者不生。其為物，無不將也，無不迎也；無不毀也，無不成也。其名為攖寧。攖寧也者，攖而後成者也。南伯子葵曰：子獨惡乎聞之？曰：聞諸副墨之子，副墨之子聞諸洛誦之孫，洛誦之孫聞之瞻明，瞻明聞之聶許，聶許聞之需役，需役聞之於謳，於謳聞之玄冥，玄冥聞之參寥，參寥聞之疑始。

[She continued,] "One who kills life does not die; one who gives life to life is not born. For such a thing, there is nothing it does not carry forward, nothing it does not draw back; nothing it does not destroy, nothing it does not bring to completion. Its name is stillness amidst turmoil. Stillness amidst turmoil means: only through turmoil can completion come."

Zikui the Count of the South asked, "From whom did you hear all this?"

She said, "I heard it from Ink's-Assistant, whose son heard it from Reciting-by-the-River's Grandson. Reciting-by-the-River's Grandson heard it from Bright-to-Behold; Bright-to-Behold heard it from Great-Embrace; Great-Embrace heard it from Awaiting-Command; Awaiting-Command heard it from Oh-Song-Chanting; Oh-Song-Chanting heard it from Dark-Obscurity; Dark-Obscurity heard it from Vast-Void; and Vast-Void heard it from Doubting-the-Beginning."

第十五段，朝徹。朝，明也；徹，通也。言胷中明通也。獨，道也。萬物未有無對者，而惟道無對，故謂之獨見。[12] 獨見ˆ，道也。無古今，道，無古今之異也。入於不死不生，道，無存亡之變也。殺生不死，殺物而不隨物而死也。[13] 生生不生，生物而不隨物而生也。[14]

The fifteenth section. In the phrase "to perceive through the dawn," "dawn" means brightness, and "perceive through" means thoroughness or penetration. Thus, "perceived through the dawn" expresses the idea of the mind becoming bright and fully clear. "Alone" refers to the Way. Among myriad things, there is none that is without a counterpart—only the Way has no counterpart. Therefore, it is said "to behold the Alone." "Beholding the Alone" refers to [attaining] the Way. "To be without past and present" means that, in the Way, there is no distinction between the past and the present.

"To enter into that which neither dies nor is born" means that in the Way, there is no transformation involving coming into existence and perishing. "One who kills life does not die" means that one that ends life does not follow [the course of ordinary] things, and so he does not die. "One who gives life is not born" means that one brings things to life but does not follow [the course of] things, and so he is not born.

其爲物，物，道也。如《中庸》其爲物不貳之物。將，送其去也；迎，迎其求也。言物之去來、成毁，無非道之所爲也。攖ˆ寧ˆ，攖，紛羅也；寧，有定也。言萬象紛羅，道有定體也。攖而後成，即象之紛羅，而見道之定體也。如《論語》一貫之旨。

In the phrase "such a thing," the "thing" refers to the Way. It is the same usage as in the *Zhongyong*, where it says, "Such a thing is not twofold."[15] "To carry forward" means to send it away, and "to draw back" means to seek its return. This shows that in all coming and going, in the completion and destruction of all things, nothing lies outside what the Way brings about.

In the phrase "stillness amidst turmoil," "turmoil" refers to a chaotic state, and stillness means that there is stability. This means that although all forms of thing are in a chaotic state, the Way possesses a stable essence within them.

[In the main text,] "Only through turmoil can completion come" means that although forms are chaotic, the stable essence of the Way can still be seen within them. This is in line with the intent of the concept of "one-threaded consistency" in the *Lunyu* (4.15; 15.3).

---

12 In the original text of the ZZ, it is written as *kyŏn tok* 見獨, instead of *tok kyŏn* 獨見.

13 It appears that, in terms of meaning of the sentence in accordance with that of the original text, the character *pul* 不 is missing before the character *sa* 死.

14 Likewise, in light of the meaning of the original *Zhuangzi* text, it appears that the character *pul* 不 is omitted before *saeng* 生.

15 The quote is from section 27 of the *Zhongyong*: "Such a thing is not twofold. That is, its giving life to other things cannot be fathomed. 其為物不貳，則其生物不測。

自見獨以下，論道極善。但其道，非吾所謂道也。此以上言，入道次第。此以下，復以聞道次第，言聞道而後入道。故先言入道，而後言聞道。
From the passage beginning with "to behold the Alone" onward, [Zhuangzi] discusses the utmost goodness of the Way. However, that Way is not the same as the Way spoken of in our [Confucian] tradition. Before this "to behold the Alone," the text speaks of the order of entering the Way; from this point onward, it discusses the order of the state after having heard the Way by proceeding in that manner. [Zhuangzi,] having heard the Way himself, speaks of how one enters into the Way. Thus, he first explains the method of entering the Way, and then discusses the state after hearing it.

副墨，文子也。文墨記道，爲言語之次，故曰副墨。副，次也。洛誦，言語也。包絡是道，而誦說之謂也。文子直載其道，故謂之子。言語遾[遞]相傳告，故謂之孫。瞻明，日月、星辰、山川、草木之可見者也。聶ˆ許ˆ，聶，包攝也；許，大也。包攝之大，即天地也。需役，需，待也；役，功也。功用所待，即造化也。於謳，於ˆ，歎美辭。謳，謳歌也；贊歎而咏[詠]歌之也。即造化微妙，不可形容處。古人言語，每說到微妙難形處，只得贊歎咏[詠]歌之而已也。
"Ink's-Assistant" refers to that which is written in characters. Writing with ink and recording the Way becomes something that follows after language, and thus it is called "Ink's-Assistant." The word "Assistant" means that which comes after. "Reciting-by-the-River" refers to speech or language. It refers to those who immerse themselves in this Way and perpetuate it by reciting the doctrines concerning it. Written characters directly contain the Way, so they are called its "sons," while speech, which transmits what is passed down or spoken, is called its "grandson." "Bright-to-Behold" refers to visible things, such as the sun and moon, stars, mountains and rivers, grass and trees. "Great-Embrace," "embrace" means "to gather in" or "to encompass," and "great" means "vast" or "large." So "encompassing greatly" refers to [the work of] heaven and earth. In "Awaiting-Command," "to await" means "to wait," and "command" means "to work" or "to act." Thus, it refers to applying effort in a process of waiting, namely, creative transformation. In "Oh-Song-Chanting," "oh" is an exclamatory particle, and "to chant" means "to sing a song." It expresses singing and chanting in praise, that is, a state where transformation is so subtle and profound that it defies description. In ancient speech, whenever one reached a realm that was extremely subtle and difficult to articulate, they would simply chant and sing in praise.

玄冥，無形也。參寥[寂]，無聲也。無形無聲，又贊歎咏[詠]歌之所不及，極言其微妙也，然亦不難乎。天地形氣[聲]而爲言也。蓋言其ˆ形氣之始也。疑始，謂之始而亦無可指以爲始者。故曰疑始，即所謂未始有始者也，周之所謂道也。
"Dark-Obscurity" means having no form, and "Vast-Void" means having no sound. [They are] a state without form and sound, a realm so subtle that even praise and song cannot reach it. This expresses the utmost subtlety in an extreme manner, so it is difficult to describe. It speaks in terms of the forming *qi* of

heaven and earth, referring to the origin of that forming *qi*.

[Lastly,] "Doubting-the-Beginning" means that there is a beginning, but it is in which nothing can be pointed to as the beginning, hence it is called "to doubt the beginning." This corresponds to what is called "there has not yet begun a beginning" (ZZ 2.8), and it is what Zhuang Zhou refers to as the Way.

言語文字，以道之所傳而言也。天地日月陰陽造化，以道之所存而言也。至於疑始，方指出道之本體，而實則不離於一陰虛靜，形氣之粗也。周於此處，又進一層，則豈不爲眞知道者哉。
[In this passage, Zhuangzi] speaks of the transmission of the Way through verbal or written language, and of the Way's mode of existence through the harmony of heaven and earth, the sun and moon, and yin and yang. Upon reaching the point of "doubting the beginning," he finally points out that the Way is substantive, yet never departs from the single yin of emptiness and stillness, never apart from the coarseness of the forming *qi*. At this point, Zhuang Zhou advances yet another step; how, then, could he not be one who knew the Way?

## Section 16 (ZZ 6.5)

> 子祀、子輿、子犁、子來四人相與語曰：孰能以無為首，以生為脊，以死為尻，孰知生死存亡之一體者，吾與之友矣。四人相視而笑，莫逆於心，遂相與為友。俄而子輿有病，子祀往問之。曰：偉哉！夫造物者，將以予為此拘拘也！曲僂發背，上有五管，頤隱於齊，肩高於頂，句贅指天。陰陽之氣有沴，其心閒而無事，跰足而鑑於井，曰：嗟乎！夫造物者，又將以予為此拘拘也！
> Master Si, Master Yu, Master Li, and Master Lai were conversing together. "Who," they said, "can take non-action as his head, life as his spine, and death as his tail? Whoever understands that life, death, existence, and disappearance are all one body, we will be his friend." The four looked at one another and laughed; their hearts were in complete accord, and they became friends.
>
> Not long after, Master Yu fell ill. Master Si went to visit him. Master Yu said, "How great indeed is the maker of things! He is about to make me into something so twisted and bent! My back is hunched, five ridges rise upon it; my chin burrows into my navel, my shoulders tower above my head, and the knotted flesh on my back points toward the sky. There is some disorder between *qi* of yin and yang." Yet he seemed clam as if nothing had happened. Dragging himself to the well, he looked into the well and said, "Ah! The maker of things is about to make me into something even more twisted and bent!"
>
> 子祀曰：汝惡之乎？曰：亡，予何惡！浸假而化予之左臂以為雞，予因以求時夜；浸假而化予之右臂以為彈，予因以求鴞炙；浸假而化予之尻以為輪，以神為馬，予因以乘之，豈更駕哉！且夫得者時也，失者順也，安時而處順，哀樂不能入也。此古之所謂縣解也，而不能自解者，物有結之。且夫物不勝天久矣，吾又何惡焉？

Master Si said, "Do you dislike it?"

Master Yu replied, "No, what is there for me to dislike? If, little by little, transformation turns my left arm into a rooster, I will use it to mark the times of night. If, little by little, it turns my right arm into a crossbow, I will use it to roast owls. If, little by little, it turns my rump into a wheel and my spirit into a horse, I will ride upon it, why would I ever need a carriage?

Moreover, to gain is a matter of timing, to lose is a matter of following along. When one is at peace with the times and rests in the flow, sorrow and joy can no longer enter. This is what the ancients called 'release from what binds'—and yet one cannot release oneself, for things are what bind one.

Besides, things have never long been able to overcome heaven—so what should I dislike?"

俄而子來有病，喘喘然將死，其妻子環而泣之。子犁往問之曰：叱！避！無怛化！倚其戶與之語曰 ： 偉哉造物！又將奚以汝為？將奚以汝適？以汝為鼠肝乎？以汝為蟲臂乎？子來曰：父母於子，東西南北，唯命之從。陰陽於人，不翅於父母，彼近吾死而我不聽，我則悍矣，彼何罪焉！夫大塊載我以形，勞我以生，佚我以老，息我以死。故善吾生者，乃所以善吾死也。今之大冶鑄金，金踊躍曰我且必為鏌鋣，大冶必以為不祥之金。今一犯人之形，而曰人耳人耳，夫造化者必以為不祥之人。今一以天地為大鑪，以造化為大冶，惡乎往而不可哉！成然寐，蘧然覺。

Soon after, Master Lai fell ill, gasping for breath and on the verge of death. His wife and children gathered around him, weeping. Master Li came to visit and said, "Out! Away! Do not disturb the process of transformation!"

Leaning against the door, he spoke to him, saying, "Marvelous indeed is the maker of things! What will he make of you this time, and where will he send you? Will he make you the liver of a mouse, or the arm of an insect?"

Master Lai replied, "When parents direct their children to go east, west, south, or north, the children follow their command. The forces of yin and yang in relation to a person are no different from parents. Now they approach my death, and if I were to refuse them, would that not be defiance? How could they be at fault? The great clod bears me with a body, toils me with life, lets me rest with old age, and gives me repose in death. Thus, one who is good at living is thereby good at dying as well. Now, when a great metalworker casts gold, and the gold leaps up saying, 'I must become a Moye blade,' the metalworker surely regards it as ill-omened gold. Likewise, when one takes on the form of a human and insists, 'I'll only be human, only be human!' the maker of things must see this as an ill-omened person. Now, if we take heaven and earth as the great furnace, and creation as the great metalworker, then where could one go that is not fitting? Thus, he lay down in sleep completely at peace, and awoke suddenly."

第十六段，以無為首，以生[首]為脊，以死為尻。此三句雖略，周之見，盡於是矣。萬物生於無，而死則復歸於無。故以無與死爲首尾。生者，居其間，自無而[以]適無，故謂之脊。然以一物之生死而言，則固生於無，而歸於無也。若以陰陽之物而言，則前未嘗有無，後亦未嘗有無也。安得以無為首哉。

The sixteenth section. In "to take non-action as his head, life as his spine, and death as his tail," these three phrases, though concise, fully convey Zhuang Zhou's view. Myriad things arise from non-being, and when they die, they return again to non-being. Thus, [Zhuangzi] takes non-being and death as the head and the tail. [He sees] life as the state of dwelling in between, coming from non-being and going back to non-being. Therefore, he calls it the "spine." However, when one speaks of the life and death of a single thing, it means that [a thing] comes from non-being and returns to non-being. [However,] if one were to speak in terms of yin and yang, there never was a time before when it did not yet exist, and there never will be a time after when it no longer exists. In that case, how could one, like Zhuangzi, take non-being as the "head"?

然則周之所謂無[言]者，可見其指天地未闢，萬物未生之前，一陰之靜者也，以是為道。非道之眞，而其無亦非至無之無也。自此至終篇，皆言得道之人，以實前段之意，如孟子道性善，而稱堯舜以實之也。
If this is so, then what Zhuang Zhou refers to as non-being is the tranquility of the sole yin before heaven and earth opened and before all things were born. He regarded this as the Way, but this is not the true Way. Moreover, the non-being he speaks of is also not the utterly ultimate non-being.

From this point until the end of the chapter, he speaks entirely about human beings who have attained the Way. By doing so, it substantializes the message of the previous passages, just as Mengzi, when discussing the goodness of human nature, always substantialized it through references to Yao and Shun (3A1).

## Section 17 (ZZ 6.6)

子桑戶、孟子反、子琴張三人相與友，曰：孰能相與於無相與，相為於無相為？孰能登天遊霧，撓挑無極，相忘以生，無所終窮？三人相視而笑，莫逆於心，遂相與友。莫然有閒，而子桑戶死。未葬, 孔子聞之，使子貢往侍事焉。或編曲，或鼓琴，相和而歌曰：嗟來桑戶乎！嗟來桑戶乎！而已反其真，而我猶為人猗！子貢趨而進曰：敢問臨尸而歌，禮乎？二人相視而笑，曰：是惡知禮意！
Master Sanghu, Mengzi Fan, and Master Qinzhang, these three people were friends to one another. They said, "Who can give each other without giving each other? Who can ascend to heaven and wander in the mists, walk in the Non-Ultimate, and forget each other in life, with no end?" The three looked at each other and laughed, their hearts in perfect accord, and so they became [true] friends with each other.

While nothing was happening, Master Sanghu died. Before he had been buried, Confucius heard of it and sent Zigong to assist with the funeral. [When Zigong arrived,] he found some composing a song and some strumming a lute. Together, they sang, "Ah, Sanghu, Ah, Sanghu. You have returned to your true form while we remain as humans."

Zigong stepped forward and asked, "May I dare to ask if this accord with ritual propriety, singing in the presence of the corpse?"

The two looked at each other and laughed, saying, "How could this person know of the [true] meaning of ritual propriety?"

子貢反，以告孔子曰：彼何人者邪？修行無有，而外其形骸，臨尸而歌，顏色不變，無以命之。彼何人者邪？孔子曰：彼遊方之外者也，而丘游方之內者也。外內不相及，而丘使女往弔之，丘則陋矣。彼方且與造物者為人，而遊乎天地之一氣。彼以生為附贅縣疣，以死為決疢潰癰。夫若然者，又惡知死生先後之所在！假於異物，託於同體，忘其肝膽，遺其耳目，反覆終始，不知端倪，芒然彷徨乎塵垢之外，逍遙乎無為之業。彼又惡能憒憒然為世俗之禮，以觀眾人之耳目哉！

Zigong returned to Confucius and asked, "What sort of people are they? They conduct with no [rules], forget their appearance, and sing beside a corpse without changing expression. I cannot even name what kind of men they are."

Confucius replied, "Such people roam beyond the realm. People like me remain within it. The beyond and the within do not meet. It was foolish of me to send you. Even now they have joined with the maker of things, wandering as men in the single breath of heaven and earth. They see life as a swelling and death as the draining of a sore. For them, there is no ranking of life before death or death after life. They borrow the forms of the ten thousand things and lodge them in one body, forgetting liver and gall, casting aside ears and eyes, turning and revolving, beginning and ending without knowing where it starts or finishes, drifting beyond dust and dirt, roaming freely in the service of non-action. Why should they be troubled by mundane rituals or perform for the ears and eyes of the crowd"

子貢曰：然則夫子何方之依？孔子曰：丘，天之戮民也。雖然，吾與汝共之。子貢曰：敢問其方。孔子曰：魚相造乎水，人相造乎道。相造乎水者，穿池而養給；相造乎道者，無事而生定。故曰：魚相忘乎江湖，人相忘乎道術。子貢曰：敢問畸人。曰：畸人者，畸於人而侔於天。故曰：天之小人，人之君子；人之君子，天之小人也。

Zigong asked, "Then upon what does the Master rely?"

Confucius said, "I, Qiu, am one of those people punished by heaven. Even so, I will share it with you."

Zigong said, "I venture to ask what it is."

Confucius said, "Fish come to life in water; human beings come to life in the Way. Those who come to life in water dig ponds and thereby receive their nourishment. Those who come to life in the Way do nothing, and thereby give rise to settled life. Thus, it is said, fish forget one another in the rivers and lakes; human beings forget one another in the arts of the Way."

Zigong said, "May I venture to ask about the sole person?"

Confucius said, "The sole person stands aloof from other human beings yet equal to heaven. Thus, it is said, the petty person of heaven is the noble person among human beings; the noble person among human beings is the petty person of heaven."

子桑戶一段，無極，與上文所謂太極，皆以形氣言，非如吾儒所謂無極太極也。世之議，周之失者（楊龜山說）。[16] 每以道在太極之先為口，實以周為若道上求道者。然此無極字，亦可作道字，看耶。周雖不知道，亦未嘗以道為有二層，以是詬厲，周豈服哉。

In this section about Master Sanghu, the term "Non-Ultimate," which corresponds to the so-called "Supreme Ultimate" mentioned in the earlier section. [For Zhuangzi,] both are spoken with the concept of form-generating *qi*. [Therefore,] it is not the same as the "Non-Ultimate and yet Supreme Ultimate" discussed in our Confucian [tradition]. There is a [common] opinion in the world, that it was Zhuang Zhou's misunderstanding.

He repeatedly invokes the claim that the Way comes before Supreme Ultimate,[17] but in truth, he portrays himself as one who looks for the Way above the

---

[16] Han Wŏnjin's original comment: "[For example,] this is the theory of Guishan 龜山 Yang Shi 楊時 (1053–1135)" 楊龜山說.

Translator's note: Han Wŏnjin's comment is so brief that it is difficult to determine precisely what he meant by this vague statement. Since Han discusses the Zhuangzi's and the Confucians' uses of the concepts of the Non-Ultimate and the Supreme Ultimate in the previous sentences, his remark appears to concern the misuse of these concepts in contrast to their orthodox interpretation in the Zhu Xi school. Here Han likely identifies Yang Shi as an example of one who made the same kind of mistake as Zhuangzi.

Yang Shi, a major Northern Song Confucian, studied under Cheng Hao and later Cheng Yi. Through his disciple Luo Congyan 羅從彥 (1072-1135) and Luo's student Li Tong 李侗 (1093-1163)—teacher of Zhu Xi—Yang became a key link in transmitting the Cheng brothers' learning to Zhu Xi (see Wu 2022). Alongside Xie Liangzuo, he was among Cheng Yi's foremost students. While Xie emphasized active moral practice, Yang focused on quietude (*jing* 靜), suspending conscious activity to attain direct inner awareness.

In this quietude-centered view, Yang held that the external world and the inner nature endowed by Heaven form a single reality: outer form and inner essence are one—expressed in his phrase, "Form and appearance are Heavenly nature" 形色天性也. He went further, aligning this unity with the Buddhist *Heart Sūtra* teaching that "form is emptiness," showing his engagement with Daoist and Buddhist thought. Though still regarding Buddhism as heterodox, Yang claimed no essential difference between "form is emptiness" and "form and appearance are Heavenly nature" (Chen 2004, 111–113).

Han Wŏnjin saw a possible connection between Yang Shi's view and Zhuangzi's conception of the Non-Ultimate and the Supreme Ultimate. He interprets Zhuangzi's Non-Ultimate as the primal non-being from which all arises and to which all returns, and the Supreme Ultimate as the first manifestation of form within yin–yang *qi*—ultimately identical with the Non-Ultimate. Han therefore views Zhuangzi's worldview as akin to Buddhism.

However, he argues that in the Confucian tradition, neither the Supreme Ultimate nor the Non-Ultimate signifies a fixed void or pure non-being; both describe a state where being and non-being coexist without sequence. Thus, Zhuangzi's concepts differ fundamentally from the Confucian view. Han adds that some Confucians, especially Yang Shi, mistakenly drew parallels between them by equating form and essence while overlooking the non-being element foreign to Confucian thought.

Notably, this comment does not appear in the Yŏam edition.

[17] It refers to a line in the ZZ 6.3: "The Way is before the Supreme Ultimate, yet it does not claim to be higher [than the Supreme Ultimate]" 夫道... 在太極之先而不為高.

Way. Yet here the word Non-Ultimate can just as well be read as the Way itself. Although Zhou did not know the Way, he never once regarded it as divided into two tiers (i.e., Non-Ultimate and yet Supreme Ultimate).[18] Even if he is reproached for this, how could Zhuang Zhou be convinced?

且周於道字，本不見得，則又安知無極太極之爲道耶。特自撰出此名[此撰出名字]，言ˆ以形容形氣之極處，此[與]無窮者耳。莫然有間，莫濶遠之意，言阻隔也。既相與友ˆ，而又不叅尋相聞者，亦言其形骸相忘之意也。
Moreover, Zhuang Zhou fundamentally failed to grasp the notion of the Way; therefore, how could he have known that the Way is both the Non-Ultimate and yet the Supreme Ultimate? Especially, this concept of the Way was invented by him, and from that concept, he described the extreme state of form-generating *qi* as the boundlessness. The phrase "While nothing was happening" means that vastness and distance imply an absence of anything, that it is blocked, and there is a gap. Though they "became [true] friends with each other," yet they neither seek nor question one another, which means they have forgotten each other's outward appearance and physical bodies.

### Section 18 (ZZ 6.7)

> 顏回問仲尼曰：孟孫才，其母死，哭泣無涕，中心不戚，居喪不哀。無是三者，以善處喪蓋魯國。固有無其實而得其名者乎？回壹怪之。仲尼曰：夫孟孫氏盡之矣，進於知矣。唯簡之而不得，夫已有所簡矣。孟孫氏不知所以生，不知所以死，不知就先，不知就後，若化為物，以待其所不知之化已乎！且方將化，惡知不化哉？方將不化，惡知已化哉？吾特與汝其夢未始覺者邪！且彼有駭形而無損心，有旦宅而無情死。孟孫氏特覺，人哭亦哭，是自其所以乃。
> Yan Hui asked Zhongni, saying, "When Mengsun Cai's mother died, he wept but shed no tears; his heart felt no grief, and during mourning he showed no sorrow. Yet despite lacking all three, he was praised throughout the state of Lu for how well he handled the mourning. Could it be that one attains a reputation without any genuine substance? I find this truly strange."
>
> Zhongni said, "Mengsun has done his utmost—he has reached the stage of understanding. Yet he is simple and easy but cannot go beyond that. There is still something more to be easier and simpler. Mengsun does not know how he came to life, nor how he will die; he does not know how to follow what precedes him, nor how to follow what comes after him. It is as if he has transformed into a thing, waiting for that transformation which he does not yet know to complete itself! If he is in the midst of transforming, how can he know that he is not yet transformed? If he is in the midst of not transforming, how can he know that he has already transformed? Perhaps you and I are like dreamers who have never awakened! Moreover, he [still] has a physical form of human,

[18] For Han, these two tiers are Non-Ultimate and yet Supreme Ultimate.

> but no injured mind; He has a temporary dwelling (i.e., a body), yet he has no feelings toward death. Mengsun is simply awake. Because others wept, he wept too, and that is why he did so."

孟孫氏，不知就先，不知就後,[19] 即所謂不知死生，先後之所在也。所不知之化，言不知化爲何物也。即所謂若人之形，萬化未始有極者也。且方將化，惡知不化，言自我化物，認物爲眞，安知非本物而未化者乎。方將不化，惡知已化，言自我視我，自謂不化，安知非自物，而已化者乎。有形骸[骸形]而無損心。有骸人之形，而無損道之心也。言母死不慽，雖骸於人，而其心，則無損於道也^。
Mengsun "does not know how to follow what precedes him, nor how to follow what comes after him." That is to say, "He does not know life and death." [Life and death] are where what comes before and after.

The phrase, "the transformation one does not know," refers to not knowing what kind of thing one will become [through transformation]. Hence, in the earlier passage (section 13; ZZ 6.2), it says: "As for the human form, the myriad transformations have never had a limit."

"If he is in the midst of transforming, how can he know that he is not yet transformed?": From oneself, one projects transformation onto external things, and then takes those external things to be real, so how could one know that what appears as external is not in fact external by nature, but has not yet transformed?

"If he is in the midst of not transforming, how can he know that he has already transformed?": When one looks at oneself from within and declares, "I have not changed," how could one know whether the self is not already an external thing and has in fact already undergone transformation?

"He [still] has a physical form of human, but no injured mind" means that although he possesses the form of a human body, the mind has not been damaged by losing the Way. That is to say, even when his mother died, he did not grieve. Although the form was still human, his mind has not lost anything with respect to the Way.

有旦宅而無情死，有一旦之宅，而無萬古之死也^。言生爲一旦之宅，而死爲萬古之生也。情，常也，實也。言無常死，無實死也。言人之變化，未始有極，人死而有所化。自其所化，而又有所化，則其死，非實死也。
The phrase "He has a temporary dwelling (i.e., a body), yet he has no feelings toward death" means that while he may have a dwelling for a morning, he has no place for death that endures for all time. It describes that life is like a place to stay for a morning; death is a life that continues through eternity.

The character for "feeling" here carries the sense of "always substantial," indicating that there is no eternal or substantial death. It says that in human transformation, there has been no end yet: when a person dies, there is a transformation; and from that transformation, yet another transformation arises. Thus,

[19] In the Yŏam edition, these two phrases quoted from the original text of the *Zhuangzi* are written as *pu chi suk sŏn suk hu* 不知執先孰後.

what is called "death" is in truth not death at all.

孟孫氏有覺於此，故以其母死爲非實死，不慼其死也。人哭亦哭，亦隨衆爲之，而欲簡而不得者也。自其所以乃爾也,[20] 所以乃爾，即指哭泣無涕以下也。自傳說爲列星至此，皆以人死，有所化爲言。蓋與釋氏輪回之見同。
Mengsun has got enlightened on this and therefore did not consider his mother's death to be a real or substantial death, hence, he did not grieve over it.

"Since others wept, he wept, too" means that he followed others in doing so. Although he wished to be simple and effortless, he could not fully achieve it, [as he could not help but follow them.]

In the phrase "that is why he did so," "he did so" refers specifically to the passage beginning with "he wept but shed no tears" and what follows.

From the section on legendary figures [such as Xiwei and Fuxi] and all the stars through this point, [Zhuangzi] discusses that all beings undergo transformation with the case of human death. This view aligns with Śākyamuni's teaching of transmigration.

**Section 19 (ZZ 6.7)**

> 且也，相與吾之耳矣，庸詎知吾所謂吾之乎？且汝夢為鳥而厲乎天，夢為魚而沒於淵，不識今之言者，其覺者乎，夢者乎？造適不及笑，獻笑不及排，安排而去化，乃入於寥天一。
> [Zhongni continued] "Besides, [people] talk to each other something like "I did this," but how would I know who this I is in the "I did this"? You dream of being a bird flying high in the sky, or a fish diving into deep waters, but you do not know that the one who is currently telling me [about the dream] is awake or still dreaming. tell me of these dreams, how can I be sure you are not still dreaming? Establishing what is right is not as good as smiling, and smiling is not as good as simply going along with things. Going along with things peacefully and being removed in change, that is the unity with the vast heaven.

吾之耳，與上文人耳人耳之語，同。言自吾其身不能喪我也。寥天一，虛靜之意，即所謂大宗師也。
The phrase "I did this" parallels the earlier expression, "I'll only be human, only human" (section 16; ZZ 6.5). Both express that, from [the standpoint of the sustained] self-identity, one cannot "lose himself." "The unity with the vast heaven" conveys a sense of emptiness and stillness, which is precisely what the

---

[20] In the extant original text of *Zhuangzi*, the phrase reads 自其所以乃, but it seems that the version Han Wŏnjin consulted read 自其所以乃爾也. In fact, the extant passage in Zhuangzi has a somewhat awkward sentence ending, and the *Zhuangzi* that Han Wŏnjin saw appears to have revised this somewhat awkward ending to make it clearer and more definite. The phrase 其所以乃爾也 carries the same meaning as 其所以乃已也.

In the Yŏam edition, *nae* 乃 occurs three times in succession, which seems to be an error.

"Great Founding Master" refers to.

**Section 20 (ZZ 6.8)**

意而子見許由，許由曰：堯何以資汝？意而子曰：堯謂我：汝必躬服仁義，而明言是非。許由曰：而奚為來軹？夫堯既已黥汝以仁義，而劓汝以是非矣，汝將何以遊夫遙蕩、恣睢、轉徙之途乎？意而子曰：雖然，吾願遊於其藩。許由曰：不然。夫盲者無以與乎眉目顏色之好，瞽者無以與乎青黃黼黻之觀。

Yi Erzi met Xu You. Xu You said, "How could Yao be an asset to you?"

Yi Erzi replied, "Yao told me: 'You must personally practice benevolence and righteousness, and clearly articulate right and wrong.'"

Xu You said, "Then why come to follow me? Yao has already branded you with benevolence and righteousness, and cut your nose with right and wrong. How then will you wander in the path of freedom, indulgence, and travelling?"

Yi Erzi said, "Even so, I wish to wander within his fence."

Xu You said, "No. A blind person cannot partake in the beauty of eyebrows, eyes, and faces; a sightless person cannot partake in the perception of blue, yellow, or patterned garments."

意而子曰：夫無莊之失其美，據梁之失其力，黃帝之亡其知，皆在鑪捶之間耳。庸詎知夫造物者之不息我黥而補我劓，使我乘成以隨先生邪？許由曰：噫！未可知也。我為汝言其大略。吾師乎！吾師乎！齏萬物而不為義，澤及萬世而不為仁，長於上古而不為老，覆載天地、刻彫眾形而不為巧。此所遊已。

Yi Erzi said, "Wu Zhuang lost her beauty, Ju Liang lost his strength, the Yellow Emperor forgot knowledge—all occurred within the span of the furnace and hammer [of the maker]. How could one know that the maker of things will not cease branding me and restore my nose, allowing me to ride upon completeness and follow you, Master?"

Xu You said, "Ah! That cannot be known. Let me tell you the broad outline of it. My teacher! My teacher! He grinds all things to dust yet does not consider himself as righteous; he bestows his grace upon all ages yet does not consider himself as benevolent; he existed long before the high antiquity yet does not consider himself as old; he covers heaven and earth, shapes all forms, yet does not consider himself as skillful. This is where he wanders."

意而子一段，承上寥天一之語，復言道體。齏萬物，殺物之義也；澤及萬世，生物之仁也。義而無意於爲義，仁而無意於爲仁，故曰不為義，不為仁。上文聖人之不失人心，不爲愛人意，亦與此同。然無所爲而爲仁義，仁義之眞，而天理之公也；有所爲而爲仁義，仁義之賊，而人欲之私也。

The section on Yi Erzi continues the concept of "unity with the vast heaven" from the previous section, once again speaking of the substance of the Way.

The phrase, "He grinds all things to dust" refers to righteousness that destroys all things, while "he bestows his grace upon all ages" refers to benevolence that gives life to them. One is righteous, yet has no consciousness of performing righteousness; one is benevolent, yet has no awareness of practicing benevolence. Therefore, he says, "[He] does not consider himself as righteous" and "does not consider himself as benevolent." This corresponds to the earlier passage: "The sage does not lose people's hearts, but also does not practice favoritism for certain people," which expresses the same idea.[21]

As such, though one performs nothing, he is considered benevolence and righteousness; such non-action is the true essence of benevolence and righteousness, and the universality of the Way of heaven. By contrast, to deliberately perform acts of benevolence and righteousness is to become a thief of benevolence and righteousness, a manifestation of private human desire.

眞者，可謂仁義；賊者，不可謂仁義。則君子於此，當辨其公私之辨[下]分而已。又何必惡其名，而幷去之哉。此周之學，所以過高，而爲異端也。長於上古以下，語奇而意正，形容道字，甚善。學者當取其言[意]，而闕其所以言，可也。

What is true may be called benevolence and righteousness, but what is thievery cannot be so named. Thus, the noble person must clearly distinguish between what is universal and what is private.

Yet again, why must one hate these names (i.e., the concepts of benevolence and righteousness) and abolish them altogether? In this way, the learning of Zhuangzi, due to its excessive loftiness, comes to be regarded as heretical.

The phrase toward the end of this passage, "long before the high antiquity," though the wording itself is strange, expresses a meaning that is upright and gives a remarkably profound description of the concept of the Way. Those who study should carefully take note of these words and examine closely what they convey.

### Section 21 (ZZ 6.9)

> 顏回曰：回益矣。仲尼曰：何謂也？曰：回忘仁義矣。曰：可矣，猶未也。他日復見，曰：回益矣。曰：何謂也？曰：回忘禮樂矣。曰：可矣，猶未也。他日復見，曰：回益矣。曰：何謂也？曰：回坐忘矣。
>
> Yan Hui said, "I have made progress." Zhongni said, "What do you mean?"
> He replied, "I have forgotten benevolence and righteousness."
> Zhongni said, "That is good, but not yet enough."
> Another day [Yan Hui] came again and said, "I have made progress."
> Zhongni said, "What do you mean?"
> He replied, "I have forgotten ritual and music."

---

[21] This line in the ZZ appears as follows: "Therefore, when the sage uses arms, states may perish but people's hearts are not lost; when benefit and grace are extended to all things, they do not do so out of love for people" 故聖人之用兵也，亡國而不失人心；利澤施於萬物，不為愛人. This line belongs to either section six or section seven of this chapter. As noted earlier, these two sections are not found in the extant versions of this work. That Han Wŏnjin is clearly referencing this passage suggests that the original version of section six or seven must have contained these sections. Why they were omitted in the current editions is unknown.

Zhongni said, "That is good, but still not enough."
Another day he came again and said, "I have made progress."
Zhongni said, "What do you mean?"
He replied, "I have entered the state of sitting in forgetfulness."

仲尼蹴然曰：何謂坐忘？顏回曰：墮肢體，黜聰明，離形去知，同於大通，此謂坐忘。仲尼曰：同則無好也，化則無常也。而果其賢乎！丘也請從而後也。
Zhongni, startled, said, "What do you mean by 'sitting in forgetfulness'?"

Yan Hui said, "I drop off my limbs and body, cast away hearing and sight, leave behind form and remove knowledge, and become one with the great thoroughfare. This is what I call sitting in forgetfulness."

Zhongni said, "Being one, there are no preferences; transformed, there is no constancy. Indeed, you are the truly worthy one! Let me follow after you."

顏淵一段，承上仁義字，言得道者，自忘仁義，忘禮樂，以至於忘其身，而至矣。墮肢體，黜聰明，即下篇去七竅爲[而]混沌之意。大道即混沌之道，而所謂大宗師者也。此蓋一篇之結語也。
The section concerning Yan Yuan continues the earlier discussion of benevolence and righteousness, explaining that one who has attained the Way naturally forgets benevolence and righteousness, forgets rituals and music, and by doing so arrives at the state of forgetting the self, thus reaching the ultimate.

The phrase "to drop off limbs and body, cast away hearing and sight" corresponds to the meaning of the story in the next chapter about boring seven holes into primal undifferentiation. The great Way is the Way of primal undifferentiation, and this is what is called the Great Founding Master. This serves as the conclusion of this present chapter.

**Section 22 (ZZ 6.10)**

子輿與子桑友，而霖雨十日。子輿曰：子桑殆病矣！裹飯而往食之。至子桑之門，則若歌若哭，鼓琴曰：父邪母邪！天乎人乎！有不任其聲，而趨舉其詩焉。子輿入，曰：子之歌詩，何故若是？曰：吾思乎使我至此極者而弗得也。父母豈欲吾貧哉？天無私覆，地無私載，天地豈私貧我哉？求其為之者而不得也。然而至此極者，命也夫！
Master Yu and Master Sang were friends. It rained without stop for ten days. Master Yu said, "Master Sang must be ill!" So, he wrapped up some rice and went to feed him. When he arrived at Master Sang's gate, he heard sounds like either singing or weeping. Master Sang was playing the zither and saying: "Is it father? Is it mother? Is it heaven? Is it man?"

Unable to contain his voice, he raised his chant and sang his poem.

Master Yu entered and said, "Why are your songs and verses like this?"

Master Sang said, "I have pondered who has brought me to this extremity, but I cannot find it. Did my parents wish me to be poor? Heaven covers all

> things without partiality; earth bears all things without preference. How could heaven and earth have singled me out for poverty? I have sought for what has caused it but cannot find it. Yet to have reached this extremity, it must be fate!"

子輿、子桑一段，在前段既結一篇之後，而又子祀、子輿數段，語意相類[雜]，恐爲錯簡，而當在子桑戶、孟子反之下。抑末句命字，與上文死生命也之命，相應而同，爲大宗師以結一篇之意耶。然ˆ亦無甚[甚無]意味矣。

This section about Master Yu and Master Sang appears after the preceding section has already concluded the chapter, and its wording and meaning align closely with sections like the one on Master Si and Master Yu (section 16; ZZ 6.5). This suggests that the original bamboo slips of the ZZ may have been compiled out of order. Most likely, this passage should have followed the section on "Master Sanghu and Mengzi Fan" (ZZ 6.6). Alternatively, in the final phrase of this passage, the notion of fate corresponds to the same as in the phrase "life and death are a matter of fate" (ZZ 6.2). [The fate] is the Great Founding Master, and with that, conclude the message of this chapter. Still, even in that case, it bears no particularly profound significance.

## Concluding Remarks

此篇始言，知道在於眞人，故其下八段，皆言眞人眞知之事，死生[+明]命也。以下五段，承上眞知，而皆言道。女偊一段，言入道、聞道之次第。子祀、子輿以下七段，皆言得道之人。周以虛無爲道，以齊物爲得道之要，故其言知道，以無心無知；言者，以虛無，知虛無也。其言得道，以一死生，外形骸。爲言者，一死生，外形骸，爲齊物之極也。

This chapter states that understanding the Way belongs to the true person; accordingly, the following eight sections all concern the true person and the matter of true knowing, that life and death are matters of fate. The five sections that follow continue the discussion of true knowing and all speak of the Way. The section on the hunched woman (ZZ 6.4) discusses the order of entering the Way and hearing the Way, and the seven sections beginning with "Master Sang and Master Yu" (ZZ 6.5) all speak about the one who has attained the Way.

Zhuang Zhou regards emptiness and non-being as the Way, and considers treating all things alike as the essential point of attaining the Way. Therefore, he says that one comes to know the Way through no-mind and non-knowing. That is to say, what he speaks of is coming to know emptiness and non-being with being empty and nothing. He also says that attaining the Way is to see life and death as one, and to cast off outer form and the physical body. What he speaks of is that to regard life and death as one, and to transcend the physical form and body, is the ultimate expression of treating all things equally.

# Chapter 7

# Being in Accord with the Way of Emperor

前篇言道，得道者，可以爲帝王，故以應帝王終之。應，猶言^合也。言合乎帝王之道也。養生主，人間世，如吾儒之修身行已。應帝王，如吾儒之治國平天下也。
The previous chapter speaks of the Way: one who attains the Way may become the emperor; therefore, [Zhang Zhou] concludes with "Being in Accord with the Way of Emperor." Here, the character for "to respond" means to correspond or to be in accord with. It refers to being aligned with the Way of the emperor.

[The message in] "The Foundation of Nurturing Life" and "Living Among People in the World" is the same as our Confucian practice of cultivating oneself, and [the message in] "Being in Accord with the Way of the Emperor" corresponds to our Confucian's ruling the state and pacifying all-under-heaven.

**Section 1 (ZZ 7.1)**

> 齧缺問於王倪四問而四不知。齧缺因躍而大喜， 行以告蒲衣子。蒲衣子曰：而乃今知之乎？有虞氏不及泰氏。有虞氏， 其猶藏仁以要人， 亦得人矣， 而未始出於非人。泰氏， 其臥徐徐， 其覺于于， 一以己為馬， 一以己為牛， 其知情信，其德甚真，而未始入於非人。
> Toothless asked Wang Ni four questions, and for each, Wang Ni said he did not know. Toothless leapt up in great joy and went to tell Master Reed Garbed.
>
> Master Reed Garbed said, "So now you understand, do you? Youyu does not compare with Tai. Youyu still hides his benevolence in order to win people; he may indeed win them, yet has never departed from what is human. Tai lies at ease and wakes with calm; at one moment he regards himself as a horse, at another as an ox. His knowing and feelings are trustworthy, his virtue utterly true—yet he has never entered into what is not human."

此篇大意以自然爲治天下之道，故篇首即擧不知二字。不知，即任其自然之貌。以不知治天下，如蘓子所謂以不治治之者也。非人，即天也。此所謂天，以天地之天言也。下文所受於天，天字以道言，與此不同。
The main message of this chapter is to view "being so of itself" as the Way to govern all-under-heaven. Thus, at the beginning, it mentions the phrase "not knowing." "Not knowing" means allowing things to follow their own course. Governing all-under-heaven through not knowing accords with what Master Su (Su Shi 蘇軾; 1037-1101) says: "to govern by not governing" (*Su Shi ji* 40.1).

The phrase "what is not human" refers to heaven, and the "heaven" mentioned here refers to heaven as part of heaven and earth. [In contrast,] in the later passage that contains the phrase "that which is received from heaven" (Section 14; ZZ 7.6), "heaven" refers to the Way, and is not the same as the heaven [mentioned here].

周蓋以天地未生之前爲道，以道爲在天地之外。故便敢小覷天地，殊不知道。不外於天地，而天地盡，得此道也。爲馬，爲牛，視其己，無辨[下]於牛馬也。
Zhuang Zhou considers the Way to precede the creation of heaven and earth, and regards the Way as existing outside of heaven and earth. Therefore, his audacity to look down upon heaven and earth clearly [shows that] he does not understand the Way. If one does not depart from heaven and earth but completes [his duties] within the bounds of heaven and earth, one will attain the Way.

The expressions "to regard himself as a horse" and "as an ox" signify perceiving oneself without drawing distinctions from an ox or a horse.

**Section 2 (ZZ 7.2)**

> 肩吾見狂接輿。狂接輿曰：日中始何以語女？肩吾曰：告我：君人者，以己出經式義度，人孰敢不聽而化諸！狂接輿曰：是欺德也。其於治天下也，猶涉海鑿河，而使蚉負山也。夫聖人之治也，治外乎？正而後行，確乎能其事者而已矣。且鳥高飛以避矰弋之害，鼷鼠深穴乎神丘之下，以避熏鑿之患，而曾二蟲之無知！
> Jian Wu met the madman Jie Yu.
>
> The madman Jie Yu said, "What did the man [named] 'Beginning at the Sun's Zenith' try to tell you?"
>
> Jian Wu replied, "He told me: 'A ruler should use himself as the model for laws, norms, morality, and standards—who then would dare not listen and be transformed?'"
>
> The madman Jie Yu said, "That is to deceive virtue! To govern all-under-heaven in that way is like trying to cross the sea by digging a canal, or making mosquitoes carry mountains. When the sage governs, does he govern externally [only]? He should first rectify himself and then act, being firm and capable in what he does—that is all. Moreover, birds fly high to escape the harm of arrows, and field mice dig deep under sacred mounds to avoid the dangers of smoke and traps—yet even such creatures are without knowing!"

第二段，鳥鼠之比，可見老莊之以傲世絶物自高者。其實全出於避患之意也。卑矣哉。
The second section. The analogy of the bird and the mouse shows that Laozi and Zhuangzi, by using such an analogy, despise the world, cut themselves off from other things, and exalt themselves. Such an attitude stems purely from intent to avoid all worries. How base it is!

## Section 3 (ZZ 7.3)

天根遊於殷陽，至蓼水之上，適遭無名人而問焉，曰：請問為天下。無名人曰：去！汝鄙人也，何問之不豫也！予方將與造物者. 為人厭則又乘夫莽眇之鳥，以出六極之外，而遊無何有之鄉，以處壙埌之野。汝又何帠以治天下感予之心為？又復問。無名人曰：汝遊心於淡，合氣於漠，順物自然，而無容私焉，而天下治矣。

Root of Heaven was wandering in the Yinyang region. When he reached the banks of the Liao River, he happened to encounter a nameless man and asked him, "May I inquire how to work for all-under-heaven?"

The nameless man said, "Stay away, you petty man! What a tedious question to ask! I am about to join with the maker of things in creating beings, and when I grow weary of being human, I shall ride upon the vast and one-eyed bird to soar beyond the six ends, wander in the land of nowhere at all, and dwell in the open and boundless wilderness. Why would you trouble my heart with talk of governing all-under-heaven?"

Root of Heaven asked again. The nameless man said, "Let your mind roam in the calm of clarity, merge your *qi* with the vast expanse, follow things as they are, and make no allowance for what is private—then all-under-heaven will be well-governed."

第三段，淡，湛一也。[1] 漠，虛靜也。湛一虛靜，即氣之太初也。周以是爲道。故言治天下，亦^當^以湛漠爲宗[無心]也。順物自然，而無容私，即湛漠無心也。[2] 非順理無私之謂也。順物自然一句，該盡一篇應帝王之意[+也]。前言不知，順其自然者也。後言混沌，自然之道也。.

The third section. The notion of "clarity" refers to clarity and unity, while "vast" signifies emptiness and tranquility. Clarity and unity, together with emptiness and stillness, represent the primordial state of *qi*. Zhuang Zhou regards this as the Way; therefore, it says that when governing all-under-heaven, one should also take clarity and stillness as the foundation [of ruling].

The phrase "follow things as they are, and make no allowance for what is private" means to be clear, tranquil, and with no mind. This is not what [our Confucian tradition] says, as following principle and eliminating what is private.

This single phrase, "follow things as they are," contains the entire message of the chapter "Being in Accord with the Way of Emperor." The "not knowing" mentioned earlier is precisely this following of being so of itself, and the "primal undifferentiation" spoken of later is the Way of being so of itself.

---

[1] In the Yŏam edition, the characters are reversed and written as *cham tam il* 湛，淡一 instead of *tam cham il* 淡，湛一.

[2] In the Yŏam edition, the passage from 順物自然 to 湛漠無心也 is omitted. It seems that a line may have been skipped.

## Section 4 (ZZ 7.4)

陽子居見老聃曰：有人於此，嚮疾強梁，物徹疏明，學道不倦。如是者，可比明王乎？老聃曰：是於聖人也，胥易技係，勞形怵心者也。

Yang Ziju visited Lao Dan and said, "There is a man here who is quick and forceful in his impulses, penetrating and keen in his understanding of things, and tireless in learning the Way. Could such a person be analogous to an enlightened king?"

Lao Dan said, "To the sage, such a person is a technician entangled in base skills, who toils with his body and agitates his mind."

第四段，胥，胥隸也。易，賤易也。枝，技巧也。係，係累也。此以聖人之憂民而勞心爲胥隸之賤技巧之累。言爲人之役，而不自適其適也。

The fourth section. The word "technician" refers to a skilled artisan. The character for "being easy" means to be cheap or insignificant. The character for branch means skill or craft.[3] "Entangled" means to be bound.

This [section] views the sage's troubling himself over the people and burdening their hearts and minds as akin to a craftsman binding others with petty skills. It implies that, although it is done for the sake of others, it does not naturally proceed as it should.

## Section 5 (ZZ 7.4)

且也虎豹之文來田， 猿狙之便、執嫠之狗來藉。如是者， 可比明王乎？陽子居蹴然曰：敢問明王之治。

[Lao Dan continued:] "Now, the markings of tigers and leopards invite hunters; the agility of apes and monkeys, and the [ability of] the dogs that chase raccoons, are all bound to be tied up. Can such things be compared to [the rule of] an enlightened king?"

Yang Ziju, startled, said, "May I dare to ask about the rule of an enlightened king?"

第五段，虎豹、猨、狗之比[譬]。比[譬]爲善之取禍。此老莊自私用智之機巧，畏禍蘄[鄿]免之本情也。

The fifth section. The analogy of the tiger, leopard, monkey, and [hunting] dog. This analogy illustrates that acting for the sake of good can bring misfortune. This is the position of Laozi and Zhuangzi: from the ruler's personal use of cunning and intelligence as techniques of rule arises the basic impulse to fear calamity and to seek escape from it.

---

3 In the original text of the ZZ, the character *chi* 枝 (tree branch) is written as *ki* 技 (skill; craft). *Chi* is likely a transcription error for *ki*.

**Section 6 (ZZ 7.4)**

> 老聃曰：明王之治，功蓋天下而似不自己，化貸萬物而民弗恃，有莫舉名，使物自喜，立乎不測，而遊於無有者也。
> Lao Dan said, "The ruling of an enlightened king is that though his achievements cover the world, he does not claim them as his own; that though his transforming influence extends to all things, the people do not rely on it; that there is no name to be mentioned [for the ruling], and [the king] let things find joy on their own; and that they stand upon what cannot be grasped and wander where nothing exists."

第六段，功蓋天下不自已，即舜有天下，不與之意也。化貸萬物民不恃，即耕食鑿飲，帝力何有之意也。有莫舉名，即蕩蕩乎無能名之意也。使物自喜，即使萬物各得其所之意也。然其如此者，在聖人，則循天理之自然者也；在老莊，則任氣化之所謂者也。循天理，則已與萬物同歸於仁壽軌道矣；任氣化，則已與萬物同歸於遙蕩、恣睢。所謂差若毫釐，謬以千里者也。自首段至此，皆言治天下，當以自然爲本。
The sixth section. The phrase "Though his achievements cover the world, he does not claim them as his own" corresponds to the idea that Shun ruled the world yet did not get involved in it (*Lunyu* 8.18). The phrase "Though his transforming influence extends to all things, the people do not rely on it" has the [same meaning of] the phrase "they plowed and ate, dug wells and drank, what need had they of the emperor's power?"[4] The phrase "[though there is achievement,] there is no name to be mentioned" means that his [i.e., the enlightened king's] being is so expansive and great that there is nothing to exactly name him. The phrase "[they] let things find joy on their own" means allowing all things to attain what properly belongs to them.

However, what it is like this, for [our Confucian] sage, is to follow the being so of itself of the heavenly principle. For Laozi and Zhuangzi, [however,] it is to entrust oneself to the so-called "transformations of *qi*." Following the heaven's principle means both oneself and all things return together to the path of benevolence and longevity. But, entrusting to the transformations of *qi* is that both oneself and all things return instead to a state of "wandering in the vast and remote, wantonly and angrily" (ZZ 6.8). This is why [Confucians] say, "A deviation as slight as a hair's breadth can lead to an error as great as a thousand *li*" (*D a Dai liji* 5.5).[5]

From the first section up to this point, [Zhuangzi] discusses how to rule all-under-heaven, and it rightly takes the course of being so of itself as the root.

---

[4] The original text is as follows: "They plowed fields and ate, dug wells and drank. What use do I have for the emperor's power?" 耕田而食 鑿井而飲; 帝力何有于我哉. See "Tei Gyo Do Tō shi" 帝堯陶唐氏 in *Jūhasshiryaku* 十八史略, 52.

[5] In the *Da Dai liji*, this quote line is attributed as a quotation from the *Yijing*, but the quote does not appear in any extant edition of the *Yijing*.

## Section 7 (ZZ 7.5)

鄭有神巫曰季咸，知人之生死存亡，禍福壽夭，期以歲月旬日，若神。鄭人見之，皆棄而走。列子見之而心醉，歸以告壺子，曰：始吾以夫子之道為至矣，則又有至焉者矣。壺子曰：吾與汝既其文，未既其實，而固得道與？眾雌而無雄，而又奚卵焉！而以道與世亢必信，夫故使人得而相女。嘗試與來，以予示之。

In the state of Cheng, there was a spirit-medium named Ji Xian, who could discern people's life or death, survival or extinction, fortune or misfortune, and longevity or early demise, fixing them to the very year, month, and day as if by divine power. When the people of Cheng saw him, they all fled.

Liezi saw him and was utterly fascinated. Returning home, he told Master Hu, saying, "At first I thought, Master, your Way was the highest, but now I have found one still higher than it."

Master Hu said, "I have shown you only its form, not its substance—how could you have truly attained the Way? If there are only females and no males, how could there be eggs? You are trying to contend with the world and make it trust you with the [half-understood] Way. That is why others are able to grasp you and read you. Go and bring him here, and I will show him [the true Way]."

第七段，吾與汝，與，[6] 以也，爲也。既，盡也。文，著於外者也。實，存乎中者也。言吾以汝爲盡其外，而未盡其內也。而固得道歟，言汝固自以爲得道歟。蓋未許之辭也。

The seventh section. In the phrase, "I have already shown you," the word for "to show" (lit. to give) is a verb meaning "to regard as." "Already" means "something that has completed," and "form" refers to [something] revealed to the outside. "Substance" is [something] that exists inside. This [phrase] means: I (Huzi) have shown you (Liezi) already the external aspect [of the Way], but not yet its internal substance. In the phrase, "how could you have truly attained the Way?" means [Huzi's questioning] whether you (Liezi) genuinely believe you have attained the Way, [implying that Huzi] does not yet affirm that [Liezi] has truly attained it.

## Section 8 (ZZ 7.5)

明日，列子與之見壺子。出而謂列子曰：嘻！子之先生死矣，弗活矣，不以旬數矣！吾見怪焉，見溼灰焉。列子入，泣涕沾襟，以告壺子。壺子曰：鄉吾示之以地文，萌乎不震不正。是殆見吾杜德機也。嘗又與來。

The next day, Liezi went with him to see Master Hu. [Ji Xian] came out and said to Liezi, "Ah! Your teacher is going to die— he has no vitality left in him.

---

[6] In the Yŏam edition, the order of the characters is reversed and written as 吾汝與汝. However, since this passage is a quotation from the original text of the ZZ, the record in the Yŏam edition is incorrect.

With that, he will not live past ten days. I saw something strange in him; I saw damp ashes."

Liezi went in, his tears soaking his robe, and told Master Hu.

Master Hu said, "Earlier, I showed him the patterns of the earth that began to sprout yet did not stir and did not align properly. This must have appeared [to him] as the sign of my virtue being blocked. Have him come again."

第八段，地文，陰也。萌乎不震不正，萌之未動未形，不可見者也。蓋示之以至陰之中生意。閉塞之機，在易，則十月坤卦，六爻純陰之象也。杜德機，杜閉之德之機也。機者，機關之可見者ˆ也。
The eighth section. The phrase "patterns of the earth" refers to the yin aspect. "That began to sprout yet did not stir and did not align properly" means that the sprout has not yet begun to move or taken on a defined shape, and cannot yet be revealed. This expresses the idea that even in the depths of the utmost yin, the stirrings of life are present. As a sign of closure and blockage, this corresponds in the *Zhouyi* to the tenth month and the Kun hexagram, where all six lines form a purely yin image. The phrase "the sign of virtue being blocked" refers to the indication that virtue is closed off and obstructed. "The sign" refers to a part of a [larger] mechanism, which is visible.

### Section 9 (ZZ 7.5)

明日， 又與之見壺子。出而謂列子曰： 幸矣！ 子之先生遇我也。有瘳矣， 全然有生矣。吾見其杜權矣。列子入， 以告壺子。壺子曰： 鄉吾示之以天壤， 名實不入，而機發於踵。是殆見吾善者機也。嘗又與來。
The next day, he again went with him to see Master Hu. [Ji Xian] came out and said to Liezi, "How fortunate! Your teacher was lucky to have met me. He is recovering—he's got his life back now whole again. I saw that I saw that his tendency toward death was now blocked."

Liezi went in and told Master Hu. Master Hu said, "Earlier, I showed him heaven and earth, where [human] names and realities do not enter, yet the sign was stirring from the very bottom. This must have appeared [to him] as a sign of goodness. Have him come again."

第九段，天壤，陽也。機發於踵，機之動於下，而可見者也。蓋示之以陽氣微動，生意鬫發之機。在易，則冬至復卦，一陽初生之象也。善者機，生意已動之機也。
The ninth section. "Heaven and earth" refers to the yang aspect. "The sign was emerging from the very bottom (lit. from the heel)" means that the sign begins to move from below, and it can now be perceived. This indicates the subtle stirring of the *qi* of yang and the sign of the emerging intent of life.

In the *Zhouyi,* this corresponds to the Winter Solstice and the Fu hexagram, which is the image of a single yang line emerging for the first time. The phrase "A sign of goodness" refers to a sign that the intent of life has already begun to move.

### Section 10 (ZZ 7.5)

明日，又與之見壺子。出而謂列子曰：子之先生不齊，吾無得而相焉。試齊，且復相之。列子入，以告壺子。壺子曰：吾鄉示之以太沖莫勝。是殆見吾衡氣機也。

The next day, he again went with him to see Master Hu. [Ji Xian] came out and said to Liezi, "Your teacher is not in a stable condition. I cannot physiognomize him. Try to let him settle into stability, and then I will examine him again."

Liezi went in and told Master Hu. Master Hu said, "Earlier, I showed him the image of the great void where nothing can prevail. This must have appeared [to him] this as a sign of my *qi* being in balance."

第十段，太，大也。冲，中也，和也。太冲猶言太和元氣也。兼陰陽天地，而言莫勝，言陰不勝陽，陽不勝陰，而陰陽適均也。蓋示之以陰陽天地之全機。在易，則乾坤合體，坎離相交之象也。半動半靜，若生未生，故曰不齊。衡，平也。衡氣機，二氣平等之機。

The tenth section. "Great" means "vast" and "void" refers to balance and harmony. [Thus,] "great void" refers to the primordial *qi* of great harmony that encompasses both yin and yang, heaven and earth. And it says "nothing can prevail," which means that yin cannot overcome yang, and yang cannot overcome yin; instead, yin and yang remain in proper equilibrium. This expresses the complete sign of yin and yang, and of heaven and earth [being in balance].

In the *Zhouyi*, this corresponds to the hexagrams of Qian and Kun being united, and [thus] the images of Kan and Li engaging with one another, where half is in motion and half at rest. It appears as though things have already arisen, yet they have not emerged. Thus, [Zhuangzi] refers to it as "not in a stable condition" or "not yet aligned."

The term "balance" means flat or even. The phrase "a sign of balanced *qi*" refers to a sign that the two *qi* are in equilibrium.

### Section 11 (ZZ 7.5)

鯢桓之審為淵，止水之審為淵，流水之審為淵。淵有九名，此處三焉。嘗又與來。

Where a whale wanders about, there is an abyss; where the still waters gather, there is an abyss; where the running waters gather, there is an abyss. The abyss has nine names, and I have shown him three. Have him come again.

第十一段，鯢，大漁也。桓，盤桓也。大漁盤桓之水，大水也。又桓水名也。鯢桓之淵，指太冲莫勝也。止水之淵，指地文也。流水之淵，指天壤也。總結上三機之意。

The eleventh section. The word "whale" refers to a large fish, and "to wander about" means to hesitate or perambulate. The water where a large fish lingers refers to a vast body of water. Additionally, the word used for "wander" is also the name of a river.[7]

"The abyss of the wandering whale" maps onto "the great void where nothing can prevail" (section ten); "the abyss of still water" onto "earth's pattern" (section eight); and "the abyss of running water" onto "heaven and earth" (section nine). Together, these summarize the meanings of the three preceding signs.

### Section 12 (ZZ 7.5)

明日，又與之見壺子。立未定，自失而走。壺子曰：追之！列子追之不及，反以報壺子，曰：已滅矣，已失矣，吾弗及也。壺子曰：鄉吾示之以未始出吾宗。吾與之虛而委蛇，不知其誰何，因以為弟靡，因以為波流，故逃也。然後列子自以為未始學而歸，三年不出。

The next day, he again went with him to see Master Hu. Before they even stood still, [Ji Xian] lost himself and ran off. Master Hu said, "Chase him!"

Liezi ran after him but could not catch him. He came back and reported to Master Hu, saying, "He has vanished—he's gone! I could not reach him."

Master Hu said, "Earlier, I showed him [the state of] not yet having emerged from my origin. I gave him [the image of] emptiness where I let myself move freely, not knowing who or what I was. He took me as mist vaporizes, as waves flow—thus he fled."

After that, Liezi considered himself as never having [truly] learned and withdrew, [staying at home] for three years without going out.

第十二段，未始出吾宗，即未始有物者，而周之所謂道者也。在吾儒見處，則爲前天地旣滅，後天地未闢，而萬物未生之時也。茅靡波流，言如茅之靡，波之流，而恍惚無象也。

The twelfth section. The phrase "[the state of] not yet having emerged from my origin" corresponds to "[the state where] there is not yet anything" (2.7). This is what Zhuang Zhou calls the Way. From our Confucian standpoint, [however,] this [only] describes [the time when] the previous heaven and earth had already perished, and the next heaven and earth had not yet opened, a moment when all things had yet to be born. The phrase "grasses bend, and waves flow"[8] evokes a state of reeds swaying in the wind and waves drifting, suggesting a vague and formless condition, devoid of any fixed pattern.

### Section 13 (ZZ 7.5)

為其妻爨，食豕如食人。於事無與親，彫琢復朴，塊然獨以其形立。紛而封

---

[7] More precisely, it refers to the Hwan River 桓水, which is now known as the Bailong River 白龍江, originating from Mount Xiqing 西傾山, a branch of the eastern end of the Kunlun Mountains in Gansu Province.

[8] In the extant text of the *Zhuangzi*, the phrase is written as 弟靡, but Han Wŏnjin wrote it as 茅靡 (reeds swaying [in the wind]) for currently unknown reason.

> 哉，一以是終。
> [Afterwards, Liezi] cooked for his wife, feed pigs as if feeding people. In affairs he had no partiality; carved and polished, he returned again to simplicity, standing alone as an unhewn lump, existing merely in his form. Confused and closed—thus he ended with oneness.

第十三段，為妻爨，爲妻屈也。言不知尊之在已，卑之在人也。食豕如食人，言不知人之爲貴，而物之爲賤也。於事無親，言物我之間，不知孰尊，孰卑，孰貴，孰賤，而心無所偏與也。總結爲妻爨，食豕如食人之意。雕琢復朴，言剝去聰明知識，而復其混沌之體也。自巫咸至此，言自然之道也。
The thirteenth section. The phrase "to cook for one's wife" implies humbling oneself for the sake of one's wife. It means he failed to understand that what is worthy of respect lies within oneself, while what is to be humbled lies with the other. "Feeding pigs as if feeding people" expresses that he failed to recognize that human beings are noble, while other things are base. "In affairs, he had no partiality" means that between things and oneself, he did not know who should be honored or humbled, or who is noble and who is lowly, and there is no bias or partiality in the mind. This summarizes the meanings of "to cook for one's wife" and "feeding pigs as if feeding people." The phrase "carved and polished, he returned again to simplicity" means stripping away cleverness and knowledge, and returning again to the substance of the primal undifferentiation.

From the spirit-medium Han up to this point, [Zhuang Zhou] speaks of the Way of being so of itself.

**Section 14 (ZZ 7.6)**

> 無為名尸，無為謀府，無為事任，無為知主。體盡無窮，而遊無朕，盡其所受於天，而無見得，亦虛而已。至人之用心若鏡，不將不迎，應而不藏，故能勝物而不傷。
> Do not make yourself the corpse of a name, nor the treasury of schemes; do not make yourself the bearer of affairs, nor the master of knowledge. Let your substance reach the utmost of the infinite, and wander without trace. Exhaust what you have received from heaven, yet see no gain in it—only emptiness. The mind of the ultimate person is like a mirror: it neither goes forth nor welcomes, it responds yet does not keep. Thus, he overcomes things without being harmed.

第十四段，四無爲。可見老莊之術，專要避事畏罪。苟蘄[鄿]免禍，蓋鄉愿之尤者也。無窮、無瞇，即混沌也。所受於天，天字亦以混沌言。言盡其所得混沌之道也。將，隨之於事之既往也。迎，迎[期]之於事之未來也。藏滯而不化也。此與孔子四無語，同。
The fourteenth section concerns four kinds of non-doing. [Here,] one can see that the techniques of Laozi and Zhuangzi are wholly concerned with avoiding involvement in worldly affairs, fearing the commission of wrongdoing, and sincerely seeking to escape calamity. This is the fault of Xiang Yuan (*Lunyu* 17.13;

*Mengzi* 7B83).

The phrases "the infinite" and "no trace" refer to primal undifferentiation.[9] In the phrase "what you have received from heaven," heaven here also signifies [the original state of] primal undifferentiation. [Thus, the phrase] means the complete attainment of the Way as primal undifferentiation. The word "to go forward" refers to following [the Way] in the affairs that have already passed, while the word "to welcome" refers to welcoming it in what has yet to come. This is because when things are concealed and obstructed, transformation cannot occur.[10] This is the same as Confucius's statement on the four things to avoid.[11]

然在聖人，順性命，中正之道也。在老莊，則任知覺起滅之機也。性命純善，知覺有善惡。此聖人之道，一主於善，而有所不爲也。老莊之道，不擇善惡，而無所不爲也。此一段，承上段，雕[琱]琢復朴之語，復申其意。
However, for the sage in [our Confucian tradition], following nature and [heaven's] mandate is the Way of balanced correctness; for Laozi and Zhuangzi, it is to entrust oneself to perceiving the sign of arising and perishing. [In our tradition], nature and mandate are purely good; but in knowing and perception, both good and evil are ever present. This is the Way of [our] sage that is consistent with good and has some that one should not do. But the Way of Laozi and Zhuangzi does not choose between good and evil, and there is nothing that one should not do. This section continues and expands upon the meaning of the previous phrase "to carve and polish oneself, and return to simplicity."

**Section 15 (ZZ 7.7)**

> 南海之帝為儵，北海之帝為忽，中央之帝為渾沌。儵與忽時相與遇於渾沌之地，渾沌待之甚善。儵與忽謀報渾沌之德，曰：人皆有七竅，以視聽食息，此獨無有，嘗試鑿之。日鑿一竅，七日而渾沌死。
> The emperor of the southern sea was named Shu, the emperor of the northern sea was named Hu, and the emperor of the center was named Hundun. Shu and Hu would sometimes meet in the land of Hundun, and Hundun treated them with great kindness. Planning to repay Hundun's virtue, Shu and Hu said, "All people have seven openings by which they see, hear, eat, and breathe. Only he has none—let us try carving them for him." So, they carved one opening each day, and after seven days, Hundun died.

末段，老莊見識，本末盡在此段。蓋老莊見處，極於天地未闢一番，混沌之時，故

---

[9] In the original ZZ text, *mu gyu* is written as *mu chim* 無朕, meaning "without sign."

[10] In the ZZ original, this passage appears as "to respond and not to conceal" (*ŭng i pu chang* 應而不藏).

[11] This refers to the four "don't" listed in the *Lunyu* 9.4 as follows: "The Master was free of four things: he had no arbitrary opinions, no certainty, no inflexibility, and no self-centeredness." 子絕四：毋意，毋必，毋固，毋我.

便以此爲至道。又見其天地萬物，皆自混沌中，分出[+而]來，而ˆ皆本同，而末異，故便以萬物之有大小貴賤，人事之有治亂是非，謂皆道之當有，而不可以相無。人之爲道，亦當以齊物爲宗，以復其混沌者。然後方可以得道，而人之有聰明，知識，辨別[分]是非者，爲喪道，是蓋不知。所謂混沌者，乃在前陽旣滅之餘一陰之靜，而非形而上者之道也。

The last section. The views of Laozi and Zhuangzi, from the beginning to the end, is fully contained in this section. Their perspectives are pushed to the extreme, back to a time before heaven and earth had ever opened; this is the age of Hundun (primal undifferentiation). Therefore, they consider this state to be the ultimate Way. They also view that heaven, earth, and myriad things all emerged from this primal undifferentiation, so that everything was fundamentally the same at the origin but became distinct in the end. As such, [they hold that] the myriad things' distinctions, such as great and small, noble and base, and human affairs' having order and disorder, right and wrong, are all said to rightly exist within the Way. Yet, [they view,] with those differences, no one can actually practice the Way, and one must regard all things being treated equally as the foundation of [practicing the Way], and by doing so, return to the original primal undifferentiation. Only then, [they say,] can one attain the Way. To possess cleverness and knowledge and to make distinctions between right and wrong is, [in their view,] to have lost the Way; such a person, [they say,] does not truly understand [the Way]. The primal undifferentiation they speak of refers to the quietude of a remaining singular yin after the previous yang has already annihilated. But this is not the Way that is beyond the form.

萬物之ˆ有大小貴賤，人事之有治亂是非，皆陰陽之爲，而非道之本然也。聖人以理爲道，故以主善去惡爲復其道之本然。老莊以氣爲道，故以不擇善惡爲復其道之本然。此其言道，與復其本然者，語雖同而實，則有薰蕕氷炭之不相八也。此一段始出混沌二字，以直指已之所謂道體，而總結上文。然實亦爲七篇之歸宿也。內外諸篇，皆當以此意推之。

The myriad things' distinction, such as great and small, noble and base, or human affairs' order and disorder, right and wrong, are all the workings of yin and yang, and they are not the original nature of the Way. The sages of [our Confucian tradition] regard principle as the Way. Therefore, we consider being grounded in good and eliminating evil as restoring the original nature of the Way. Laozi and Zhuangzi, [on the other hand,] regard *qi* as the Way. Thus, they see not choosing between good and evil as restoring the original nature of the Way. As such, they say of "the Way" and "restoring the Way's original nature," and these languages may sound the same [with our Confucian ones,] but in substance, [theirs and ours] are as incompatible as incense and foul weeds, ice and charcoal.

In this section, the phrase primal undifferentiation appears for the first time, and with it, [Zhuangzi] directly points to what he calls the substance of the Way, thereby summing up the preceding sections. If so, in substance, this concept of primal undifferentiation becomes the point to which the seven Inner

Chapters ultimately lead. All the chapters, both Inner and Outer, should rightly be understood by inferring the meaning of this concept.

## Concluding Remarks

篇首齧缺所問，即治天下之術也。王倪所不知，即不知治天下之術也。不知所以治之，則亦任其自然而已。此即治天下之大道也。蒲衣子言，乃今知之者，即知治天下之道，在於無知也。有虞氏不如泰氏，即以其有虞氏有知，而泰氏無知也。下文日ˆ中始、陽子居所稱，即有虞氏之有知也。無名人[氏]，老聃所答，即泰氏之無知也。巫咸之相壺子，即知之者之爲不知，而不可知者之爲道，道即混沌之謂也。
At the beginning of this chapter (ZZ 7.1), what Toothless questions is an art of ruling the world. Wang Ni's reply that he does not know means that he does not know such an art of ruling the world. That he does not know how to rule the world with means one should only entrust matters to [the course of] being so of itself. This, then, is the great Way of ruling the world. What Master Reed Garbed says, "Now you understand" means that the Way of knowing the art of ruling the world lies in no-knowledge. [Also, when the Master says] "Youyu was not better than Tai," it means that Youyu possessed knowledge, whereas Tai did not.

The man Beginning at the Sun's Zenith (7.2) or Yang Ziju (7.4) who are mentioned in the subsequent sections, represent the state of having knowledge, like You Yu. [In contrast,] the nameless man (7.3) and Lao Dan (7.4), whom responded, correspond to the state of having no knowledge, like Tai. When the shaman Ji Xian read the physiognomy of Master Hu, it suggests that those who [claim to] know do not know, while those who [claim to] not know are the ones truly practicing the Way. The Way is none other than the primal undifferentiation.

蓋篇首不知二字已含篇末混沌之意，中間所說無非此意也。一篇之中，屢更[變]其端，面目常新，若無倫序，而指意所存，卻自不亂，一串貫來，條理整暇，而變化出沒，藏其妙用，使人驟看莫覺其然。此政[正]莊生爲文高處，手段能處，他篇倣此。
The two characters "not knowing," which appear at the beginning of this chapter, already contain within the meaning of primal undifferentiation that appears at the end of the chapter. Among the sections presented in the middle of the chapter, none deviates from this meaning. The middle sections of this chapter are restatements and reworkings of what was said at the beginning, each time renewing its aspect. Though they may appear to lack order, the messages are consistently present; far from being confused, the text is seamlessly interconnected, its logic arranged with coherence and clarity. The transformations come and go, yet the subtle workings are so well concealed that they allow the reader to proceed without obstruction, all the while unaware of how it unfolds. This is why Zhuangzi's writing is considered refined and his literary craft so masterful. Other chapters follow in imitation of this.

# Appendix

## Preface to *Changja sok pyŏnhae*

道，一太極也。孔孟老莊，一陰陽也。有陽必有陰。有吾道，必有異端。故聖人尊陽抑陰，而不能使無陰閒。聖道闢異端，而不能使無異端。所以析陰陽之分，明吾道異端之辨，使人不迷於向背也。
The Way is the one single Supreme Ultimate. Confucius and Mengzi [on the one hand], and Laozi and Zhuangzi [on the other], constitute a single pairing of yin and yang. Where there is yang, there must also be yin; where there is our Way, there must be heterodox teachings as well. Thus, the sage honors yang and restrains yin, but cannot entirely eliminate its presence. [Likewise,] the sage's Way repels heterodoxy, yet cannot bring about its complete disappearance. It is by distinguishing yin from yang, and by clearly delineating our Way from heterodox teachings, that [the sage] prevents people from falling into confusion about what ought to be pursued and what ought to be rejected.

嗚呼。孔子之道不尊，則莊周之道不闢。莊周之道不辨，則孔子之道不明。然周之書，皆吊詭之言爾。架空鑿虛，若無倫脊。諸家箋解，皆隔靴爬癢耳。其文章關鍵，亦無人發揮。況其道乎。
Alas! Unless the Way of Confucius is held in reverence, the Way of Zhuang Zhou cannot be refuted; and unless the Way of Zhuang Zhou is properly discerned, the Way of Confucius cannot be made fully clear. Thus, the book of Zhuang Zhou is nothing more than lofty, dangling words that deceive. It is vainly contrived and vacuous, seemingly lacking in order and coherence. Though numerous specialists have written commentaries and offered interpretations, all of them have amounted to nothing more than scratching the sole of the foot with a shoe on—that is, they were neither sufficient nor penetrating. His literary style is the key, yet no one has demonstrated the strength truly to grapple with it. All the more so when it comes to his Way.

噫。吾道異端之不明，未必不由於此也。往往主心主氣之學，浸浸乎莊周之道，而其因是因非之說，又爲占便宜者篙矢，則可無辨乎。南塘先生爲是之懼，爲辨解一篇。於是吾道異端之辨，若日星于天矣。覩乎秋冬之爲陰，而春夏之陽，益明矣。察乎陰陽之爲氣，而太極之理，益尊矣。猗歟先生之意，其在斯歟。
Ah! The lack of clarity in distinguishing our Way from heterodoxy surely stems from this. From time to time, there have been teachings [even in our Confucian tradition] that place emphasis either on the mind or on the *qi*, and this is because they had become deeply immersed in the Way of Zhuang Zhou. And his theory

that right and wrong are mutually dependent has come to serve as both banner and weapon for those seeking convenience and advantage. Then, would it be acceptable that no one has critically examined his doctrines? Master Namdang Han Wŏnjin feared precisely this point, and thus composed the *Changja pyŏnhae*. With this, the distinction between our Way and heterodoxy has become as clear as the sun and stars in the sky. Upon reflection, it has become all the more evident that autumn and winter (i.e., Zhuang Zhou) are of yin, while spring and summer (i.e., Confucius) are of yang. Upon further thought, one comes to hold in even greater esteem the teaching that yin and yang pertain to *qi*, and that the Supreme Ultimate is principle. Ah, such was the intention of the Master.

余於庚戌之秋，客金陵。金君愼夫請受以莊子書。余誦先生之說以授之，愼夫請記其說。余曰，先生有辨解，吾敢贅乎。愼夫請之固，余念先生辨解，詳於辨而畧於解。雖續爲之解，而不爲贅也。遂使執筆，口呼以記之。雖或不中於先生之說，亦不遠矣。
In the autumn of the kyŏngsul year (1730), I was staying in Kŭmnŭng (modern-day Kimhae), when Kim Sinbu (b. 1712) requested instruction in the ZZ. I memorized all the theories [on the ZZ] by my teacher, Master Han, and instructed him with them. When Sinbu asked me to write down those theories, I said: "Since Master Han had already composed a work, *Pyŏnhae*, how could I dare to do it superfluously?" Yet Sinbu's request was insistent. So, I carefully read through Master Han's *Pyŏnhae* [again], elaborated upon his critical analysis, and streamlined his explanatory notes. Though this may be regarded as a supplementary interpretation, it is not a superfluous one. In the end, I took up the brush and recorded the content aloud as I wrote. Even if, in some places, what I have written does not exactly align with my teacher's views, it is by no means far removed from them.

然朱子曰，莊老註解，無一人說得本義。某若拈出便別，只是不欲。朱子之所不欲，先生發之。小子續之，盖亦不得已也。是書也，與孔子之書並傳，亦安得無辨乎。是歲剝之朏，南塘門人姜奎煥序。
Master Zhu once said that among the many commentaries on Laozi and Zhuangzi, not a single one had truly grasped their original meaning. Each interpretation merely pointed out how one person's views differed from another's. I sought only to avoid falling into the same pattern. This was precisely what Master Zhu wished to guard against. Master Han initiated this endeavor, and I humbly have continued it, with all the limitations that may entail. This book (i.e., ZZ) has been transmitted alongside the works of Confucius; how, then, could one possibly treat it without discernment?

On the first day of the ninth month, under the new moon of the kyŏngsul year (1730), Written by Kang Kyuhwan, a disciple of Master Namdang Han Wŏnjin.

# Bibliography

## Primary Sources[1]

*Changja pyŏnhae* 莊子辨解 (Analytic Interpretation of the *Zhuangzi*), by Han Wŏnjin 韓元震 (1682–1751), dat. 1716. Manuscript (Kyujanggak edition): https://kyudb.snu.ac.kr/book/mfPdf.do?book_cd=GK01648_00&vol_no=0001); Metal-type print (Yŏam edition): https://www.nl.go.kr).

*Chuci* 楚辭 (Songs of the South).

*Da Dai liji* 大戴禮記 (Record of Rituals by Elder Dai).

*Daode zhenjing jijie* 道德真經集解 (Collected Explanations of the *Perfect Scripture on the Dao and Its Virtue*), by Dong Sijing 董思靖 (fl. 1246–1260).

*Daode zhenjing jieyi* 道德真經解義 (Explanations of the Meanings of the *Perfect Scripture on the Way and Its Virtue*), by Song Huizong 宋徽宗 (r. 1100–1125).

*Daode zhenjing lun* 道德真經論 (Discussion on the *Perfect Scripture on the Way and Its Virtue*), by Sima Guang 司馬光 (1019–1086).

*Daxue* 大學 (Great Learning).

*Er Cheng yishu* 二程遺書 (Collected Posthumous Writings of the Two Cheng Brothers), by Cheng Hao 程顥 (1032-1085) and Cheng Yi 程頤 (1033-1107).

*Fayan* 法言 (Model Sayings), by Yang Xiong 揚雄 (53 BCE-18 CE).

*Guishan ji* 龜山集 (Collected Works of Guishan Yang Shi), by Yang Shi 楊時 (1053–1135).

*Han Feizi* 韓非子 (Book of Master Han Fei).

*Huian ji* 晦庵集 (Collected Writings of Master Huian), by Zhu Xi 朱熹 (1130-1200).

*Huian xiansheng Zhu Wengong wenji* 晦菴先生朱文公文集 (Collected Writings of Master Huian, Zhu Wengong), by Zhu Xi. https://www.shidianguji.com/zh/book/SBCK218/

*Jūhasshiryaku* 十八史略 (*Shiba Shilüe*; Eighteen Histories in Brief), by Zeng Xianzhi 曾先之 (late 13th c.). Tokyo: Gosha-ro, Shobakudo, 1870.

[1] Unless otherwise noted, all Chinese primary texts were accessed through ctext.org, and all Korean texts through db.itkc.or.kr. All digital versions were used only after close comparison and crosschecking with scanned images of the original texts and/or their printed counterparts.

*Kubong sŏnsaeng-jip* 龜峯先生集 (Collected Works of Master Kubong), by Song Ikp'il 宋翼弼 (1534–1599).

*Laozi Daodejing* 老子道德經 (Laozi's Scripture on the Way and Its Virtue).

*Laozi Heshang gong zhangju* 老子河上公章句 (Chapters and Phrases of the *Laozi* by the Master on the River), by Heshang gong 河上公 (2nd c. BCE).

*Laozi jie* 老子解 (Explanation of the *Laozi*), by Su Che 蘇轍 (1039–1112).

*Liezi* 列子 (Book of Master Lie).

*Lunyu* 論語 (Analects).

*Mengzi* 孟子 (Book of Master Meng).

*Namdang sŏnsaeng munjip* 南塘先生文集 (Collected Works of Master Namdang), by Han Wŏnjin.

*Pisujae sŏnsaeng munjip* 賁需齋先生文集 (Collected Works of Master Pisujae), by Kang Kyuhwan 姜奎煥 (1697–1731).

*Pyŏnggye sŏnsaeng-jip* 屛溪先生集 (Collected Writings of Master Pyŏnggye), by Yun Ponggu 尹鳳九 (1683–1767).

*Sambong-jip* 三峰集 (Collected Works of Sambong), by Chŏng Tojŏn 鄭道傳 (1342–1398).

*Shijing* 詩經 (Classic of Poetry).

*Shujing* 書經 (Classic of Documents).

*Shuowen jiezi* 說文解字 (Explaining Graphs and Analyzing Characters), by Xu Shen 許愼 (58-148).

*Songja taejŏn* 宋子大全 (Complete Works of Master Song Siyŏl), by Song Siyŏl 宋時烈 (1607–1689).

*Su Shi ji* 蘇軾集 (Collected Works of Su Shi), by Su Shi 蘇軾 (1037-1101).

*Sunŏn* 醇言 (Purified Words), by Yi I 李珥 (1536-1584). ca. 1580. Manuscript (Kyujanggak edition: https://kyudb.snu.ac.kr/book/mfPdf.do?book_cd=GK07743_00&vol_no=0001)

*Taiji tushuo* 太極圖說 (Explanation on the Diagram of the Supreme Ultimate), by Zhou Dunyi 周敦頤 (1017–1073).

*Tang Song badajia wenchao* 唐宋八大家文鈔 (Selected Writings of the Eight Great Prose Masters of the Tang and Song), by Mao Kun 茅坤 (1512-1601).

*Ximing* 西銘 (Western Inscription), by Zhang Zai 張載 (1020-1077).

*Yŏam yugo* 旅菴遺稿 (Collected Posthumous Writings of Yŏam), by Sin Kyŏngjun 申景濬 (1712–1781).

*Yŏam chŏnsŏ* 旅菴全書 (Complete Works of Yŏam), by Sin Kyŏngjun, edited by Sin Chaehyu 申宰休, copy-edited by Chŏng Inbo 鄭寅普 and Kim Ch'undong 金春東. Kyŏngsŏng (Seoul): Sin Chosŏn. 1940. See also https://www.nl.go.kr.

*Yulgok sŏnsaeng chŏnsŏ* 栗谷先生全書 (Complete Works of Master Yulgok), by Yi I.

*Zhangzi quanshu* 張子全書 (Complete Works of Master Zhang), by Zhang Zai.

*Zhongyong* 中庸 (Balanced Harmony in Daily Life).

Zhongyong zhangju 中庸章句 (Commentary on the *Balanced Harmony in Daily Life*: Chapters and Phrases), by Zhu Xi.

*Zhouyi* 周易 (Zhou Book of Changes).

*Zhuangzi* 莊子 (Book of Master Zhuang).

*Zhuzi quanshu* 朱子全書 (Complete Works of Master Zhu), by Zhu Xi.

*Zhuzi yulei* 朱子語類 (Categorized Sayings of Master Zhu), by Zhu Xi.

## Translations

*Ch'irwŏn ch'aegi* 漆園采奇 (Selections of Wonders from the Lacquer Garden), by Kwŏn Hae 權瑎 (1639–1704).

Im Ch'ae-u 임채우 trans. 2014. *Kwŏn Hae ŭi* Changja 권해의 장자. Seoul: Sae-munsa. 2014.

*Ch'owŏn tamno* 椒園談老 (Chowŏn's Discourses on the *Laozi*), by Yi Ch'ung'ik 李忠翊 (1744–1816).

Kim Yunkyŏng 김윤경 trans. 2013. *Ch'owŏn tamno* 초원담노. Seoul: Yemun Sŏwŏn.

Kim Hangmok 김학목 trans. 2014. *Ch'owŏn Yi Ch'ung'ik ŭi* tamno *yŏkju* 초원 이충익의 담노 역주. Seoul: T'ongnamu.

*Chŏngno* 訂老 (Rectifying with the *Laozi*), by Hong Sŏkju 洪奭周 (1774–1842).

Kim Hangmok 김학목 trans. 2001. *Hong Sŏkju ŭi* Noja 홍석주의 노자. Seoul: Yemun Sŏwŏn.

*Munjang chunch'ik Changja sŏn* 文章準則莊子選 (Selected Writings from the *Zhuangzi* as a Model of Composition), by Sin Kyŏngjun.

Kim Namhyŏng 김남형 trans. 2014. *Yŏam Sin Kyŏngjun ŭi* Changja 여암 신경준의 장자. Sŏul: Yemun Sŏwŏn.

*Namhwagyŏng chuhae sanbo* 南華經註解刪補 (A Commentary and Editing of the *Nanhua Scripture*), by Pak Sedang 朴世堂 (1629–1703).

Chŏn Hyŏnmi 전현미. 2012. *Pak Sedang ŭi Changja: Namhwagyŏng chuhae sanbo naep'yŏn* 박세당의 장자: 남화경주해산보 내편. Sŏul: Yemun Sŏwŏn.

Pak Hŏnsun 박헌순. 2012. *Pak Sedang ŭi Changja ikkki: Namhwagyŏng chuhae sanbo* 1 박세당의 장자 읽기: 남화경주해산보 1. Sŏul: Yurich'ang.

*Sinju todŏkkyŏng* 新註道德經 (A New Commentary on the *Scripture on the Way and its Virtue*), by Pak Sedang.

Kim Hangmok 김학목 trans. 1999. *Pak Sedang ŭi* Noja 박세당의 노자. Seoul: Yemun Sŏwŏn.

*Sunŏn* 醇言 (Purified Words), by Yi I.

Yi Chuhang 이주항 trans. 1993. *Sunŏn* 순언. Sŏul: In'gan Sarang. 1993.

Kim Hangmok 김학목 trans. 2001. *Yulgok Yi I ŭi* Noja 율곡 이이의 노자. Sŏul: Yemun Sŏwŏn.

Yu Sŏngson 유성손 trans. 2002. *Sunŏn* 순언. Koyang: Kukhak Charyowŏn.

Cho Kiyŏng 조기영 trans. 2022. *Sunŏn* 순언. Sŏul: Chisigŭl Mandŭnŭn Chisik.

Sŏ Myŏngja 서명자 trans. 2023. *Sunŏn* 순언. Sŏul: Ch'am.

*Todŏk chigwi* 道德指歸 (A Corollary of the *Daodejing*), by Sŏ Myŏng'ŭng 徐命膺 (1716–1787).

Cho Minhwan 조민환 trans. 2008. *Todŏk chigwi* 도덕지귀 Sŏul: Yemun Sŏwŏn.

Kim Hangmok 김학목 trans. 2023. *Todŏk chigwi* 도덕지귀. Sŏul: Hakkobang.

## Secondary Studies

Chen Lai 陈来. 2004. *Song Ming lixue* 宋明理学. Shanghai: Huadong shifan.

Choi Seok-Ki 최석기. 2010. *Chosŏn sidae Chungyong tosŏl* 조선시대 중용도설. Sŏul: Pogosa.

_____. 2007. "Namdang Han Wŏnjin ŭi Chungyong haesŏk ŭi t'ŭkjing kwa kŭ ŭimi" 南塘 韓元震의 中庸해석의 特徵과 그 意味. *Tongbang Hanmunhak* 동방한문학 32.1:271–303.

Glomb, Vladimír. 2016. "Yulgok and Laozi: Integration of the *Daodejing* into 16th Century Confucian Discourse." In *Integration Processes in the Circulation of Knowledge: Cases from Korea*, edited by Marion Eggert and Florian Pölking, 15-47. Frankfurt: Peter Lang.

Ivanhoe, Philip J. 2016. *Three Streams: Confucian Reflections on Learning and the Moral Heart-Mind in China, Korea, and Japan*. New York: Oxford University Press.

Kalton, Michael C. 1988. *To Become a Sage: The Ten Diagrams on Sage Learning.* New York: Columbia University Press.

______. 1994. *The Four-Seven Debate: An Annotated Translation of the Most Famous Controversy in Korean Neo-Confucian Thought.* Albany: State University of New York Press.

______. 2019. "Toegye: His Life, Learning and Times." In *Dao Companion to Korean Confucian Philosophy*, edited by Young-Chan Ro, 159-78. Dordrecht, the Netherlands: Springer.

Kang Soonae 강순애. 2024. "*Yulgok sŏnsaeng chŏnsŏ* wa *yulgok sŏnsaeng chŏnsŏ sŭbyu* ŭi p'yŏnch'an kwa kanhaeng ŭl wihan Yulgok chŏnsŏja ŭi chosŏng mit sŏjijŏk t'ŭkjing e kwanhan yŏn'gu" 栗谷先生全書와 栗谷先生全書拾遺의 편찬과 간행을 위한 율곡전서자의 조성 및 서지적 특징에 관한 연구. *Sŏjihak Yŏn'gu* 서지학연구 97:5-26.

Kim Hangmok 김학목. 2001. "*Sunŏn* e taehan Hong Kyehŭi ŭi ipjang" 순언에 대한 홍계희의 입장. In *Yulgok Yi I ŭi* Noja 율곡 이이의 노자, edited by Kim Hangmok, 133-44. Sŏul: Yemun Sŏwŏn.

______. 2024. "*Namhwagyŏng chuhae sanbo* wa *Changja pyŏnhae* ŭi sanggwan kwan'gye" 남화경주해산보와 장자변해의 상관관계. *Minjok Munhwa* 민족문화 68:47–76.

Kim Jung Yeup. 2019. "Sŏ Kyŏngdŏk and the Rise of the Philosophy of *Ki* 氣." In *Dao Companion to Korean Confucian Philosophy*, edited by Young-Chan Ro, 135-58. Dordrecht, the Netherlands: Springer.

Kim Kilhwan 김길환. 1976. "Yulgok ŭi *Noja* Kwan: Chŏn Yulgok chak *Sunŏn* ŭl chungsimŭro" 율곡의 노자관: 傳栗谷作 醇言을 중심으로. *Hanguk Hakbo* 한국학보 2.4:4059–4105.

Kim Tae-neon 김태년. 2006. "Namdang Han Wŏnjin ŭi chŏnghak hyŏngsŏng e kwanhan yŏn'gu" 남당 한원진의 '정학' 형성에 관한 연구. Ph. D. dissertation, Korea University.

Kim Wŏnil 김원일. 2010. "Han Wŏnjin ŭi *Changja* Chemullon haesŏk e kwanhan yŏn'gu" 한원진의 장자 제물론 해석에 관한 연구. M.A. thesis, Sungkyunkwan University.

Kim Yun'gyŏng 김윤경. 2003. "Sŏ Myŏngŭng ŭi *Noja* Sasang e kwanhan yŏn'gu" 서명응의 노자 사상에 관한 연구. M.A. thesis, Sungkyunkwan University.

______. 2006. "Sŏ Myŏngŭng ŭi *Todŏk chigwi* e nat'anan T'aegŭkkwan" 서명응의 道德指歸에 나타난 태극관. *Tongyang Ch'ŏrhak Yŏn'gu* 동양철학연구 48:145–72.

Kŭm Changt'ae 금장태. 2006. *Hangguk yuhak ŭi* Noja *ihae* 한국 유학의 노자 이해. Sŏul: Seoul National University Press.

______. 2009. "Han Wŏnjin ŭi *Changja* haesŏk kwa pip'an nolli" 한원진의 장자 해석과 비판 논리. *Tong'a Munhwa* 동아문화 47:125-56.

Kwak Shinhan. 2019. "Song Siyŏl: The Revival of a *Qi*-Oriented Approach to the Interpretation of the Mind." In *Dao Companion to Korean Confucian Philosophy*, edited by Young-Chan Ro, 197-209. Dordrecht: Springer.

Lee Sangyong 리상용. 2013. "Chosŏn sidae haeje mongnok e nat'anan toga sŏjŏk yŏn'gu" 조선시대 해제 목록에 나타난 도가 서적 연구. *Hanguk Pibŭllia Hakhoeji* 한국비블리아학회지 24.1:63–81.

Liu Gusheng 劉固盛. 2024. "Lun Dong Sijing de Laoxue Sixiang" 論董思靖的老學思想. *Daojia wenhua yanjiu* 道家文化研究 1:329-50.

Muller, A. Charles. 2015. *Korea's Great Buddhist-Confucian Debate: The Treatises of Chŏng Tojŏn (Sambong) and Hamhŏ Tŭkt'ong (Kihwa)*. Honolulu: University of Hawaii Press.

Mun Sŏgyun 문석윤. 1993. "Namdang Han Wŏnjin ŭi Changja ch'ŏrhak pip'an" 남당 한원신의 장자 철학 비판. *Ch'ŏrhak Non'gu* 철학논구 21:39–71.

Ro, Young-chan. 1989. *The Korean Confucianism of Yi Yulgok*. Albany: State University of New York Press.

______. 2019. "Yi Yulgok's Life and His Neo-Confucian Synthesis." In *Dao Companion to Korean Confucian Philosophy*, edited by Young-Chan Ro, 179-95. Dordrecht: Springer.

Watson, Burton. 2013. *The Complete Works of Zhuangzi*. New York: Columbia University Press.

Wu Furui 吴福瑞. 2022. *Yang Shi yu Zhu Xi yuan yuan lu* 杨时与朱熹渊源录. Fuzhou: Fuzhou renmin chubanshe.

Yi Sanggon 이상곤. 2009. *Han Wŏnjin* 한원진. Sŏul: Sungkyunkwan University Press.

Yoon Chun-Keun 윤천근. 2021. "Yulgok ŭi *Sunŏn* e taehan koch'al: 16 segi Chosŏn sidae munhwa ŭi chŏn'gae wa yŏnggwanhayeo" 율곡의 순언에 대한 고찰: 16세기 조선 시대문화의 전개와 연관하여. *Yulgokhak Yŏn'gu* 율곡학연구 46:69-113.

# Index